The Preservation of Open Spaces, and of Footpaths, and Other Rights of Way

A Practical Treatise on the Law of the Subject

ROBERT HUNTER

CAMBRIDGE
UNIVERSITY PRESS

CAMBRIDGE UNIVERSITY PRESS

Cambridge, New York, Melbourne, Madrid, Cape Town,
Singapore, São Paolo, Delhi, Tokyo, Mexico City

Published in the United States of America by Cambridge University Press, New York

www.cambridge.org
Information on this title: www.cambridge.org/9781108036740

This edition first published 1896
This digitally printed version 2011

ISBN 978-1-108-03674-0 Paperback

THE PRESERVATION OF OPEN SPACES,

AND OF FOOTPATHS,

AND OTHER RIGHTS OF WAY.

CAMBRIDGE LIBRARY COLLECTION

Books of enduring scholarly value

History

The books reissued in this series include accounts of historical events and movements by eye-witnesses and contemporaries, as well as landmark studies that assembled significant source materials or developed new historiographical methods. The series includes work in social, political and military history on a wide range of periods and regions, giving modern scholars ready access to influential publications of the past.

The Preservation of Open Spaces, and of Footpaths, and Other Rights of Way

Sir Robert Hunter (1844–1913) became a leading legal authority on common land. As solicitor to the Commons Preservation Society, where he first met Octavia Hill, he was instrumental in saving Hampstead Heath, Epping Forest and the New Forest for the nation, and he developed the principles of protection upon which the National Trust would be founded. First published in 1896, and informed by a lifetime of experience, this work was devised specifically to instruct 'those who are interested in preserving the open lands of the country'. Covering iconic English landscapes ranging from cliff tops to forests and from village greens to allotments, each chapter explores real cases and the statutes that shaped their conclusions. The result is an account of the nineteenth-century legal developments that provided the foundations which both government and charitable bodies have since used in preserving the heritage – both natural and man-made – of the nation.

Cambridge University Press has long been a pioneer in the reissuing of out-of-print titles from its own backlist, producing digital reprints of books that are still sought after by scholars and students but could not be reprinted economically using traditional technology. The Cambridge Library Collection extends this activity to a wider range of books which are still of importance to researchers and professionals, either for the source material they contain, or as landmarks in the history of their academic discipline.

Drawing from the world-renowned collections in the Cambridge University Library, and guided by the advice of experts in each subject area, Cambridge University Press is using state-of-the-art scanning machines in its own Printing House to capture the content of each book selected for inclusion. The files are processed to give a consistently clear, crisp image, and the books finished to the high quality standard for which the Press is recognised around the world. The latest print-on-demand technology ensures that the books will remain available indefinitely, and that orders for single or multiple copies can quickly be supplied.

The Cambridge Library Collection will bring back to life books of enduring scholarly value (including out-of-copyright works originally issued by other publishers) across a wide range of disciplines in the humanities and social sciences and in science and technology.

THE PRESERVATION OF OPEN SPACES, AND OF FOOTPATHS, AND OTHER RIGHTS OF WAY.

A Practical Treatise on the Law of the Subject.

BY

SIR ROBERT HUNTER, M.A.,

Solicitor to the Post Office, Formerly Honorary Solicitor to the Commons Preservation Society.

EYRE AND SPOTTISWOODE,

Law and General Publishers,

LONDON—EAST HARDING STREET, FETTER LANE, E.C

1896.

PREFACE.

THE object of this work is to furnish those who are interested in preserving the open lands of the country, and the footpaths and other means by which rural England may be enjoyed, with a sketch of the law by which such enjoyment is secured and regulated. Some care has been taken to avoid the unnecessary use of technical terms, and thus to make the book intelligible to laymen, without, it is hoped, sacrificing accuracy and precision of language.

Common rights have been the subject of many legal treatises, and the Lectures of the late Mr. Joshua Williams deal exhaustively with the topic from an abstract point of view.

This volume treats rather of the several descriptions of land which are subject to common rights, and of those rights as the means by which such lands may be protected from inclosure. Thus, it has not been thought desirable to deal elaborately with such questions as that of surcharge between commoner and commoner, or those arising upon the partition of common lands under a Parliamentary inclosure. But attention has been drawn to the peculiarities attaching to common fields and pastures and to the common lands of forests; for, there can be little doubt, that in the past, the interests of the commoners and of the public have often been prejudiced by the tendency to treat all common land as of the same character, and to neglect the special history of the particular open space under consideration. Notably, it has not always been borne in mind, how large a part of England was formerly under Forest law, and consequently subject to the exercise of exceptional rights.

The law of footpaths is of course the law of highways; and that law has been very carefully digested in such works as those of Mr. Glen and Mr. Pratt. There are, nevertheless, certain questions which most frequently arise in the case of footpaths, while others relate almost exclusively to roads and streets. It is seldom, for example, that the public right of way along a carriage-road is challenged, while, on the other hand, the question, highway or no highway, is of constant occurrence and controlling interest in the case of footpaths. It seems useful, therefore, to apply the law of highways to footpaths, and, at the same time, to draw attention to various exceptional ways, such as fords and towing-paths, with reference to which the public right is not unlikely to be called in question, and which may perhaps be less jealously guarded by local authorities than the main ways of the country. The public is also keenly interested in the use of the cliffs and fore-shores of the country, and of its rivers and lakes, and chapters on these subjects seemed to be an appropriate pendant to those on footpaths.

In short, the aim of the writer has been to bring together the provisions of the law which bear especially upon the use of the rural districts for purposes of recreation. Owing to the constant growth of large towns, and to the increasing facilities for escape from their smoke and noise, the importance of rural England as a recreation-ground for all classes becomes more obvious, and is more fully realized, every day. So far as the author is aware, no attempt has yet been made to give an account of the principles upon which the enjoyment of the many and varied beauties of England is recognized by the law; the present volume is an attempt to supply that deficiency. In this connection it should not be forgotten that the public owe much to the generosity and good sense of land-owners; but the use of the country for purposes of recreation should not be left to depend entirely upon the goodwill of a limited class, while on the other hand privileges freely accorded will be the more keenly appreciated, when the limits of public rights are understood.

What may be called the movement for the enjoyment of the country, or, to use a more familiar phrase, the open-space movement, took definite form about thirty years ago, when the Commons Preservation Society was established at the instance of Mr. Shaw Lefevre, the late Mr. Philip Lawrence, and the late Mr. Cowper Temple (afterwards Lord Mount Temple). The immediate object was to prevent the wholesale inclosure of London commons by Lords of Manors ; and to the remarkable skill and foresight with which Mr. Lawrence organized the defence of those commons is due, not only their preservation, but much of the subsequent success of the open-space movement generally. Subsequently the late Mr. Fawcett brought within the scope of the movement the New Forest, and rural commons,—working a revolution in the practice of the Inclosure Commission and of Parliament in relation to Statutory Inclosure and, with the aid of the New Forest Association, arresting the wholesale destruction of the most conspicuous specimen still left of the old English Forests. About the same time the Corporation of London by energetic and timely action rescued Epping Forest, and thus supplied the Capital with a singularly beautiful recreation ground of some six thousand acres. The strides taken by public opinion since the struggle first began are shown notably by two pieces of recent legislation. Inclosure by the Lord of the Manor under the authority (vouched in almost every instance) of the Statute of Merton has been forbidden, unless the Board of Agriculture can be satisfied, that it is for the public benefit.* And the newly constituted and popularly

* The Law of Commons Amendment Act, 1893, 56 & 57 Vict. c. 57.

elected Local Authorities of the rural districts have been enjoined to protect rights of way and roadside wastes, and authorised to preserve common lands.* These enactments mark an epoch in the movement; and render the present an opportune time to review the legal position, as thus materially modified.

During the whole of the thirty years which have seen the gradual realisation of the public interest in the open lands and natural scenery of the country, the author has been called upon to give his aid in the direction of the movement, in the earlier days in a professional capacity, and more recently as a member of the various societies now existing to protect the public in this relation. This long connection with the subject must be his excuse for publishing the present volume.

Mr. Shaw Lefevre and Mr. Percival Birkett (the Honorary Solicitor to the Commons Preservation Society) have kindly read the proofs of these pages; and the author has to thank Mr. John Okell for assistance in preparing the usual Tables of Reference. To Sir John Brunner, Bart., M.P., the author is also indebted for several suggestions bearing upon the utility of the work from a practical point of view.

* The Local Government Act, 1894, 56 & 57 Vict. c. 73. s. 26.

CONTENTS.

PART II.

Of Footpaths and other Rights of Way.

APPENDICES.

LIST OF CASES.

LIST OF STATUTES.

TABLE OF ABBREVIATIONS.

NOTE.—Most of the older Reports of Decided Cases are referred to by the names of the Reporters alone; thus, Adolphus and Ellis (contracted into Ad. & Ell. or A. & E.) means Adolphus and Ellis' Reports; and Beavan (contracted into Beav.) means Beavan's Reports. The more modern Reports are distinguished by the name of the Court in which the cases were decided. For instance, Common Bench (C.B.) means Reports of cases in the Court of Common Pleas; Chancery Division (Ch. D. or Ch. Div.) means Reports of cases in the Chancery Division of the High Court of Justice.

Abr., Abridgment.
Ad. & Ell. or A. & E., Adolphus and Ellis.
App. Cas., Appeal Cases.
Atk., Atkyn's Reports.
B. & Ad., Barnewall and Adolphus.
B. & Ald. or B. & A., Barnewall and Alderson.
B. & C., Barnewall and Cresswell.
B. & S., Best and Smith.
Beav., Beavan.
Bing., Bingham.
Bos. & Pul., Bosanquet and Puller.
Bulst., Bulstrode.
Bur. or Burr., Burrows.
c., Chapter.
C. B., Common Bench.
C. L., Common Law.
C. M. & R., Crompton, Meeson, and Roscoe.
C. P., Common Pleas.
C. P. Div., Common Pleas Division.
C. & P., Carrington and Payne.
Campb., Campbell.
Ch., Chancery.
Ch. App., Chancery Appeals.
Ch. D. or Ch. Div., Chancery Division.
Co. Litt., Coke on Littleton.
Cowp., Cowper.
Cr. Cas., Crown Cases.
Cro. Eliz., Croke's Reports, *temp.* Elizabeth.
Cro. Jac. or Cro. Jas., Croke's Reports, *temp.* James I.
Cro. Car., Croke's Reports, *temp.* Charles I.
Dearsley Cr. Cas., Dearsley's Crown Cases.
E. & B., Ellis and Blackburn.
East, East's Reports.
Eq., Equity.
Ex. or Exch., Exchequer.
Ex. D., Exchequer Division.
F. & F., Foster and Finlason.
H. L., House of Lords.
H. L. Cas., House of Lords Cases.
Hawk. P. C., Hawkins' Pleas of the Crown.
Hob., Hobart.
Hurlst. & Colt. or H. & C., Hurlstone and Coltman.
Hurl. & Norm., Hurlstone and Norman.
Hy. Bl. or H. Bl., Henry Blackstone's Reports.

Ir. Rep., Irish Reports.
J. P., Justice of the Peace.
Keble, Keble's Reports.
L. J., Law Journal.
L. R., Law Reports.
L. T., Law Times.
Leon., Leonard.
Lev., Levinz.
Lord Raym., Lord Raymond.
M. & S., Maule and Selwyn.
Macq., Macqueen.
Mag. Cas., Magistrates' Cases.
Mee & W. or M. & W., Meeson and Welsby.
Mod., Modern Reports.
Moo. & Rob., Moody and Robinson.
Moore's P. C., Moore's Privy Council Cases.
N. S., New Series.
P. C., Privy Council.
Q. B., Queen's Bench.
Q. B. D. or Q. B. Div., Queen's Bench Division.
R. R., Revised Reports.
Rep., Reports, *i.e.* Coke's Reports.
Salk., Salkeld.
Show., Showers.
Stark. N. P. C., Starkie's Nisi Prius Cases.
T. R., Term Reports.
Taunt., Taunton.
Tit., Title.
Times L. R., The "Times" Law Reports.
Vern., Vernon.
Vin. Abr., Viner's Abridgment.
W. Bl. or W. B., Sir William Blackstone.
W. R., Weekly Reporter.
Wils., Wilson.
Wms. Saunders, Williams' Edition of Saunders' Reports.

PART I.

OF COMMONS AND OTHER OPEN SPACES.

CHAPTER I.

Of the Nature of a Common and the Rights thereon.

In popular language a common is an open piece of rough ground, generally traversed by a road and several footpaths. It is covered with turf and dotted with gorse and bushes, and generally has a few trees growing here and there. There is nothing to prevent any passer-by from wandering over any part of the common; and it is looked upon in a general way as public property. The parishioners and neighbours, however, are aware that, while anyone can wander over the common, it is not lawful for anyone from a distance, any stranger to the neighbourhood, to turn out cattle upon it, or to cut the bushes or trees. Rights of this character are confined (we are speaking in popular language) to those living in the neighbourhood of the common, generally to those living in the parish.

The term "common," however, as meaning a piece of land, is not a legal term. The distinguishing feature in law of that kind of land which is ordinarily referred to as a common, or as common land, is, that it is land subject to a right of common. What, then, is a right of common? A right of common is the right to take a profit out of the land

A

of another man. The most usual and widely known right of common is that of common of pasture, *i.e.*, the right to take grass and other eatable products of a common by the mouths of cattle turned out thereon. Another right is that of cutting and carrying away, generally for use in the house or land of the person taking it, furze or bushes growing on the common. Another right is that of digging sand, gravel, or loam on the common, and taking it away for similar uses.

The persons who take these rights are called commoners.

Land which is ordinarily known as a common may therefore be defined as land the soil of which belongs to one person, and from which certain other persons take certain profits.

Common rights are mostly attached to, or enjoyed, with certain lands or houses. Thus a right of common of pasture usually consists of the right to turn out as many cattle as a certain farm or plot of ground belonging to the commoner can support in winter. Such cattle are said to be levant and couchant, that is, up-rising and down-lying, on the land, and no doubt in early days the cattle which were turned out on the common were actually stalled and fed on the land to which the right was attached. But at the present day a commoner may turn out any cattle belonging to him, wherever they are kept, provided they do not exceed in number the number which can be supported on the land in winter, that is to say, which can be supported by the stored summer produce of the land together with any winter herbage it produces.* In many places this measure of the number of cattle which may be turned out is replaced for practical purposes by a rule or bye-law specifying the number of

* Robertson *v.* Hartopp. 43 Ch. Div. 516, and the authorities there cited.

cattle or sheep which may be turned out to the acre, *e.g.*, two sheep to the acre. This rule does not generally affect the strict legal measure of the right, which is still levancy and couchancy.

Common of pasture which is attached to land in the way we have described is said in law to be common of pasture appendant, or appurtenant, to such land. Into the distinction between "appendant" and "appurtenant" it is not necessary at this moment to enter.

Where common of pasture is not appendant or appurtenant to land, it is said to be common of pasture in gross; and in this case it consists of the right to turn out a fixed number of cattle. This right is comparatively rare.

Common of pasture is often confined to what is known in law as "commonable cattle." Commonable cattle are defined in the old books as "horses and oxen to plough the land, and cows and sheep to compester (*i.e.*, manure) it."* The animals which were necessary to farm the lands of the parish or vill were those which had the enjoyment of the common. But by special usage, common of pasture may be enjoyed by other animals, such as donkeys, pigs, and geese. A goose green or goose common is an ordinary feature of rural England.

Just as common of pasture is usually appendant, or appurtenant, to particular land, so rights of cutting bushes, gorse or heather, or of lopping trees—known in law as rights of common of estovers or botes (from the Norman-French *estouffer*, and the Saxon *botan*, to furnish)—are usually attached or appurtenant to certain lands or houses. Thus, a right of taking gorse and bushes or of lopping

* Tyringham's case, 4 Rep. 37*a*; and see Second Institute, 85.

trees for fuel, called fire-bote, is limited to the taking of such fuel as may be necessary for the hearths of a particular house, and no more may be taken than is thus required.

Similarly, wood taken for the repairs of buildings (house-bote) or of hedges (hedge-bote or hey-bote) must be limited in quantity with reference to the requirements of the house, farm-buildings, and hedges of the particular property to which the right is attached. And heather taken for litter cannot be taken in larger quantities than would be necessary for manuring the lands in respect of which the right is enjoyed. It would be illegal to take the wood or heather from the common and to sell it to anyone who had not himself a right to take it.*

In the same way a right of taking sand, gravel, clay, or loam, must be exercised with reference to the repair of the roads or the improvement of the soil of the particular property to which the right is attached.

As in the case of common of pasture, rights of taking wood, heath, or sand, gravel, clay, or loam, may be enjoyed without reference to any lands or houses, that is, in gross. But in this case they must be limited by some distinct measure, as, for example, by a certain number of cart-loads.

Such is, speaking generally, the nature of rights of common. There is much legal learning connected with the subject—the different classes of persons entitled to exercise such rights, the manner in which they may be exercised, the effect of such rights in preventing inclosure and restraining other acts of ownership on the part of the owner of the soil of the common. Much of this learning will henceforth be of less importance, owing to the passing of the Law of Commons

* See the leading authorities on rights of estovers and similar rights, cited in Chap. V.

Amendment Act, 1893,* which forbids, save with the sanction of the Board of Agriculture, the most usual form of inclosure of common land. So far as the rules and principles of law relating to the subject still have a practical bearing upon the preservation of commons, they will be noticed when we deal with the means of resisting inclosure and otherwise protecting commons.

It will be seen that there is no reference in the legal definition of a common to any interest enjoyed by the public or nation at large. The public enjoyment of a common has arisen in practice from the fact that the owner of the soil of the common could not inclose it, because other persons had rights of common upon it, while the commoners could not inclose, because the common does not belong to them. From century to century the common has lain open to all comers, because no one who had any legal interest in the common could inclose it.

Most commons are what is known as "waste land of a manor." The Lord of the Manor is owner of the soil of the common. The trees and bushes on the common belong to him, subject to any rights of lopping or cutting which the commoners may possess; but, if there are such rights, the lord cannot destroy the trees or bushes so as to prevent the use of them by the commoners. The gravel, sand, and subsoil, again, belong to the lord; and even the grass on the common is his, though the commoners have the right to take it by the mouths of their cattle. The lord can turn out cattle of his own (or his tenants can turn out their cattle) to feed on the grass together with the commoners' cattle, though not in such numbers as to make the feed worthless to the commoners. It follows from the large interest possessed by

* 56 & 57 Vict. c. 57.

the lord that he can prevent any inclosure of the common, or any building upon it. Not a single tree can be felled upon the common without his leave.

Unfortunately, however, the Lord of the Manor has been often the enemy rather than the protector of a common. He wishes to inclose, in order to enlarge his fields or his game-preserves; or he seeks to make a profit by taking and selling wholesale the gravel, sand, or surface-soil of the common; or he digs clay and makes bricks upon the common. In these cases it is necessary to protect the common by means of the rights of common. These, in the case of an ordinary manorial common, are usually enjoyed by the freehold and copyhold tenants of the manor. But other persons are not infrequently entitled to rights; and before it is inferred that no rights exist, the history of all the land in the parish should be examined. We shall see subsequently the several grounds on which rights of common may be claimed, how the common may be protected by means of such rights, and how the local authorities are enabled to assist in the work.

There are other cases where the lord himself does not inclose or destroy a common, but neglects to prevent encroachments and depredations by others. It is no doubt a burden upon the lord to have to defend land from which he is making little or no profit; and it is very desirable that this duty should be assumed by some local authority. Recent enactments furnish local authorities with powers for this purpose.

In former times Parliament favoured the inclosure of commons, for the sake of increasing the food-producing area of the country. It passed a series of Acts providing means by which the lord and a majority of the commoners could inclose the whole common, even though some of the commoners objected. The latest of these Acts, those passed between 1845 and 1868, are not repealed, though their provisions are much modified by an Act of recent years, the Commons Act, 1876. No inclosure of a common can now be made under the Inclosure Acts without the consent of the Board of Agriculture and of Parliament. It will be hereafter explained what proceedings are taken in order to obtain the approval of the Board and of Parliament to an inclosure of this kind, and how the local authorities can protect a common from such an inclosure.

CHAPTER II.

Of the Inclosure of a Manorial Common by the Lord of the Manor.

IT has been stated in the preceding chapter, that the Lord of a Manor sometimes attempts to inclose the common or waste of his manor without obtaining any Parliamentary authority for so doing. These attempts have been a fruitful source of litigation in the past. During the last thirty years a most determined effort to inclose the commons in the neighbourhood of London without Parliamentary authority was made by the Lords of Manors. It was resisted by the commoners in many costly law-suits, which confirmed old legal decisions and settled many new points of law. The general result of these suits was to show that a lord could not legally inclose without obtaining an Act of Parliament. But this general conclusion depended upon many propositions of law of a technical character, and in each case, in order to obtain the benefit of these decisions, it was necessary to examine with great care and at considerable expense the history of the common and the extent and nature of the common rights. In future, the protection of a common against inclosure by the lord without Parliamentary authority will be rendered much more easy and less expensive, by reason of a recent enactment already referred to—the Law of Commons Amendment Act, 1893.* This Act is of such importance with reference to the whole subject of in-

* 56 & 57 Vict. c. 57. This Act was introduced and passed through the House of Lords by Lord Thring, at the instance of the Commons Preservation Society.

closure without the sanction of Parliament, that it is convenient to commence the consideration of the subject by an examination of its provisions.

By this statute, then, it is thus provided:—

Sec. 2.—"*An inclosure or approvement of any part of a common* purporting to be made under the Statute of Merton and the Statute of Westminster the Second, or either of such statutes, shall not be valid unless it is made with the consent of the Board of Agriculture.*"

Sec. 3.—"*In giving or withholding their consent under this Act the Board shall have regard to the same considerations, and shall, if necessary, hold the same enquiries as are directed by the Commons Act,* 1876, *to be taken into consideration and held by the Board before forming an opinion whether an application under the Inclosure Acts shall be assented to or not.*"

It will be seen that the kind of inclosure with which this Act deals is an inclosure or approvement under certain Acts of Parliament known as the Statutes of Merton and Westminster the Second.

The Statute of Merton,† which was passed in one of the early Parliaments of Henry III., before the people of England, as distinguished from the Barons, were represented, is to the following effect:—

"*Also because many great men of England (which have enfeoffed knights and their freeholders of small tenements in their great manors) have complained that they cannot make their profit of the residue of their manors as of wastes woods and pastures, whereas the same feoffees have sufficient pasture as much as belongeth to their tenements, it is provided and*

* We shall examine, as we proceed, what lands are included under the term "common." We are at present considering only the case of manorial waste.

† 20 Hen. III. c. 4.

granted that whenever such feoffees do bring an Assize of Novel Disseisin for their common of pasture, and it is knowledged before the Justices that they have as much pasture as sufficeth to their tenements, and that they have free egress and regress from their tenements into the pasture, then let them be contented therewith; and they of whom it was so complained shall go quit of as much as they have made their profit of their lands wastes woods and pastures."

Turned into modern English, this statute provides, that a Lord of a Manor may inclose part of his manorial common, if he can prove that he has left sufficient pasture for the freehold tenants of his manor.

The Statute of Westminster the Second* (passed in the year 1255) was an extension of the principle of the Statute of Merton.

It recited that statute, and then proceeded thus:—

"*And forasmuch as no mention was made between neighbour and neighbour many lords of wastes woods and pastures have been hindered heretofore by the contradiction of neighbours having sufficient pasture, And because foreign tenants have no more right to common in the wastes woods or pastures of any lord than the lords' own tenants, It is ordained, That the Statute of Merton provided between the lord and his tenants from henceforth shall hold place between lords of wastes woods and pastures and their neighbours, [so that the lords of such wastes woods and pastures, saving sufficient pasture to their tenants and neighbours, may make approvement of the residue].† And this shall be*

* 12 Ed. I. c. 46.

† In the passage in brackets I have slightly departed from the order of the English translation. The Latin runs thus:—"Ita quod domini hujus-modi vastorum boscorum et pasturarum salva sufficienti pastura hominibus suis et vicinis appruare se possint de residuo."

observed for such as claim pasture as appurtenant to their tenements. But if any do claim common by special feoffment or grant for a certain number of beasts [or in any other manner than of common right he ought to have], whereas covenant barreth the law he shall have his recovery as he ought to have by form of the grant made unto him."*

The statute then continues:—

"*By occasion of a windmill, sheepcote, dairy, enlarging of a court necessary or curtilage from henceforth no man shall be aggrieved by Assize of Novel Disseisin for common of pasture.*" †

The two statutes in question lay down a principle which has been of the highest importance in all controversies respecting the inclosure of manorial commons.

In law, a right of common over the waste of a manor (or over any other defined area) is exerciseable over every part of the common.‡

Consequently, in the absence of statutory authority, when once a right of common had been created, no part of the common could be inclosed by the owner of the soil without the assent of the commoner. The Statutes of Merton and Westminster the Second expressly modified this legal doctrine and authorised inclosures to be made against the several classes of commoners described in the statutes, provided

* In the English version of the statute the passage bracketed runs thus: "or otherwise which he ought to have of common right." The late Mr. Joshua Williams points out that this is obviously a mistranslation of the Latin, "vel alio modo quam de jure communi habere deberet," and that the proper English rendering is that given above. "Rights of Common," p. 111; and see Statute 3 & 4 Edw. VI. c. 3. s. 2.

† The Statutes of Merton and Westminster the Second were confirmed by a statute passed in the reign of Edward VI. (3 & 4 Edw. VI. c. 3.), and certain supplemental provisions not now of importance were enacted.

‡ "The common," Lord Coke says, "issued out of the whole waste and of every part thereof." Second Institute, part 1, 85.

sufficient pasture with convenient access were left for the commoners.

Accordingly, whenever, up to the passing of the recent Act, a Lord of a Manor inclosed, and the inclosure was challenged by commoners, the lord has practically had two lines of defence open to him, and only two. He could justify his inclosure by showing that no rights of common whatever existed over the land inclosed, or by showing that he had complied with the provisions of the Statutes of Merton and Westminster the Second, and left sufficient pasture for the commoners. Wherever any right of common of pasture existed—that is to say, in the vast majority of cases—the defence under the statutes was vital to the lord.

Hence it may be imagined that much learning and ingenuity have been exercised upon the construction of the statutes, and many cases have been decided upon them by the Courts. It is not necessary now to examine these at great length, because in future, however clearly the lord may establish that his inclosure is justified by these old statutes, it will not be lawful, unless he also obtains the consent of the Board of Agriculture, and that body is directed to consider (as we shall see) whether the inclosure is in the public interests.

But, as the lord will still have to prove that his inclosure is lawful under the Statutes of Merton and Westminster the Second before he can ask for the consent of the Board, we will briefly indicate the more important points decided upon the statutes.

In the first place, then, it has been held that the statutes enable owners of wastes, other than Lords of Manors, to inclose.*

* Glover *v.* Lane, 3 T.R. 445. See also Patrick *v.* Stubbs, 9 Mee. & W. 830, 836.

Secondly, the statutes do not entitle anyone to inclose land over which a right of common for a particular number of beasts, not attached to a tenement, is enjoyed.*

Thirdly, the Lord of the Manor, or the owner of the soil of the common, must prove affirmatively that he has left sufficient pasture for the commoners.†

Fourthly, in proving sufficiency the lord must have regard not only to the cattle actually turned on to feed during recent years, but to the number which might be turned on if all the commoners exercised their rights. This point has been much argued in recent years, and there have been decisions contradictory in tendency; but it appears to be now definitely decided in the sense above stated by the judgment of the Court of Appeal in the great suit relating to the Banstead Commons.‡

Fifthly, the Statute of Merton applies as between a Lord of the Manor and his copyholders, although the language of the statute is scarcely appropriate to copyholders.§

Sixthly, if an inclosure is made under the statutes, and there is not sufficient pasture left, "the commoner may break down the whole inclosure, because it standeth upon the ground which is his common." ||

* Second Institute, part 2, 475. See on this subject Robinson *v.* The Maharajah Duleep Singh, L.R. 4 Ch. Div. 798. But it would probably not be safe to press the observations of L. J. Cotton beyond the point involved in the actual case.

† Arlett *v.* Ellis, 7 B. & C. 369, 370. Betts *v.* Thompson, L.R. 6 Ch. 732, 741.

‡ Robertson *v.* Hartopp, L.R. 43 Ch. Div. 484, 516, overruling in effect Lascelles *v.* Lord Onslow, L.R. 2 Q.B.D. 433. The case of Robinson *v.* Duleep Singh may be referred to as a case in which the lord did succeed in establishing that he had left sufficient pasture for the commoners after a small inclosure (L.R. 11 Ch. D. 798).

§ Shakespear *v.* Peppin, 6 T.R. 741; and see the opinion of the late Mr. Joshua Williams, "Rights of Common," p. 123.

|| Second Institute, part 1, 88. Arlett *v.* Ellis, 7 B. & C. 346, 362, 372, 377; Smith *v.* Earl Brownlow, L.R. 9 Eq. 241.

Seventhly, the Statutes of Merton and Westminster the Second do not enable the Lord of a Manor, or the owner of the soil of a common, to make any inclosure of a common which would injure any commoner in the exercise of any right of common of estovers, or of turbary, or of digging gravel, or, indeed, of any other right of common than common of pasture.* It has been held, however, that if the land inclosed cannot in the ordinary course of nature produce any product of the kind to which the right claimed relates, *e.g.*, any wood, where the right is common of estovers, any turf, where the right is common of turbary, any gravel, where the right is to dig gravel, the inclosure is not bad as against the commoner.†

Eighthly, the special power of inclosing for a "windmill, sheepcote, dairy, or enlarging of a court necessary or curtilage," has been held to extend to other inclosures of a like nature, *e.g.*, the building of a house for a beast-keeper. The particular objects of inclosure mentioned are said not to constitute a complete list, but to be given by way of example.‡

In future, then, as in the past, a Lord of a Manor, or other owner of the soil of a common, wishing to inclose under the Statutes of Merton and Westminster the Second, must prove affirmatively that he has left sufficient pasture for the commoners in accordance with the rules laid down by the Courts, and summarised in the preceding paragraphs.

And it is assumed that the Board of Agriculture, when its consent is applied for, will, if requested by any commoner,

* Second Institute, part 1, 87; Fawcett *v.* Strickland, Willes 57, 60, 61 (followed in Shakespear *v.* Peppin, 6 T.R. 741, 747); Duberley *v.* Page, 2 T.R. 391, 392; Grant *v.* Gunner, 1 Taunt. 435.

† Peardon *v.* Underhill, 16 Q.B. 120.

‡ Second Institute, part 2, 476; Patrick *v.* Stubbs, 9 Mee. & W. 830, 836.

require the lord or owner of the common to prove that his inclosure is in accordance with the statutes as thus interpreted.

But the Board will require far more than this.

The Law of Commons Amendment Act, 1893, provides that—

"*In giving and withholding their consent under this Act, the Board shall have regard to the same considerations, and shall, if necessary, hold the same enquiries as are directed by the Commons Act,* 1876, *to be taken into consideration and held by the Board before forming an opinion whether an application under the Inclosure Acts shall be acceded to or not.*"

Now the Commons Act, 1876,* lays down as a cardinal principle that inclosure in severalty shall not be allowed, unless it can be shown to be for the benefit of the neighbourhood.

The Act recites that the Inclosures Commissioners (now merged in the Board of Agriculture) † were empowered under certain circumstances by provisional order to authorise the inclosure of a common, provided that the Commissioners were of opinion that such inclosure would be expedient, "having regard as well to the health, comfort, and convenience of the inhabitants of any cities, towns, villages, or populous places in or near any parish in which the land proposed to be inclosed, or any part thereof, might be situate (in the Act afterwards included under the expression 'the benefit of the neighbourhood'), or to the advantage of the persons interested in the common (in the Act afterwards included under the expression 'private interests')," but that

* 39 & 40 Vict. c. 56.

† See Settled Land Act, 1882 (45 & 46 Vict. c. 38), sec. 48, and Board of Agriculture Act, 1889 (52 & 53 Vict. c. 30.); and see *post*, p. 107.

the provisional order had no validity until the Commissioners certified to Parliament that the inclosure was expedient, having regard to the benefit of the neighbourhood as well as to private interests, or until an Act of Parliament had been passed confirming the order and affirming the certificate of the Commissioners.

The Act then further recites (amongst other things) that it is desirable to make further provision for bringing under the notice of the Commissioners and of Parliament any circumstances bearing on the expediency of allowing the inclosure of a common, and that it is desirable "that inclosures in severalty as opposed to regulation of commons should not be made unless it can be proved to the satisfaction of the Commissioners and of Parliament that such inclosures will be of benefit to the neighbourhood as well as to private interests, and to others who are legally interested in any such commons."

These recitals give the keynote to the Act. Throughout its provisions the Commissioners are constantly directed, in dealing with any application for the inclosure or regulation* of a common, to have regard to the benefit of the neighbourhood, and, speaking shortly, they are prohibited from recommending to Parliament any inclosure of a common unless they can certify that the inclosure will be of benefit to the neighbourhood, that is to say, will tend to the health, comfort, and convenience of the inhabitants of the district.† In

* For an explanation of what is meant by the regulation of a common, see *post*, Chap. XXI., p. 237.

† The provisions specially referring to the benefit of the neighbourhood are secs. 7, 10 (4) and (6), 11 (7), 12 (1) and (9); but the whole procedure of the Commissioners, as prescribed by the Act (secs. 2 to 14), is framed with a view to the prevention of inclosure unless some public benefit can be shown to be derived from it. We shall deal more in detail with the Act in treating of Parliamentary inclosures.

practice, under the guidance of the Select Committee of the House of Commons to which all proposals of the Board of Agriculture are referred, the Board have construed the Act in a thoroughly liberal spirit, and the controlling question with regard to any Parliamentary inclosure, at the present day, is, Can it be shown that any public benefit will result from the inclosure? If not, the Board will not entertain the proposal.

It is clear that under the Law of Commons Amendment Act, 1893, the same question must be put by the Board and answered in the affirmative to its satisfaction, before the assent of the Board will be given to any inclosure or approvement under the Statutes of Merton and Westminster the Second. This is unquestionably the true construction of the statute; and it is the construction which the Board of Agriculture have themselves put upon it. For the Board have already issued a notice* calling attention to the Act of 1893 and other enactments (which we shall presently notice), and continuing thus:—

"It follows from the above enactments that an inclosure of part of a common, whether purporting to be made under the Statutes of Merton and Westminster the Second, or either of them, by way of approvement on the ground of sufficient pasture being left for the commoners, or under copyhold grant founded on a custom of the manor,† cannot now be legally made without the consent of the Board of Agriculture, who in giving or withholding their consent are to have regard as well to the benefit of the neighbourhood as to private interests, and any person intending to make such an inclosure should publish notice of his intention in the local newspapers."

* See "The Times" of Friday, Dec. 29, 1893.

† As to inclosures under a copyhold grant, see *post*, Chapter XI., p. 93.

The concluding passage of the above notice refers to the 31st section of the Commons Act, 1876, which provides as follows:—

"*Any person intending to inclose or approve a common or part of a common otherwise than under the provisions of this Act shall give notice to all persons claiming any legal right in such common or part of a common by publishing, at least three months beforehand, a statement of his intention to make such an inclosure for three successive times and in two or more of the principal local newspapers in the county town or district in which the common or part of a common proposed to be inclosed is situate.*"

From the reference to this provision in the notice of the Board of Agriculture, it is clear that the Board will not entertain any application for its consent to inclose or approve under the Statutes of Merton and Westminster the Second, unless it is proved to them that notice of the intention to inclose has been advertised as above specified.*

It follows, then, that public notice must be given of any application to the Board, and that anyone thus becoming aware of the application may represent to the Board any objections to the inclosure on public grounds.

Notice by public advertisement is not, however, the only notice which the local authorities of the district will receive of the intended inclosure of part of a common under the Statutes of Merton and Westminster the Second.

The Local Government Act, 1894,† provides that "notice of any application to the Board of Agriculture in relation to a common shall be served upon the Council of every parish

* Production of a newspaper containing the advertisement is proof under the Act that the advertisement was issued by the party intending to inclose. See Commons Act, 1876, sec. 31.

† 56 & 57 Vict. c. 73. s. 8 (4).

in which any part of the common to which the application relates is situate."

If, therefore, a common runs into several parishes, and it is proposed to apply to the Board of Agriculture for leave to inclose under the old statutes a portion of such common, the Council of every parish into which the common extends must be served with notice of the application.

There is no express power given to a Parish Council to take proceedings in consequence of such notice. And some question might possibly arise as to any charge on the rates in relation to such proceedings. But it will clearly be competent for the Parish Council to make, through their clerk or any member of their body, any representations to the Board of Agriculture that the inclosure is objectionable on public grounds—especially in relation to the health, comfort, and convenience of the inhabitants of their parish. Such representations would be made to the Board in writing, and would give rise to no expense or charge upon the rates. If the Board of Agriculture should, as they have power to do, hold a local enquiry by an Assistant Commissioner,* the Parish Council would again be entitled to attend, by their clerk or members of their body, and to point out any objections to, or considerations arising in respect of, the proposed inclosure.

A District Council has similar powers. Notice of any application to the Board of Agriculture in relation to any common within the district of the Council must be served upon the Council,† and the Council will, like a Parish Council, have power to address itself to the Board of Agriculture or to an Assistant Commissioner of the Board holding a local enquiry on the subject of the inclosure.

* See Commons Act, 1876, secs. 10 and 11; Law of Commons Amendment Act, 1893, sec. 3.

† Local Government Act, 1894, sec. 26 (2).

A District Council may also (with the consent in some cases of the County Council),* exercise other very important powers in relation to inclosures by Lords of Manors. These we shall notice presently.†

We have seen, then—

(1.) That the Lord of a Manor cannot in future inclose under the Statutes of Merton and Westminster the Second without obtaining the consent of the Board of Agriculture.

(2.) That in order to obtain such consent, he must prove to the satisfaction of the Board not only that he has complied with the provisions of those Statutes, but also that the inclosure will be for the benefit of the public.

(3.) That the lord must advertise his intention to apply to the Board three months beforehand in two local papers.

(4.) That the Parish Council and District Council will have notice of the application, and can oppose it on the ground that the inclosure will not be of benefit to the public.

If a Lord of the Manor ventures to inclose without the consent of the Board of Agriculture, he cannot justify his inclosure under the Statutes of Merton and Westminster the Second, and must rely on his only other possible defence,‡ viz., that there are no common rights which can be exercised over the land inclosed.

If there are no such rights, he is discharged also from the obligation to advertise his intention to inclose under sec. 31 of the Commons Act, 1876. For it is there expressly enacted that the provisions of the section shall not apply

---

* See *post*, pp. 80–88.
† See Chapter X., p. 79.
‡ See *ante*, p. 12.

to any commons or waste lands whereon the rights of common are vested solely in the Lord of the Manor.*

The main question, then, in future, when a Lord of a Manor incloses a piece of common land without the consent of the Board of Agriculture, will be, does any right of common whatever exist over the land?

Now here a question of much practical importance arises, viz., will the lord be called upon to prove that the land is discharged from all rights of common? or will those who object to the inclosure be called upon to prove the existence of some such right? In legal phrase, upon whom will the burden of proof be held to fall?

This question seems to be answered by a consideration of the procedure which would be necessary to challenge the inclosure. A Lord of a Manor making an inclosure without advertising his intention as required by sec. 31 of the Commons Act, 1876, might, it would seem, be indicted for a misdemeanour for disobeying a statute.†

On such a proceeding *primâ facie* evidence would be required by any Court that the land inclosed was subject to common rights. A Court investigating a criminal charge would hardly be satisfied with statements that the land inclosed was always reputed and thought to be a common. It would probably require some evidence of the actual existence of some right of common.

But an enquiry concerning rights of common is hardly the proper function of a criminal court. And, therefore, the more convenient mode of challenging an inclosure, either on the ground that the intention to inclose has not been advertised, or that the consent of the Board of Agriculture

* See 39 & 40 Vict. c. 56. s. 31.

† 1 Hawk. P.C. c. 22. s. 5; 2 Hawk. P.C. c. 25. s. 4.

has not been obtained, will be by way of information in the name of the Attorney-General, filed on the relation of some person interested, and claiming an order (in legal phrase a mandatory injunction) for the removal of the inclosure. In any such proceeding the Attorney-General would be called on to prove that the land inclosed was subject to common rights of some kind.*

It is important, therefore, to consider somewhat more in detail, in what persons or classes of persons common rights over a manorial common may be expected to be found. This will be the subject of the following chapter.

* It is to be noticed that sec. 31 of the Commons Act, 1876, does not in terms require notice by advertisement of the intention to inclose, to the public, but only to "all persons claiming any legal right in such common or part of a common."

CHAPTER III.

Of Rights of Common connected with the Manorial System.

IN considering any question connected with a manorial common it is important to bear in mind, that the common belongs to the lord, because it is waste of his manor.

From this connection of the common and the manor divers rights of common also spring. To understand them, it is necessary to give a very brief sketch of the nature of a manor.

A manor in theory of law consists of certain lands in the actual possession of the lord, known as demesnes, and of lands which are said to be held freely of the lord by certain services. The demesnes consist partly of the land in the actual occupation of the lord, such as the manor house and park, partly of land formerly farmed by his villeins or serfs,* subsequently known as copyhold tenants, and partly of the wastes or commons of the manor. The lands held freely of the manor by certain services are what are now known as freehold lands. They do not belong to the lord, or, in legal phrase, the soil is not vested in him; but the owners are said to hold their lands of the Lord of the Manor. Originally the leading condition of the tenure was, that the freehold tenant did homage and took the oath of fealty to the lord. The form of homage and the oath of fealty both declared that the tenant would bear faith to the lord of life and limb,

* See Coke's "Compleat Copyholder," 10–15, and see p. 57.

saving the faith due to the king; and the oath of fealty further bound the tenant to perform the services which belonged to the lord for the tenements held of him.* The services rendered were of two distinct kinds. Tenants who held by military or knight service were bound to follow their lord to the wars. Tenants who held in fee socage—or, as we may translate it, by the service of the plough—were bound to certain definite services connected with the tillage of the land—services which in time were converted into money payments. There were many differences in the incidents of the two tenures, certain feudal burdens being much more onerous in cases of tenure by knight service. In both cases, if from failure of heirs the land became untenanted, or if from the commission of any breach of the conditions on which it was held the land became forfeited, the Lord of the Manor, by whom in theory it was supposed to have been granted, was entitled to take possession of it.

In modern times, when the practice of making wills has become general, the failure of both heirs and devisees is comparatively rare, and forfeiture is most exceptional. Hence, the reversion of the lord in freehold lands is usually of no value. At the same time, by the conversion of tenures by military service into tenures by plough service,† and by gradual substitution of money payments (now, by reason of the rise in prices, of very small amounts) for other services, the incidents of freehold tenure have in many cases wholly lapsed, while in others they are represented only by the payment of a small fixed quit-rent, and sometimes by an equally small sum (called technically a "relief") payable upon the death of the tenant or a change in the ownership of the land. Thus, for example, in the manor of Plumstead (near Wool-

* "Britton," Book iii. Ch. 4.

† By an Act of Parliament passed in the reign of Charles II., 12 Car. II. c. 24.

wich), in Kent, where the freehold tenants of the manor succeeded in restraining the lords (Queen's College, Oxford) from inclosing the commons.* the only dues payable by the freeholders consisted of small annual quit-rents varying from about 2*s.* 6*d.* to about 30*s.*, and reliefs of the same amounts. But however trivial the service now rendered by a freeholder, and even when such services have wholly ceased to be performed, the tenure remains, and the tenant is entitled to enjoy all such rights as are incident to the tenure.

Speaking generally, therefore, it follows from the constitution of a manor, that within its bounds—which are often, though by no means always, coterminous with those of the parish—three classes of persons interested in the land exist, viz.:—

(*a*) Persons holding land freely of the manor, or freehold tenants;

(*b*) Persons holding land of the manor by copy of court roll, or copyhold tenants;

(*c*) Persons holding land from the Lord of the Manor by lease or agreement, or from year to year.

Amongst the first two classes we usually—though, as we shall see, there are commoners of many other descriptions—find the majority of the commoners; for important rights of common attach both to land held freely, and to land held by copy of court roll of the manor.

These rights, though generally similar in their actual exercise, are of a very different character, from a legal point of view.

To every freehold tenant of a manor belongs a right of common of pasture upon the waste lands or commons of the

* Warrick *v.* Queen's College, Oxford, L.R. 6 Ch. App. 716.

manor. This right is said to be "appendant" to the land which the tenant holds freely of the manor, and is known in law as "a right of common appendant." It differs from most other rights of common in the important characteristic that actual exercise of the right need not be proved. When once it is shown that certain land is held freely of the manor, it follows of necessity* that a right of common of pasture for commonable cattle attaches to the land, and therefore belongs to the owner of the land, and may be exercised by its occupant. "Common appendant," says Lord Coke,† "is of common right, and commences by operation of law, and in favour of tillage; and therefore it is not necessary to prescribe therein as it would be if it was against common right."

To prescribe means to found a claim upon usage dating from before the time of legal memory;‡ and it is, of course, of the essence of such a claim that long usage should be proved. The right of common of pasture appendant is not founded on long usage, but on the legal doctrine that such a right is necessarily exercised over the commons of a manor by the owners and occupiers of the land held freely of such manor. The right, in fact, grew, as Lord Coke intimates, from the necessities of the case. When the fields of the vill were under crop, and the meadows laid up for hay, the only place where the villagers could house their stock was the waste land. Thus every villager, as a matter of course, enjoyed the right of having his cattle on this waste; and this ancient usage is represented at the present day by the right of common appendant enjoyed by the freehold tenants of a manor. The right is of the greatest importance for the purpose of

* Save perhaps in the case of the total conversion of the land so that it cannot be used to raise any fruit of the earth. See *post*, p. 77.

† Tyringham's case, 4 Rep. 37*a*; see also Co. Litt. 122*a*, and Second Institute, part 1, 85.

‡ *i.e.* from before the first year of Richard I.

protecting a common, because, as we have seen, its existence is proved as soon as the tenure of the land is established. Modern methods of stock-farming do not lead to the free exercise of common rights by the larger farmers of a parish; and where a common becomes suburban (and hence of the highest value as an open space), the pasturage is likely to become almost valueless. Hence, it is often difficult to prove actual exercise of common rights in respect of any considerable acreage of land; and the existence of rights which do not depend upon actual user becomes of exceptional importance.

The right of common appendant extends to common of pasture alone. It has been defined to be "the right which every freehold tenant of a manor possesses to depasture his commonable cattle, levant and couchant, on his freehold tenement, anciently arable, on the wastes of the manor."*

From this definition we see that the right is subject to two limitations. It is confined to commonable cattle, and to cattle levant and couchant on the freehold tenement.

Commonable cattle are either beasts of the plough, such as oxen and horses, or animals which manure the land, such as cows and sheep.† Swine, goats, donkeys and geese are not commonable, though special rights founded on long usage may justify their feeding on a common.

The expression "levant and couchant" means literally rising up and lying down, and no doubt originally the animals which the freehold tenant turned out were those which he actually kept on his land, when not on the common.‡ The

* Williams on "Rights of Common," edition 1880, p. 31.

† Tyringham's case, 4 Rep. 37*a*.

‡ In the Isle of Purbeck, Dorsetshire, certain singular rights of quarrying are enjoyed by the inhabitants. In the ancient rules regulating the industry, it is provided that the apprentices of a quarryman must be "levant and couchant" in his house.

words, however, gradually came to have reference rather to the number of cattle which the land was capable of maintaining than to those which it actually maintained. As population increased, and the boundaries of each vill or manor became more sharply defined, wastes and commons became in some places scarcely productive enough to satisfy the wants of the community. It became necessary, therefore, to have some rule by which each tenant of the manor should be prevented from overburdening the common and taking more than his share of the feed. The rule which naturally suggested itself was, that each tenant should turn out the number of beasts which his own lands were capable of supporting. This rule, when reduced by lawyers to precise terms, was stated thus—that the number of animals to be turned out was the number which could be supported on the land, to which the right of common was attached, in winter *—that is, during the season in which, the grass not growing, the right of common is of no benefit to the cattle. And the number to be supported in winter is the number which will live on the stored produce of the land in summer, plus the winter eatage, or growing produce of the winter,† so that, it would seem, the full measure of the right is the number of cattle which could be kept on the commoner's own land if it were devoted entirely to the maintenance of cattle, the common being used in aid during the growing times of the year when the land is under crop. It is now, however, well decided in law that the cattle turned out on the common need have no actual connection with the commoner's own land. The rule of levancy and couchancy, as obtaining at the present day, is a mere measure, by reference to the capacities

* Robertson *v.* Hartopp, 43 Ch. Div. 516, and the authorities there cited.

† Whitelock *v.* Hutchinson, 2 Moody & Robinson 206; Scholes *v.* Hargreaves, 5 T.R. 46, 48.

of the tenant's land, of the number of animals he may turn out.*

It is further to be noticed that the right was originally attached only to ancient arable land. This is perfectly intelligible when we consider that the main work of a village community in the Middle Ages was to cultivate the arable land of the vill, and that this work was carried on, not by each member of the community on his own plot of land according to his own pleasure, but on large fields, owned in strips by the several villagers, and by means of large ploughs pulled by 12 or 16 oxen, and according to fixed rules. Only those beasts which took their share in ploughing and manuring the large common fields could be turned on to the waste land, and only those persons who had a share in these fields could claim any right on the wastes. The same idea is expressed by Lord Coke, in the language of the feudal lawyers, when he explains the origin of common appendant in the case to which we have already referred.†

But though a right of common appendant was necessarily attached to arable land, the right is not lost by the conversion of the land into pasture, wood, garden, or orchard, or by its being in part built over. If the land is wholly built over or turned into a reservoir, so that it is rendered absolutely incapable of producing fruits on which to keep cattle, it is a question, not at present decided, whether the right of common would be extinguished, or, if not extinguished, temporarily suspended. But so long as part of the land is in such a condition that it may still be used to raise eatage for cattle (although not actually so used)—the rule of levancy and couchancy having reference to the capabilities of the land

* Carr *v.* Lambert, 3 Hurlst. & Colt. 499, affirmed L.R. 1 Ex. 168.

† Tyringham's case, 4 Rep. 37*a*. Common appendant may be claimed for a manor, for demesnes must be taken to include arable land. Same case.

and not to any actual lying down or getting up of the cattle thereon—the right of common is unaffected.*

A right of common appendant cannot, however, be exercised in respect of a house which has no land of any kind connected therewith and no means of housing cattle.†

The endeavour has sometimes been made to put the freehold tenant of a manor claiming a right of common appendant to proof that his land was originally arable. It would appear, however, that no such proof is necessary, for the judgment of Lord Coke in Tyringham's case ‡ shows, that every freehold tenure, other than a tenure by knight service, was a tenure by the service of the plough, and the lands held of the manor must therefore have consisted in part at least of arable land.

Such, then, are the rights enjoyed, with reference to the commons of the manor, by the first class of persons interested in land within the manor, the freehold tenants.

Copyhold tenants as a rule possess an interest in the common of equal importance. Their rights of common do not, like those of freehold tenants, exist by virtue of any legal doctrine of general application. But in practice it is very rarely, if ever, that copyhold tenants do not possess rights of common over the wastes of the manor of which they hold; while, from the nature of the tenure, the existence of copyholds is more easy to prove than that of freeholds of the manor.

Copyholders, as we have already said,§ had their origin in the villeins or serfs (*villani*) who tilled the lord's own demesne. They held their homesteads and crofts or pightles of land, their gardens and orchards, and their strips in the

* Carr *v.* Lambert, 3 L.R. 1 Ex. 168.

† Scholes *v.* Hargreaves, 5 T.R. 46, 2 R.R. 532; Benson *v.* Chester, 8 T.R. 396, 4 R.R. 708.

‡ 4 Rep. 37*c*.

§ *Ante*, p. 23.

arable common fields, at the will of the lord,* to whom they were bound to render services in kind, such as to plough his lands and to carry grain to his mill. They were attached to the soil (*adscripti glebae*) and could not be sold by the lord, except upon a sale of the manor; but they could not themselves depart from the manor, and were liable to disabilities and obligations of the most onerous kind. By degrees, however, their services became for the most part commuted into money payments, and it came further to be recognised that a copyholder was not to be disturbed in the occupation of his land so long as he performed his services. He was, however, still considered in law to be a mere occupier or tenant at will of the lord's land, and the freehold interest in his land was considered to belong to the lord; and this is the law at the present day. When a copyholder wishes to sell his land he must surrender it into the lord's hands, and the lord thereupon re-grants the land to the purchaser; and when a copyholder dies, his heir or the person claiming under his will must apply to the lord to be "admitted" or put in possession of the land. These transactions formerly entailed an attendance at the court of the manor, and though this is no longer necessary, a record of every dealing with the land must be entered on the court rolls of the manor, and copies of these entries are the copyholder's title deeds. The copyholder also has to pay not only quit-rents and other dues, but, in many manors, on every death or sale of the tenement, a fine calculated on the improved value of his premises, and amounting sometimes to two years' purchase of such value.

To the copyholder, equally with the freeholder of the

* There are copyholders who do not hold "at the will of the lord." The necessary condition of the tenure is, that the land passes by surrender and admittance at the lord's court, and not by feoffment or deed out of Court; see Duke of Portland *v.* Hill, L.R. 2 Eq. 765, 776, 783. Copyholders holding otherwise than at will are, however, very rare.

manor, the possession of rights of common was formerly a matter of necessity. When his lands were under crop, he must have a place to depasture the cattle which he used in his tillage, and to supply milk and other necessaries of life to his family. He therefore turned out his cattle on the common of the manor, and when the law conferred upon him a certain fixity of tenure in his land, it also continued to him the enjoyment of such rights of common as he had previously used. Such rights could not, however, be considered to exist (like the freeholder's right of common appendant) as of common right, or by the general law of the land, since by the general law the copyholder had no rights whatever. They were ascribed, therefore, to local law, or the custom of each manor.*

In order, therefore, to establish the enjoyment of a right of common of pasture (or other right of common) by a copyholder in connection with (or, in legal phrase, as appurtenant to) his copyhold tenement, it is not necessary to prove long usage in respect of the particular tenement. What must be proved is, that a custom has existed within the manor from time immemorial, that all the copyhold tenants have had and enjoyed the right of pasture or other right in question. To prove the custom, entries in the court rolls of the manor † showing the exercise of the right, and statements by old copyholders and inhabitants of the manor to the effect that they have heard from their ancestors and other old persons that the right existed, may be used; and

* Custom is defined to be local law by the late Sir George Jessel, Master of the Rolls, in Hammerton *v.* Honey, 24 W.R. 603. This is the only instance in which the right to take a profit in the soil of another can be claimed by custom. This exception to the ordinary rules of law was evidently made to prevent the grievous wrong of excluding copyholders from rights which they had long enjoyed, on account of technical rules of law. (See Mr. Joshua Williams' opinion on this point, "Rights of Common," p. 17.)

† See *post*, p. 74.

evidence of the exercise of the right by particular copyholders will be received as evidence that the right belongs to the class generally. In point of fact, the proof which is necessary is proof of enjoyment of the right by the class generally, and not by the owners and occupiers of a particular property.

The right of common of pasture enjoyed by a copyholder by custom in respect of, or appurtenant to, his copyhold land does not differ greatly in its extent and mode of enjoyment from the right of common of pasture appendant, enjoyed by the freehold tenant of a manor. The right cannot be claimed for an unlimited number of cattle,* and it is usually limited in the same way as the freehold tenant's right, viz., by the number of animals levant and couchant on the copyhold tenement, or, as we have explained, the number which the copyhold tenement can maintain in winter. As in the case of freeholds, the cattle need not be actually kept on the copyhold.

The right of pasture is not, however, necessarily confined to commonable cattle, that is, horses, oxen, cows, and sheep. As the right depends entirely on the local custom, if it has been usual to depasture donkeys, goats, swine, or geese, the right of the copyholders to turn out such animals may be established.

Nor is the right confined by law to land anciently arable, though it is probable that as a matter of history the tenement occupied by the copyholder, equally with that owned by the freeholder, must have consisted at least in part of arable land.

Copyhold tenure has given rise in modern times to a third description of land which will be found to exist in nearly every manor, viz., land which was formerly copyhold of the manor, but which has by the process of enfranchisement been converted into freehold.

* A right alleged to be unlimited is always held to be limited by levancy and couchancy (Chapman *v.* Cowlan, 13 East 10).

Enfranchisement consists in the release by the Lord of the Manor of his lordship over the land enfranchised, and is effected, apart from Statutes, by the conveyance of the soil and freehold of the copyhold tenement to the copyholder.

The copyholder thus becomes possessed of a part of the demesnes of the manor previously owned by the lord. He stands in the shoes of the lord, and if the lord previously held his manor of the lord of some other manor, the owner of the tenement formerly copyhold becomes a tenant of that manor, and not of the manor of which he was formerly a copyholder. Thus, if we call the manor of which he was a copyholder A, and the superior manor B, the enfranchised copyholder is a freehold tenant, not of manor A, but of manor B. He cannot, therefore, claim on the commons of manor A the rights of common which are enjoyed thereon by the freehold tenants of that manor; while, on the other hand, being no longer a copyholder, he cannot claim to enjoy any right on such commons by the custom of the manor.* Thus he would, as a matter of dry law, lose all his rights on the commons of A. This result would, however, in most cases be so contrary to the intentions of the parties to the enfranchisement (both lord and copyholder), that the Courts have decided, that, though the common rights are technically gone, a Court of Equity will, where it has apparently been intended to preserve them, protect the enfranchised copyholder in their enjoyment, as if he had not enfranchised.† The deed of enfranchisement, however, often contains some express reference to common rights. If the fee simple of the commoner's tenement is conveyed "together with all commonable rights therewith used or enjoyed," the rights

* Marsham *v.* Hunter, Cro. Jac. 253.

† Styant *v.* Staker, 2 Vern. 250.

are considered to be continued or revived,* and in many cases much more definite words, embodying an express regrant of common rights, are used. On the other hand, there may be an express surrender or extinguishment of the common rights in the deed of enfranchisement, and then of course the enfranchised copyholder will no longer enjoy any such rights.

Enfranchisement is at the present day carried out in many cases under the provisions of the Copyhold Acts by means of an award of the Board of Agriculture. In such cases, it is expressly provided that the common rights shall be unaffected by enfranchisement.†

There is one species of copyhold which demands particular notice.

In many manors, particularly in the south of England, a custom has obtained of making grants of small portions of the waste to be held as copyhold of the manor freed from common rights. Such portions are inclosed ‡ and treated in all respects as other copyhold tenements of the manor. The question has been often discussed, but not yet decided by the Courts, whether these waste-hold copyholds (as they are sometimes called) are entitled to the same rights of pasture on the common of the manor as ancient copyholds. In a case relating to the Manor of Harrow Weald, in Middlesex,§ in which it was first clearly decided that copyholds could be created by such grants, it was laid down that, "although the premises in question had been newly granted by copy of court roll, yet that having been granted by virtue of an

* Worledge *v.* Kingswil, Cro. Eliz. 794; Bradshaw *v.* Eyre, Cro. Eliz. 570. And see *post*, p. 39, as to the words necessary to continue a right of common lost through the extinguishment of the tenure of the land.

† Copyhold Act 1894 (57 & 58 Vict. c. 46.) sec. 22.

‡ This subject is treated of in a later chapter from the point of view of the inclosure effected.

§ Lord Northwick *v.* Stanway, 3 Bos. & Pul. 346.

immemorial custom to demise parcels of the wastes as copyhold, they were to be considered as much copyhold tenements as if they had been immemorially holden by copy of court roll." The inference from this dictum would seem to be, that waste-hold copyholders are entitled to the same common rights as other copyholders of the manor.* The question was raised in a prominent form in the suit against Sir Thomas Maryon Wilson, to protect Hampstead Heath, and an issue was directed by Lord Romilly, then Master of the Rolls, to be tried on the subject by a jury; but owing to the purchase of the Heath by the Metropolitan Board the questions in the suit were not fought out.

The third class of persons whom one may generally expect to find in a manor—or, to use another expression, in the parish in which a common is situate—are the farmers and tenants of the lands belonging to the Lord of the Manor, —partly, probably, ancient demesnes of the manor, and partly lands purchased by him and his predecessors from freeholders, copyholders, or strangers. Now, it is of course possible, that part of this land may be held under leases which confer in actual terms, or by necessary implication, a right of common on the commons of the manor. But it is not usual to find any such provisions, even where a lease exists, and agricultural land in England is usually held on a tenancy from year to year. In such cases the occupancy of the land gives no right upon the commons of the manor, although the tenant may regularly depasture his cattle thereon. A man cannot claim a right against himself; he cannot have common in his own land;† and therefore no right of com-

* The late Mr. Joshua Williams was of this opinion, "Common Rights," p. 33; and see Swayne's case, 8 Rep. 63.

† Grymes *v.* Peacock, Bulst. 17; and see Austin *v.* Amhurst (Hackney Commons, 1877), 7 Ch. Div. 689, where a claim of common by occupiers, as such, and as against their own landlords, was held to be impossible in law.

mon can attach to land which is owned by the owner of the common, however long may have been the enjoyment of the pasturage of the common in fact.* Even under the Prescription Act, where the enjoyment by occupiers, and not by owners, is relied on to prove the right claimed, it has been held that, as the owner of the common could not have an enjoyment as of right against himself, so neither can any right be founded upon the enjoyment of pasture by the tenant of a farm owned by the owner of the common † There is a case, indeed, in which it was held that a right of common appurtenant might be assumed from long user to have been granted by the owner of the common to his tenants of a particular farm; ‡ but in this case the injury complained of by the commoner was committed by another commoner, not by the lord. As a rule, no right can be claimed on a common, for the purpose of protecting it from inclosure or injury at the hands of the lord, in respect of farms and lands owned by the lord.

There are, however, in many manors lands which were at one time owned by the lord, but which have been (since the 18th year of Edward I.) sold by him. To these lands a right of common may, or may not, be attached. They are not freehold of the manor for the following reason. In the 18th year of Edward I. a statute, known from its opening words as the Statute of Quia Emptores,§ was passed,

* It seems somewhat inconsistent with this statement that on a statutory inclosure of a common the Lord of the Manor obtains an allotment in respect of his farms, if he can show that cattle have actually been turned out from them (Arundell *v.* Viscount Falmouth, 2 M. & S. 440; Lloyd *v.* Earl Powys, 4 E. & B. 485; Musgrave *v.* the Inclosure Commissioners, L.R. 9 Q.B. 162). But this practice must be held to be merely a convenient way of assessing the lord's interest in the waste, which is taken to be greater, for practical purposes, when he has depastured cattle than when he has not.

† Warburton *v.* Parke, 2 Hurl. & Norm. 64.

‡ Cowlam *v.* Slack, 15 East 108, 13 R.R. 401.

§ 18 Edw. I. c. 1.

altering the mode of selling or alienating land. Before the statute, when a Lord of a Manor sold or otherwise parted with land, he usually granted it to the purchaser and his heirs, to hold it as tenant of his manor; a process known as sub-infeudation. The Statute of Quia Emptores forbade sub-infeudation, declaring that when henceforth a man conveyed land the purchaser should hold of the same lord and by the same services as the vendor. Consequently, since the 18th year of Edward I., it has not been possible for any subject to create a freehold tenure; and all the freehold tenements of a manor must date from before that time. Sales of land by a Lord of a Manor since that time sever the land sold from the manor. The land sold cannot, therefore, enjoy a right of common appendant which is only attached to land held freely of a manor, or, if attached to other ancient arable lands, must date from time immemorial. Again, the land is not copyhold, and cannot claim rights of common by custom. It may, indeed, before its purchase by the lord have been either freehold or copyhold of the manor. But the tenure was extinguished upon the lord's purchase—since the manor and the tenement held of the manor then came into the same hands, and with the extinguishment of the tenure in this way all rights incidental to the tenure were likewise extinguished.* Nor can there be attached to such land a right of common appurtenant by reason of immemorial usage as of right, since usage as of right could only commence after the sale by the lord, and this sale took place within the time of legal memory, that is, since the first year of King Richard I. The

* Marsham *v.* Hunter, Cro. Jac. **253**; Worledge *v.* Kingswil, Cro. Eliz. 794; Bradshaw *v.* Eyre, Cro. Eliz. 570. The enfranchisement of a copyhold does not in equity and for practical purposes extinguish common rights (see *ante*, p. 34); and the grant of the lord's rights in a freehold does not extinguish such rights even at law. Baring *v.* Abingdon, 2 Ch. (1892) 374; Broome *v.* Wenham, 9 Times L.R. 346.

only foundation (apart from the Prescription Act, to which we shall presently refer) on which a right of common in respect of such land can rest, is that of a grant of the right by the Lord of the Manor within the time of legal memory. Such a grant may be presumed from long user,* and where the land was sold by the lord at a very early date (although necessarily since the 18th year of Edward I.), proof of long user alone would no doubt establish a right. But the more usual case is that of a comparatively modern sale by the lord. In such a case, unless of course actual continuous user of a right of common can be proved under the Prescription Act—a user difficult of proof, as we shall see subsequently—some evidence of an actual grant will be necessary. Sometimes a considerable acreage of land in a manor is sold by the lord with an express grant of common rights. In the Manor of Wimbledon, during the elaborate investigations made before Lord Spencer sold his interest in the common to the public, it was found that such was the case. More often the conveyance from the lord contains general words referring to common rights enjoyed with the land. These words have in certain cases been held sufficient to re-create rights of common.

It is not easy to deduce a clear rule from the various decisions on this question. But the general result seems to be—

(1.) That the question whether any right of common is kept alive or re-created is to a large extent a question of the intention of the parties to the conveyance, such intention being gathered—

(*a*) from the general words used in the deed;

(*b*) from the contemporaneous and subsequent use and enjoyment of the right claimed.

* Cowlam *v.* Slack, 15 East 108.

(2.) That the conveyance or grant should extend to all commons "occupied," "used," or "enjoyed" with the premises conveyed, as distinguished from commons "belonging," or "appertaining," or "appurtenant" to the premises.*

(3.) That even these words will not be sufficient to keep alive or revive any right formerly belonging to the premises, unless there was actual use and enjoyment of the right or quasi-right at the date of the conveyance of the property. Enjoyment of the pasturage or other commodity since the conveyance will also be very material evidence in support of the right claimed, and absence of enjoyment would probably be admitted as evidence against the claim.

Apparently a grant of "all commons profits and commodities at the date of the conveyance or at any time theretofore used occupied or enjoyed" with the premises conveyed by the lord, would have the effect, without contemporaneous or subsequent user, of reviving or re-creating any right formerly existing; but there is no decision on these words.†

It may be added, perhaps, that the general words imported into a conveyance of land by the Conveyancing Act, 1881,‡ would appear to be sufficient, on the authority of the

* In Doidge *v.* Carpenter, 6 M. & S. 47, the words "belonging or appertaining" were considered sufficient to pass or create a right of common. But in this case the lord granted the reversion of a lease, and there was very strong evidence of user both before and after the grant. The Court therefore held that "although there was no right of common which could be transferred, the intention of the parties, as is obvious from their position, must have been to create and confer upon the grantee that right of common which, in fact, he had been enjoying." See the remarks on this case in Baring *v.* Abingdon, 2 Ch. (1892) 374.

† On this subject generally see Bradshaw *v.* Eyre, Cro. Eliz. 570; Worledge *v.* Kingswil, Cro. Eliz. 794; Marsham *v.* Hunter, Cro. Jas. 253; Clements *v.* Lambert, 1 Taunt. 205; Doidge *v.* Carpenter, 6 M. & S. 47; Hall *v.* Byron, 4 Ch. Div. 671–2; Baring *v.* Abingdon, 2 Ch. (1892) 374. Doidge *v.* Carpenter certainly does not seem to be consistent with the other cases, but the case is explained by the Court of Appeal in Baring *v.* Abingdon.

‡ 44 & 45 Vict. c. 41, s. 6 (1).

decided cases, to maintain or revive a right of common previously belonging to the land, if there is contemporaneous user, but not otherwise.

When, therefore, it is found that lands in the parish or manor in which a common is situate have been purchased from the lord, it is important to examine the exact terms of the deeds of conveyance, and to ascertain both the status of the land before it came into the lord's hands, and whether, in fact, rights have been usually, and were, at the time of the purchase from the lord, exercised in respect of the land.

CHAPTER IV.

Of Rights of Common not connected with the Manorial System.

WE have now examined the mode in which rights of common * arise from the constitution of a manor and the relations existing between the manor, or the Lord of the Manor, and the lands in the neighbourhood of a common. As a rule, at least in the south of England, it is in connection with lands which either are or were formerly held of the manor, either freely or by copy of court roll, that rights of common can be most easily proved.

But rights of common, even over a manorial common, may exist quite independently of the manorial system.

In the first place, a right of common over any common may be enjoyed as an appurtenance (or thing belonging) to any land, quite independently of the question whether such land was at any time connected with the manor of which the common is waste.

Such a right must be proved either by the production of the actual grant of the common right, or by long user. A grant to a man and his heirs, owners and occupiers of a certain farm, of a right to depasture on a certain waste or common a certain number of cattle or sheep, or as many cattle or sheep as are levant and couchant on the tenement,

---

* It may be taken that the foregoing and the present chapter apply, for the most part, to any rights of common, and not merely to common of pasture, though, for convenience, that right is referred to. The rules especially applicable to rights other than common of pasture will be discussed in Chapters V. and VI.

would establish a right of common on the waste or common designated.* It is rarely that in modern times an ancient grant of this character is found; but modern grants occur occasionally in connection with the settlement of claims or actions in relation to common rights.

Usually, however, the claim of common appurtenant to land not connected with the manor, of which the common, on which the right is claimed, is waste, must be proved by user of the rights claimed, such user being deemed in law to prove that a grant of the right claimed and enjoyed was once made, though the deed evidencing the grant has been lost. In connection with such claims, however, a curious distinction arises. The claim may either be founded on immemorial usage, or, as it is called in law, prescription—in which case no reference to any grant is made in the form of claim—or upon a modern and lost grant. "Immemorial usage" means usage dating "from time whereof the memory of man runneth not to the contrary." But the memory of man in this phrase is not confined to the memory of living men (though, as we shall see, in actual proof such memory is of great importance); the phrase has a technical meaning. It refers to the whole period which has elapsed since the first year of King Richard I. Any event happening before that date is said to have happened before the time of legal memory; any event happening since, within that time. In order, therefore, to establish a right of common by immemorial usage, it is not considered necessary to prove actual user from the first year of Richard I.—a thing usually impossible of proof—but it is necessary that there should be no proof of the commencement of the right since that time.

* Williams on Rights of Common, 118; and see Co. Litt. 121*b*; Sacheverell *v.* Porter, Cro. Car. 482, Sir William Jones, 396.

Now if the land in respect of which the right is claimed has at any time since the first year of Richard I. been in the same ownership as the common on which the rights are claimed, the rights claimed could not have existed during this period—whether long or short—since a man cannot exercise a right of common over his own land.* In such a case, therefore, there cannot have been an unbroken user as of right from time immemorial, and the claim by prescription fails. But in the absence of any bar of this sort to immemorial enjoyment, a right of common which has been actually enjoyed without reference to manorial considerations is properly claimed by prescription, and is established by reasonable proof of user. Usage for the last twenty years is, in such a case, deemed to be enough to throw upon the party opposing the claim the burden of proving that the right has arisen since the first year of Richard I.† In practice it is usual to support such a claim by the evidence of the oldest inhabitants as to the actual exercise of the rights claimed, and by the production of any entries in court rolls or other documents proving such exercise before the time of living memory. Such evidence conclusively establishes the right.

Wherever it can be shown, that the right claimed must, if it exists, have commenced within the time of legal memory, the claim must be founded, apart from the Prescription Act, to which we shall shortly refer, upon the theory or presumption, that a grant of the common right claimed was made by the owner of the soil of the common, at or before the time, when it can be shown that the right commenced, and that the deed evidencing such grant has been since lost. It is now

* Grymes *v.* Peacock, Bulst. 17; and see Warburton *v.* Parke, 2 Hurlst. & Nor. 64.

† Rex *v.* Jolliffe, 2 B. & C. 54, 59.

established that evidence of continuous user will establish such a presumption.*

There is a third way of claiming common of pasture appurtenant on a common independently of any connection with any manor, viz., under the provisions of the Prescription Act.† This Act was intended to protect rights which had been long enjoyed, but were nevertheless liable to be defeated by proof of their commencement since the first year of King Richard I. It provides in effect that when enjoyment of a right of common claimed in respect of land has been enjoyed as of right without interruption for thirty years, it shall not be defeated merely by showing that the enjoyment commenced prior to such period of thirty years, though it may be defeated in any other way; and that where the right has been enjoyed for sixty years, it shall be deemed

* The most remarkable case on this subject arose with reference, not to a right of common, but to the right of the owner of a building to support from the earth belonging to his neighbour. One of two adjoining owners built a heavy stack of chimneys on his land. After this had stood more than twenty years, the other of the two owners made considerable excavations in his land with a view to the reconstruction of the buildings upon it. The result of these excavations was to let down the chimney. The owner of the chimney brought an action for relief against his neighbour's acts, and the case was carried to the House of Lords, where the Judges were asked for their opinion. It was assumed throughout the case, that the right to support for buildings was not covered by the Prescription Act (though Lord Selborne, in the House of Lords, was inclined to hold otherwise), and consequently the claim of the owner of the chimney was based upon a prescriptive right arising from a lost modern grant or covenant. The House of Lords held that twenty years' uninterrupted enjoyment—the enjoyment being peaceable and without deception or concealment, and so open that it must have been known that the enjoyment in fact existed—is sufficient to confer a prescriptive right without reference to the Prescription Act, and on the theory of a lost modern grant or covenant (Angus *v.* Dalton, 6 App. Cas. 740).

In applying this case to common rights, it would probably not be safe to assume that less than thirty years' enjoyment of the right would establish a lost grant, thirty years being the time prescribed by the Statute in relation to a right of common; but this question is undecided.

See, for a common right established on the theory of a lost modern grant or covenant, Cowlam *v.* Slack, 15 East 108, 13 R.R. 401.

† 2 & 3 Will. IV. c. 71.

absolute and indefeasible unless it appears that the right was enjoyed by some consent or agreement expressly made or given for the purpose by deed in writing. The periods of thirty and sixty years are to run immediately before the date when an action challenging or asserting the right is brought, and no act shall be deemed to be an interruption, unless it has been acquiesced in for one year after the party interested shall have had notice of the interruption and of the person responsible for it. Thirty years' enjoyment will not avail, if part of it has taken place during any disability of the owner of the common to defend his rights, or during the time any action challenging the right was pending; but, if sixty years enjoyment can be proved, these considerations may be disregarded (sec. 7).

As the Prescription Act enables a right of common to be established by user and by user alone, it is natural that the proof of user demanded should be full and exact. It must be carried back for the full period of thirty or sixty years, as the case may be; * and though cesser of user for a time is not fatal if it can be accounted for,† it would seem desirable, if not necessary, to prove some enjoyment of the right in the year next before the action is brought. Exercise of a right on part of a common may, however, be sufficient to establish a right over the whole.‡

In practice, the Prescription Act is not of much service in establishing rights of common. In the first place, manors usually form part of settled estates. Hence, in the case of manorial commons, the common is more often than not in

* Baily *v.* Appleyard, 8 Ad. & Ell. 161.

† Carr *v.* Foster, 3 Q.B. 581.

‡ Peardon *v.* Underhill, 16 Q.B. 120, 123; and see per Tindal, C.J., in Doe dem Barrett *v.* Kemp, 7 Bingham 335. See Williams on "Rights of Common," pp. 176–182, for a summary of the rules established as to claims under the Prescription Act.

the ownership of a tenant for life. But we have seen that the thirty years do not run during a tenancy for life. It is usually, therefore, necessary to prove user for sixty years. This is a very long period, and it is necessary to prove the exercise of the right at the very commencement of the period, since the Act provides that no presumption in favour of the right shall arise from an enjoyment for any shorter periods than those prescribed. It requires a man of over seventy to prove exercise of a right sixty years ago. Supposing this difficulty to be got over, another arises from the nature of a right of common of pasture and its diminished value for farming purposes in modern times. For some years no cattle suitable to be depastured on the common may have been kept on the lands of the claimant; of late years the breeds of cattle mostly kept by farmers are often deemed too valuable to be subjected to the risks of an open common,—risks greatly increased by the removal of the gates which formerly stood across roads traversing commons, and which prevented the straying of cattle, but which have been considered too irksome to traffic. But under the Prescription Act, though interruption for a year or two during the period is excused, it is of great importance to prove user at both ends, and it is just at these points that the difficulty arises.

From these causes it happens, that, while the Prescription Act is universally relied on to prove rights of light (a right the enjoyment of which is, so to speak, automatic), and is also of great use in proving private rights of way, it is of comparatively little service in establishing rights of common. As a practical matter, immemorial usage, or usage establishing the presumption of a lost modern grant, is generally easier to prove than usage for the thirty or sixty years required under the Prescription Act. Still, the Act may, in exceptional cases, be of great use, as, *e.g.*, when a common has been inclosed under an Act of Parliament and all rights extinguished, but has been allowed to remain in fact open and uninclosed, so that other rights have sprung up.*

Common of pasture appurtenant to land not connected with a manor, or claimed in respect of such land under the Prescription Act, may extend to any kind of animal, such as swine, goats, donkeys, and geese, and not only to commonable animals, *i.e.* oxen, horses, cows, and sheep.† The usage alone determines the right.

Such common may also be claimed for a fixed number of animals,‡ and, in that case, it is not necessary to consider the capacities of the land in respect of which the right is claimed for supporting animals, or, in technical terms, to prove that the animals turned out are levant and couchant on the land.§ But the enjoyment of the right must have been consistent with the limitation of the claim to a fixed number. Rights of common for a fixed number of animals seem to have been not uncommon in the Middle Ages, especially in connection with common fields.‖ They are comparatively rare over manorial commons; but such a right has recently been found to exist in a metropolitan common. In the Manor of Banstead, Surrey, a right of common for 200 sheep over the wastes of the manor has been found to belong to the Manor of South Tadworth.¶ Usually a right of common of pasture attached to lands not connected with a manor is

* A most important right, that of cutting litter, was established in Ashdown Forest by means of the Prescription Act (De la Warr *v.* Miles, 17 Ch. Div. 535, 584).

† Bacon's Abridgement, Tit. Common, A; Co. Litt. 122*a*.

‡ Co. Litt. 122*a*.

§ 1 Williams' Saunders, 28*d*. Sir John Thornel *v.* Lassels, Cro. Jac. 27; Stevens *v.* Austin, 2 Mod. 185; Richards *v.* Squibb, 1 Lord Raymond, 726.

‖ As to Common Fields generally, see *post*, Chapter XIV. p. 126; and see especially p. 140.

¶ Robertson *v.* Hartopp, 43 Ch. Div. 489, 490, 515.

measured by levancy and couchancy, like a manorial right of common.*

A right of common of pasture appurtenant to a tenement, but enjoyed not for cattle levant and couchant on that tenement, but for a fixed number of cattle, may be severed from the tenement and enjoyed by a purchaser independently of the tenement to which the right was originally appurtenant.†

When severed, however, the common appurtenant becomes common in gross.

A right of common in gross is a right enjoyed irrespective of the ownership or occupancy of any lands.‡ It may exist by express grant, or by user implying a modern lost grant, or by immemorial usage or prescription. A right of common in gross must be limited to a certain number of cattle, unless the right is claimed by actual grant. In some parts of the country, mainly in the north, an interest in a pasture known as a cattle-gate or beast-gate exists. This interest is sometimes a right of common in gross, though sometimes it is a right of sole pasture, and sometimes an interest in the soil of the pasture.§

* As to the meaning of levancy and couchancy, see *ante*, pp. 2, 27.

† Daniel *v.* Hanslip, 2 Lev. 67.

‡ Co. Litt. 122*a*. See Drury *v.* Kent, Cro. Jac. 15; Spooner *v.* Day, Cro. Car. 432.

§ As to cattle-gate, see *post*, p. 140.

CHAPTER V.

Of Common of Estovers and Common of Turbary.

COMMON of pasture is the right of the most general prevalence over commons; and there is no other right which is in any case assumed by the law to exist without proof of user.

But rights of cutting furze or gorse, heather, fern or brake, and bushes, for fuel, for repairs, and, so far as applicable, for litter, and rights of cutting and digging turf and peat on heaths and moors, for fuel, are very common. Indeed, it is obvious that in early days, when the waste lands of the village community perhaps furnished the only supply of such articles obtainable, the practice of freely taking them must have been as necessary to the life of the community as the practice of depasturing cattle. In the Alpine districts at the present day, the wood of the mountains is of equal importance with their pastures, and a village community in the mountains of the Grisons is esteemed rich or poor according to the quantity and quality of the forests it possesses. One can easily see, however, that as means of communication increased and habits changed, the rough material furnished by the common for fuel, litter, and repairs, would become of much less value in some places than in others, and that the practice of resorting to the common for such products would often fall entirely into desuetude. The great cheapening of coal in the present century has had much to do with the abandonment of peat and turf for fires,* while the use of baker's bread has led to the disuse of the large ovens which were formerly attached to nearly every house and cottage for baking home-made bread, and which were well and quickly heated by a blaze of furze from the common. Hence rights of the character we are describing have been less generally maintained than the right of pasture, though usually to be found existing on any common of importance.

The right of cutting wood and bushes is, as we have seen, known as common of estovers, and the right of cutting and digging turf for fuel is known as common of turbary.

Estovers is a word derived from the Norman-French *estouffer*, to furnish, and common of estovers is the right of taking the loppings of trees, or the gorse or furze, bushes or underwood, heather or fern of a common for fuel to burn in the commoner's house or for the repairs of the house and farm-buildings, hedges, fences, and instruments of husbandry.† The English word corresponding to estovers is bote, and common of estovers comprises fire-bote or house-bote, *i.e.*, a necessary supply of wood for fuel and also for the repair of the house, plough-bote and cart-bote, which respectively relate to the repair of ploughs and other implements of husbandry, and of carts, and hey-bote or hedge-bote, which relates to the repair of hedges or fences.

Common of turbary is the right of taking turf or peat fit for burning—not green turf—for use as fuel in the commoner's house. It exists, not on grass-commons, but on heaths or peat moors. Turf usually means the growing

* It is a common thing to hear from old men, when interrogated on the subject of these rights, that in their youth every cottage and farm-house burnt peat and turf on open hearths, but that the grates now used make such a thing impossible.

† Williams, "Rights of Commons," 186.

heather taken to a slight depth only, so that earth and roots together, when dried, burn slowly with a smouldering flame. Peat is composed of the black earth which consists of old heather and other vegetable matter more or less decomposed. It is dug out to a considerable depth with a spade. Both turf and peat are usually stacked on the common to dry, before being carted home.

Common of estovers and common of turbary, as we have said, are never presumed to exist unless usage is shown. In legal phrase, they cannot be claimed as appendant to land or houses. They usually exist as appurtenant or attached to a tenement, but they may exist in gross, that is, apart from the enjoyment of any house or land.

When claimed as appurtenant or attached to houses or land, they may, like common of pasture, be claimed either by prescription, that is, by reason of immemorial usage, or by a modern grant either actually produced or presumed from long and uninterrupted usage; or they may be claimed under the Prescription Act. The observations already made with reference to this subject when discussing common of pasture apply equally to the rights of common now under consideration.

Like common of pasture, also, common of estovers and common of turbary will generally be found to be enjoyed in respect of lands and houses now or formerly held of, or otherwise connected with, the manor of which the common on which they are exercised forms part. Thus, they are generally enjoyed by the freehold and copyhold tenants of the manor and by persons holding lands formerly copyhold, but subsequently enfranchised; and they will be found attached to lands which at one time belonged to the lord, but have been sold by him, either with an explicit grant of the rights, or with such a grant of the appurtenances as will be held to re-create the rights, if their enjoyment at the time of the grant is proved.*

Such rights may, also, like common of pasture, be attached to lands and houses which are not shown to have had at any time any connection with the manor.†

But there are other rules which apply especially to these rights, and which must now be noticed.

Fire-bote and common of turbary can only be claimed in respect of a house,‡ since the object is to obtain fuel for domestic purposes.

When claimed by prescription, or immemorial usage, they can only be claimed in respect of an ancient house, that is, a house which is not shown to have been built since the first year of Richard I., or in respect of a house built on the site of an ancient house.§ If an old house is pulled down and rebuilt on a larger scale, the supply of wood is limited to that required for the use of the old house.||

But if fire-bote or common of turbary is claimed by modern grant, express or implied, there seems to be no reason why it should not be claimed for use in new houses, since a grant of wood to be burnt in a new house or in all the houses to be built on a certain field could clearly be made at the present day, and such a grant can therefore be proved by long usage.¶ It is probable, however, that user of too large a description would be held invalid to prove any grant, on

* See *ante*, pp. 37–41.

† See Chapter IV.

‡ Tyringham's case, 4 Rep. 37*a*; Co. Litt. 121*b*.

§ Luttrell's case, 4 Rep. 86, 87 (and see interpretation of this case by Hobart, C.J., in Cowper *v.* Andrews, Hob. 39); Costard and Wingfield's case, 2 Leon, 44, 45.

|| Luttrell's case, 4 Rep. 86, 87.

¶ See Countess of Arundel *v.* Steere, Cro. Jac. 25. This case is said to be inconsistent with other authorities, and, so far as regards a prescriptive right, this would be so. But the reasoning of the Court seems really to have had in view a right claimed under a modern grant, express or implied.

the ground that every such grant must be assumed to have been reasonable, and not to have gone to the destruction of the whole commodity claimed.*

There is very little in the authorities about that species of house-bote which relates to the repair of a house, but it is assumed that the rules relating to fire-bote apply equally to this species of estovers.

The rights of plough-bote, cart-bote, and hey-bote, not having any relation to a house, may, it is assumed, be claimed in respect of any land, though of course, if claimed by prescription or immemorial usage, the land must be ancient enclosed land, and not land taken in from the common itself since the first year of Richard I.†

Common of estovers usually extends only to undergrowth, but it may comprise the right to lop trees and even to cut oaks.‡ Thorns and windfalls may be the subject of such a right.§

A right of turbary will not extend to the cutting of green turves for forming grass-plats and similar uses, such a practice being held to be unreasonable and tending to the destruction of the pasture of the common.||

The right of cutting furze, fern, heather, and other small growth for fodder and litter for cattle and subsequently for

* Wilson *v.* Willes, 7 East 121, 8 R.R. 604; and see the remark of the dissenting judge in Countess of Arundel *v.* Steere, Cro. Jac. 25. But compare the view of the House of Lords in Corporation of Saltash *v.* Goodman, 7 App. Cas. 633, where it was held that the possibility that the exercise of the right claimed might destroy the subject-matter of the right was no ground upon which to negative the presumption of a modern grant or condition in favour of the claimant. See p. 68 for some account of this Case.

† We have already alluded to the question which arises in the case of wastehold copyholds, a question which applies to these rights as well as to common of pasture.

‡ Russel and Broker's case, 2 Leon. 209, and 3 Leon. 218; Fisher *v.* Wren, 3 Mod. 250 (as to willows); and see Willingale *v.* Maitland, 3 Eq. 103.

§ Duke of Portland *v.* Hill, L.R. 2 Eq. 768.

|| Wilson *v.* Willes, 7 East 121, 8 R.R. 604; see note * above.

manuring the land of the commoner does not seem to come within the definition of estovers in the law-books. But it is a right which is well established, and is sometimes of great importance. In the recent litigation relating to Ashdown Forest, in Sussex, it was shown that a large body of commoners had been accustomed to mow down the heather, fern, and other small growth with a short scythe, to stack it for drying, then to litter with it their cattle kept upon their tenements, and in the ensuing autumn to cart the litter trampled and manured by the cattle on to their lands, where it formed a very valuable dressing. The existence of the right was challenged by the owner of the soil of the waste, as being contrary to law, but it was established by the Court of Appeal as existing in respect of particular tenements under the Prescription Act, and was subsequently admitted by the owner to exist with reference to all the lands which enjoyed a right of common of pasture on the waste—a right defined by ancient documents.*

In the modern suit relating to Berkhampstead Common, Herts, the freehold and copyhold tenants of the manor were declared to be entitled (amongst other rights) to a right appurtenant to their respective freehold and copyhold tenements held of the manor, "to cut so much furze, gorse, fern, and underwood on the common in question as may be required for the purpose of fodder and litter for all commonable cattle and swine levant and couchant on their tenements, and for fuel, and other purposes of agriculture and husbandry necessary for the beneficial and profitable enjoyment and use of the said tenements."†

* See De la Warr *v.* Miles, 17 Ch. Div. 538, 584. The right in this case could not be clearly shown to have existed from time immemorial in its modern form, and thus the commoners were driven to rest their case on the Prescription Act.

† Smith *v.* Earl Brownlow, L.R. 9 Eq. 241.

In the suit relating to the commons of Plumstead Manor, in Kent, the freehold tenants of the manor were declared to be entitled to a right of common appurtenant to their freehold lands held of the manor, "to cut turf for use as fuel in their dwelling-houses, and to cut such furze, gorse, and fern upon the said common as may be required for fuel to be consumed in the said hereditaments so held by them, and for the purpose of fodder and litter for cattle levant and couchant on the said hereditaments."*

Rights of fodder and litter being annexed substantially to land and not to houses, may, it is assumed, be claimed for any anciently inclosed land without reference to the consideration, whether there is any ancient house, or any house at all, on the land. The decrees to which we have called attention are evidently framed on this view.

Rights of this character when claimed, as is usual, as appurtenant to a house or land must be claimed for use upon such house or land. A right to take such commodities and sell them, and even to take a limited quantity without reference to use on the property in respect of which the claim is made, is bad,† unless, possibly, a distinct grant of such a right be produced.

But a right to take wood, turf, or small growths may be granted in gross irrespective of its use on any tenement.‡ If the grant itself is produced the right may, it would seem, be

---

* Warrick *v.* Queen's College, Oxford, L.R. 6 Ch. 716. See also Hollinshead *v.* Walton, 7 East 485, 8 R.R. 662, where a right of "cutting and taking brackens" was recognised without question. A similar right was established in the case of Banstead Common (Robertson *v.* Hartopp, 43 Ch. Div. 484, 516).

† Valentine *v.* Penny, Noy. 145; Hayward *v.* Cannington, 2 Keble, 290, 311, 1 Lev. 231; Baily *v.* Stephens, 12 C.B. N.S. 91.

‡ Williams, "Rights of Common," 190; Hayward *v.* Cannington, 2 Keble, 311; Lord Mountjoy's case, Co. Litt. 164*b*, 1 Anderson, 307; Queen *v.* the Chamberlains of Alnwick, 9 A. & E. 444.

practically unlimited in extent.* But if the grant is only implied by long usage, although there seems to be no reason why an unlimited grant, being possible, should not be presumed, it would undoubtedly be far more easily established, if the claim and user were definitely limited, as, *e.g.*, to so many cart-loads of wood or turf.

It has been held (as noticed above)† that rights of estovers and turbary cannot be asserted to prevent the inclosure of part of a common, if the land inclosed is of such a nature, that it cannot produce the product to which the right claimed relates. For example, if the land inclosed is a piece of light, sandy, grass-grown soil incapable of producing turf or peat, no right of turbary (in the strict sense) would prevail to prevent an inclosure; and, on the other hand, if the land were of a peaty character, no right of taking gravel could be asserted for the like purpose. Hence it does not absolutely follow, that because rights of turbary or estovers are proved to exist over a common, the inclosure of any particular part of a common would be bad without the consent of the Board of Agriculture. It is probable, however, that, at the present day, the Courts would bear rather against, than for, inclosure on such a question, and would put the lord to proof with some strictness, that growth of the product to which the right related was in the ordinary course of nature impossible. Proof of the existence of the right on the common generally would certainly raise a *primâ facie* presumption against the lawfulness of the inclosure, and it would rest upon the lord to justify his act.

---

* See Lord Mountjoy's case.

† See *ante*, p. 14; Peardon *v.* Underhill, 16 Q.B. 120.

CHAPTER VI.

Of Rights of Digging Gravel and other species of Subsoil.

THE rights we have hitherto been considering relate to the growing vegetation of a common, or, in the case of peat, to that species of soil which may be expected to renew itself.

Rights, however, sometimes exist of taking gravel, sand, loam, clay, and other species of subsoil, and even coal, upon a common. The rules relating to such rights are similar to those affecting common of estovers and common of turbary.

Like those rights, and like common of pasture, they are, in the case of manorial commons, usually, but not necessarily, found in connection with the manorial system, that is to say, enjoyed by freehold or copyhold tenants of the manor of which the common forms part, by enfranchised copyholders or by persons holding land formerly belonging to the Lord of the Manor. But they may exist independently of any manorial relation.

Such right may be claimed by actual grant,* or by long user; and such user may establish either a modern lost grant or a grant made before the time of legal memory. But the right is never assumed to exist without either grant or user.

The right may be claimed as appurtenant to a tenement,

* For instances of such grants see Lord Mountjoy's case, Co. Litt. 164*b*, 1 Anderson, 307; the Queen *v.* the Chamberlains of Alnwick, 9 A. & E. 444; Rex *v.* Warkworth, 1 M. & S. 473.

or in gross. In the latter case, unless a grant were actually produced, some reasonable limitation must probably be shown. Where the right is claimed as appurtenant to a tenement, in the absence of an actual grant, the right must be of a reasonable kind—not calculated to destroy the whole common—and must be confined to taking the commodities claimed for use on the land or in the house (according to the nature of the thing taken) of the claimant. Thus, a claim to take clay without limit for use in a brick-kiln was held to be a bad claim;* and a claim by a copyholder to take sand, loam, and gravel from a common for the necessary repairs of the claimant was defeated on the ground, that there was no allegation "that the house in respect of which the right was claimed was in want of repair, that the claimant entered [the common] for the purpose of digging for and carrying away the sand and other materials claimed for the necessary repairs of the house, and that he used the materials for that purpose."† In the Manor of Harrow, otherwise Sudbury, Middlesex, a right to dig and take sand and gravel in and from Harrow Weald Common for the necessary repairing and amending of the ways, paths, and walks of, and the gardens, orchards, and yards of and belonging to the messuage of the claimant, and for the necessary repairing and amending of the ways in, upon, and belonging and appertaining to the land of the claimant was established. Here the right was claimed and found to exist by prescription—that is, by usage from time immemorial in respect of a freehold house and land within the manor.‡

* Clayton *v.* Corby, 5 Q.B. 415.

† Peppin *v.* Shakespear, 6 T.R. 748; but this case seems to have been little more than a decision on the proper form of pleading.

‡ Duberley *v.* Page, 2 T.R. 391, 392; and see Williams, "Rights of Common," p. 139, where an extract from the pleas in the case is given.

A right to dig coal on a common, for their own uses, claimed by the copyholders of a manor was held to be confined to coal to be consumed on the copyholders' tenements.* In this case, however, there were presentments on the Court Rolls for selling out of the manor, and the decision had regard to these presentments.

Most of the gravel-digging which is seen on commons and wastes is due to the highway authorities. Under the Highway Acts,† surveyors of highways and highway boards are entitled to enter upon waste lands, and to search for, dig, get, and carry away gravel, sand, stone, and other materials for the repair of the highways under their care. Similar powers were conferred upon turnpike trustees by the Acts relating to turnpike roads.‡ These rights, however, are of no use for the protection of a common from inclosure, since it has been held that they only apply to land which is *de facto* open and waste, and that the highway authorities are not justified in breaking down a fence to give access to common land which has been recently inclosed.§

* Duke of Portland *v.* Hill, L.R. 2 Eq. 765, 779.

† See especially the Highway Act, 1835 (5 & 6 Will. IV. c. 50.), sec. 51; and see *post*, p. 102, for a fuller description of the powers of highway authorities.

‡ See especially 9 Geo. IV. c. 126. ss. 80, 87, 89.

§ See per Willes, J., in Tongue *v.* the Plumstead Board of Works, *Times*, 5 Nov. 1866. The judgment on the rule for a new trial is not reported.

CHAPTER VII.

Of Rights of Sole Vesture and Sole Pasture.

ALL the rights which have hitherto been described are rights of common—that is, rights which are exercised in common with, and not to the exclusion of, the owner of the soil.* But there may be rights over a common which, without giving an interest in the soil, exclude the owner of the soil from all enjoyment of some particular product of the common, and are, therefore, not in strictness rights of common, though for practical purposes they are of that nature. There are several varieties of such rights.

The largest in kind is the right of enjoying the sole vesture of a common or other land. This right is defined by Lord Coke to extend to the enjoyment of the corn, grass, underwood, sweepage (*i.e.* everything which falls to the sweep of the scythe), and the like, but not to houses, timber, trees, or mines, or in any way to the land itself.† This right may be enjoyed throughout the whole year, or during part only of the year, and in either case excludes the owner of the soil during the period for which it is enjoyed.‡ The person or persons enjoying the sole vesture may bring an action

* Co. Litt. 122*a*. Usually they are also exercised in common with other persons enjoying like rights. This is obviously the case when a right is claimed by a freeholder or copyholder of a manor; the nature of the case implies that there are, or at least have been, other freeholders and copyholders of the manor entitled to like rights.

† Co. Litt. 4*b*.

‡ Co. Litt. 4*b*, 122*a*.

of trespass against any person entering upon the land,* and may let the vesture, reserving a rent.† The owners of the vesture cannot dig upon the land, as they have no interest in the soil,‡ but they can inclose.§ The owner of the soil during the time when the vesture is exclusively enjoyed by others, cannot bring an action of trespass for a mere entry on the land which affects the surface herbage alone; but he may bring such an action against anyone who drives stakes into the ground, and thus disturbs the soil.‖

Sole vesture may be limited with reference to the growth of the products to be taken. Thus, the first mowing, *prima tonsura* or *prima vestura*, may be enjoyed.

Again, a particular kind of growth,¶ and not all kinds, may be exclusively enjoyed. Thus, an exclusive right to take all the thorns growing on certain land, to be consumed in and about a house and three acres of land, has been upheld.

A more limited right than that of sole vesture is sole pasturage.

Sole pasturage is the exclusive right to take everything growing on the land in question by the mouths of the cattle of the person or persons entitled, but not in any other way.**

* Co. Litt. 4*b*.

† Co. Litt. 47*a*.

‡ Owen, 37.

§ Dyer, 285*b*, pl. 40; Vin Abr., Tit. Herbage (*a*).

‖ Cox *v.* Glue, Cox *v.* Moulsey, 5 C.B. 533.

¶ Dowglass *v.* Kendal, Cro. Jac. 256. It may be doubted whether the limitation to use on a tenement which appears in this case is necessary, since if the right exists to take all the thorns, it cannot matter to the owner of the soil how they are used. Compare Hoskyns *v.* Robins, 2 Wms. Saunders, 320.

** Hoskyns *v.* Robins, 2 Wms. Saunders, 320. In the case of Potter *v.* North, 1 Wms. Saunders, 347, which came before the Courts two years earlier, there was no actual decision on the validity of the claim made, because the facts could not be proved, but the Court inclined to hold the claim good. In the recent case of De la Warr *v.* Miles, 17 Ch. Div. 535, 584, sole common pasturage and herbage was,

This right, like that of sole vesture, may extend throughout the whole year, so that the owner of the soil is excluded from depasturing any cattle at any time, or may apply to part of the year only, so that the owner can put on his cattle at other times. The owners of the sole pasturage may take it with any cattle, and not only with those levant and couchant upon their lands, and may license other persons to put their cattle on,* and may bring an action of trespass against anyone entering the land and treading down the pasturage.† Whether the owner of the soil can bring an action of trespass against a person merely entering on the land and treading down the grass seems doubtful, but he clearly, as in the case of sole vesture, can bring such an action when the soil is disturbed.†

All the exclusive rights to which we have alluded may be claimed either by reason of an actual grant,‡ or, it is presumed, by user establishing a lost modern grant, or by immemorial usage or prescription; § and they may be claimed either as appurtenant to land or houses (according to their nature ||) or in gross—that is, irrespective of the possession of other property. As to the latter mode of claim, there is a

by a decree of the Duchy of Lancaster Court of 3 July 1793, given to a certain class of commoners. It is not quite clear, however, from the remarks of the Court of Appeal, whether in this particular case the right conferred carried with it all the characteristics of sole pasturage, or whether it was merely the ordinary right of common of pasture coupled with the right to exclude the lord from taking any feed by his cattle. The practical question in the action was whether the right of "sole common pasturage and herbage" included the right to cut the surface growth with a scythe and to carry it away for litter. The Court held that it did not, *i.e.*, that the words used did not confer a right of sole vesture.

* Hoskyns *v.* Robins, *ubi supra.*

† Cox *v.* Glue, Cox *v.* Moulsey, *ubi supra.*

‡ Co. Litt. 4*b*.

§ Co. Litt. 122*a*; Sir George Sparke's Prescription, Winch, 6; and see per Wilde, C.J., in Cox *v.* Glue, Cox *v.* Moulsey, 5 C. B. 548.

|| For a claim appurtenant to land, see Hoskyns *v.* Robins, 2 Wms. Saunders, 320; for a claim appurtenant to a house and land, see Dowglas *v.* Kendall, Cro. Jac. 256.

remarkable case in the books in which a right of sole pasture from the 4th of September in every year till the following 5th of April was proved to have been enjoyed by a man and his heirs, and by persons to whom they had by deed sold and leased the right.* And there is another case in which the freemen of Colchester, claiming through the Corporation, were upheld in the enjoyment of such a pasturage right.† Both these are instances of the enjoyment of exclusive rights of pasturage irrespective of any other property; in both cases, also, it was established that such a right might be sold, either in whole or in part, and be enjoyed by the purchaser.

Such exclusive rights may be enjoyed by the freehold or copyhold tenants of a manor,‡ or by any other defined class, such as the owners and occupiers within the bounds of a forest.§

* Welcome *v.* Upton, 6 M. & W. 536.

† Corporation of Colchester and Johnson *v.* Barnes, L.R. 7 C.P. 592, 8 C.P. 527. In Mellor *v.* Spateman (1 Wms. Saund. 343, 346*d*) it was held, that a Corporation could not claim common in gross without number upon a common field during certain times (*i.e.* between harvest and seed-time for two years, and during the whole of the third or fallow year); but that they could lawfully claim for cattle levant and couchant within the town. Probably the right possessed by the Corporation was sole and several pasture (exercisable by the burgesses) during the times mentioned. It is singular, that this case, and those of Cox. *v.* Glue and Cox *v.* Moulsey, all relate to the Burgesses of Derby. Again, in Rex *v.* Churchill, 4 B. & C. 750, the Burgesses of Nottingham were found (in 1825) to be entitled to exclusive rights of pasturage during certain periods of the year over certain large fields, known as the Sand Field, the Clay Field, and the Meadows. Although the Judges who decided this case (which related to rating) speak of the right as a right of common, Blackburn, J., points out in Johnson *v.* Barnes, L.R. 8. C.P. 532, that without doubt the right was one of sole pasturage.

‡ Hoskyns *v.* Robyns, Potter *v.* North.

§ See the case of Earl De la Warr *v.* Miles, 17 Ch. Div. 535, 584. The claim in this case, however, was laid in a class of commoners particularly ascertained by a previous litigation.

CHAPTER VIII.

Of Claims by the Inhabitants of a District to enjoy Rights on a Common.

WE have seen that within the district in which a common is situate, rights over the common may be claimed on many grounds, and enjoyed by many different classes of persons. Thus, the freehold tenants of the manor, and the occupiers of their lands on their behalf, invariably enjoy a right of common of pasture, and often rights of estovers and other rights. The copyhold tenants of the manor, and the occupiers of their lands on their behalf, usually enjoy the same rights as the freehold tenants, where both classes of tenants exist, and a right of common of pasture, and often other rights, where there are copyholders only. The holders of lands formerly copyhold, but enfranchised—or, as they are called for shortness, enfranchised copyholders—and the occupiers of their lands on their behalf, usually enjoy the same rights as the copyholders. The owners and occupiers of lands which have passed through the hands of the Lord of the Manor not infrequently enjoy rights similar to those of the freehold and copyhold tenants. And, finally, the owners and occupiers of lands which cannot be shown to have had at any time any connection with the manor often enjoy rights of common of pasture, of common of estovers, and other rights of common, by virtue of actual grants or long user. We have also seen that a right of common may be claimed in gross—that is, as a separate hereditament or piece of property, passing by devise or descent, and by deed from vendor to purchaser. By these several modes of enjoyment large classes of persons may assert an interest in the common of their district. But, as a rule, the inhabitants of a district, as such, cannot make good a claim to any right of common. This was decided in the time of Queen Elizabeth,* and in a comparatively recent case it was held that the poor, necessitous, and indigent householders residing within a township could not establish a right to take rotten wood to be burned in their houses within the town.† This case seems to have occurred within a chase—the Chase of Whaddon, in the county of Bucks. In Cranbourne Chase, in Dorset and Wilts, a right was in recent years claimed by the inhabitants of the parish of Tollard Farnham to cut furze upon Tollard Farnham Common to burn in their houses in the parish. The claim was supported by very singular evidence, obtained from the parish books relating to the relief of the poor. It appeared, that the overseers had been accustomed to send persons applying for relief on to the common to cut furze, and that furze had been consumed from time immemorial in every cottage in the place, including cottages maintained out of the rates for the use of the poor. The Court, however, found that no right such as that claimed could exist in law.‡

There are cases, however, in which a claim by inhabitants in the nature of a right of common has been held good on exceptional grounds. Thus, in the fen country it has been

* Gateward's Case, 6 Rep. 594.

† Selby *v.* Robinson, 2 T.R. 758. See also Grimstead *v.* Marlowe, 4 T.R. 717 (relating to the Common Meadow at Leatherhead); Att.-Gen. *v.* Mathias, 579, 590, 594 (relating to the Forest of Dean, where, however, the rights of the free miners condemned by the Court had previously been recognized by Parliament, 1 & 2 Vic. c. 43); Chilton *v.* Corporation of London, L.R. 7 Ch. Div. 735.

‡ Lord Rivers *v.* Adams, L.R. 3 Ex. D. 361.

assumed, that grants (it would appear from the Crown) of rights of pasture were made in early times to encourage residence.* And in Royal Forests grants by the Crown in derogation of its forestal rights have been assumed to explain practices of lopping and taking wood which would otherwise have been contrary to the doctrines of the law.† A grant by the Crown to the inhabitants of a vill or district is considered to incorporate those to whom it is made for the purpose of enjoying the benefit of the grant;‡ and corporations may, as we have seen, enjoy rights of common and rights of sole vesture and sole pasture.§

It is seldom that the inability of the inhabitants of a parish or vill to claim a right of common as inhabitants is fatal to the preservation of a common. For though they cannot enjoy the right as inhabitants, most of them enjoy it as occupiers of land to which the right is attached—a fact to which attention was called by the judges who decided against the claim of inhabitants in the time of Elizabeth. After explaining that a right of common ought to be claimed in the name of the owner of the tenement to which it is attached, and that any limited owner, tenant, or occupier ought to claim in the name of the owner, the Court concludes: "So that there is none that hath any interest, though it be but at will, and who ought to have common, but by

* Weekly *v.* Wildman, 1 Lord Raym. 405; and see Dean and Chapter of Ely *v.* Warren, 2 Atk. 189.

† See *post*, p. 163.

‡ Willingale *v.* Maitland, L.R. 3 Eq. 103. It is to be noted that in the Epping Forest Arbitration Lord Hobhouse (now a member of the Judicial Committee of the Privy Council), who was endowed with statutory powers to decide such questions, held, notwithstanding the previous case of Rivers *v.* Adams, that the inhabitants of the parish of Loughton were entitled to take lopwood from the forest.

§ Where such a right is vested in the corporation of a town, the right is exerciseable by the freemen and burgesses of the town.

good pleading may enjoy it."* And the same fact probably explains the constant reference in old Acts of Parliament and other documents to the enjoyment of rights of common by "tenants and inhabitants." But there are some cases in which the inability of inhabitants as such to make a valid claim to a right of pasture or estovers has very serious consequences. A Lord of a Manor not infrequently purchases a great portion of the land to which rights of common over the common of his manor are attached. The occupiers of such land have been accustomed before the purchase to exercise rights, and they probably continue to exercise them after the purchase; while not infrequently the tradition and talk of the place is that all inhabitants enjoy the right. But, if the lord incloses, the occupiers of his own land can, as such, claim no right on the common against their own landlord, while as inhabitants they are precluded from claiming by the law. Hence, a whole district may be suddenly deprived of an open space and of rights which they have, without gainsaying, enjoyed over it from time immemorial. Such was the case in the village of Tollard Farnham, to which reference has been made. Happily, it is rarely that some landowner entitled to rights cannot be found.

There are, moreover, two recent cases in which Courts of the highest authority have decided in favour of claims of inhabitants to rights somewhat akin to common rights.

The first case arose in a litigation between the Corporation of Saltash and the free inhabitants of certain ancient tenements in the borough. The Corporation, which was an ancient one, holding many Royal Charters, established a prescriptive right to an oyster fishery in the navigable river Tamar. The Corporation claimed that this right

* Gateward's Case, 6 Rep. 596 (see Mr. Joshua Williams' translation, "Rights of Common," p. 17).

was exclusive against everyone. But the free inhabitants of certain ancient tenements in the borough claimed the right to dredge for oysters from the 2nd of February to Easter Eve, and to catch oysters and carry them away for sale. It was proved that such inhabitants had, in fact, acted in accordance with their claim from time immemorial without interruption and as of right; but the Corporation disputed, that the right claimed could exist in law, and cited Gateward's case and the decisions following it down to that in the Tollard Farnham case. A special case was stated for the opinion of the Court, and in this it was found, amongst other things, that the usage of the free inhabitants (inasmuch as it extended to the sale of the oysters) tended to the destruction of the fishery. The Courts below decided against the claim of the inhabitants, but the House of Lords (consisting of Lord Selborne, Lord Cairns, Lord Bramwell, Lord Watson, and Lord Fitzgerald, Lord Blackburn dissenting) held that a lawful origin for the usage ought to be presumed, if reasonably possible; and that the presumption which ought to be drawn, as reasonable in law and probable in fact, was, that the original grant to the Corporation was subject to a trust or condition in favour of the free inhabitants of ancient tenements in the borough in accordance with the usage. The House further excluded the application of Gateward's and other similar cases, by pointing out that the claim was not to a *profit à prendre* in the soil of another, inasmuch as the free inhabitants could not claim independently of and against the Corporation, of which they were, in fact, members, but only through the Corporation and under a trust in favour of such inhabitants.* The claim of the inhabitants was thus upheld.

* Corporation of Saltash *v.* Goodman, 7 App. Cas. 633.

This decision has been recently followed by the Court of Appeal (Lord Esher, M.R., and Lindley and Lopes, L.JJ., affirming Mr. Justice Charles) in another case arising under somewhat singular circumstances. A road was set out as a public highway under an Inclosure Act of 1774. There was no allotment of the soil of the road in the Award, and no evidence as to the ownership; but the pasturage on the road had for many years been let annually by the inhabitants in Vestry assembled, and the persons to whom it was let had turned out animals to graze on the road. The Lord of the Manor brought an action for trespass against the tenants of the Vestry. The Court held that a lawful origin for the acts of the Vestry must be presumed from the long usage, and that the presumption was, that the road was vested in some person or persons as trustees for the parishioners. There was the special difficulty in this case, that inasmuch as a trust in favour of the parishioners would create a charity, the deed (which must have been made in modern times) ought to have been enrolled; and no enrolment was produced. The Court held, however, that it might be presumed either that the grant had been enrolled and the enrolment lost, or that the grant had been made for some purpose which had since been lost sight of, but which did not require the deed to be enrolled.*

With reference to the existing trustees, it was further decided that the Churchwardens and Overseers might, under the Poor Relief Act, 1819,† and the Statute of Limitations, maintain a title to the soil of the road on behalf of the parish by virtue of undisturbed possession for more than a century.

These two cases, the one dealing with a claim founded on

* Haigh *v.* West, 1893, 2 Q.B. 19.
† 59 Geo. III. c. 12.; see sec. 17.

immemorial usage, the other with a claim founded on a lost modern grant, and both establishing a right in an unincorporated body of inhabitants, show how far the Courts are disposed to go in the direction of upholding actual and long-continued usage, even by what has been designated in the older cases as an uncertain and fluctuating body of persons. They do not, of course, overrule Gateward's case, and it may be difficult to establish a trust against an ordinary Lord of a Manor who produces the grant of his manor, and who has exercised such acts of ownership over a common as clearly establish his interest in the soil. But when, as is sometimes the case, there is a singular lack of direct evidence of ownership by the lord, and the evidence points on the contrary (as in the Tollard Farnham case) to a practical ownership of the common by the inhabitants, there seems to be no reason why (as in Haigh *v.* West) the common should not be presumed to have been vested in some person or persons as trustees for the whole of the parishioners. By this or some other method the cases in question will, it is hoped, be utilized in the future to prevent the destruction of interests which have existed for centuries, and are as much entitled to the protection of the law as that interest in the soil of waste places which has been ascribed to the Lord of the Manor.*

* The case of the Corporation of Saltash is the subject of some remarks by Lord Selborne in Neill *v.* Duke of Devonshire, 8 App. Cas. 154. And in Smith *v.* Andrews [1891], 1 Ch. 678, an endeavour was made to found upon it a right of fishing by the public in a non-tidal river; the original title of the plaintiff's predecessors to a several fishery must, it was argued, be held to have been displaced by some abandonment or dedication to the public, or some conveyance to trustees for the public of the right to fish. This argument was, however, set aside by North, J.; see 700–702.

CHAPTER IX.

Of the Mode of Ascertaining Common Rights, and of the Loss or Extinguishment thereof.

IN the previous chapters we have endeavoured to classify the persons who are likely to be found to enjoy rights of common over an ordinary manorial common.

They may be thus summed up:—

(1.) Freehold tenants of the manor of which the common is waste, or, in other words, persons owning land held freely of the manor.

(2.) Copyhold tenants of the manor, or persons owning land held of the manor by copy of court roll.

(3.) Enfranchised copyholders of the manor, or, in more exact language, persons owning land which was formerly held of the manor by copy of court roll, but which has been enfranchised.

(4.) The owners of land which has been purchased or otherwise acquired from the Lord of the Manor since the passing of the Statute of Quia Emptores, and in respect of which a grant by the lord of a right of common can be proved to have been made in express terms, or will be presumed to have been made by reason of the long user of the right, and the words of the conveyance.

(5.) The owners of any land who can prove a grant of a right of common either—

(*a*) by production of the grant (a very rare case), or

(*b*) by continuous and uninterrupted user from time immemorial, or

(*c*) when the history of the land precludes the existence of the right from time immemorial, by continuous and uninterrupted user for such a period as will raise the presumption of a lost grant.

(6.) The owner or occupier of any land in respect of the occupation of which uninterrupted user can be shown in the terms of the Prescription Act (2 & 3 Will. IV. c. 71).

We have also seen that in certain cases classes of persons are entitled to all the surface growth, or to the pasturage of a common, to the exclusion of the Lord of the Manor or other owner of the soil; and, that though the inhabitants of a district cannot as a rule claim rights of common, there are exceptional cases in which they may successfully assert an interest in common land.

We will now indicate some practical means of ascertaining what rights are enjoyed over a common, the whole or part of which has been inclosed.

One of the first steps is to enquire, whether any persons have been in the habit of turning out cattle or other animals on the land enclosed, or of cutting gorse or bushes, or of cutting turf (not green sward, but heather with the roots and soil), or of digging peat, gravel, sand, or loam. If any such user is found to exist, the lands from which the cattle or animals have been turned out, or the lands or houses upon which the products of the common have been used, should be ascertained, and an endeavour should be made to find out whether any past or present connection with the manor exists, or under which of the categories described above the user of the common can be placed.

Contemporaneously with this enquiry into the actual use of the land enclosed, it is well to look at any account of the parish or district which is to be found in any county or local history. Not infrequently mention will be found of some manor which has been forgotten of recent years, or reference will be made to valuable sources of information.

If the land enclosed is waste of a manor, it becomes important to obtain access to the rolls of the manor. Occasionally these will be found in the Public Record Office, open to public inspection; but usually they are in the hands of the steward of the manor, who, as a rule, is also the solicitor to the lord. This officer may be found willing to produce the rolls for inspection. If not, inspection can be compelled at the instance of any freehold or copyhold tenant of the manor.* Upon the rolls will usually be found presentments of the rights of the tenants of the manor over the wastes, of encroachments on the wastes, perhaps also of grants of portions of the waste to be held as copyhold with the consent of the homage. Court rolls are usually written in Latin up to the middle of the last century, subsequently in English.

It may be that no actual use of the common of recent years can be ascertained; or only use by cottagers whose cottages belong to the lord, or by dairymen or others whose premises are far too small to bear the cattle they have turned out according to the rule of levancy and couchancy; or, owing to other difficulties, the actual use of the common may not seem to be of a nature to support any legal right of common.

It does not follow even in this case that no right of common exists.

The right of common enjoyed by freehold tenants of the manor depends in no way upon user, but is enjoyed by the common law. Again, it may appear from the court rolls or other documentary evidence that rights of common were

* The King *v.* Shelley, 3 T.R. 141–2, 1 R.R. 673.

formerly exercised by copyhold tenants of the manor, or other persons, or were granted to be enjoyed in connection with particular lands or by particular persons. In all these cases the question then arises, have the rights of common which can be clearly shown * to have formerly existed been lost or extinguished?

Now a right of common may be extinguished by the release of the right by deed in favour of the Lord of the Manor, or other owner of the soil of the common. In a recent case, relating to the commons of the Manor of Banstead, the Lord of the Manor set himself to acquire all the rights of common. He offered various inducements to commoners—the payment of money, the enfranchisement of their copyhold lands, the conveyance of a portion of the common land—and many commoners by deed released their rights to him.† It is more usual to find that common rights have been extinguished by the purchase of the lands to which the rights are attached. As we have seen, when the common itself, and the land to which a right over the common is attached, come into the same hands, the right is extinguished. The extinguishment in this case is commonly said to be effected by unity of possession. Similarly, if a commoner were to take a lease of the waste in which he has a right of common, his right would be suspended during the lease. It has also been held, that, if a commoner entitled to a right of common, appurtenant to his tenement, over lands belonging to different owners, purchases the land of one of such owners,

* We say "clearly shown," for, when there is no recent user, the Courts require strict proof of the existence of the right claimed. The absence of user is considered as some evidence, though not conclusive, against the existence of the right.

† Fortunately, after a large sum of money had been spent by the lord, when he attempted to inclose, it was found that ample rights of common still remained to make any inclosure illegal. See Robertson *v.* Hartopp, 43 Ch. Div. 484, 513.

his right is extinguished over the whole;* but this doctrine does not apply to common appendant, and does not, therefore, affect the right enjoyed by a freehold tenant of the manor.

If, however, a right of common has not been released by deed, or extinguished by unity of possession, it will be held to be still in existence, unless evidence be adduced amounting in the opinion of the Court to proof that the commoner has abandoned his right. Mere non-user will not prove the loss of the right, unless it is coupled with such circumstances as raise a presumption of an abandonment. It is not so much the cessation of the enjoyment, or the period of such cessation, as the nature of the act done by the owner of the right of common, or of the adverse act acquiesced in by him, which is material to a consideration of the question whether or not the right has been lost.† In a very remarkable case relating to a right of light, it was proved that the owner of certain ancient windows had closed them for nineteen years, but that he had re-opened them when a neighbouring owner erected a building which would have obstructed them. It was held, that the mere closing of the windows for nineteen years did not in itself prove the loss of the right of light, but that the question whether the right was lost must depend upon whether the owner of the windows had so closed them as to manifest an intention of permanently abandoning his right, or so as to lead the adjoining owner to incur expense or loss in the reasonable belief that the right of light had been

* Tyringham's Case, 4 Rep. 385; it must be remembered that in this case the common was claimed over two tracts of land belonging to different persons, and that the commoner had purchased the whole of one tract, thus throwing the whole burden of the common rights on the other. The writer is not aware that the doctrine has ever been applied to the purchase by the commoner of a small portion of a large manorial waste.

† Reg. *v.* Chorley, 12 Q.B. 515. This case related to a private right of way, but the law as to the loss or abandonment of easements and of rights of common is based upon the same considerations.

permanently abandoned.* In another case, where a wall containing ancient lights was pulled down and buildings were erected by an adjoining owner inconsistent with the ancient lights, and expenses incurred upon the buildings, no right of action in respect of the ancient lights was allowed, the pulling down of the wall being taken as evidence of an intention to abandon the ancient windows.† And there is an important case in relation to common rights to the same effect. A right of common appurtenant found to exist in respect of a tenement formerly in a condition to support cattle was held not to have been lost or suspended because for thirty years the tenement had been in such a condition that no cattle had been or could be actually maintained thereon. If, it was said by the Court, the character of the tenement had been completely altered "so that it could not be applied to the purpose of providing fruits on which to keep cattle—if, for instance, a house of considerable extent had been built upon the land and its neighbourhood, or if it was turned into a reservoir—it might be a question whether the right of common were not extinguished or suspended." This question the Court did not decide, but they held that changes in the use of the land which fell short of such a complete conversion would not affect the right.‡

Speaking generally, then, it may be assumed that if a common right can be clearly shown to have existed—for example, if it should be proved (*a*) that certain lands are held

* Stokoe *v.* Stinger, 8 E. & B. 31.

† Moore *v.* Rawson, 3 B. & C. 332.

‡ Carr *v.* Lambert, 3 Hurlst & Colt. 499, affirmed L.R. 1 Ex. 168; see also on the question of abandonment, Ward *v.* Ward, 7 Ex. 838; Cooke *v.* Corporation of Bath, L.R. 6 Ex. 177, and Crossley and Sons *v.* Lightowler, 3 Eq. 278, 2 Ch. 478. In a recent case Mr. Justice Charles held that a right of common was lost over a part of a waste of a manor, where such part had long since ceased to produce any grass or herbage, and no attempt had been made to exercise the right of pasture upon it. See Scrutton *v.* Stone, 9 Times L.R. 478.

freely of the manor, or (*b*) that certain lands are held by copy of court roll, and the rolls show a custom for all copyholders to exercise a specified right of common—the fact that the right has not been exercised for many years, even for the whole period of living memory, will not in itself destroy the right. It follows, therefore, that in such a case the lord cannot inclose without the consent of the Board of Agriculture, and is put to proof that his projected inclosure is for the public benefit.

It is to be borne in mind, however, that the Courts are disposed to look unfavourably upon a right that has not been exercised. Though non-user will not deprive a commoner of his right when the existence of the right is established, if there is any doubt, whether it ever existed, the fact of non-user will be admitted as important evidence against its existence. It is, therefore, most important to exercise common rights, if only, so to speak, nominally, as by turning out cattle, or cutting a little gorse, once a year. The user should, of course, be open, and of a character to be known by the Lord of the Manor, or his agents, if they care to enquire. It should also be a user strictly justified by the right, and not in any way excessive or irregular. In the case of a right of common of pasture no more cattle should be turned out than the tenement can maintain, according to the rules previously described. If it is a right to cut bushes, or dig gravel, for use on the commoner's holding, the bushes or gravel should be taken to the house or land and used there. A right need not, however, be exercised over the whole of a common; exercise on part is evidence of a right on the whole.*

* Peardon *v.* Underhill, 16 Q.B. 120, 123; per Tindal, C.J., in Doe dem. Barrett *v.* Kemp, 7 Bing. 335.

CHAPTER X.

Of the Power of Local Authorities to prevent Inclosures by the Lord of the Manor.

We have now seen, that, speaking generally, the Lord of a Manor cannot inclose any part of a manorial common without the consent of the Board of Agriculture, provided it can be shown that any rights of common exist over it.*

The various persons and classes of persons who may be expected to possess rights over a manorial common have been indicated,† and some suggestions offered as to the enquiries which should be instituted to ascertain what rights exist.‡

It has also been shown that common rights clearly proved to have existed are not lost by mere non-user, but that such a state of facts must be proved as to establish an intention on the part of the commoner to abandon his rights.§ At the same time it has been pointed out, that neglect to exercise common rights throws great difficulties in the way of this proof, and that the exercise should be open and in accordance with the rights claimed.‖

We have now to consider how local authorities can aid in maintaining rights of common, and in preventing inclosure by the lord on the ground that no such rights exist.

We will take, first, the case of what used to be called Urban Sanitary Authorities, that is, the municipal

* *Ante*, Chap. II.
† *Ante*, Chap. IV. to VIII.
‡ *Ante*, Chap. IX., p. 73.
§ *Ib.* p. 76.
‖ *Ib.* p. 78.

authorities of Corporate Boroughs, and Urban District Councils.*

The Commons Act, 1876 † (sec. 8), provides that the Town Council or Urban District Council (we use the terms sanctioned by the Local Government Act, 1894 ‡) of any borough or urban district possessing 5,000 inhabitants according to the last published census, may, in relation to a common which is situate either wholly or partly in the town over which the Council has jurisdiction, or within six miles of any such town (in the Act named a suburban common), do the following (amongst other §) acts:—

(1.) *It may acquire the common by gift and hold it without licence in mortmain on trust for the benefit of the town.*

(2.) *It may similarly acquire and hold "any rights in the common."* ||

(3.) *It may purchase and hold on trust for the benefit of the town, with a view to prevent the extinction of the rights of common, any saleable rights in common or any tenement of a commoner having annexed thereto rights of common.*

* A Corporate Borough is a town possessing a Royal Charter of Incorporation. The head officer of such a borough is invariably a Mayor or Lord Mayor, and the governing body is a Town Council, consisting usually of a Mayor, Aldermen, and Town Councillors. The legal name of such governing body is usually "the Mayor, Aldermen, and Burgesses of the Borough of ——— acting by the Council." An Urban District (not a Corporate Borough) is either an Improvement Act District or a Local Government District. Improvement Act Districts have generally been constituted by special Acts of Parliament. Local Government Districts are constituted by the Local Government Board under the Local Government Acts. Henceforth Improvement Act Commissioners and Local Boards will be known as Urban District Councils, and their districts as Urban Districts. (See Public Health Act, 1875, 38 & 39 Vict. c. 55. s. 6; Local Government Act, 1894, sec. 21.)

† 39 & 40 Vict. c. 56. ‡ 56 & 57 Vict. c. 73.

§ The functions of the local authorities not here noticed relate to proceedings before the Board of Agriculture, and are dealt with elsewhere, see *post*, pp. 117, 246.

|| Having regard to the next paragraph of the enactment, these words probably refer to limited estates in the soil of the common—*e.g.*, the interest of a tenant for life. They would enable a local authority to take a lease of a common. Probably they do not refer to common rights.

Expenses incurred by a Town Council or Urban District Council under this enactment will be defrayed "out of any rate applicable to the payment of expenses incurred by such authority in the execution of the Public Health Act, 1875, and not otherwise provided for."*

In ascertaining whether a common is "within six miles of the town" (the language of the enactment), distances are to be measured in a direct line to the nearest part of the common from the town hall, or if there be no town hall, from the cathedral or church, or if there be no cathedral and more churches than one, from the principal market place. And when part only of the common is situate within six miles of the town as thus measured, such part shall be deemed for the purposes of the enactment to be a common separate and distinct from the rest of the common.†

We see, then, that a Town Council or Urban District Council has two important means of precluding inclosure by the Lord of the Manor. If some owner of the manor is willing to part with his interest in the common by way of gift to the Corporation or District Council, all danger of any inclosure by him or his successors in title will be removed. Similarly, if the lord is willing to make a lease of the common at a nominal rent, the common would be secured during the term of the lease.‡

Such arrangements between Lords of Manors and local

* Commons Act, 1876, sec. 8.

† Commons Act, 1876, sec. 8. The effect of these words last quoted would be to prevent the purchase of any part of the soil of a common lying beyond six miles from the town. But they have no meaning in relation to the purchase of common rights, because a right over the part of a common within six miles would also be exerciseable over the part beyond six miles.

‡ Under the Public Health Act, 1875 (38 & 39 Vict. c. 55.), sec. 164, any Urban Authority (*i.e.* any Urban District Council) may purchase or take on lease lands for the purpose of being used as public walks or pleasure grounds. Apparently a common of moderate size might be purchased or leased under this enactment, as well as under the provisions of the Commons Act, 1876.

authorities are not by any means out of the question. The Lord of the Manor of Banstead was anxious in 1865 to make over to the public his interest in Banstead Downs; but there was then no local body capable of receiving and holding it. Had it been otherwise, the long and costly litigation which was necessary to protect the commons of Banstead would probably have been avoided. Many lords would be very glad to be relieved of the trouble and expense of taking care of their commons, if they were sure that they would be transferred to safe keeping.

If a Corporation or Urban District Council acquires the soil of a common, it would, it may be assumed, have a right to apply the appropriate rates to the protection, maintenance, and improvement of the common as a piece of property belonging to the Corporation or District Council.

But to set at rest any question of the application of rates, and also to secure full powers of keeping order, it would be well that the Corporation or Council in any such case should apply to the Board of Agriculture for a provisional order for the regulation of the common under the Commons Act, 1876. Power to apply for such an order is conferred by sec. 8 of the Commons Act, 1876, if the consent of persons representing one third in value of the interests in the common be obtained. As the Council would already possess the interest of the Lord of the Manor, in many cases it would itself represent the necessary proportion of interests; in others there would be little difficulty in obtaining the concurrence of a sufficient number of commoners. Upon any such application the Corporation or Council would naturally ask to be invested with powers of management under the provisional order and the Commons Act provides that such powers may be conferred upon them by the Board of Agriculture.*

* Commons Act, 1876, sec. 8, par. 7.

The scope of a provisional order for regulation, and its consequences, will be discussed in a later chapter. For present purposes it is sufficient to point out that such an order, when confirmed by Parliament, precludes subsequent inclosure by the Lord of the Manor, even when the local authorities are not owners of the soil.*

We have, however, to consider the case where the Corporation or District Council is unable to obtain from the Lord of the Manor a gift of the soil of his common. If, nevertheless, as we have just seen, they are able to obtain a provisional order, confirmed by Parliament, for the regulation of the common, they may in this way preclude inclosure; but this also may be impracticable. The remaining means open to them to protect the common is to purchase some right of common. As we have seen, the Act enables them to purchase either "a saleable right in † common," or "a tenement having annexed thereto rights of common." The only rights of common which can be said to be saleable apart from the tenements to which they are attached, are rights of common for a fixed number of animals, or rights of common in gross.‡ Such rights are rare in the South of England, but in the Midlands and North, where gated or stinted pastures are not uncommon, they may often be found. A right of common in gross is, as we have seen, a right to turn out a certain specified number of beasts on a common, or a right to take a certain specified quantity of some product, such as firewood, or litter, or gravel. It would hardly, speaking generally, be safe for a local authority to buy such a right, unless it had previously been the subject of separate sale and purchase, and had been exercised by or on behalf of successive owners. When such a right is clearly established in this

* Commons Act, 1876, sec. 36.

† Probably a misprint for "of."

‡ See *ante*, pp. 49, 56, 59.

way, there can be no better safeguard against inclosure, and no right which would be more valuable in the hands of a local authority.

In the South of England, at least, however, it will more often be found that all the rights over a common are attached to lands and houses. In this case it will be necessary for the local authority to buy the land or house in order to acquire the right. Where the right in question is a right of common of pasture, care should be taken to purchase sufficient land to maintain at least one animal, commonable on the particular common, levant and couchant. And where the right has been exercised in respect of a considerable farm or estate, it should be ascertained, that the right is attached to the particular portion of the estate proposed to be purchased; since it not infrequently happens, that, of a large estate, part can be clearly shown to be held of the manor or otherwise entitled to rights, while no such proof can be given with reference to other parts. When the right proposed to be purchased is a right to take firewood (fire-bote), or wood for the repair of a house (house-bote), it will be necessary to buy the house or cottage in which the wood has been used, and it must be ascertained that the house is an ancient one, or stands on the site of an ancient house. It should also be borne in mind that the purchase of a right of this kind may not prevail to prevent the inclosure by the lord of a portion of the common (if there be such) incapable in the ordinary course of nature of producing wood.* Similar considerations apply to a right of taking turf for fuel. Rights of taking heather and undergrowth for litter and manure, and bushes for the repair of hedges, and gravel or loam for the repair or dressing of land, would appear to attach generally to all the land in the holding

* See *ante*, p. 14, Peardon *v.* Underhill, 16 Q.B. 120.

entitled to the right, and may, it would appear, be apportioned like common of pasture, on the division of the tenement; so that purchase of a part of the tenement would carry with it a right to take a proportionate quantity.

When a Corporation or District Council has purchased a right of common, the right should be exercised sufficiently to enable evidence of such exercise to be given, if necessary, on any enquiry by the Board of Agriculture, or in any legal proceedings. The remarks previously made as to the mode of exercising common rights apply to such a case.*

Where land or a house has been purchased in order to carry the right, the land or house may be used in any manner convenient to the local authority, provided its character be not so altered as to raise a presumption that it is intended to abandon the right.†

If after such a purchase the Lord of the Manor attempts to inclose any part of the common, the Corporation or District Council should at once give him notice, that they object to the inclosure as an infringement of their rights, and should also warn him, that the inclosure cannot be legally made without the consent of the Board of Agriculture, or without previous advertisement in the local papers.‡ If the lord still persists in the inclosure, appropriate legal proceedings should be taken.§

The Commons Act, 1876, does not apply to any metropolitan common, *i.e.*, any common within the Metropolitan Police District.||

The powers of local authorities in relation to such commons will be separately dealt with.

---

* See *ante*, p. 78.

† See *ante*, p. 77.

‡ See *ante*, Chap. II.

§ See *ante*, p. 21.

|| Commons Act, 1876 (39 & 40 Vict. c. 56.), sec. 35; Metropolitan Commons Act, 1866 (29 & 30 Vict. c. 122.), sec. 4.

The Local Government Act, 1894,* gives to District Councils generally the same powers to prevent inclosure by a Lord of a Manor as those enjoyed by Corporations of Boroughs and Urban Councils of districts of 5,000 inhabitants under the Commons Act, 1876, with these differences:—

(1.) The powers are to be exercised "in relation to any common *within* their district."†

(2.) They can only be exercised with the consent of the County Council.‡

(3.) In addition to other powers, District Councils may, with the consent of the County Council, "*aid persons in maintaining rights of common where, in the opinion of the Council,§ the extinction of such rights would be prejudicial to the interests of the district.*"‖

In considering the effect of these variations from the terms of the Commons Act of 1876, it is important to distinguish between—

(1) Urban District Councils for districts of more than 5,000 inhabitants; ¶

(2) Urban District Councils for districts of less than 5,000 inhabitants;

(3) Rural District Councils.

District Councils coming under the second and third heads take no powers directly under the Act of 1876; and

---

* 56 & 57 Vict. c. 73. s. 26 (2) and (3). † Sec. 26 (2). ‡ *Ib.*

§ Grammatically it is doubtful whether "the Council" here means the District Council or the County Council. The question is not of much importance, since substantially both Councils must arrive at the opinion indicated in the Act in order to sanction the necessary action.

‖ Sec. 26 (2).

¶ The Council of a County Borough (*i.e.* a Borough which is a County of itself) is expressly clothed with all the powers enjoyed by a District Council (Local Government Act, 1894, sec. 26 (7)); and being a County Council it does not, of course, require the consent of any other County Council.

they must, therefore, depend wholly upon the powers conferred by the Act of 1894.*

It would seem clear, therefore, that a Rural District Council, and what may be called a small Urban District Council, will have no power of resisting inclosure by a Lord of a Manor on a common wholly without its district. Its powers do not, as in the case of a large Urban District Council, extend to a common which, though outside the district, is within six miles of the centre.

When a common is situate partly within and partly without the district, the powers of the Council to resist inclosure will apply to the following extent. The Act of 1876, as we have seen, provides that the part of a common within the area described by the Act shall be deemed to be a separate common. It seems probable that this provision would be deemed to be incorporated in the Act of 1894. Assuming that this is so, it would not be competent for the Council of a rural district to accept the gift of a part of a common outside their district. But the purchase of a right of common over a portion of a common inside their district would, as a rule, put them also in possession of a right over the portion of the common outside their district. In such cases it would seem to follow that they would have a right to defend their property (*i.e.*, their right of common) by resisting an inclosure outside their district, which would undoubtedly tend to the injury of their property.

Neither a Rural District Council nor a small Urban Council will be able either to take a gift of a common, or to purchase a common right, without the consent of the County

* But see *ante*, p. 81, note, as to the power of any Urban District Council to purchase land (and therefore, it is presumed, a common) for a pleasure ground, under the Public Health Act, 1875, sec. 164.

Council; nor will they be able to aid persons in maintaining rights of common without such consent.

The Council of a large urban district will henceforth have the powers conferred both by the Act of 1876 and by the Act of 1894. In addition, therefore, to the various powers conferred by the former Act—which it will be able to exercise without the consent of the County Council—it may also, with that consent, aid persons in maintaining rights of common.

This power (which, as we have seen, may also be exercised, with the consent of the County Council, by a Rural or small Urban District Council) enables the local authority, without itself possessing common rights, to defray the expenses incurred by commoners or other persons in maintaining such rights. Thus, if a Lord of a Manor makes an inclosure, and a committee of residents is formed to resist it by the assertion of some right of common over the land enclosed, the District Council will (with the consent of the County Council) be able to contribute towards the expenses of the committee. And it is to be noticed that this power of aiding in the assertion and maintenance of rights of common is not confined in its exercise to commons within the district. The only condition is that, in the opinion of the Council, the extinction of the rights would be prejudicial to the inhabitants of the district.

It is further provided* that a District Council—that is, either a Corporation, Urban District Council, or Rural District Council—may, for the purpose of carrying into effect the section of the Act of 1894 under consideration, institute and defend any legal proceedings, and generally take such steps as they deem expedient.

* Local Government Act, 1894, sec. 26 (3).

Clearly therefore, the local authority may, when in possession of any right of common, bring an action to enforce such right for the protection of the common, or may, when not in possession of such a right, contribute towards the expense of any litigation commenced by a committee of residents for similar purposes.

A Parish Council is in a somewhat different position from a District Council with reference to the protection of commons.

It is not endowed with the powers specified in sec. 8 of the Commons Act, 1876.

By the Local Government Act, 1894, however, it is provided* that notice of any application to the Board of Agriculture in relation to a common shall be served upon the Council of every parish in which any part of the common is situate.

Hence, notice of an application under the Law of Commons Amendment Act by a lord to inclose under the Statute of Merton must be served upon the Council of every parish into which the common extends. And it follows that the Council may make such representations on the subject of the application as they think well.

Further, the Parish Council may acquire land for a recreation ground or for public walks;† and may accept and hold any gifts of property, real or personal, for the benefit of the inhabitants of the parish or any part thereof.‡

A Parish Council will thus be able to acquire by gift either a common or any right of common, and no doubt it can defend such common or right of common when acquired, indeed it would be bound to protect in any reasonable

* Sec. 8 (4).

† Local Government Act, 1894, sec. 8 (1) (*b*).

‡ *Ib.* (*h*).

way any property of the ratepayers. If, therefore, the Council can obtain a gift from a commoner of a right of common, or of a tenement having annexed thereto a right of common, it will be able to prevent inclosures under the Statute of Merton without the consent of the Board of Agriculture; and doubtless its views will have great weight with the Board on any application for the consent of the Board to an inclosure.

It does not seem, however, that a Parish Council has any right to purchase a right of common, or a tenement having a right of common annexed thereto.

But a Parish Council may purchase a common for a recreation ground, either under the power conferred by the Local Government Act itself,* or under the Public Improvements Act, 1860,† if that Act is adopted by the Parish Meeting.‡ The Act last referred to enables lands to be purchased, leased, or accepted by way of gift, for the purpose of public walks and exercise or play grounds. The expenses incurred under this Act would not be treated as part of the general expenses of the Parish Council,§ but would be defrayed by a special rate levied in pursuance of a resolution of the Parish Meeting. No such rate can, however, be levied unless half the estimated expense of the proposed improvement is raised by voluntary contribution; two-thirds in value of the ratepayers of the parish present at a meeting must agree to the rate; and the rate can in no case exceed sixpence in the pound.|| These conditions would probably make it somewhat difficult in practice to acquire a common under the Public Improvements Act, 1860; but there may be

* Sec. 8 (1) (*b*).

† 23 & 24 Vict. c. 30.

‡ Local Government Act, 1894, sec. 7.

§ See the parenthesis in sec. 11 (3) of the Local Government Act, 1894.

|| Public Improvements Act, 1860, secs. 6, 4, 7.

exceptional cases in which it would be convenient to proceed under the Act. The Act can only be adopted in a parish having, according to the last census, a population of more than five hundred persons.*

It is possible that a Parish Council might even be authorised to acquire a common for purposes of recreation by the exercise of compulsory powers. Such powers may be conferred upon the Council by an order of the County Council, or of the Local Government Board, made after proper notice and enquiry.† In order to obtain such a right of compulsory purchase, it would probably be necessary to show that no other ground was available for recreation, and that the common could not be acquired by other means. And even under such conditions the power would probably be confined to comparatively small commons. Looking also at the expense attending any such purchase, no Parish Council could be advised to enter upon it, save under very unusual circumstances.

The powers of a Parish Council to purchase or enter upon legal proceedings will be limited in practice by the narrow scope of their rating powers. The sum raised in any one financial year by a Parish Council for their expenses (other than expenses under the Adoptive Acts) is not to exceed 6*d.* in the pound on the rateable value of the parish at the commencement of the year; and the term "expenses" includes any annual charge, whether of principal or interest in respect of any loan.‡

In a parish where there is no Parish Council, the Parish Meeting may obtain from the County Council any of the

* Public Improvements Act, 1860, sec. 1.

† Local Government Act, 1894, sec. 9 (2), and following sub-sections.

‡ Sec. 11 (3). If, however, a common were acquired under the Public Improvements Act, 1860, the expense, as we have said, would be allowed over and above the 6*d.* rate.

powers of a Parish Council.* In this way, therefore, a Parish Meeting may obtain—

(*a*) Power to acquire by gift

(1) A right of common or any tenement having annexed thereto a right of common, or

(2) The interest of the Lord of the Manor, or other owner, in the soil of the common; or

(*b*) Power to purchase common land for a recreation ground.

As every parish of a population of 300 must have a Parish Council,† the Public Improvements Act, 1860, cannot be adopted in a parish where there is no Parish Council.

* Local Government Act, 1894, sec. 19 (10).
† Local Government Act, 1894, sec. 1 (1).

CHAPTER XI.

Of the Inclosure of a Manorial Common by way of Copyhold Grant.

THE inclosures by a Lord of a Manor which we have been considering hitherto are enclosures for his own benefit—assertions by himself of the right to appropriate a portion of the common for his own exclusive use.

There has, however, in the past been an alternative method of inclosure, equally removed from the supervision and moderating power of Parliament. In many manors the lord has claimed the right to grant portions of the waste (or common land) of his manor by copy of court roll—in other words, he has claimed the right to create copyholds out of the common—to be held of him as Lord of the Manor. These grants have been made in favour of inhabitants of the parish or other persons, and the lord has received rents and fines upon them.

Sometimes these grants have been made by the lord alone of his grace and pleasure; sometimes with the consent of the homage, or jury, of the freehold and copyhold tenants of the manor.* But as copyholds are regulated in all respects by long use and custom, in both cases it has been considered necessary to establish that there has been a custom in the manor, time out of mind, to make such grants.† The right to create such copyholds was indeed challenged early in the

* See *ante*, Chap. III., pp. 23, 30, as to meaning of freehold and copyhold tenants.

† The Courts, however, have in some cases inferred such a custom from comparatively few grants.

century, on the ground that the land alleged to be copyhold had not been such time out of mind, whereas it was of the essence of copyhold tenure that the premises should have been demised or demiseable by copy of court roll from time immemorial. The Court, however, upheld the custom on the ground that "although the premises in question had been newly granted by copy of court roll, yet that having been granted by virtue of an immemorial custom to demise parcels of the waste as copyhold, they were to be considered as much copyhold tenements as if they had been immemorially holden by copy of court roll." *

There appears to be this difference between grants of waste to be held as copyhold, made with, and made without, the consent of the homage. In the latter case no inclosure can be made, unless it be proved that the lord at the time of the grant left sufficient pasture for the commoners.† In the former case the consent of the homage has generally been held to be a bar to the rights of common of the several classes of tenants represented by the homage, on the ground that the representatives of those tenants considered that the inclosure would do such tenants no harm—that, in fact, there would be sufficient common left for such tenants.‡ The assent of the homage will apparently bind persons owning lands formerly copyhold of the manor but enfranchised, although such persons cannot attend the manorial courts or be chosen on the homage.§ But such assent does not bind

* Lord Northwick *v.* Stanway, 3 Bos. & Pul. 346; the case related to the Manor of Harrow Weald, in Middlesex.

† Arlett *v.* Ellis, 7 B. & C. 346, 368, 373.

‡ See Folkard *v.* Hemmett (Manor of Hampstead), 5 T.R. 417*n.*, 2 William Blackstone, 106, and the remarks of Mr. Justice Bayley on this case in Arlett *v.* Ellis, 7 B. & C. 368; Lady Wentworth *v.* Clay and others, Cases *temp.*, Finch, 263.

§ Ramsey *v.* Cruddas, L.R. 1 Q.B. (1893) 228; see also Lascelles *v.* Onslow, L.R. 2 Q.B. Div. 433, as to freeholders who are summoned to attend a manor court.

persons not tenants of the manor, or claiming common rights by virtue of a former tenancy (as in the case of enfranchised copyholders), but claiming common rights by some title wholly independent of manorial tenure and customs.*

However, the exact effect of a grant of waste as copyhold in barring common rights will not in future be of great practical importance. For, by the Copyhold Act, 1894,† it is provided ‡ as follows:—

"(1.) *It shall not be lawful for the lord of any manor to make grants of land not previously of copyhold tenure to any person to hold by copy of court roll, or by any customary tenure, without the previous consent of the Board of Agriculture.*

"(2) *The Board of Agriculture in giving or withholding their consent to a grant under this section shall have regard to the same considerations as are to be taken into account by them in giving or withholding their consent to an inclosure of common lands.*

"(3.) *When a grant has been lawfully made under this section the land therein comprised shall cease to be of copyhold tenure, and shall be vested in the grantee thereof to hold for the interest granted as in free and common socage.*"

This enactment places inclosures by way of copyhold grant on the same footing as inclosures under the Statutes of Merton and Westminster the Second. In order to justify such an inclosure, it must be shown—

(1.) That the grant is in accordance with a custom of the manor, and is effectual, in accordance with the principles above indicated, to bar the rights of all commoners.

---

* Commissioners of Sewers *v.* Glasse, L.R. 19 Eq. 134.

† 57 & 58 Vict. c. 46.

‡ Sec. 81.

(2.) That the inclosure will be for the benefit of the public.

The lord, or the person to whom the grant is made and who proposes to inclose, must also advertise his intention to apply to the Board of Agriculture for its consent three months beforehand in two local papers.* The Parish Council and District Council will have notice of the application to the Board,† and may oppose it on the ground that it will not be of benefit to the public.

The provision quoted above is a reproduction of an enactment of the year 1887.‡ The Board of Agriculture have therefore administered the provision in question for some years. Their practice has been to allow only very small inclosures, and such as are clearly of benefit to the public.

* Commons Act, 1876, sec. 31; and see notice of Board of Agriculture previously quoted, p. 17, "Times" of Friday, Oct. 29, 1893.

† Local Government Act, 1894, secs. 8 (4) and 26 (2).

‡ 50 & 51 Vict. c. 73. s. 6.

CHAPTER XII.

Of the Disfigurement of a Manorial Common; and, herein, of the Powers of Highway Authorities.

ALTHOUGH inclosure is the most serious evil which can befall a common, since it altogether excludes the public from its enjoyment, a common may suffer great injury while in an open condition.

For example, the subsoil, where it consists of any marketable substance, such as gravel, sand, marl, or peat, may be removed to an excessive extent and without regard to the precautions necessary to the safe enjoyment of the common. In such cases the common suffers not only by the destruction of the surface, where the gravel or other substance is actually dug, but by the multiplication of tracks through carting away the material dug out, and by the leaving of holes and banks.

Still worse injury is inflicted on a common where the surface soil—perhaps under the name of loam—is taken away, or the turf stripped off, for sale. The actual feed of the commoners is in such cases destroyed, while the common is rendered most unsightly.

Injuries of this kind may be inflicted upon a common

(1) by the Lord of the Manor,

(2) by commoners,

(3) by persons having no legal right on the common, *e.g.* gipsies and tramps,

(4) by the highway authorities.

(1.) The law relating to the taking of gravel and other substances by the Lord of the Manor differs from that relating to inclosures made by him. The lord is not bound to obtain the consent of the Board of Agriculture before digging on the common. Nor is he bound to show that he has left sufficient pasture for the commoners. He cannot dig in such a way as to materially injure the rights of the commoners. But the burden of proving injury rests upon the commoners. The lord is held to be exercising a right which flows from the ownership of the soil of the common; it is for those possessing rights in or over the soil to show that the lord is acting in such a way as to injure their rights.*

It has been held, however, in a recent case in which the law was exhaustively discussed, that in considering the effect on the commoners' rights of such acts as the taking of loam and surface soil from the common, regard must be had not merely to the number of cattle commonly turned out, but to the number which might be turned out, if every one fully exercised his rights.† The commoners have an interest in the pasturage of the common, to the full extent of their rights, and that interest is not to be prejudiced because they have not in recent years fully exercised such rights.

Whenever, therefore, a Lord of the Manor digs gravel excessively upon a common, or otherwise injures the surface, action to restrain him should be taken in the names of commoners. But it must be proved, that the rights of common existing over the common in question are so numerous, that the digging complained of cannot be carried on without impairing the feed, which would be required, if all the cattle,

* Hall *v.* Byron, L.R. 5 Ch. Div. 667, 680; Robinson *v.* Duleep Singh, L.R. 4 Ch. Div. 798, 831.

† Robertson *v.* Hartopp, L.R. 43 Ch. Div. 497, 516. This case practically overruled Lascelles *v.* Lord Onslow, L.R. 2 Q.B. Div. 433.

which the commoners are entitled to turn out, were in fact turned out.

If the commoners' rights extend to the digging of gravel or other substances which the lord is taking, and they can show, that he is not leaving them sufficient to satisfy such rights, the commoners would have a right of action against the lord on this ground, apart from the question of damage to the feed. But such proof would probably in most cases be somewhat difficult.

There are other rights which may be exercised by Lords of Manors upon the condition that the commoners are not injured, *e.g.*, planting trees,* and making rabbit burrows: † that is to say, the lord may do these things if he does not injure the commoners, and if the commoners wish to prevent them, they must show they are injured. The same rule would, upon principle, seem to apply to the making of roads and gravelled footpaths upon a common, by the lord.‡

It is to be borne in mind that the commoners' only remedy against the lord for acts of disfigurement, or interference with a common short of inclosure, is by way of action. The commoner cannot kill rabbits put in by the lord, or distrain or drive out the lord's cattle,§ or cut down his trees.

The powers which we have described as enjoyed by Urban Authorities, Rural District Councils and Parish Councils, in relation to commons,‖ may be exercised to restrain the disfigurement of a common by the Lord of the Manor, as well

* Kirby *v.* Sadgrove, 1 Bos. & Pul. 13, 17; per Bayley, J., in Arlett *v.* Ellis, 7 B. & C. 362.

† Cooper *v.* Marshall, 1 Bur. 259.

‡ See Mr. Justice Stirling's remarks on this class of cases in Robertson *v.* Hartopp, 43 Ch. Div. 500 *et seq.*

§ See Coney's Case, Godbolt 122, 2 Leon. 201; Kirby *v.* Sadgrove, *ubi supra.*

‖ *Ante*, Chap. X., p. 79.

as to prevent inclosure. If common rights are acquired by the local authority, they may, under the conditions before described, be used to restrain such acts; and a District Council may, with the consent of the County Council, help commoners to restrain such acts, without themselves possessing common rights.

(2.) Commoners may injure a common either by exercising excessively or irregularly some right to which they are entitled, or by doing some act quite outside their rights. Thus, a commoner entitled to cut bushes or dig gravel is not entitled to take more than is sufficient for the requirements of the tenement to which the right is attached. If he takes large quantities for sale he is committing a trespass on the common, and the Lord of the Manor can restrain him by an action of trespass. He is equally a trespasser, and liable to an action by the Lord of the Manor, if having, for example, a right of common of pasture, he cuts any bushes or digs any gravel on the common.

Indeed, apart from his user of his right, a commoner is, with regard to intermeddling with a common, in the same position as a stranger. It has been held that he cannot cut mole-hills, or make fish-ponds, or clear the common of bushes or other growth to improve the pasturage; he cannot fill up a trench, even though it is by way of improving the common;* and the same doctrine would undoubtedly apply to the making of a metalled road.

Thus commoners' rights, while most valuable for protecting a common, cannot be lawfully used to injure it. The interests of the commoners and the public are, save in very rare instances, identical.

Any commoner by intermeddling with a common may

* Potter *v.* North, 1 Wms. Saunders, 353*a*, note; Howard *v.* Spencer, 1 Siderfin, 251.

injure other commoners as well as the lord. The other commoners cannot, however, bring an action of trespass, as neither the soil nor the surface of the common belongs to them. If they are injured, they may bring an action for damages and for an injunction to restrain the wrong-doer, but in such an action they would have to prove, that they are prevented from enjoying their right in as ample and beneficial a manner as they otherwise would, though no actual damage from the particular act need be shown.* It is much better, therefore, in any such case that the action should be brought in the name of the lord.

(3.) The same rules hold good of damage by persons having no right whatever on a common, such as gipsies and tramps. Although the pasturage or other product of the common in which the commoners are interested may be injured by such acts, yet the commoner, not having possession of the common, cannot complain of the acts as a trespass. But he may bring an action against the stranger for hindering him from enjoying his common in so ample and beneficial a manner as he might otherwise, and he need not prove any specific damage.† He may also distrain the foreign cattle, if he finds them on the common, and will be justified in so doing though he prove no actual damage.‡ And either remedy may be had, though the cattle are not turned on the common by the stranger, but merely stray there.§

* Comyns' Digest, Tit. Common (I).; Robert Marys' case, 9 Rep. 111*b*; Wells *v.* Watling, 2 W. Bl. 1233; Hobson *v.* Todd, 4 T.R. 71; Pindar *v.* Wadsworth, 2 East 154; and see Mr. Justice Stirling's remarks on these cases in Robertson *v.* Hartopp, L.R. 43 Ch. Div. 498.

† See authorities cited in last note; and per Littledale, J., in Williams *v.* Morland, 2 B. & C. 916.

‡ Robert Marys's Case, 9 Rep. 112*b* (and see note D on p. 204 of Thomas and Fraser's Ed., 1826); Morris's Case, Godbolt 185.

§ Robert Marys's Case, 112*a*, 113*b*; Morris's Case, *ubi supra*. See also Vin. Abr. Tit., Distress (C.) 1.

It is different, however, where certain persons other than the lord have a right to the sole vesture of the common, or to the sole pasturage, even for a part of a year only.* This sole right is held to give possession of the surface, and to entitle the holders to bring an action of trespass against anyone unlawfully injuring the surface, to however small an extent, as, for example, by riding over it.† The owners of the soil have, at the same time, a right of action for any trespass upon the subsoil, as by driving in posts, but not for a trespass upon the surface merely.

The duty of preventing trespasses upon a common by gipsies, tramps, and other casual marauders is often considered burdensome by the Lord of the Manor, who is practically less interested in protecting the common than the inhabitants of the district. Hence it is convenient to place a common under the management of some local authority, which shall have summary powers of preventing such disfigurement. We shall deal with these powers in treating of the regulation of commons.‡

(4.) One of the most common causes of the disfigurement of common land is the digging of gravel by the highway authorities. Under the Highway Act, 1835,§ any surveyor of highways may "search for, dig, get, and carry away gravel, sand, stone, or other materials" for the repair of roads, in any waste land or common ground within the parish for which he is surveyor, or within any other parish, if materials are wanting in the first parish, and sufficient is left in the second parish for the repair of the roads of that parish. No compensation is paid to the Lord of the

* See *ante*, p. 61.
† Cox *v.* Glue, Cox *v.* Moulsey, 5 C. B. 533.
‡ See *post*, Chap. XX., p. 221, and Chap. XXI., p. 237.
§ 5 & 6 Will. IV. c. 50. s. 51.

Manor or commoners for the materials taken from the common, or for the injury done to the common.

All the powers of surveyors of highways are conferred upon Highways Boards by the Highway Acts. (See Highway Acts, 1862 and 1864.*)

The highway authority is, however, bound † to take the following precautions for the benefit of the common and the public:—

(1.) They must forthwith fence off any pit or hole, and support and repair such fence while the pit or hole is open.

(2.) When a pit or hole is opened and no materials are found, it must, within three days, be filled up, levelled, and covered with the turf or clod dug out of the same.

(3.) Where a pit or hole is opened and materials are found, within fourteen days after sufficient materials are dug out, the pit or hole must, if it is so required by the Lord of the Manor or any commoner, be filled up or sloped down and fenced off.

Surveyors of highways are also enjoined within twenty-one days after appointment to their office to fill up or slope down all pits and holes not likely to be further useful, and to secure those still required by posts and rails or other fences, to prevent accidents to persons or cattle.

These duties are enforced by penalties recoverable before justices.

The precautions thus enjoined are, however, very imperfectly observed, and many commons are much injured, not so much by one or two large pits as by indiscriminate digging, and by trial holes left open and absolutely unprotected.

Turnpike trustees had formerly the same powers as high-

* 25 & 26 Vict. c. 61.; 27 & 28 Vict. c. 101.

† Highway Act, 1835, sec. 55.

way authorities;* and by the Turnpike Trusts Continuance Act, 1869,† their powers devolve upon highway authorities where turnpike roads are thrown on highway districts.

Questions have from time to time arisen as to what is waste land or common ground within the meaning of the enactment above quoted.

By the Highway Act of 1841,‡ it was provided that lands and grounds "in the exclusive occupation of one or more persons for agricultural purposes" should be deemed to be inclosed lands and grounds within the provisions of the Highway Act relating to the taking of materials for roads, "although not separated from any adjoining lands or grounds of other persons or from the highway by any fence or other inclosure."

The effect of this provision is to take such lands out of the category of waste lands and common grounds, and to necessitate a justices' order, made on notice to the owner and occupier, before any materials can be taken.

Common fields and common meadows, therefore, which are owned in severalty during a portion of the year, would not be subject to the right of highway authorities to dig without a justices' order.

It would appear that highway authorities lose their right to enter upon land which is *de facto* inclosed, though it may have been wrongfully inclosed.§

Highway authorities may not search for or take material for the roads from any common which is

(*a*) regulated pursuant to the Commons Act, 1876, by

* See 9 Geo. IV. c. 126. ss. 80, 87, 89.

† 33 & 34 Vict. c. 73. s. 11.

‡ 4 & 5 Vict. c. 51.

§ See per Willes, J., in Tongue *v.* Plumstead Board of Works, *Times*, 5 Nov. 1866. There is no report of the judgment on the argument of the rule nisi, said to have been granted for a new trial.

a Provisional Order of the Board of Agriculture confirmed by Parliament,* or

(*b*) the subject of a scheme confirmed by Parliament under the Metropolitan Commons Act,† or

(*c*) the subject of any private or local Act of Parliament having for its object the preservation of the common as an open space,

without the consent of the person or persons having the regulation or management of the common, or an order of justices in petty sessions, and the justices, if they grant such an order, may prescribe such conditions as to mode of working and restitution of the surface as they may think fit.‡

By the Public Health Act, 1875,§ every urban authority (*i.e.* every municipal corporation, and every urban district council) is directed to exercise within its district the office of surveyor of highways, and is clothed with the powers, authorities, duties, and liabilities of surveyors of highways.

And under the Local Government Act, 1894, the powers, duties, and liabilities of every highway authority in a rural district are transferred to the District Council of such district.||

Henceforth, therefore, the rights of digging on commons for the repair of highways will be exerciseable by Urban Councils in urban districts, and by Rural District Councils in rural districts. It is to be hoped that these bodies, being directly elected by the ratepayers, and especially empowered to protect open spaces,¶ will be amenable to public opinion in relation to the disfigurement of commons.

* See Chap. XXI. † See Chap. XX.

‡ Commons Act, 1876 (39 & 40 Vict. c. 56.) sec. 20.

§ 38 & 39 Vict. c. 55. s. 144.

|| Local Government Act, 1894, sec. 25; the date of transfer may be postponed for a short time, see sec. 25 (1), proviso. Main roads are under the care of the County Council, Local Government Act 1888 (51 & 52 Vic. c. 41.), sec. 11.

¶ Local Government Act, 1894, sec. 26 (2).

CHAPTER XIII.

Of the Inclosure of a Manorial Common by the Authority of Parliament.

THE greater part of the common land of the country has been converted into inclosed land by Act of Parliament.

We have seen that even in very early times an Act of Parliament was considered necessary to effect inclosure.* The Statutes of Merton and Westminster the Second were, however, designed to enable the lord or owner of the soil to inclose against the wishes of the commoners. The aim of modern Inclosure Acts is to facilitate inclosure where it is the general wish of those interested in a common to inclose. Owing to the number of the commoners, the frequent uncertainty as to their rights, and the fact that amongst the commoners were usually some persons who could not give a binding consent to an inclosure—persons under age, married women, or lunatics—it was found, as soon as the endeavour was made to inclose with the consent of all parties, that no legal inclosure could be effected without the aid of Parliament. Private Bills authorising the inclosure of particular commons were accordingly passed in great numbers during the last century and the first half of the present; and some seven millions of acres of common and common fields were inclosed under their provisions. At length, to diminish

---

* See *ante* Chap. II.

the cost of the process and further facilitate inclosure, a public general Act, the Inclosure Act, 1845, was passed, and a permanent body, at first styled the Inclosure Commission, was constituted to consider proposals for inclosure, to submit them to Parliament, and subsequently to carry them into effect. Six hundred and eighteen thousand acres were enclosed by the Inclosure Commission under this Act; * and the process continued unchecked till 1869, when inclosure was arrested at the instance of the late Mr. Fawcett, on the ground that it was in the interests of the country to preserve open lands for health and recreation, rather than to inclose them with the object of increasing the food supplies of the country. This view was completely endorsed by the Conservative Government of the day, when, in 1876, the Commons Act of that year was passed into law. This Act, without repealing the Act of 1845 and the various Inclosure Acts, laid down new principles to guide the Inclosure Commission in dealing with proposals for inclosure, provided an alternative method of dealing with commons—that of their regulation as open spaces—and introduced many alterations of procedure in the interests of the public.

Since the passing of this Act, the Inclosure Commissioners, after being rechristened the Land Commissioners for England,† have been merged in the Board of Agriculture,‡ which is represented by a responsible Minister in the House of Commons. At the present time, therefore, inclosure by Act of Parliament cannot be effected except with the approval, first of the Board of Agriculture, and then of the Legislature; and the procedure up to the time when Parliament, by special

* See Annual Report of Board of Agriculture, 1895, (C. 7660), p. 17.

† By the Settled Land Act, 1882 (45 & 46 Vict. c. 38.), sec. 48.

‡ By the Board of Agriculture Act, 1889 (52 & 53 Vict. c. 30.).

Act, authorises an inclosure, is regulated mainly by the Commons Act, 1876.*

No metropolitan common, however – that is, no common within the Metropolitan Police District—can be inclosed under the machinery of the Commons Act, 1876, and the Inclosure Acts.†

Persons contemplating the inclosure of a common usually communicate with the Board of Agriculture in the first instance in an informal way. They will then receive information and directions as to the mode in which an application for inclosure can be made, and a form of application.‡

Before submitting their formal application, the applicants must advertise in a local paper their intention to apply,§ and must serve notice on the Council of the urban or rural district in which the common is situate,|| and also on the Council of every parish in which any part of the common is situate.¶ The local authority thus has the earliest opportunity of considering how the proposal affects the interests of the neighbourhood, and what measures it should take to oppose or watch it.

The application for inclosure must be in writing, in such form as the Board of Agriculture may from time to time direct, and must be accompanied by a map of the common, or part thereof.** It must be signed by, or on behalf of, persons representing at least one third in value of the legal

* 39 & 40 Vict. c. 56.

† Metropolitan Commons Act, 1866 (29 & 30 Vict. c. 122.), secs. 4 and 5. The Metropolitan Police District is almost identical with the Greater London of the Registrar General, and extends from Potter's Bar on the north to Banstead on the south, and from Erith on the east to Staines and Uxbridge on the west.

‡ Commons Act, 1876 (39 & 40 Vict. c. 56.), secs. 9, 10 (2).

§ Commons Act, 1876, sec. 10 (1).

|| Local Government Act, 1894, sec. 26 (2)

¶ *Ib.* sec. 8 (4).

** Commons Act, 1876, sec. 10 (2).

interests in the common.* In other words, the interest of the Lord of the Manor and the interests of the various commoners must be roughly valued in proportion to each other, and it must be made clear that the interests of the persons making the application amount to at least one third of all the legal interests in the common.

For the purpose of this calculation, the public at large are not taken to have any interest in the common, nor is any local authority, merely as such, credited with such an interest. The persons interested are the lord and commoners alone. The lord's interest in the soil of the common is usually, in the case of an ordinary manorial common, put at one sixteenth; † but over and above this interest he is held to be entitled to share with the commoners in the feed of the common in respect of the acreage of his inclosed land from which cattle have been in fact turned out on the common.‡ The relative value of the lord's interest (apart from the

* Commons Act, 1876, sec. 2.

† The lord may obtain a larger allotment in respect of the minerals under the common; or the right to work minerals under the allotments to commoners and others may be reserved to him (Inclosure Act, 1845, 8 & 9 Vict. c. 118. s. 76; and see Inclosure Commissioners Act, 1851, 14 & 15 Vict. c. 53. s. 9; Inclosure Act, 1859, 22 & 23 Vict. c. 43. ss. 1 to 7).

‡ Musgrave *v.* The Inclosure Commissioners of England and Wales, L.R. 9 Q.B. 162, 173. The case turned upon the construction of sec. 27 of the Inclosure Act, 1845. This section directed the Commissioners to make an allotment to the lord in respect of his right in the soil, exclusively or inclusively of minerals, and inclusively or exclusively "of any rights of pasturage which may have been usually enjoyed by such lord or his tenants." The Court held that the Act referred to rights of pasturage which would have been rights of common in the hands of anyone but the lord, and that, to satisfy the expression "usually enjoyed," it was not necessary to prove continuous enjoyment to the time of the claim, but it was sufficient to give such evidence of user as would, as applied to anyone but the lord, prove a right of common from time immemorial (see *ante*, p. 43). Sec. 27 of the Act of 1845 was repealed by sec. 34 of the Commons Act, 1876 (39 & 40 Vict. c. 56.); but the ruling of the Court no doubt still holds good to justify allotments to Lords of Manors in respect of pasturage actually enjoyed. See also Arundell *v.* Falmouth, 2 M. & S. 440, 15 R.R. 305; Lloyd *v.* Earl Powys, 4 E. & B. 485, 24 L.J. Q.B. 145.

ownership of the soil) and of the interests of the commoners is estimated by reference to the comparative acreage of the land held to carry common rights. Thus, if in a parish of 2,000 acres the common extended to 500 acres, the lord's inclosed land from which cattle had been turned out to 500, and the commoners' lands to the remaining 1,000, the lord alone would own, for the purposes of an inclosure, more than one third in value of the interests in the common, and an application by him alone would comply with the requirements of the Act. Probably, however, in such a case the Board would be loth to consider the proposal, unless, at least, some commoners joined in it. The Board cannot proceed until the necessary proportion of interest in the applicants is proved. Consequently, if there is any serious dispute as to the rights, *e.g.*, if rights of common are claimed, but denied by the lord, in respect of a large acreage of land, the Commissioners must either suspend proceedings, or hold a preliminary enquiry upon the question of right.

Any local authority desiring to stop an inclosure will therefore do well to consider what rights exist over the common, whether any doubts exist on the subject, and what proportion of commoners have concurred in the application.

In the case of a manorial common, the Lord of the Manor has a veto upon inclosure.* This veto, in strictness, does not operate until the provisional order for inclosure is in draft; but it is improbable that the Board would entertain the proposal to inclose at all, if the lord expressed himself as resolutely opposed to it. In fact, it may be taken, that no application for the inclosure of a manorial common is ever likely to be made without the concurrence of the lord.

* Commons Act, 1876 (39 & 40 Vict. c. 56.), sec. 12 (5).

The applicants for an inclosure must furnish the Board of Agriculture with very full information touching the expediency of the application "considered in relation to the benefit of the neighbourhood as well as to private interests."*

The following are items of information mentioned in the Commons Act:—

(*a.*) The number and occupation of the inhabitants of the parish or place in which the common is situate.

(*b.*) The population of the neighbourhood, and the distance of the common from any neighbouring towns and villages.

(*c.*) The intention of the applicants to propose the adoption of all or any of the statutory provisions for the benefit of the neighbourhood.†

(*d.*) Whether any other ground is available for the recreation of the neighbourhood.

(*e.*) The site, extent, and suitableness of the allotments, if any, proposed to be made for recreation grounds and field gardens.‡

(*f.*) The advantages which the applicants anticipate from the inclosure of the common as compared with its regulation, and the reasons why an inclosure is expedient when viewed in relation to the benefit of the neighbourhood.

(*g.*) The extent and nature of the common.

(*h.*) Any questions of boundary.

(*i.*) The parties legally interested, and the numbers and interest of those who have consented to, or dissented from, the application.§

---

* Commons Act, 1876, sec. 10 (3) to (5).

† As to the nature of these, see *post*, p. 116.

‡ As to these allotments, see *post*, p. 114.

§ See *ante*, p. 108.

(*j.*) Any other information which, in the judgment of the Board, may assist them in forming an opinion upon the application, having regard to the benefit of the neighbourhood and to private interests.

It is the duty of the Board of Agriculture to consider whether, upon any application, a *primâ facie* case for inclosure has been made out.

From the annual reports of the Board to Parliament, it is clear that at this initial stage every application for inclosure is narrowly scrutinised, and that the Board will not proceed unless a strong case is made out. Any local authority wishing to oppose an inclosure should not fail, therefore, to communicate with the Board as soon as the application for the inclosure becomes known.* Great weight will no doubt be given to their representations, and not improbably an end will be put to the scheme of inclosure without further expense to anybody.

If, however, the Board of Agriculture consider that a *primâ facie* case for an inclosure has been made out, they are then required by the Act to "order a local enquiry to be held by an Assistant Commissioner." †

This local enquiry consists, mainly, in an inspection of the common, and in holding one or more public meetings in the locality.‡

---

* The right so to communicate is expressly given (subject in certain cases to the consent of the County Council) to Urban and Rural District Councils by the conjoint operation of the Commons Act, 1876 (39 & 40 Vict. c. 56.), sec. 8 (first par.), and the Local Government Act, 1894, sec. 26 (2). But no doubt any representation of a Parish Council would also be considered by the Board. The expression used in the Commons Act in reference to communications with the Board is "appear before the Commissioners"; but the most convenient form of communication at the initial stage of an application is a communication in writing, either by way of memorial under the seal of the local authority, or of letter signed by the presiding officer or clerk of the authority.

† Commons Act, 1876, sec. 10 (6).

‡ *Ib.* sec. 11 (1).

Of the first of such meetings twenty-one days' notice must be given by the Assistant Commissioner,* and such notice must be posted on the principal door of the parish church, on or near the common, at every post office of the parish or district, at any town hall or vestry hall, or other building or room maintained out of any local rates, and at all places where notices are usually posted. The notice must also be advertised or otherwise made public, as the Board may direct;† and it is to contain an invitation to all persons interested to attend the enquiry.‡ The meetings must be held at a suitable time and place for securing the attendance of the neighbouring inhabitants, and of all persons claiming interest in the common; and one of such meetings must be held in the evening between 7 and 10 o'clock. § It is the practice of the Board to hold two meetings, one in the morning and the other in the evening. The Assistant Commissioner, as directed by the Act,‖ presides at such meetings and conducts the proceedings.

He is bound to hear all persons desirous of being heard in relation to the subject matter of the enquiry; and may adjourn any meeting from time to time or from place to place as he may think fit.¶

If, then, a local authority has failed to stop a projected inclosure by representations to the Board of Agriculture in the first instance, it should attend the local enquiry and oppose the scheme in the usual manner. It should be remembered, that the burden of proving that the inclosure of the common, as compared with its regulation as an open space, is for the benefit of the neighbourhood, lies on the applicants. The local authority should, therefore, put the applicants to strict

* Commons Act, 1876, sec. 11 (2).
† *Ib.* sec. 11 (4).
‡ *Ib.* sec. 11 (3).
§ *Ib.* sec. 11 (1).
‖ *Ib.* sec. 11 (5).
¶ *Ib.* sec. 11 (5).

proof on this point, by cross-examining their witnesses; and should also adduce positive evidence that the common is of value to the neighbourhood, both for purposes of recreation and, if the fact be so, as a means to enable the cottagers and small holders of the district the better to maintain themselves in independence and comfort. The importance of fostering small holdings is now generally admitted, and evidence of the importance of the common from this point of view will probably have much weight. On the other hand, it not infrequently happens, that though the increase of the food supply is made a pretext for inclosure, much of the common when inclosed is converted into a game preserve, whilst in other cases fair and even good pasturage is converted into very inferior arable land. When any such result seems probable, this consideration should be urged upon the Assistant Commissioner. And, of course, all facts connected with the population of the district, and the need of open spaces, should be proved. In practice, the morning meeting is generally conducted in the more formal manner, the promoters being heard in the first instance, and then the opponents; while at the evening meeting an endeavour is made to elicit the popular opinion of the neighbourhood. A local authority opposing an inclosure would, of course, take care to be present at both meetings.

Some representative of the local authority may also properly accompany the Assistant Commissioner on his inspection of the common.

Not only the expediency of the inclosure, but the provisions to be made for the public benefit, should the inclosure be sanctioned, will be discussed at the local enquiry.

The Inclosure Act, 1845, empowered the Inclosure Commission, in the case of any "common which was waste land of a manor" or subject at all times of the year to rights of common not limited by number or stints, to set out allotments for the exercise and recreation of the inhabitants of the neighbourhood, and for field gardens to be worked by the labouring poor.* Other Inclosure Acts amended these provisions, and the Commons Act, 1876, enlarged in many respects the powers of the Commissioners in this relation.† As we have seen, the applicants for an inclosure are bound to furnish the Commissioners, in the first instance, with the particulars of any allotments they may propose to set out.‡ And, in practice, it may be taken that the Board of Agriculture will require ample provision to be made, both for recreation and for field gardens, on any inclosure they may sanction, even though the provisions as to allotments do not in terms apply to the species of common which it is proposed to inclose.§ In some cases, however, where the commons which it is sought to inclose are of wide extent and more or less mountainous in character, the Board of Agriculture, instead of reserving specific allotments for recreation, has reserved to the public a general right of roaming over the land to be inclosed so long as it is not actually tilled or planted.‖ This is a privilege of great value, and one which should be obtained wherever the circumstances admit of it.

The Commons Act, 1876, further provides¶ that the Board of Agriculture shall insert in any provisional order

* 8 & 9 Vict. c. 118. ss. 30 and 31.

† See secs. 21 to 28.

‡ Commons Act, 1876, sec. 10 (4).

§ Where commons subject to public allotments, and other land, are included in the same application to enclose, the allotments may be made by the Commissioners out of the other land, subject to an adjustment of interests (Commons Act, 1876, sec. 23).

‖ See Reports of Inclosure Commissioners as to Hendy Bank Common and Llandegly Rhos Common, in the county of Radnor, House of Commons Papers, 1880, No. 77, and many subsequent Reports.

¶ Sec. 7.

for the inclosure or regulation of a common, certain terms and conditions, designated collectively "statutory provisions for the benefit of the neighbourhood," so far as such terms and conditions are applicable.

These conditions are as follows:—

(1.) That free access is to be preserved to any particular points of view.

(2.) That particular trees and objects of historical interest are to be preserved.

(3.) That there is to be reserved, where a recreation ground is not set out, a privilege of playing games or of enjoying other species of recreation at such times and in such manner and in such parts of the common as may be thought suitable, care being taken to cause the least possible injury to persons interested in the common.

(4.) That carriage roads, bridle paths and footpaths over the common are to be set out in such directions as may appear most commodious.

(5.) That any other specified thing is to be done which may be thought equitable and expedient, regard being had to the benefit of the neighbourhood.

The applicants, as we have seen, are bound to inform the Board in their application, how they propose to deal with these statutory provisions for the benefit of the neighbourhood; and the Assistant Commissioner is bound to make special enquiry on the subject.*

When, therefore, a local authority is not wholly opposed to an inclosure, or fears that it may be unable to resist it, endeavour should be made to secure to the public not only

* Commons Act, 1876, secs. 10 (4), 11 (7).

the reservation of large allotments for field gardens, but some measure of enjoyment of the common, not only in the way of recreation grounds for the playing of particular games, but in the way of a right of access to the more beautiful or frequented parts of the common. Local authorities are especially empowered to assist in securing advantages of this kind. They may contribute out of their funds for or towards the maintenance of recreation grounds or of paths or roads, or the doing of any other matter or thing for the benefit of their town or district in relation to the common to which an application for inclosure relates.*

But this remark is perhaps of more importance to individual opponents of an inclosure than to local authorities, for it may be safely assumed, that, where a local authority closely interested in a common offers a resolute opposition to an inclosure, either the Board of Agriculture or Parliament will refuse its sanction to the scheme.

The Assistant Commissioner, when he has inspected the common, held his local meetings, and made any other enquiries he may think fit,† reports in writing to the Board of Agriculture the result of the local enquiry, with very full information both as to the several details dealt with in the original application, and as to the attendance at the meetings and the feeling of the neighbourhood. His report must be accompanied by a map, with a sketch of any allotments to be made for recreation grounds and field gardens.‡

* Commons Act, 1876, sec. 8, par. 2; and see also par. 3. District Councils have all the powers specified in this enactment, but Councils for rural districts and for urban districts of less than 5,000 inhabitants must obtain the consent of the County Council to the exercise of such powers. See *ante*, Chap. X.

† *Ib.* sec. 11 (6).

‡ *Ib.* sec. 11 (7) and (8).

The Board of Agriculture then again takes the subject into consideration, and if satisfied that "having regard to the benefit of the neighbourhood as well as to private interests" it is expedient to proceed, frames the draft of a provisional order for the inclosure of the common.* In this order they are bound to insert all such of the statutory provisions for the benefit of the neighbourhood as are applicable to the case, and, if the common is waste of a manor, the quantity and situation of the allotments (if any) to be made for recreation grounds and field gardens.† The order is also to show how the interest of the Lord of the Manor and any interest in minerals are to be dealt with.‡ The draft order must be deposited in the parish or parishes in which the common lies, for consideration, and due public notice of such deposit, and of the intention of the Board to certify the expediency of the order, if the necessary consents are obtained thereto, must be given.§

A provisional order cannot be certified by the Board to Parliament, unless persons representing at least two thirds in value of the interests in the common consent thereto.|| We have already explained ¶ what is meant by interests in the common, and by the value of such interests, in dealing with the application for an inclosure; and the same rules apply in relation to a provisional order, two thirds in value being substituted for one third.

It is also (as we have already noticed **) necessary at this stage to obtain the consent of the Lord of the Manor to a

* Commons Act, 1876, sec. 12 (1).

† *Ib.* sec. 12 (2).

‡ *Ib.* sec. 12 (3).

§ *Ib.* sec. 12 (4).

|| *Ib.* sec. 12 (5). The exact words of the statute are, "two thirds in value of such interests in the common as are affected by the order." In the case of an inclosure, however, all interests must necessarily be affected, except possibly interests in minerals.

¶ See *ante*, p. 109.

** See *ante*, p. 110.

provisional order.* Where there is more than one person interested in the manor, the actual consent need not be obtained, but the Board cannot proceed, if such persons, or the majority of such persons, signify their dissent within a time limited by the Board.†

We have seen ‡ that there are cases in which the freemen, burgesses, or inhabitant householders of a corporate town are entitled to exercise common rights over a common in the name of the Corporation. In any such case (whether the rights exercised are strictly common rights or in the nature of some other interest, such as an interest in the soil of the common §) the Board of Agriculture cannot certify a provisional order, unless two thirds in number of such of the freemen and burgesses as may be resident in the city, borough, or town, or within seven miles thereof, or of the inhabitant householders (as the case may be) consent to the order.|| The consent of two thirds is to be deemed the consent of the whole class.¶

To obtain the necessary consents, or to ascertain the interests of consenting or dissenting parties, the Board may hold meetings by an Assistant Commissioner; and they may modify the draft order at any time before it is certified, provided any modifications are duly consented to.**

When the necessary consents to a draft provisional order have been obtained, the order is to be deemed final.†† The Board then, as directed by the Act, certify to Parliament that it is expedient that the order be confirmed by Parliament. This certificate must be contained in a report, in which they must give their reasons for recommending the inclosure,

* Commons Act, 1876, sec. 12 (5). † *Ib.* ‡ See *ante*, pp. 64, 67.

§ This could hardly happen in the case of a manorial common.

|| Commons Act, 1876, sec. 12 (6). ¶ *Ib.*

** *Ib.* sec. 12 (7) and (8). †† *Ib.* sec. 12 (9).

and must furnish Parliament with the fullest information on all the subjects dealt with in the original application and at the local enquiry, and on the subject of the inclosure generally.* The provisional order is appended to the report of the Board.

Early in each session of Parliament, a Committee of the House of Commons is appointed to consider all reports from the Board of Agriculture recommending the inclosure or regulation of any common.† Before this Committee a member of the Board of Agriculture, the Assistant Commissioner who held the local enquiry, and one or two local witnesses, are usually examined in support of any inclosure recommended by the Board to Parliament; and any persons opposed to the inclosure are also examined.

The Committee may recommend that the provisional order be confirmed, or not confirmed, by Parliament. In the first case a Bill is subsequently introduced by the Secretary of State for the Home Department. This Bill sets out in a schedule the provisional order of the Board of Agriculture, and enacts its confirmation. It passes through Parliament as a public Bill, and is not referred to a Select Committee. But it may of course be opposed on second reading, or at any other stage, in either House, in the same manner as any other public Bill.

If the Committee recommend that the provisional order be not confirmed, the proposal drops entirely.

The Committee may, however, take a middle course. They may recommend that the provisional order be not confirmed by Parliament except subject to certain modifications.‡ In this case the order is referred back to the Board

* Commons Act, 1876, sec. 12 (9).

† This step is contemplated by the Commons Act, 1876; see sec. 12 (11).

‡ See Commons Act, 1876, sec. 12 (11).

of Agriculture, and the Board may modify the order accordingly.

But the modification must be assented to in the same manner in all respects as an original draft provisional order. If the necessary proportion of the parties interested will not consent to the modification, the proposal drops. If they do consent, the Board make a special report to Parliament presenting and recommending the modified order; and in such case the report is referred to the Standing Committee of the House for consideration. If the Committee then report that the order should be confirmed, a Bill is introduced in the manner above described.*

It does not appear that the Act of 1876 contemplates that Parliament should itself by Act modify a provisional order of the Board—a practice not unusual in the case of provisional orders of other departments, such as the Board of Trade and the Local Government Board.

The Standing Committee of the House, as a matter of fact, scrutinise every provisional order for inclosure with great rigour. In the early years after the passing of the Act of 1876, when the then Inclosure Commissioners rather favoured inclosure, more than one scheme was rejected or amended, the Committee insisting in some cases on larger allotments for recreation and for field gardens. So decidedly adverse was the tone of the Committee to any inclosure, unless it could be shown to be for the clear advantage of the public as distinguished from those who had private interests in the land (*i.e.*, the Lord of the Manor and the commoners), that the Board of Agriculture has practically ceased to make provisional orders for inclosure, save occasionally in wild upland districts, where planting or an improvement in sheep

* See Commons Act, 1876, sec. 12 (11).

farming is the object, or under very exceptional circumstances.* The machinery remains, however, and may at any moment be put into action; and it is therefore necessary that local authorities and all persons desiring to preserve open spaces should be acquainted with its working, and should know what are their powers and opportunities of opposing inclosure by Act of Parliament. Shortly, it may be said, that, if a local authority interested in a common offers a determined opposition before the Board of Agriculture, both by written representation and deputation to the Board, and at the local enquiry, there is little chance that the Board will certify the expediency of the inclosure to Parliament; and that, should the Board do so, the Standing Committee of the House of Commons would, upon proper evidence by the local authority, in all probability reverse the Board's decision. Even if the Select Committee passed the inclosure, it is probable that no Government would care to force an Inclosure Bill through the House against strong local opposition.†

* It appears from the last Report of the Board of Agriculture, 1895, (C. 7660), p. 17, that about 26,600 acres have been authorised to be inclosed under the Act of 1876. This is about the quantity annually inclosed, until Mr. Fawcett interposed. Occasionally the machinery of inclosure is used to vest a common in a local authority, to be preserved as an open space.

† A local authority, interested in any inclosure scheme certified to Parliament, should either subscribe for the Parliamentary Votes, in which the appointment of the Standing Committee and the presentation of the report of the Board of Agriculture will be found recorded, or communicate with the Member for the borough or division, who will give the desired information. When the Standing Committee is about to sit, a communication should be made to the Committee Clerk, stating that it is desired to give evidence for or against the scheme, and the Member may also be asked to use his influence to secure the hearing of the desired witnesses. A certain small allowance for expenses and loss of time is made to witnesses examined before a Select Committee.

The Commons Preservation Society examines with care all proposals of the Board of Agriculture for the inclosure of commons, and local authorities interested will do well to communicate with the secretary of the Society, E. W. Fithian, Esq., of 1 Great College Street, Westminster, or the honorary solicitor, Percival Birkett, Esq., of 4 Lincoln's Inn Fields.

A Parish Meeting in a parish where there is no Parish Council is not entitled to notice of applications to the Board of Agriculture in relation to commons. But probably in any such case the District Council would give the Chairman of the Parish Meeting notice of the application, and, upon becoming aware of it in this or any other way, the Parish Meeting would be entitled to take such steps as a Parish Council could take, if one existed in the parish. It will be remembered that a Parish Meeting (where there is no Council) has a continuous existence through the Chairman and the Overseers of the Parish.*

In a work treating of the means of preserving open spaces, it is unnecessary to discuss at length the steps taken to carry out an inclosure after the Act confirming the provisional order is passed. It is sufficient to say that a valuer is appointed by the parties, subject to the approval of the Board of Agriculture.† To this official special instructions are given as to the carrying out of the inclosure.‡ The subjects dealt with comprise drains and watercourses, both public and private, the provision of allotments for public purposes, the adoption or preparation of a map for the purposes of the inclosure, the payment of the expenses of the proceedings, and generally any matter concerning the interests of the public or of the persons interested in the inclosure as a class. These instructions must not be inconsistent with the provisional order, and must be approved by the Board of Agriculture. The valuer may also ascertain and set out the boundaries of the parishes or manors in which the land to be inclosed is situate,§ and may straighten the

* Local Government Act, 1894, sec. 19.

† See Inclosure Act, 1845 (8 & 9 Vict. c. 118.), sec. 33; Commons Act, 1876 (39 & 40 Vict. c. 56.), sec. 32.

‡ 8 & 9 Vict. c. 118. s. 34.

§ Secs. 39 to 44.

boundary of the lands to be inclosed, with the consent of the adjoining owners.*

The valuer then holds meetings for the examination of claims, and all persons claiming any right or interest in the lands to be inclosed must deliver their claims in writing to him.† A statement of claims is deposited, opportunity given for objections, and the claims are then heard and determined by the valuer, subject to an appeal to the Board of Agriculture,‡ and a trial at the assizes in an action brought by any dissatisfied person.§

The steps to be taken in the public interests and the rights of the parties being thus ascertained, the valuer proceeds—

(*a*) to set out the necessary roads,‖

(*b*) to effect any other public works or improvements which have been directed,¶

(*c*) to allot a portion of the land to be inclosed to the Lord of the Manor in respect of his interest in the soil, in accordance with the directions of the provisional order,**

(*d*) to sell, if so directed, a portion of the land to pay the expenses of the inclosure,†† and

(*e*) to divide and allot the residue of the common amongst the persons legally interested, in proportion to the extent and value of their rights as ascertained.‡‡

When the work is completed, the valuer draws up a report,§§ which is deposited for the inspection of the persons interested,‖‖ is considered at a meeting held by the Board of

* Sec. 45.
† Secs. 46 and 47.
‡ Sec. 48.
§ Sec. 56.
‖ Secs. 62, 65, 68.
¶ Secs. 72 and 73.
** Sec. 76.
†† Sec. 77.
‡‡ Sec. 77 and following sections.
§§ Sec. 102.
‖‖ Sec. 103.

Agriculture, or an Assistant Commissioner,* and is approved by the Board when they have heard all objections and made all necessary enquiries.*

Upon the basis of this report the award of the Commissioners is drawn up.† This document specifies the several allotments made and other steps taken, and is binding and conclusive upon all parties‡; the special Act and the award constituting together the title to all hereditaments, rights, and privileges derived under the enclosure. A copy of the award is deposited with the Clerk of the Peace of the County, and another copy with the Churchwardens of the parish § in which the common or the greater part thereof is situate, or with such other fit person as the Board may approve; and all persons interested are entitled to inspect such copies, and to be furnished with copies and extracts on the payment of specified fees. A copy or extract signed by the Clerk of the Peace is received as evidence.||

Local authorities or other persons interested in past inclosures made under the Act of 1845 may thus see the award on application to the Clerk of the Peace, and valuable information may often be so obtained.

---

* Sec. 103. † Sec. 104. ‡ Sec. 105.

§ Probably in future this deposit would be with the Clerk of the Parish Council, see Local Government Act, 1894, secs. 6 (1) (*b*) and 17 (7). See also sec. 17 (8) as to the custody of Awards already deposited.

|| Inclosure Act, 1845, sec. 146.

CHAPTER XIV.

Of Common Fields, Meadows, and Pastures.

We have hitherto dealt with the rights existing in relation to an ordinary manorial common, where the soil belongs to the Lord of the Manor, and the commoners mostly trace their common rights to some connection with the manor. We have considered the various forms in which inclosure may threaten such a common,* the mode in which the common may be disfigured, the means of resisting inclosure and disfigurement, and especially the powers of the local authorities to prevent these evils.

But though a manorial common is the form of common land most usually met with, especially in the South of England, there are other kinds of common land which are by no means unusual. Foremost amongst these are the common fields, common meadows, and common pastures which formerly existed throughout the country—constituting the usual form of agriculture—but most of which have been enclosed by Act of Parliament.

Common fields and meadows are distinguished from commons in this, that whereas a common is waste land, land which has never been occupied in severalty and never subjected to any course of husbandry, common fields and meadows are, as a rule, parcelled out in separate strips or other plots at certain times of the year, and are always during such periods,

* Certain exceptional forms of inclosure are dealt with more conveniently later, see Chap. XVIII., p. 197.

which may be referred to as the close time, either tilled or shut up for hay. The several strips or plots in which the land is held during the close time are owned by different persons, though during the open time the whole field is depastured in common.

Common pastures stand in a somewhat different position. As a rule they are not parcelled out in severalty, like common meadows, but are always depastured in common. They are, however, usually more or less completely inclosed, and they are devoted exclusively to pasture and not, like a common, to the supply of wood and other purposes. And from their systematic use as pastures, they are apt to lose the appearance of waste land and to acquire that of managed ground. Moreover, they are not waste of a manor in the technical sense. Sometimes the soil is vested in the lord, subject to well-ascertained common rights in a limited class of persons. Sometimes the soil belongs in undivided shares to the persons who have a right to depasture cattle.

There is no doubt that a large part of England originally lay in common fields. In each vill or township there were usually three large fields (or, perhaps, two or more sets of such fields) in which the three-course system of husbandry was followed, one field in each year being under wheat, one field under barley, and the third lying fallow. These fields formed the whole, or the bulk, of the arable land of the township. Each field was divided into small strips—originally, apparently, an acre or half an acre in extent*—separated one from another by strips of turf, known as balks, linches, lanchards, or lanchets.

The arable strips were owned and tilled in severalty by the owners, but as soon as the corn was carried, the whole

* Seebohm's "Village Communities," edition 1883, pp. 2 and 3.

field was thrown open to indiscriminate pasturage, by all the householders of the village. A most interesting account of the open common fields in the parish of Hitchin, Herts, will be found in the opening chapter of Mr. Seebohm's "English Village Communities." * And in the first report of the Inclosure Commissioners under the Commons Act, 1876,† will be found a description of the common fields of Barrowden and South and North Luffenham, in Rutlandshire, from which it may be worth while to quote a few sentences by way of illustration. In the three parishes together, the Commissioners state, there are no less than 4,600 acres of open field. In Barrowden "the number of owners is 40 (out of a population of 636). Their buildings are all congregated in the village, and the arable land is divided into 2,790 strips, each averaging less than an acre, some not more than 12 feet wide, each divided from its neighbour by a green balk, the different owners, according to their interests, possessing less or more of these strips in all the different varieties of soil and locality which the parish affords." In South Luffenham 784 acres were held by 22 persons, in 1,238 separate strips, averaging a little over half an acre each; and in North Luffenham 1,493 acres were held in 1,631 strips. "When the corn is cut," the Commissioners say, "the whole land is thrown open to be roamed over by all the live stock as a common pasturage for the parish." In Barrowden and South Luffenham there also existed 391 acres of ordinary common land, waste land of a manor subject to the manorial rights of pasturage. In Barrowden was also a tract of common land known as the Cow Pasture, and in North Luffenham 143 acres of common pastures and meadows. The cow pasture was held in severalty for the purpose of getting a crop of hay and "stocked only

* Longman, 1883.

† 1877 [C.—No. 213].

after the hay crop is removed;" and probably, although the Commissioners do not state the fact, the same rules applied to the North Luffenham meadows. Thus we have in these parishes instances alike of ordinary commons or manorial wastes, of open and common arable fields, and of common pastures and meadows; and down to comparatively recent times parishes so arranged and agriculturally worked might have been found everywhere. The common field system was probably, indeed, almost universal in England down to the time of the dissolution of the monasteries. The agrarian risings of the Tudor period originated mainly in the attempts of large landowners to substitute extensive sheep pastures for open arable fields; and the inclosures so bitterly complained of by Latimer, Sir Thomas More, and other writers of the time, unquestionably related rather to such fields than to commons in the present acceptation of the term. In spite of these protests, considerable inroads on the area of the land under open field cultivation were no doubt made at this time. Nevertheless, much remained until the commencement of the last century, when the movement for Parliamentary inclosure set in. The first private Inclosure Act was passed in 1704, and between that date and 1869 nearly eight millions of acres have, as we have seen, been inclosed. Of the land inclosed since 1845 the Inclosure Commissioners estimated in 1870 * that more than one-third was common field or pasture, as distinguished from common; and probably in the earlier Acts the proportion of common field land was much greater. The quantity of common field, meadow, or pasture land now remaining is consequently comparatively small, and for purposes of public enjoyment such land is not, as a rule, so valuable as common land. From the fact that it is tilled, common field land in particular is not so pleasing to the eye and not so fully

* 1870 [C. 39].

available for purposes of recreation as common land. Still it may provide a wide open space, and, from the necessity of access to the several strips, it is usually traversed by abundant tracks. In the neighbourhood of London such important spaces as the Hackney Downs and Hackney Marshes are not commons, but common fields or meadows, occupied in severalty during a part of the year.

From what has been said, it will be gathered that the two distinguishing features of common field or meadow land (distinguishing it from private land on the one hand and from common land on the other) are—

(1) That it is owned by several persons in strips or plots lying unfenced from each other, but well ascertained and marked by small bound-stones or other marks;

(2) That during a part of the year the whole field or meadow is used in common.

The periods during which common fields and meadows are thrown open for pasturage vary considerably in different cases. But they may be said always to have reference to the possibility of producing the crop to which the field or meadow is devoted during the close time.* Thus we usually find in the Inclosure Commissioners' Reports, that the cattle are admitted after the corn or hay, as the case may be, is carried; but the reports do not show clearly the date at which the fields or meadows are closed. At Hackney, where the Downs appear to have been an arable field, while the marshes and other lands were common meadows, the open time extended, for all alike, from old Lammas Day, the 12th of August, to old Lady Day, the 6th of April. In these cases the days of opening and closing were originally Lammas Day, the 1st of August, and Lady Day, the 25th of March,

* See some instances of open and close times in Appendix I, p. 345.

which was also, up to 1752, the first day of the civil year. Thus the open time would be from Lammas Day to the end of the civil year. The Act for the correction of the Calendar * refers expressly to the fact that "certain lands and grounds are on particular nominal days and times in the year to be opened for common of pasture and for other purposes, and at other times the owners and occupiers of such lands have a right to inclose or shut up the same for their own private use"; and it thereupon provides that such lands and grounds should after the 2nd of September, 1752, be opened and inclosed or shut up upon the same natural days and times on which the same events would have happened if the Act had not passed. Thus the opening of the common fields and meadows, which formerly took place on Lammas Day, was postponed to the 12th of August, and the closing, which formerly took place on Lady Day, was postponed to the 6th of April. It appears, however, from an amending Statute,† that some grounds were opened and shut upon or with reference to the moveable feasts (such as Easter and Whitsuntide), and in such cases no change was to be made, the method of ascertaining such feasts having been itself corrected. No case, however, in which the use of common fields or meadows is regulated by the moveable feasts has come under the writer's notice.

A common field, meadow, or pasture may be threatened with inclosure at the hands of the owners of the soil by virtue of their legal rights, without the assistance of Parliament; or it may be the subject of an application to the Board of Agriculture for inclosure by the sanction of Parliament.

If the owners of the soil propose to inclose without the sanction of Parliament, they must advertise their intention in the local newspapers in the manner already described as

* 24 Geo. II. c. 23. s. 5.

† 25 Geo. II. c. 30.

applicable to a manorial common.* Further, as the provision as to advertisement extends expressly to a "part of a common," one owner of part of a common field wishing to inclose his parcel in perpetuity against his co-owners† must advertise his intention to do so.

Thus the local authorities, and all persons interested in the common field, meadow, or pasture, will have ample notice of the projected inclosure. Or, if notice is not given, the inclosure may be opposed on the grounds already indicated in the case of a manorial common.‡

Whether notice of the intention to inclose common field, meadow, or pasture land need be served on the Parish Council or District Council, is a somewhat nice point. This notice is prescribed by the Local Government Act, 1894,§ and that Act contains no definition of "a common." As we have said,|| the term "a common," as applicable to a piece of land, is not a strictly legal term, and much argument might be raised before the Courts as to the exact meaning to be assigned to it. Probably, however, the Courts, finding the term used in an Act of Parliament, would construe it with reference to the Acts of Parliament relating to the same subject matter, and would thus import the definition of "a common" contained in the Commons Act, 1876. Parish and District Councils may, therefore, reasonably advance a claim to receive notice of any projected inclosure of a common field, meadow, or pasture, or any part thereof.

There is no question that the powers conferred by the

* See *ante*, p. 18. Commons Act, 1876, sec. 31. The term "a common" in the Commons Act, 1876, means any land subject to be inclosed under the Inclosure Acts, 1845 to 1868, and the definition in the Inclosure Act, 1845, of land subject to be inclosed under that Act, covers every description of common field, meadow, or pasture. See 8 & 9 Vict. c. 118. s. 11.

† See *post*, p. 138.

‡ See *ante*, Chap. II., p. 8.

§ 56 & 57 Vict. c. 73. ss. 8 (4) and 26 (2).

|| *Ante*, p. 1.

Commons Act, 1876,* on Urban Sanitary Authorities (now Urban District Councils) in reference to commons within six miles of their towns † extend to common fields, meadows, and pastures. The Local Government Act, 1894, confers these powers (by reference to the Act of 1876) upon all District Councils (acting with the consent of the County Council) in relation to any common within the district of the Council. Here, again, though there is no definition of a common in the Act of 1894, the definition contained in the Act of 1876 would, it can scarcely be doubted, be imported; and it may therefore be assumed that the powers specified in sec. 8 of the Act of 1876 may be exercised by any District Council with reference to any common field, meadow, or pasture within the district of the Council. These powers, as we have seen,‡ extend to the acquisition by gift of the soil of the common field, meadow, or pasture, and to the acquisition of common rights over such field, meadow, or pasture by purchase or gift.

It would seem, however, that the veto of the Board of Agriculture on inclosure, conferred by the Law of Commons Amendment Act, 1893,§ does not extend to common fields or meadows, though possibly it may in some cases extend to common pastures.

That veto, it will be remembered, applies to "an inclosure or approvement purporting to be made under the Statute of Merton and the Statute of Westminster the Second, or either of such statutes." These statutes authorise the Lord of a Manor to inclose his wastes, woods, and pastures, leaving sufficient pasture for the commoners. The whole language of the Act is inappropriate to lands such as common fields and meadows where the land is cultivated, and where the soil

* Sec. 8.

† See *ante*, p. 81, as to this limit.

‡ See *ante*, p. 80.

§ 56 & 57 Vict. c. 57. See *ante*, p. 9.

belongs (in parcels) to the very persons who (with or without others) depasture their cattle over it during the open season.

Speaking generally, an inclosure of common field, meadow, or pasture land could not be justified under the Statutes of Merton and Westminster the Second; and therefore the veto of the Board of Agriculture does not apply.

There are two grounds on which such an inclosure may be justified.

The one is, that the only persons who have any legal interest in or right over the land inclosed consent to the inclosure.

The other, that a custom exists enabling the owner of any plot in the common field to inclose and enjoy his plot in severalty, on condition that he abandons his right of depasturing over the rest of the field during the open season.

If an inclosure is justified on the first ground, the important questions to be considered are—

(1.) Who are the owners of the field or meadow?

(2.) What class of persons is entitled to rights of depasturing the field or meadow during the open season?

(1.) The ownership of a common field or meadow may be in many or in few hands. Originally, without doubt, every householder in the village who gained an independent living had his holding in each of the common fields of the vill or parish; he could not raise grain on any other land. But from the time that the absolute ownership of particular strips in each field was recognised, there would doubtless be changes of ownership by way of sale and exchange. Agricultural writers of the Tudor period are emphatic in their recommendations to consolidate holdings.* Hence the number of owners in a common field or meadow varies indefinitely, and

* The exchange of lands lying in common fields was expressly authorised and facilitated by the statute 4 & 5 Will. IV. c. 30.

may be reduced very low. This is especially the case in the neighbourhood of towns, where the old usages of the common field system are alien to the habits of the place, and where the land is beginning to acquire a building value. On the other hand, in rural districts, where the system is still understood, and the common fields and meadows are greatly used, the number of owners will still be found to be considerable. Of course the danger of inclosure increases as the number of owners diminishes. It is difficult to get even a dozen persons to agree upon so radical a measure as inclosure, and, moreover, amongst the dozen will probably be found some who are trustees, under age, or otherwise incompetent to consent to such a step.*

One owner in a common field or meadow may, apart from any custom of inclosure, prevent the inclosure of the whole.

* The following are examples of the ownership of common fields and meadows:—

Place.	Common Field or Meadow.	Acreage.	No. of strips where stated.	Number of owners.	Sources of information.
Hackney Parish, Middlesex, population very large.	Lammas Lands:—				Pleadings in Baylis v. Tyssen-Amherst, reported 6 Ch.Div. 500. The pleadings are in the possession of Messrs. Horne & Birkett, solicitors to the Commons Preservation Society.
	Hackney Downs -	40	The strips, in any uniform size or shape, had practically disappeared in these cases.	6	
	London Fields -	27		1	
	Well Street Common.	21		3	
	North Mill Field -	30		5	
	South Mill Field -	30		5	
	Hackney Marshes -	320		27	
Barrowden, Rutlandshire, population 636.	Common Fields -	—	2,790	40	Special Report of Inclosure Commission.
South Luffenham, Rutlandshire, population 359.	Common Fields -	784	1,238	22	House of Commons Papers, 1877, No. 213.
North Luffenham, Rutlandshire.	Common Fields -	1,493	1,631	—	
Steventon, Berkshire, population 829.	Common Fields -	1,162	1,000	20	House of Commons Papers, 1880, No. 77.
Riccall, Yorkshire, (N.R.), population 795.	Common Fields -	691	1,127	43	—

It will be seen that the strips average roughly about an acre in some cases, about half an acre in others, as suggested by Mr. Seebohm.

It is therefore of great importance to acquire some holding, however small; and if a District Council can induce any owner to make over his holding to the Council by way of gift,* any danger of an inclosure against the wishes of the neighbourhood may be averted.

(2.) The user of the common field or meadow during the open period is subject to great differences of practice—differences which, however, are easily explained by the original connection of the land with the village community. As we have said, every independent householder in the community originally had his holding in the common fields and meadows. Consequently, when the crops were carried, the persons who turned in their cattle were the same as those who during the close period held the fields (in strips) in severalty. The holders of the strips constituted the village, and therefore to say that the whole village depastured the common fields was only another way of saying, that all the owners depastured them in common.† But as time went on, new-comers arrived in the community. No separate holding in the common fields and meadows could be given to them, because all the holdings were occupied. But in some communities they appear to have been allowed to depasture the fields and meadows during the open time, while in others they appear to have been rigidly excluded.‡ Hence in some cases the rights of pasture during the open season are exercised by a class much larger than that which holds the fields in severalty—by the householders of the parish, or the tenants of a

* Commons Act, 1876, sec. 8, 4th par.

† When the right of common is claimed in respect of land lying in the common field, it is correct to claim that it is a right of common of pasture for cattle levant and couchant, on the strips of the owner; and each owner is entitled to turn out the number of cattle his strips will support. Cheeseman *v.* Hardham, 1 B. & A. 706.

‡ In Swiss Communes, until very recently, the most pointed distinction was made between the burghers or old inhabitants and the *nieder-gelassene* or new-comers, the property in the common woods and pastures belonging to the former, although certain rights were allowed to the latter.

manor (though we believe the latter qualification to be one of modern creation), while in other cases only those who hold the several strips depasture the fields in common.*

It need hardly be added that where the class of persons entitled to depasture is larger than the owners of the common fields or meadows, no valid inclosure can be made against the rights of the persons so entitled; and as the question of sufficiency does not arise, any one commoner during the open season may stop the inclosure. Hence, if a local authority can acquire a common right under the Commons Act, 1876, inclosure may be prevented.†

* The following are a few cases illustrative of the classes entitled to depasture common fields and meadows during the open season:—

Common Field.	Class entitled.	Remarks.
Common Fields of Barrowden and North and South Luffenham, Rutlandshire.	"A common pasturage for the parish" after harvest, *i.e.* the right enjoyed by the owners and occupiers of all lands in the parish.	—
Common Fields of Riccall, Yorkshire, N.R.	Owners of strips - - -	—
Do. of Steventon, Berks. -	Owners of strips - - -	Note. In this case the persons entitled to common on the common pastures and wastes are about the same in number as the owners of the strips in the common fields, this fact indicating that they represent the original village community.
Totternhoe, Beds - -	Owners of strips - - -	The same remark applies.
Orford, Suffolk - - -	The rated inhabitants of the Corporate Borough of Orford.	In this case the common field was owned by Sir Richard Wallace and the Corporation of Orford.
Lammas Lands of Hackney, Middlesex.	Either the owners and occupiers of lands in the parish of St. John, Hackney, or the freehold and copyhold tenants of the manor of Lord's Hold, Hackney.	It was the main question in the action to which class the right belonged, but the action was not tried out. It was agreed, however, that the class was much larger than the owners of the Lammas lands, and that the turning out was regulated by the annual value of the holdings of the persons entitled, according to a scale. ‡

The statute 13 Geo. III. c. 81., for the better cultivation of common fields, expressly saves the rights of persons having rights of common over a common field, without having any land therein (secs. 8–10).

† Sec. 8, 5th par.

‡ See Baylis *v.* Tyssen-Amhurst, 6 Ch. Div. 500; and the pleadings, in this Case, see p. 135.

Inclosures in common fields may in some cases be justified by special custom. A custom may exist in a common field, that any owner may inclose his portion in perpetuity, and so keep out his neighbours, giving up his right of common over the rest of the field. Such a custom has been upheld in several decided cases.*

It would seem that such a custom can only exist (though the point does not seem to have been decided) when the right to depasture in common during the open period is confined to the owners of parcels in the field; since in this case the custom is in the nature of a give-and-take arrangement, while in any other the commoners during the open time are deprived of their feed without any equivalent.† And whether in the first case such a custom exists must depend entirely on the evidence. Thus, if inclosures have been made, and during a long course of years the right of common over them has not been asserted by other owners in the field, the custom will be deemed to have been proved; but if the commoners have, notwithstanding the inclosure, gone in "by bars or gates" and depastured their cattle, then there is no proof of such a custom.‡

We have said enough to show that the exact character of the rights subsisting over common fields and meadows varies within very wide limits in different cases. No such general directions for ascertaining such rights as are possible in the case of commons proper can be given.§ But in any investigations touching on open spaces of this description, it is nevertheless important to bear in mind that the common field

* Sir Miles Corbet's Case, 7 Rep. 5; Barber *v.* Dixon, 1 Wils. 44; How *v.* Strood, 2 Wils. 269.

† See Mr. Justice Bayley's remarks in Cheeseman *v.* Hardham, 1 B. & Ald. 712.

‡ Per Lord Coke in Sir Miles Corbet's Case, 7 Rep. 5.

§ The remarks contained in Chap. IV. on rights of common existing apart from the manorial system, whether claimed by immemorial usage, by modern grant, by usage giving rise to a presumption of such a grant, or under the Prescription Act, apply to rights claimed over a common field or meadow.

or meadow was in all probability enjoyed originally by all the householders of the parish or vill in which it lies. Where such an open space is still owned in severalty by many persons, there is little practical risk of inclosure. Where it has passed into one or two hands, rights of pasture during a portion of the year, perhaps fallen more or less into disuse, may often be found to have existed in the owners and occupiers of lands within the parish or district; and such rights may be used to prevent inclosure.

In the case of common pastures, also, the rights vary considerably, but, as a rule, they are well ascertained. Common pastures, as distinguished from common meadows, are not held in severalty during any part of the year, but are always depastured in common according to fixed rules. They fall under two categories. In the first case, the soil is jointly owned by the persons who turn out on the pasture. Such persons are said to be entitled to the land as tenants in common in undivided shares, such shares corresponding to their interest in the surface as measured by the number of cattle they can turn on.* In the second case, the soil of the pasture belongs to some one person (who may or may not also own certain of the rights of pasturage), the persons entitled to turn in cattle being owners of the pasturage only.† In the latter class of cases, the owner of the soil is not infrequently the Lord of the Manor. Although, perhaps, absolutely excluded from the pasturage, he is entitled to sport over the land, and also to the minerals

---

* The King *v.* The Inhabitants of Whixley, 1 T.R. 137. Here the cattle-gates (see next page) passed by lease and release.

† Earl of Lonsdale *v.* Rigg, 11 Ex. 654, 1 Hurlst. & Norman, 923. Here the cattle-gates were of customary tenure, and the right of pasture was from 26th of May to 24th of April each year. The distinction in the text is noticed in the Inclosure Act, 1845, under the description of land subject to be inclosed under the Act. See 8 & 9 Vict. c. 118. s. 11.

lying under the land, though he is unable to work the latter, unless he can do so without injury to the pasturage.

A right of turning cattle into a common pasture is often called a cattle-gate or beast-gate.* Each cattle-gate gives the right to turn on a fixed number of animals, and the whole pasture is divided or held in a fixed number of gates. Another word to express the same thing is "stint"; and the Land Commissioners often speak of a "gated or stinted pasture." For example, in the parish of Steventon, Berks (already referred to), the Commissioners found two stinted pastures, the soil of which was claimed by the Lord of the Manor, but which were depastured exclusively by 24 persons, owners of 117 stints of equal value. In this case each stint entitled the owner to depasture cows during a specified period of each year, and afterwards sheep for a short time. How nearly a stinted pasture may approach in appearance to a common, and how far it may be removed, are illustrated by this case. The two stinted pastures were known as the Cow Common and the Green. The Green, extending to 27 acres, had been used for recreation, and apparently was more or less in the nature of a village green. The Cow Common, 54 acres, is described as "a large fenced field, to which the public have no admittance."

Where a right of common of pasture is regulated by fixed number, as distinguished from levancy and couchancy, it may be alienated without the tenement to which it was originally appendant or appurtenant; † and it thereupon becomes a right of common in gross. Consequently, it follows that the rights of common over a common pasture, which is gated or

* The word obviously refers not to any material gate, but to the going or gait of the beasts on the pasture.

† See Drury *v.* Kent, Cro. Jac. 15; Spooner *v.* Day, Cro. Car. 432; Daniel *v.* Hanslip, 2 Lev. 67.

stinted to a definite number of beasts held in a fixed number of rights, may at any moment, if not so already, be converted into rights of common in gross.*

Whether rights over a stinted pasture (not being an interest in the soil †) are rights of common in gross, or rights to an undivided share of a several pasture, will depend upon whether the owner of the soil has any right to turn cattle on to the pasture. If he has, the rights of the owners of stints are rights of common in gross; if not, they are rights to an undivided share of a several pasture.‡

There is one class of gated or stinted pasture which should be noticed.

Under the Inclosure Acts, commons (wastes of manors) may be converted into gated or stinted pastures;§ and the same process was formerly authorised by private Acts. In such cases the ancient rights of common are extinguished by Act of Parliament; and the Lord of the Manor and the commoners are converted into owners of the pasture in undivided shares in proportion to their liability for the rate to be levied for the maintenance of the pasture, such liability being in turn regulated by the number of stints or rights of pasture held by such persons respectively.||

* The Land Commissioners, in reporting upon the proposed inclosure of the common fields and pastures of Steventon (near Abingdon), in Berkshire, say, "the stints are not necessarily attached to or held in respect of other land, but are sometimes dealt with as held in gross, and are bought and sold apart from any other property." (1880 [C. — No. 77].)

† See *ante*, p. 139. Where the persons depasturing have an interest in the soil, no right of sporting or right to minerals will as a rule be found to exist in any other person.

‡ See *ante*, p. 62, as to sole or several pasturage.

§ See Inclosure Act, 1845, secs. 113–122; Inclosure Act, 1854, sec. 6; Commons Act, 1876, secs. 15–17. The same process may now be accomplished by a provisional order for regulation under the Commons Act, 1876; see secs. 2–4.

|| Inclosure Act, 1845, secs. 116, 115.

It will be remembered that a local authority is expressly authorised by the Commons Act to purchase a saleable right of common.* To preserve a gated or stinted pasture from inclosure, therefore, the surest means is to purchase one of the gates or stints. Where the stints are undivided shares of a several pasture, the owner of any one such share may prevent an inclosure. Where there are rights of common in gross, no inclosure (whether under the Statutes of Merton and Westminster the Second or otherwise) can be made by the owner of the soil against any such right.† The opposition of any one commoner is fatal to an approvement or inclosure.

One form of inclosure noticed in relation to manorial commons, that of inclosure by way of copyhold grant,‡ is inapplicable, from the nature of the case, to common fields. But, if it were in any case attempted, the provision of the Copyhold Act, 1894, which gives the Board of Agriculture a veto upon any such grant, would apply.§

We have now dealt with the inclosure of common fields, meadows, and pastures by the owners without the authority of Parliament.

There have been many statutes passed from time to time to facilitate the inclosure of common fields, meadows, and pastures.‖ But at the present day, it is probable that any proposal to enclose would be made under the Inclosure Acts, 1845 to 1882, and that the proceedings would, therefore, be subject to the provisions of the Commons Act, 1876. All that has been said in relation to the Parliamentary inclosure of a manorial common ¶ may therefore be taken to extend

* Commons Act, 1876, sec. 8, 5th par.

† See *ante*, p. 13.

‡ See *ante*, p. 93.

§ See *ante*, p. 95.

‖ There are also statutes to facilitate the cultivation of common fields; see 13 Geo. III. c. 81.; 4 & 5 Will. IV. c. 30.

¶ See *ante*, Chap. XIII.

to the same process as applied to common fields, meadows, and pastures. There is, indeed, one distinction. The Board of Agriculture cannot compel the persons legally interested in such land to agree to allotments for exercise and recreation and for field gardens. The provisions as to such allotments apply only to land which is either

(*a*) waste land of any manor on which the tenants of such manor have rights of common, or

(*b*) land subject to any rights of common at all times of the year for cattle levant and couchant, or

(*c*) land subject to any rights of common which may be exercised at all times of the year and are not limited by number or stints.*

This distinction is, however, of no great practical importance at the present day. For the Board of Agriculture will not recommend any inclosure to Parliament, unless they are convinced, that it is for the public benefit; and if in their opinion it would be to the advantage of the neighbourhood to have allotments for recreation and field gardens, they would obviously be unable to certify, that the inclosure was beneficial, unless these allotments were made. The parties promoting such inclosure can of course consent to such allotments, and when they are authorised by the provisional order, all other persons interested in the land will be bound.†

We have said nothing as to the disfigurement of common fields, meadows, and pastures. From their nature they are not liable to the same depredations as commons. Near London some harm was done to an open space which was a common field, Hackney Downs, by gravel digging carried

* Commons Act, 1876 (39 & 40 Vict. c. 56.), sec. 10 (4) and 37.

† There is, indeed, a special provision of the Commons Act, 1876 (sec. 23), enabling allotments to be made out of common field land where such land is included in the same application as common land.

on by the Lord of the Manor, who was also owner of parcels of the Downs. But in this case the common field system had fallen into disuse, and many irregularities occurred. It seems probable, that no owner of any parcel of a common field can properly use it except in the way which has been authorised by custom from time immemorial, *i.e.*, for the growth of certain crops at certain times of the year, and for pasturage in common with others at other times. And the same observation may be held to apply, according to the character of the land, to common meadows and common pastures.

CHAPTER XV.

Of the Waste and Commonable Lands of a Forest.

MANY of the largest tracts of open and commonable land remaining in England are, or were, the waste or commonable lands of a royal forest.

An appreciable proportion of the whole soil of England must at one time have been subject to forest laws. Manwood gives a large number of Royal Forests, all of them, except the New Forest and Hampton Court Forest, so ancient, that no record of their commencement existed. It would probably be a laborious task to compile a complete list of these forests and to account for their disappearance or present condition. During this century more than a dozen Acts disafforesting particular forests have been passed; and no doubt other forests would be found to have been dealt with by private Inclosure Acts, and, more anciently, by letters patent, by which the Crown made away with its rights, supplemented by a decree of the Court of Chancery, which divided the land amongst the commoners and others interested.* Probably, in other cases, forests have ceased to exist from mere non-exercise of forestal rights. To trace the fate of each forest would be interesting from an historical point of view. But it is a question of practical importance, whether a particular

* Malvern Chase (comprising the well-known Malvern Hills) and Ashdown Forest (in Sussex) were partitioned and partly inclosed in this way.

tract of open land ever was part of a forest; for the rights of common in a forest belong to, and are exercised by, different classes of persons from those in which such rights are usually found in the case of non-forestal commons. The best illustration of this statement is furnished by the recent history of what is popularly known as Epping Forest—the splendid tract of 5,600 acres of open lawn and woodland lying on the threshold of London, and now preserved for ever for the public enjoyment. Epping Forest was part of the Royal Forest of Waltham or Essex, an extensive tract of country comprising a large acreage of inclosed lands and many villages, as well as two large tracts of waste and wood, the one known as Hainault, the other as Epping, Forest. Hainault Forest was disafforested by an Act passed in 1851, and its open lands were subsequently for the most part inclosed. In Epping Forest the Crown first neglected to enforce its rights, and then sold them over large portions of the Forest. The proximity of the Forest to London gave its open land an exceptional value, and the lords of several manors in the Forest set themselves to inclose. Now, in this case, it was undoubtedly the fact, that the soil of the waste land belonged to the lords of the several manors in the Forest, each lord owning as much as lay within the bounds of his manor.* On the other hand, the lords could not deny that the open Forest was subject to rights of common of some sort; but they alleged, that these rights were only those of the tenants of their respective manors, and that the tenants of each manor were entitled to depasture their cattle only on those parts of the open Forest which lay within such manor, and had no

* The manors were originally for the most part in the hands of religious houses, such as the Abbey of Waltham. They came into the hands of the Crown at the Reformation, and were granted again to subjects.

rights in any other parts. Accordingly they claimed to exercise all such powers of inclosure as were till recently claimed by the lord in an ordinary manor.* They made grants of portions of the forest to be held as copyhold, and they inclosed other portions for their own use under the alleged authority of the Statutes of Merton and Westminster the Second; and so energetically did they proceed, that in 1871, out of 7,000 acres, 4,000 had been inclosed. The Corporation of London then came to the relief of the commoners and the public.† The history of the Forest and the nature of the common rights were fully investigated, and a suit was commenced against one of the lords of manors who had inclosed. The right alleged in this suit was not that of any tenants of any manor, but that of all the owners and occupiers of lands within the legal bounds of the Forest ‡ to depasture their cattle upon the wastes of the forest without regard to manorial limits. Such a claim was obviously fatal to all the lords' inclosures, since the class in whom the right was alleged was, for practical purposes, unlimited, and it could not be pretended that the consent of the members of this class had been obtained to any inclosures, or that sufficient pasture for their wants had been left. The claim was, therefore, stoutly resisted, on the grounds, first, that such a right could not exist in law, and, secondly, that it did not exist in fact. The Court of Appeal (Lords Justices James and Mellish) decided the first question without hesitation; § and the late Master of the Rolls, Sir George Jessel, found that

* See *ante*, Chap. II., p. 8.

† We are not here telling in detail the history of the rescue of the forest. This will be found in Mr. Shaw Lefevre's recent book on "English Commons and Forests," Cassell & Co., Limited, 1894.

‡ Speaking broadly, Epping Forest comprised the land between the rivers Roding and Lea.

§ Commissioners of Sewers *v.* Glasse, L.R. 7 Ch. App. 456.

the evidence in favour of the right was so clear and abundant, that it ought to have been known to the lords.* He pronounced against all the inclosures, and ordered the lords to pay the costs of the suit. Thus Epping Forest was saved for London by means of the character of the common rights exercised over it.

From the above sketch of the Epping Forest case, it will have been seen, that a forest in the legal sense comprises far more than the actual open land to which the name is popularly applied.

Manwood, in his "Treatise of the Forest Laws," defines a forest as "a certain territory of woody grounds and fruitful pastures, privileged for wild beasts and fowls of forest, chase and warren to rest and abide there, in the safe protection of the King, for his delight and pleasure."† It is not (he says) inclosed, but is "meered and bounded with unremoveable marks, meers, and boundaries,"‡ such as hills, rivers, highways, and sometimes remarkable trees.§ Within its circuit there may be many inclosed grounds, villages, and even towns. Thus, within Waltham Forest were the old market towns of Waltham and Epping, besides many villages. The essential peculiarity of the district does not consist in being woodland,|| or even a wild open district (though, no doubt, both these characteristics may generally be expected), but in being subject to the forest laws. And the main object of these laws was to keep the place *in statu quo*. Thus, speaking generally, pasture land could not be turned into

* Commissioners of Sewers *v.* Glasse, L.R. 19 Eq. 137.

† Ed. 1717, "Pl. Forests," p. 143.

‡ Manwood, *ubi supra.*

§ *Ib.* p. 140.

|| There are forests which are almost destitute of trees, and which it is difficult to believe ever contained much wood, *e.g.*, Dartmoor and Exmoor, in the county of Devon.

arable, inclosed woods could not be felled except under conditions which would ensure their restoration, buildings could not be erected, and open uninclosed grounds could not be inclosed. The roam of the deer was preserved throughout the whole district, inclosed and uninclosed land, cultivated and waste land, alike. No landowner or farmer could erect a fence high enough to keep out a doe with her fawn, and to kill or chase out the deer even from amongst standing corn was a high misdemeanour. In time, as the Forest laws were relaxed, the roam of the deer over the farms and gardens of the forest became in practice curtailed, and the open waste lands came to be looked on as the district specially set aside for them, while the owners of inclosed lands set at naught the restrictions of the Forest law. But in the controversies respecting Epping Forest, old witnesses spoke to the inroads made by the deer on fields adjoining the open Forest, and pointed to particular spots where they might generally be found by the keepers at certain hours. And the records of the last century of the Court of Attachments of Waltham Forest are full of the applications of landowners in the Forest for leave to fell their inclosed woods or groves.

Incident to a forest there seems commonly to have been a general right in the inhabitants of the district* to depasture their cattle (not offensive to the deer) over the whole tract of uninclosed waste and woodland comprised within the forest bounds. Of the legal origin of the right it is not possible to speak with confidence, but it has often been viewed as a compensation for the burden imposed upon the inhabitants by the roam of the deer over their inclosed lands, and the restrictions to which they were subject in

* The exact limits of the right seem to have varied. See *post*, pp. 157-160.

the beneficial occupation of such lands.* The right did not extend to sheep, and could not be exercised during the fence-month, fifteen days before and fifteen days after old Midsummer Day (July 6th), when it was important to preserve quietude for the does and their fawns. In some forests another close-time has also been enforced, known as the winter-heyning. This period extends from the 22nd of November to the 4th of May, and its express object seems to have been to preserve the pasturage exclusively for the deer during the winter months, when it was scantiest. However, this restriction does not appear to be of the same general obligation as the fence-month. It was never observed in the Forest of Waltham.†

In addition to the right of common of pasture for horses and cows, there also exists in most royal forests a right of pannage for pigs. Pannage is a word which has been used in two senses, meaning sometimes the feeding of hogs with mast, *i.e.* the fruit of the oak and beech, and sometimes the payment made to the King, or other owner of the wood, for the liberty to send pigs there so to feed. In Waltham Forest it was found ‡ that the class of persons entitled to common of pasture (the owners and occupiers of lands in the Forest) had also a right to send their pigs into the Forest to take the mast fallen from the trees. In the New Forest this right is a very valuable one, and was found to

* The language of the Ordinatio Forestæ (33 Edw. I. c. 5.) confirms this view. Another view is that the large rights of common found in forests are rights which existed in many parts of the country before the Conquest, and which have been preserved by the forest system, whereas in other places they have yielded to narrower manorial customs. The late Mr. W. R. Fisher, in his valuable work on "The Forest of Essex" (Butterworths, 1887), holds this view, and adduces many facts and arguments in its favour.

† It is singular, that in the New Forest the winter-heyning has during recent years (and before the passing of the New Forest Act, 1877) been much more strictly observed than the fence-month.

‡ By the Epping Forest Commissioners' Final Report, p. 4.

exist in a large class of persons by the Commissioners appointed by Statute * to compile a register of commoners. The right is only exerciseable in time of pannage, that is, when there is mast on the ground. In the King's woods the time of pannage, according to ancient law, was from Holy-rood day (fifteen days before Michaelmas) to Martinmas (forty days after Michaelmas); but in the woods of subjects it might be at any convenient times when the mast is ripe, subject only to this condition, that where such woods adjoined the King's woods, the latter must be agisted first, and private persons were not at liberty to take pigs into their woods until that agistment was over, that is, about Martinmas.† The right of pannage is a right to take by the mouths of the pigs such mast as has fallen; and the owner of a wood is not impeded by the existence of the right in the proper husband-like management of his trees.‡ It was, in ancient times, an exceedingly valuable right, woods being esteemed not for their timber, but for the number of pigs they could support.§ And even at the present day it is, as we have said, much valued in the New Forest, where herds of pigs are turned out in the autumn by the adjoining small tenants and freeholders. A similar right is said to be systematically exercised in the forests of Germany.||

Speaking generally, then, an ancient royal forest was a district devoted to the preservation of deer and other game for the delight of the sovereign, and, with that view, kept as far as possible in a stationary condition as to the advance of cultivation and the increase of towns, villages, and dwell-

* 17 & 18 Vict. c. 49.

† Manwood, ed. 1717, Tit. Pannage, pars. 11–15.

‡ Chilton *v.* Corporation of London, L.R. 7 Ch. Div. 562.

§ Furley's "Weald of Kent," pp. 70, 77–8, and the Laws of King Ina, quoted on p. 78.

|| Head's "Bubbles from the Brunnen of Nassau."

ings—a district in which there was always a large tract of waste land (generally wood-land interspersed with heath), which was the special resort and nursery of the deer, and over which large numbers of cattle and pigs belonging to the adjoining inhabitants roamed and fed.

The soil of this tract of waste was not necessarily vested in the Crown, but might be held by subjects. In some cases we find the Crown the sole owner, as in the New Forest * and the Forest of Dean; in other cases there is a joint ownership of the Crown and private persons, as in the Hainault Division of Waltham Forest, and formerly in Windsor Forest; or, again, as in Epping Forest, the Crown may not hold a single rood of waste land. The forest rights of the Crown, when exercised over the lands of subjects, are technically known as rights of forest, and are sometimes defined as rights of vert and venison, that is, rights of preserving the deer (venison) and the woods and herbage (vert) of the Forest for the use and protection of the deer.

The peculiar laws applicable to a Forest were administered by courts existing specially for the purpose. These courts were of three grades: (1) the Court of Attachments, Woodmote, or Forty-day Court, (2) the Court of Swainmote, and (3) the Court of the Chief Justice in Eyre, or Justice Seat. The Court of Attachments and the Swainmote Court were presided over by the verderers, four gentlemen chosen by the freeholders of the county in which the Forest lay, and holding office for life. The Court of Attachments had summary jurisdiction over offences in the Forest where the value of the trespass was not more than fourpence; but its main function was the committal and bail of offenders

* Even in the New Forest, the soil of certain small portions of the open waste is claimed by private persons.

attached, or charged, by the foresters or keepers of the forest. At the Court of Swainmote (which, since the Charta de Foresta of the 9th year of King Henry III., could not lawfully be held more than three times a year), the offenders bailed to appear there by the Court of Attachments were tried by a jury of freeholders in the Forest. If convicted, the fact of the offence could not afterwards be traversed. But no sentence was pronounced at the Swainmote; the offender was again bound over to appear at the next Justice Seat. At this court the verderers produced the rolls of the Swainmote, showing the various offences there tried. An offender might still plead any matter of law or special exemption in justification of his conduct, and final judgment was then pronounced. A Justice Seat could not be held more often than once in three years; but it would hardly seem, from the various records extant, that it was commonly held so often. In the case of Waltham Forest, only the records of isolated courts, kept at very considerable intervals, have been preserved. Not only were convicted offenders sentenced at a Justice Seat, but a general enquiry was made as to all the circumstances connected with the Forest. For this purpose a jury of freeholders, from eighteen to twenty-four in number, was sworn, and a charge of great length and minuteness of detail was delivered to them by the Chief Justice in Eyre. The claims of all persons enjoying any special rights or exemptions in the Forest (other than the right of common of pasture) * were also brought in, considered, and, if found valid, enrolled. In short, every step was taken to obtain a full and correct account of the state of the Forest and the various rights existing therein.

* It was not necessary to claim the right of common of pasture at the Justice Seat (Manwood, ed. 1717, p. 99; Sir William Jones' Rep. 291).

There were two Chief Justices in Eyre for the royal forests, one acting on this (the south) side, and one on the other side of the River Trent. They were peers, appointed rather for their rank than for their knowledge of the Forest laws, and they were, therefore, assisted by some of the judges of the King's Courts at Westminster.

The officers of the Forest, whose duty it was to put this elaborate legal machinery in motion, consisted commonly of a lord warden, with a staff of chief foresters or master keepers, and under-foresters or under-keepers. It was the duty of these officials to watch the Forest as a gamekeeper watches a preserve, noting all offences, and apprehending offenders, whose appearance at the Court of Attachments they had power to ensure by attaching them either by their goods, by pledges, or by their bodies. Of course, in practice, the duty was performed by the under-foresters.

There was still another set of officers of a forest, called regarders. Their duty it was to traverse the whole forest every third year, before the holding of the Justice Seat, to make an independent survey of all offences, and of the state of the forest, and to note any breaches of duty on the part of the foresters. The result of this inspection they entered formally on a roll, which they delivered at the Swainmote Court (in order that the offenders named in it might there be tried), and subsequently at the Justice Seat. Amongst the matters to which their attention was directed was the expeditation or lawing of mastiffs, *i.e.* the cutting off of three claws of the forefeet, so that they might not be able to pursue the deer.

Another officer playing an important part in some forests is the reeve. The term reeve appears to denote a person having the charge and responsibility of a district for certain purposes, *e.g.*, the shire-reeve or sheriff, the person accountable to the Crown for the preservation of its rights in a particular shire or county. The reeve of a parish or vill within a forest was, no doubt, selected by the Crown as a suitable person to make accountable for the proper exercise by the inhabitants of their rights within the forest. At an early date * we find that townships and villages in a forest were respectively represented at the forest courts by a reeve and four men, who were there sworn in to be of good behaviour to the vert and venison, and especially to assist in driving the forest and to prevent improper commoning. In Waltham Forest the reeve was appointed by the parish vestry, and sworn in at the Court of Attachments; and his chief duty was to mark with a special mark all beasts commonable upon the forest turned out in respect of lands lying within the parish for which he acted. The marks consisted of a crown and a letter of the alphabet, the parishes being lettered in order throughout the Forest.

Such is a sketch of the Forest system in its integrity. In the reigns of Henry VII., Charles I., and Charles II., records exist for Waltham Forest, giving a vivid picture of the procedure at the courts and of the peculiar rights and liabilities attaching to residence in a forest. No doubt similar records may be found for other royal forests. In Sir William Jones' Reports are collected a number of decisions given at a Justice Seat held for Windsor Forest in the years 1632 and 1633.

The feature of the Forest system which most concerns those interested in open spaces is, as we have said, the invariable existence of extensive rights of common. The characteristic of these rights is, that they depend upon locality and not upon tenure. We have not, as is mostly

* See Records of the Justice Seat for Waltham Forest of 4 Hen. VII. (1489), Duchy of Lancaster Miscellaneous Records; and Swainmote Roll of the same forest, 36 Eliz., preserved in the Bodleian Library.

the case when asserting rights over an ordinary manorial common, to show that the lands in respect of which the right is claimed are, or were, held of any particular manor. In Epping Forest, as we have seen, the attempt to show such a connection completely failed. Enquiry should be directed rather to some district within which the lands entitled to rights are to be found. In Epping Forest this district was the forest itself. It was conclusively proved that the owners and occupiers of all lands within the Forest were entitled to a right of common of pasture for horses and oxen.* In Hainault Forest, the other portion of the Forest of Waltham, the Court of Common Pleas (confirming a finding of an Assistant Inclosure Commissioner) held, that in two parishes, Woodford and Navestock, where there were detached wastes, rights of common over these wastes were confined to the parishioners, but that with respect to the residue of the open Forest the right was exercised indiscriminately by all the parishes over the whole waste.† The Hainault case was, however, decided without reference to the history of the Forest, or to the practices prevailing in Epping Forest; it had reference to the practical use of the Forest wastes, and the mode in which they should be allotted on inclosure. Inter-commoning between Hainault and Epping could never have been largely practised, owing to the division of the two wastes by the valley of the Roding. But two parishes extended into both divisions; and the reeves' marking irons were lettered throughout for all the parishes, without reference to their situation in one or other division. These divisions, indeed, never existed in law, and all the documentary evidence goes to show that a right of common, enjoyed over all the

* Commissioners of Sewers *v.* Glasse, L.R. 19 Eq. 137.

† *In re* Hainault Forest Act, 1858, 9 C.B. N.S. 648.

open lands of the Forest of Waltham (including both Epping and Hainault), existed in all the owners and occupiers of lands within the bounds of that forest.

The class of commoners cannot, however, in every forest be defined with reference to the bounds of the forest. In the New Forest the inclosed lands within the bounds extend to less than 30,000 acres, while the open wastes are more than 60,000 acres. A register of commoners on this Forest has been compiled under statutory authority,* and the total acreage registered as entitled to common rights exceeds the total acreage of the Forest wastes.† It follows, therefore, that more than half of the lands entitled to common of pasture in the Forest wastes are situate outside the present bounds of the Forest.

In the Forest of Exmoor, the Act of Disafforestation ‡ indicates that the owners and occupiers of lands in twenty-five parishes in Somerset and Devon had rights of pasture on the Forest, upon payment of certain small sums, while certain landowners in two parishes (Hawkridge and Withypoole, in the County of Somerset) had rights without payment. All these landowners are said to owe suit to the Court of Swainmote, *i.e.* (probably) they were bound to appear, either individually or by their parish representatives, at the Forest courts. The landowners in Hawkridge and Withypoole were known as *free* suitors. In this Forest the right of pasture extended to sheep.

In the Forest of Dartmoor the right of pasture (which again extends to sheep) is enjoyed by the owners and occupiers of lands in all the parishes bordering on the Forest, such

* 17 & 18 Vict. c. 49; see this Act referred to in Mill *v.* Commissioners of the New Forest, 18 C.B. 60. For Extract from Register, see Appendix, p. 346.

† The register has always been alleged to have been compiled with some harshness to the commoners, and it is probable that many rights previously existing were not registered and were thus lost.

‡ 55 Geo. III. c. 138.

parishes being said to be "venville parishes," or "in venville," *i.e.*, perhaps, parishes which were bound to come (Lat. *venire*, or Fr. *venir*) by their representatives to the Forest courts.*

In the Forest of Whittle-wood or Whittle-bury, which extended into the counties of Northampton, Oxford, and Buckingham, the owners of lands in sixteen parishes are said by the Disafforestation Acts † to have rights of common in the Forest. Seven of these are said to be known as in-towns, and nine as out-towns, but it is not stated whether any difference in the nature of the rights existed. In-towns were, no doubt, parishes or vills within the bounds of the Forest, and out-towns parishes or vills outside those bounds. Thus, it would seem, that common rights were extensively enjoyed in respect of lands outside the Forest.

In another forest of the Midlands, that of Salcey (Northampton and Bucks), the landowners of six parishes (it appears from the Disafforestation Act ‡) had rights of common in the Forest; but it is not clear whether these parishes were wholly within the legal bounds of the Forest or not. Many parishes were also interested in the rights of pasture in the Forest of Whichwood, Oxfordshire; but the Disafforestation Act § does not state whether they were, or were not, within the bounds of the Forest.

In a recent case ‖ the rights of common over Ashdown Forest, in Sussex, were elaborately investigated. Ashdown Forest was granted as a free chase to John of Gaunt in 1372 (25 June), and from that time onwards the full system of forest courts has not been in force in the Forest, though

* Another view of the origin of the term venville is that it is a corruption of "fines villarum." See Mr. Percival Birkett's Paper on the History of Dartmoor.

† 5 Geo. IV. c. 99.; 16 & 17 Vict. c. 42.

‡ 6 Geo. IV. c. 132.

§ 16 & 17 Vict. c. 36.

‖ De la Warr *v.* Miles, 17 Ch. Div. 535.

certain courts known as Avise, Eves, or Evesfeld Courts, and as Woodmote Courts, and being of the nature of forest or chase courts, were regularly held. The wastes and woods of the forest were at one time surrounded by a pale, but the forest was considered to extend beyond the pale. The rights of common were specified from time to time in ancient presentments or verdicts of juries made at Avise Courts in return to commissions issued from the office of the Duchy of Lancaster. According to these documents, the rights were enjoyed by a large class of persons known as "customaries" or "customers." Some of these held their lands solely of the duchy, and were described as "the King's customary tenants"; others whose lands were not so held were styled "foreign customaries"; but the rights of the two classes differed but very slightly. Both enjoyed common of pasture all the year round, except between Michaelmas and Martinmas (11th November),* for as many beasts as they could keep on their tenements in winter (*i.e.* for their beasts levant and couchant on their tenements), and for two mares and one colt for every draft of oxen they kept,† on payment of certain small fees—fees which probably corresponded to the marking fees in Epping Forest and the New Forest. Subsequently, in the time of William III., the then owners of the soil of the forest, wishing to effect a partition between themselves and the commoners, brought a suit ‡ in Chancery against no less than 144 persons. In the decree made in the suit the holdings of all the defendants were detailed; and thus a register of commoners was constructed. The holdings lie in eight parishes in Sussex, into seven of which the open forest (before the partition) extended. For the purpose of the

* The time of pannage.

† Notice this curious reference to the connection of rights of common with the tillage of the soil.

‡ Earl of Dorset *v.* Newnham.

recent litigation it was not necessary to go behind the register compiled in 1691, or to discuss the class originally entitled to common of pasture. But all the facts suggest that the right was originally exercised by the owners and occupiers of lands in the parishes into which the open forest extended, or upon which it bordered. Possibly in early Norman days all these parishes were subject to the Forest laws.

A comparison of the classes of persons ascertained, or appearing, to be entitled to common of pasture on forest wastes in the cases above mentioned, and in others, rather tends to strengthen the conclusion arrived at by the late Mr. W. R. Fisher in his valuable work on "The Forest of Essex."* Mr. Fisher thinks that the exercise of rights of common over the wastes of forests by large classes of persons independently of manorial tenure indicates not a special grant by the Crown in compensation for the burden of the forest laws, but the preservation, by means of the Forest system, of rights existing from the earliest times of agricultural occupation. Around a large district of wood and waste lay a number of village communities, each with its own houses, common arable fields, and common meadows. All turned out their cattle on the great waste at their doors. This waste, being found suitable for hunting, was gradually placed under special game laws, which culminated in the severe forestal code of the early Norman sovereigns. To have driven out the cattle of the surrounding villages would have been impracticable; nor was so severe a measure necessary, for the cattle did not harm the deer. The usage of turning out was therefore recognised and put under regulations, such, for example, as those relating to (1) the marking of the cattle to prevent beasts from a distance being driven in, as communication became more easy, and (2) the exclusion

* Butterworths, 1887.

of the cattle at certain times, such as the fence-month and the winter-heyning. The forest system being more authoritative in the district than the manorial, which sometimes scarcely existed, the rights were not as they were elsewhere, gradually confined in their exercise to the limits of the manor and associated with manorial tenures, but were preserved in their ancient form to the present day. And, if at any time such rights were challenged, the law came to their assistance, not speculating unnecessarily upon the origin of rights unconnected with the manorial system, but holding that the existence of a forest was quite enough to account for the existence within it of unusually extensive rights.

Whatever, then, the history of forestal rights of common may be, wherever the existence of a forest can be traced, it may be safely assumed, that rights formerly existed over its whole wastes, and that these rights were attached to a large acreage of land lying either within the ancient legal bounds of the forest or within certain parishes or districts adjacent to the forest waste. Such rights are far more easily proved than rights depending upon the connection of particular lands with a particular manor.

Perhaps the only right invariably found in a forest is that of common of pasture for horses and neat-beasts, *i.e.* oxen, cows, heifers, and calves. Sheep are, as a rule, not commonable in a forest. It is sometimes stated that they spoil the pasture for the deer, but probably the main reason is that their bite is so much closer than that of horses and cattle.* Nevertheless, sheep are commonable all over Dartmoor, and were commonable on Exmoor. In the Forest of Waltham certain limited rights of depasturing sheep in

* See some statements on the subject in litigation respecting Waltham Forest of the time of Charles I. Fisher's "Forest of Essex," p. 294.

certain places seem formerly to have existed by charter;* but sheep have not been turned out in modern times. In Whichwood Forest, in Oxfordshire, "sheep-walks" existed at the time of the disafforestation; † in other words, there were rights of pasturing sheep in certain places, probably the lawns or open glades of the forest.

Speaking generally, a right to depasture sheep must not be expected in a forest; ‡ but it may exist by special usage, founded on a charter or long exercise.

Goats and geese are never commonable in a forest. Indeed, they are not, as we have seen, commonable on an ordinary common, except by special usage.

Pigs, as we have seen, are usually commonable in a forest during the time of pannage. In Ashdown Forest they were commonable all the year round except during the fence-month, when hogs above six months old were excluded.§

It is by no means unusual to find rights of cutting wood for fuel in a royal forest, but such rights stand on a very different footing from the right of common of pasture. They do not exist in every forest; and where they are found, they do not, as a rule, exist throughout the whole wastes of the forest, but only in particular places. And under the old Forest law, while a right of pasture for horse-beasts and neat-beasts was recognised as attached to inclosed lands within the forest without special claim, it was necessary to make special claim to any right of wood-cutting, and to obtain an

* See Forest Records quoted in Fisher's "Forest of Essex," p. 291.

† See the Disafforestation Act, 16 & 17 Vict. c. 36.

‡ A formal decision that commoning with sheep was illegal was given at the Justice Seat held for the Forest of Essex in 1630, the Chief Justice of the King's Bench and the Barons of the Exchequer being parties to the decision. Chancery Forest Proceedings, 6 Car. I. No. 130.

§ See a reference to a right of pannage in Duke of Portland v. Hill, L.R. 2 Eq. 768.

allowance of such claim at the several Justice Seats held for the Forest.*

In Epping Forest the most remarkable right of woodcutting was that which existed in the Parish of Loughton. This right, as found both by the Epping Forest Commissioners and by the Epping Forest Arbitrator in almost identical terms, was "that the occupiers of houses in the Manor and Parish of Loughton had the right to cut, under the name of 'lopwood,' for the proper use and consumption of the inhabitants of such houses as fuel, from the hour of 12 o'clock at night on the 11th day of November (All Saints, Old Style) in each year to the same hour on the 23rd day of April (St. George's Day) in each succeeding year, the boughs or branches of the trees growing upon the waste lands of the Forest within the precinct of the said manor and parish (except upon Monks Wood and Loughton Piece), in such manner as not to destroy or unnecessarily injure the trees, and at such a height from the ground as not to destroy the covert or browsing of the deer of the Forest." †

In two other manors in Epping Forest, those of Sewardstown and Waltham Holy Cross, certain rights to cut lopwood under the name of fuel assignments were found to exist by the Epping Forest Commission, and were purchased by the Corporation of London on the final settlement of the Forest question. These rights were at one time attached to ancient messuages and the lands held with them, and were exercised in specific parts of the Forest. In 1878 there were thirty-two such areas in Waltham Holy Cross, and thirty-three in Sewardstown, each area being known as "an assignment,"

* Sir William Jones' Reports, 291, Case of the Tenants of the Manor of Bray.

† Final Report of the Epping Forest Commission, p. 4 (1 March, 1877); Report of the Epping Forest Arbitrator. The two findings differ only in the omission from that of the Commission of the clause referring to the covert or browsing of the deer. The legality of the claim was established many years before in the Court of Chancery; see Willingale *v.* Martland, L.R. 3 Eq. 103.

and being marked and distinguished by one or more letters on the parish map.* On each assignment the tenant entitled to it had the exclusive right of lopping, the period of lopping and the restrictions under which it was exercised being precisely the same as in the Parish of Loughton.

In another manor, that of Theydon Bois, there was evidence before the Epping Forest Commission, that a right similar to that of the inhabitants of Loughton had formerly existed; † and in the Hainault Division of Waltham Forest assignments similar to those in Waltham and Sewardstone were found,‡ with this important difference, that the areas of Forest in which the lopping took place were not permanently assigned to particular properties or particular persons, but were made yearly, in Barking, on or about Candlemas Day, by the delivery through the steward of the Forest of a ticket bearing the distinguishing letter of the assignment. The forest keepers in the month of November marked off the place of the assignment; and when the faggots were set up, the keeper checked the quantity before they were carried away.§

The fuel assignments (*i.e.* the areas in which the wood might be cut) were not inclosed, either in Hainault or Epping, but their boundaries were indicated by marks on trees or by posts. Originally the loppings were not allowed to be sold, but could only be used as fuel on particular properties. But in later times the right to lop on the assignments was sold and conveyed apart from any house or land, and was also let on lease for terms of years; and the loppings

* Epping Forest Act, 1878, Schedule 1; and see 15th Report of Land Revenue Commissioners, 1793, App. No. 12.

† Proceedings of Epping Forest Commission, evidence of Maynard, Salmon, Wade, Parish, pp. 3417–29.

‡ 34 in Barking and 39 in Dagenham, each entitling the holder to 5 loads or 500 faggots. See 15th Report of Land Revenue Commissioners, 1793, No. 10.

§ Attachment Rolls of Waltham Forest, 28 April 1829; Epping Forest Arbitration Proceedings, evidence of Alfred Saville.

themselves were sold or dealt with as the person exercising the right chose.* Kindlings for the fires of the House of Commons were, it was proved before the Epping Forest Arbitrator, largely supplied from the Epping Forest assignments.

There seems to be a strong probability that all these customs of lopping in Waltham Forest originated, like the right of pasture, in ancient usages of the vills surrounding the Forest waste, confirmed and regulated by the Forest laws. We have seen how essential to the wants of an early community was the right to take wood from the neighbouring wastes. The right maintained in Loughton down to the present day probably preserves the ancient usage in a very early form, while the system of assignments shows how the usage became modified by the endeavour to shut out new-comers and to confine it to ancient houses. In both cases the usage had been adapted to the Forest system, and placed more or less under the supervision of the Forest courts and Forest officers, and had thus been regulated and preserved. In the Alpine communes of Switzerland parallel customs exist, each householder being entitled to take a certain fixed quantity of wood according to certain regulations; while the distinction between "*bürger*," or old inhabitants, and *nieder-gelassene*, or new settlers, has played an important part in the history of many a commune.

Other instances of wood-rights in Forests may be given.

In the New Forest the system of assignments to particular persons prevails. The assignments are bought and sold, and tend to accumulate in a few hands. But the assignment does not at the present day give the right to

* Epping Forest Arbitration Proceedings, evidence of S. Mill, 145–152, Salmon, 159, and others. The right appears to have been gradually converted from a right appurtenant to a particular tenement to a right in gross.

enter the Forest and cut in a particular place, but only the right to require at the hands of the Forest keepers a certain number of loads of wood.*

In Ashdown Forest the earliest records show that each "customer" was entitled to "two loads of birch wood or alder, to be felled by him and carried home to his house against Christmas."†

In the Hainault Division of Waltham Forest another somewhat curious wood-right existed at the time of the disafforestation. Every poor widow in those parts of Barking and Dagenham which lay in the Forest, who was not in receipt of parochial relief and whose husband had been dead a year, was "usually allowed" one load of wood out of the King's woods on Easter Monday, or 8*s.* in money, if she could not procure a team to carry the wood out of the Forest on that day.

Customs relating to dead wood also obtained in certain forests.

In Ashdown Forest the customers were entitled to take in the spring, and according to certain regulations, all manner of windfall and rotten wood. The right is repeated in all the commoners' claims, and was evidently considered to be of value.

In Whittlewood Forest the poor inhabitants of both the in-towns and the out-towns claimed the right to gather sere and broken wood in the Forest on two days of the week in every year.

Upon disafforestation, both the right of the widows in Hainault and that of the poor inhabitants in Whittlewood were compensated by money or land granted to the vicars and parish officers of the respective parishes, to be laid

* See Appendix, p. 348.

† Duchy of Lancaster Records.

out either in fuel or generally for the benefit of the poor.*

Rights of turbary and other rights are also sometimes found in forests.

In the New Forest the right of cutting turf for fuel is highly valued. As in the case of an ordinary common, it is not cut on the grass lawns, but on the wide expanses of heather which form so large a part of the Forest. All rights to cut turf are registered, and the turf must be burnt in the house for which it is taken. On Dartmoor similar rights exist; and on Exmoor the free suitors were entitled, the Disafforestation Act states, to cut and take certain quantities of turf, heath, and fern to consume in their houses.†

In Wolmer Forest, also, it appears from an old Act ‡ that rights of turf-cutting obtained. In fact, it is probable that such a right exists in most forests where the soil is suitable.

In Ashdown Forest the customers claimed from very early times the right to take many products of the Forest suitable for the better enjoyment of their holdings. In an old presentment of 1520 these rights were thus enumerated:—

(1.) Frith and tenet, that is, stakes and binders, for inclosing their lands.
(2.) Marl for mending their lands.
(3.) Heath to thatch their houses.
(4.) Loam to daub their walls.
(5.) Stone to underpin their houses.
(6.) Fern to mend their lands.

* Hainault Forest Disafforestation Act, 1851 (14 & 15 Vict. c. 43.), sec. 8; Whittlewood Forest Disafforestation Acts, 5 Geo. IV. c. 99. s. 31, 16 & 17 Vict. c. 42. s. 21. A right to take thorns and windfalls is referred to in Duke of Portland *v.* Hill, L.R. 2 Eq. 768, as existing in the Manor of Bolsover, Derbyshire, where some kind of forestal or chase rights would seem to have obtained. And in Whaddon Chase, in the county of Bucks, a custom to take rotten wood for fuel formerly obtained, though it was decided that it could not be pleaded as a custom; see Selby *v.* Robinson, 2 T.R. 758.

† 55 Geo. III. c. 138.

‡ 52 Geo. III. c. 71.

These rights are continually presented, and no objection seems to have been made to them; but they do not seem to have survived to modern times precisely in the form presented. Out of them, however, no doubt grew the right to cut heather and fern for litter and for use subsequently as manure, which was established in the recent litigation between Earl De la Warr and the commoners. This right, as exercised and justified, is to cut bracken (the common brake-fern) with a sickle, and to cut with a scythe what is commonly known as litter, *i.e.* bracken, heather, furze or gorse, broom and coarse grass, everything, in fact, which falls to the scythe. Both bracken and litter, when cut, are taken to the cattle yards and spread down there, and subsequently, when well trodden and manured, are carted out and put upon the land. Occasionally they are used in the first instance for covering roots or other like purposes, but always finally for manure. The right was challenged by Earl De la Warr, and was defended by the commoners, to whom, upon the partition of the Forest by a decree of the Court of the Duchy of Lancaster made in 1693, the sole common pasturage and herbage of the parts left open was conferred. There were two grounds of defence. The first was, that the right was included in the sole common pasturage and herbage of the land; the second, that the right had been continuously enjoyed for sixty years and upwards, and was therefore legally established under the Prescription Act.* The Court of Appeal decided against the commoners on the first ground, and in their favour on the second.† The right is much valued by the owners of the estates round the Forest, and freely exercised.

* As to this Act, see *ante*, p. 45.

† Lord De la Warr *v.* Miles, 17 Ch. Div. 535. A decree was subsequently made by consent in a cross action of Hale *v.* Earl De la Warr, by which the right to cut litter was established in favour of all the commoners entitled to sole herbage under the decree of 1693.

Such is the nature of the rights existing over the wastes of royal forests. There are other districts containing large areas of open land, known by the name of "Chase." Malvern Chase in Worcestershire,* Cannock Chase in Staffordshire,† and Cranborne Chase in Dorsetshire,‡ may be given as examples.

A chase is of the same character as a forest, a region devoted to the nurture of wild animals; but the owner of the chase has no right to hold the peculiar Forest courts which have been described above.§ If a royal forest is granted to a subject without an express grant of the right to hold forest courts, it becomes a chase.‖

As regards rights of common, a forest and a chase are in a similar position. The rights may be expected to depend upon locality rather than upon any manorial connection. The foregoing remarks upon common rights in a forest may therefore be taken to apply generally to such rights in a chase.

The waste lands of forests and chases are exposed to many of the same dangers as ordinary manorial commons. The owner of the soil, whether the Crown or a subject, may attempt to inclose without any Parliamentary authority; the land may be disfigured by excessive gravel-digging, or beautiful woods may be felled or marked for felling; and an application to the Board of Agriculture for an inclosure by Act of Parliament may be made. The New Forest and the Forest of Dean, two of the most important royal forests still remaining, cannot, however, be made the subject of such an

* This Chase was partitioned in the time of Charles I., but the open lands on the Malvern Hills are part of its wastes.

† Now inclosed by Act of Parliament, though a great part is still actually lying waste, and is accessible to the public.

‡ Now inclosed. Some particulars of this Chase will be found stated in the Reported Case of Lord Rivers *v.* Adams, 3 Ex. Div. 361.

§ See *ante*, p. 152.

‖ Fourth Institute, p. 314.

application as that last mentioned; these forests are expressly excepted from the operation of the Inclosure Acts.*

It does not seem clear that the Statutes of Merton and Westminster the Second ever applied to a royal forest. The language of the statutes is certainly not applicable to cases where the Crown is owner of the soil of the wastes, since they refer expressly to manors in the hands of subjects ("great men"). In cases where manors in a forest had been granted out, and the soil of the waste was in the hands of subjects, the Statute of Westminster the Second, which holds between Lords of Manors and their neighbours having common rights, may possibly apply, though the Statute of Merton, which applies only to commoners who are such by virtue of their tenancy of a manor, certainly does not. And even the language of the later statute is not very apt to a case where the common rights have been either granted or confirmed by the Crown in consideration of the burden of the deer.† There is a case where the statute was held to apply in Epping Forest; ‡ but this case was decided upon a very imperfect statement of the circumstances, and, having regard to the subsequent elaborate investigation of Forest law and of the history of Epping Forest in the litigation prosecuted by the Corporation of London,§ its authority may be questioned.|| At one time no doubt the Courts were disposed to give a very elastic interpretation to the Statutes of Merton and Westminster the Second;¶ but, except so far as they are bound by authority, they would hardly at the present day travel beyond the words of the statutes.

* General Inclosure Act, 1845, 8 & 9 Vict. c. 118. s. 13.

† See *ante*, p. 149.

‡ Lake *v.* Plaxton, 10 Ex. 196.

§ Commissioners of Sewers *v.* Glasse, L.R. 19 Eq. 137.

|| See the remarks on Lake *v.* Plaxton in Robertson *v.* Hartopp, 43 Ch. Div. 517.

¶ See Glover *v.* Lane, 3 T.R. 445.

So far as the Statutes of Merton and Westminster the Second apply to the wastes of a forest or chase, the Law of Commons Amendment Act, 1893, will also apply, subject to this remark, that the last-mentioned Act clearly does not, on general principles, bind the Crown. Consequently, if it were held (though, it is submitted, it could not be so held), that the Crown could inclose the wastes of a forest under the Statutes of Merton and Westminster the Second, there would be no obligation upon the Crown to obtain the consent of the Board of Agriculture. In any other case the owner of forest waste wishing to inclose must prove, that his inclosure is for the benefit of the neighbourhood, in the manner previously described.*

There is, however, apart from the veto of the Board of Agriculture, little risk of waste lands of a forest or chase being lawfully inclosed under the Statutes of Merton and Westminster the Second. The class of commoners is usually so large, that any attempt on the part of the Crown or other lord of the soil to show that sufficient pasture had been left for the commoners would be hopeless.

When the soil of the wastes of a forest belongs to private Lords of Manors, as in the case of Epping Forest, there is another restraint upon inclosure, besides the existence of common rights. No inclosure is valid without the licence of the Crown. This question was much discussed in Epping Forest, where it was contended on the part of the lords, that the open forest might (as regards the Crown) be inclosed with a low hedge and ditch not sufficient to obstruct the passage of deer. But a full investigation of the Forest law and customs seemed to show beyond doubt, that this limited form of inclosure embodied a restriction upon the enjoyment

* See *ante*, pp. 15–17.

of private lands, and did not apply to the forest wastes. The question was not submitted for judicial decision, but the Epping Forest Commissioners appointed by Act of Parliament to report upon the rights existing in the Forest and the validity of the inclosures which had been made, found that all inclosures made on waste land, where the Crown still retained Forest rights, were bad against the Crown.

The powers conferred upon certain Urban District Councils by the Commons Act, 1876,* and upon all District Councils (acting with the consent of the County Council) by the Local Government Act, 1894,† apply to waste and commonable lands of forests. To prevent inclosure by the Crown or by any Lord of a Manor, the District Council may, therefore, take by gift any waste lands of a forest, or purchase any right of common.‡ Such powers as are enjoyed by Parish Councils in relation to commons would apply also to wastes of forests. And both the District and the Parish Council will be entitled to notice of any application to the Board of Agriculture for the inclosure or approvement of any part of any forest waste within the district or parish, and may oppose such application.

Inclosure by way of copyhold grant§ has, no doubt, sometimes taken place on forest wastes; but it may be doubted whether such inclosures were ever really lawful. Inasmuch as the common rights do not depend upon tenancy of a manor, but upon locality, it seems impossible that any custom of any manor could have authorised such inclosures. Only the tenants of the manor in which the custom obtains are bound by any such custom; the rights of all other commoners are untouched by any such grant. In Epping Forest

* Sec. 8.

† Sec. 26 (2).

‡ See *ante*, p. 80.

§ See *ante*, Chap. XI.

large areas of the Forest waste were during the twenty years prior to the institution of the Corporation suit, in 1871, inclosed by way of copyhold grant; but all such inclosures became illegal, and were so treated by Parliament in consequence of the decision of the Court, which established a right of common of pasture in the owners and occupiers of all lands within the bounds of the Forest.*

However, as we have seen, no new inclosure by way of copyhold grant can be made without the consent of the Board of Agriculture, and any District or Parish Council can oppose such inclosure on the ground, that it is not for the benefit of the neighbourhood.

Under the forest system, properly kept up, no serious disfigurement of the waste lands of a forest could take place. Any considerable digging of gravel, and still more any paring of the surface, would damage the food of the deer, and would be clearly contrary to Forest law. Nor could any trees be felled without the licence of the Crown. In the New Forest, although the deer have been removed, the trees and vert of the Forest are still under the protection of the Crown.

But where the soil of the forest wastes is in private hands, and the Crown rights have been sold (as in parts of Epping Forest, before the Corporation proceedings), there may be considerable difficulty in protecting the trees, if threatened by the owner of the soil. Where any right of estovers exists, the lord or owner of the trees must leave

* Commissioners of Sewers *v.* Glasse, L.R. 7 Ch. App. 456. Certain of such inclosures were in the hands of the lords, and were directly found to be unlawful by the decree in this suit. All others within the period of twenty years were found to be unlawful by the Epping Forest Commission, and were dealt with as such by the Epping Forest Act, 1878, and the Award of the Arbitrator thereunder.

† Unfortunately the Crown officials, in their anxiety to make a revenue from the Forest, have sometimes been inclined to sacrifice the trees and vert.

sufficient standing to satisfy such right.* But in the absence of any such right, the trees would be at the disposal of the Lord of the Manor or other owner of the soil, as in the case of a manorial common. It is therefore very desirable that any local authority desiring to secure any fragment of an old forest, bearing, as is often the case, large and picturesque trees, should, when possible, acquire the ownership of the soil, with a view to preserving the trees.

The powers of local authorities with respect to Parliamentary inclosure are the same in the case of forest wastes as in the case of manorial commons; and the remarks already made on this subject † apply equally to such wastes.

* Fourth Institute, 298.

† See *ante*, Chap. XIII., p. 106.

CHAPTER XVI.

Of Village Greens.

WE all know what is meant, in popular parlance, by a village green. It is a small open space covered with turf, traversed generally by one or two footpaths, usually surrounded or crossed by roads, and lying in the midst or on the outskirts of a rural village. Very often it has a pond in one corner; in another an old tree, with a bench in its shade; sometimes the signboard of the village inn stands upon its edge; and sometimes the village sawyer stacks his wood upon it. A few geese and chickens, perhaps, stray about it, and it is seldom free from children. Before all things, it is the village playground.

So familiar is the expression "village green," that it has found its way into Acts of Parliament, and even into the utterances of the Courts. Yet the term "village green," like the term "common," as applied to a piece of land, has no exact legal definition, unless it be that of a green situate in a village. It does not follow, that, because a piece of land is what is usually called a village green, it is therefore subject to peculiar rights. It may be subject to such rights, but in each case the existence of the right, as a fact, has to be proved.

Apart from any peculiar rights, a village green may be subject to the same rights as an ordinary manorial common. This is almost certain to be the case, where, as not infrequently happens, the green is a corner—the corner nearest the village—of a larger common. And where it is an altogether separate open space, yet, if there are other commons in the same manor, the common rights may be taken, in the absence of direct evidence to the contrary, to extend to the green. Usually the soil of the green, as part of the waste, belongs to the lord of the principal manor in the parish. But this is not always the case. Sometimes the ownership may be claimed by the lord of a smaller manor—*e.g.*, a manor attached to the rectory—and sometimes by someone who is not lord of any manor. Sometimes a village green may be a stinted pasture;* or it may be waste land of a forest.†

Whenever, then, there is any question of inclosing or damaging a village green, enquiries similar to those made in the case of a manorial common should be set on foot. Common rights should be asserted, if possible, and the various remedies existing in the case of a common or common field or forest waste, as the case may be, should be resorted to. In particular, the necessity of the consent of the Board of Agriculture, if the inclosure is made under the Statutes of Merton and Westminster the Second, should be borne in mind.

In some cases, however, it is impossible to prove that any right of common exists over a village green. It may be impossible to trace its connection with any manor of which tenants can be found; and the actual turning out upon it may be of such a character as will not found any legal right. In such cases it is most important to consider whether a right of recreation over the green can be established.‡

* *E.g.*, The Green, Steventon, Berks, see Inclosure Commissioners Report, 1880; see *ante*, p. 140. In this case the soil was vested in the Lord of the Manor.

† *E.g.*, Woodford Green in Epping Forest.

‡ We say, "in such cases"; however, as will be seen from the following remarks, it is not very easy to prove a right of recreation; and where clear common rights can be ascertained it will, the author is of opinion, generally be found better to protect the green by their means; or advantage may be taken of the statutory remedies described later, see pp. 185–7.

As we have said, it is of the very nature of a village green that it should be used for recreation; cricket, and games of all sorts, have probably been played on it from time immemorial. Happily, also, the right to play games upon such a spot is recognised by the law. So long ago as the time of Charles II. it was held that a custom, "that all the inhabitants of a vill, time out of memory, had used to dance on a certain close at all times of the year at their free will for their recreation," was held to be a good custom, the Court sententiously observing that "it is necessary for inhabitants to have their recreations."* In this case an action for trespass had been brought against an inhabitant for breaking into the plaintiff's close† and dancing thereon, and the Court upheld the defendant in this act on the ground of the custom we have quoted.

More than a hundred years afterwards‡ a similar action was brought against certain persons for playing cricket on a certain piece of ground at Steeple Bumstead, in Essex. The playing of cricket was justified under a custom "for all the inhabitants of the parish to play at all kinds of lawful games, sports, and pastimes on the ground in question at all seasonable times of the year at their free will and pleasure." This custom the Court held was good. One of the defendants, however, pleaded a similar custom "for all persons for the time being being in the said parish." This custom the Court held was bad, on the ground that it was in reality a custom for all mankind to play on the ground in question, and that such a custom cannot exist in English law. A custom, it was held, must be local, and confined to a limited class of persons;

* Abbot *v.* Weekly, 1 Lev. 176, *temp.* 1665.

† It does not follow that the ground was inclosed, because it is spoken of in the pleadings as a close. It may have been an open village green.

‡ The decision of the Court was given on the 4th February, 1795.

a usage which extends to all the subjects of the realm must be justified not by exceptional custom, but by the common law.*

This decision has since governed all claims to a right of recreation. It has been repeatedly mentioned with approval† and followed, and may, together with the earlier case we have cited, be taken as settling the law on the subject.

There are several reported cases of recent years in which a right of recreation has been established on the authority of the old decisions. In 1863, a custom for the freemen and citizens of a town on a particular day in the year to enter upon a close for the purpose of holding horse-racing thereon, was held to be a good custom.‡ And more recently (1875), "a custom for the inhabitants of a parish to enter upon certain land in the parish to erect a may-pole thereon and dance round and about it, and otherwise enjoy on the land any lawful and innocent recreation at any times in the year," was upheld.§

Much discussion has taken place in these cases upon the question whether the right of recreation may be claimed at all times of the year, or only at seasonable times. But it seems now to be settled that the right may be claimed at all times.‖ Nevertheless, the custom must be used reasonably,

* Fitch *v.* Rawling, Fitch and Chatteris, 2 H. Bl. 393–9; 3 Revised Reports, 425.

† See Mayor of London *v.* Cox, L.R. 2 H.L. 239, 274; Warrick *v.* Queen's College, Oxford, L.R. 10 Ex. 105, 129; Bourke *v.* Davis, 44 Ch. Div. 110, 120.

‡ Mounsey *v.* Ismay, 1 Hurlst. & Coltm. 729. This case related to the races at Carlisle. In the same case it was held, two years later, that such a right could not be enjoyed under the Prescription Act. (See Mounsey *v.* Ismay, 3 H. & C. 486, 494.)

§ Hall *v.* Nottingham, L.R. 1 Ex. Div. 1. This case related to a piece of glebe land situate in an inclosed field, and called the Maypole Piece, in the parish of Ashford Carbonell, Salop.

‖ See Mounsey *v.* Ismay, 1 H. & C. 729; Hall *v.* Nottingham, L.R. 1 Ex. Div. 1. A case of Bell *v.* Wardell (Willis, 202), and the case of Millichamp *v.* Johnson, there cited (p. 205), seem practically to have been overruled by the Court.

and no wanton damage committed. Thus, it was held that it was not a lawful exercise of the custom found to exist at Steeple Bumstead, Essex, to enter upon the land when the grass had been allowed to grow and had been cut for hay, and to throw the hay about and mix it with gravel and spoil it.* No doubt in this case the inhabitants might, in the fair use of the green for sports, have prevented the grass yielding any crop; but having allowed it to grow, so that a crop of hay was obtained, they had no right to spoil the hay.

But notwithstanding that it is clear law that the inhabitants of a parish or other defined district may enjoy a right of recreation over a village green by custom, it is by no means easy to prove such a custom. It has been pointed out that the custom must be limited to the inhabitants of the district. Now, it is seldom that on any open green any restriction is imposed upon the persons using it. All comers resort to it at their will and pleasure. But if the only evidence which can be given relates to the indiscriminate use by all persons, there is great danger that the Court will hold that no special custom for the inhabitants of the district has been established. Thus, the late Master of the Rolls, in a case relating to Stockwell Green,† in the parish of Lambeth, held that no custom in the inhabitants of the vill or hamlet of Stockwell was proved, because the evidence showed that all persons who wished had played upon the green. In this case Sir George Jessel laid down the law with his usual clearness and emphasis. "A custom," he explained, "is local common law, the law of the place before the time of legal memory, that is, the time of Richard I. It is proved by usage; and the evidence must establish a

* Per Holt, J., Fitch *v.* Fitch, 2 Espinasse, 543–5; a sequel to the case of Fitch *v.* Rawling.

† Hammerton *v.* Honey, 24 W.R. 603.

reasonable usage, and a continuous usage without serious interruption acquiesced in. The usual evidence to prove the custom is that of old people, who can testify to the usage for some fifty years. But this evidence must not prove a usage wider than the custom which is alleged to exist. Thus, if the custom alleged is for certain persons to dance on a green, and the evidence proves that anyone, whether belonging to that class of persons or not, has done so, it is too wide. But a usage generally legal (that is, restricted) is not made useless to establish a custom because an occasional illegal use (*i.e.* usage by other persons than those said to be entitled) is shown to have existed. A custom being local law, when once established, can only be got rid of by Act of Parliament. But persistent interruption of the user, as by the inclosure of the land and the exclusion of the persons claiming the right for some time, is strong evidence against the existence of the custom." In the case under the consideraticn of the Master of the Rolls, the land had been inclosed for more than nineteen years before the commencement of the litigation. This, coupled with a failure to show that the Green, when open, had been used by the inhabitants of Stockwell in particular as distinguished from mankind generally, Sir George Jessel held to be fatal to the claim.*

In reality, therefore, to protect any village green or other open space by asserting a right of recreation, it is of especial

* In Sowerby *v.* Coleman (1867), L.R. 2 Exch. 96, it was held by the Court (Kelly, C.B., and Channel and Pigott, BB.) that the inhabitants of a parish cannot enjoy by custom the right to exercise and train race-horses at all seasonable times in a place not within the parish. The Court seemed to indicate that if the claim had been limited to certain days in the year it might have been good. In Edwards *v* Jenkins (1895 W.N. 142) Kekewich, J., held that a custom laid in the inhabitants of three parishes to use a certain plot of land for purposes of recreation was bad. Three parishes could not, he considered, be regarded as one district. There seems, however, to be no reason, why a custom should not be laid in a district comprising many parishes, such, for example, as the City of London, or an ancient Hundred, Manor, or Honor.

importance to give some proof of special enjoyment by the inhabitants of the district selected. It is usually impossible to show systematic exclusion of the general public. But some kind of assertion of right on the part of the inhabitants over and above the mere use in common with others should be forthcoming. Perhaps a may-pole has been placed by them on the green; perhaps a portion has been specially preserved for cricket; perhaps the villagers, or some village club, have exercised the right to play cricket or some other game on the green in preference to other persons, when the claims came into competition. Possibly the vestry-books may contain entries on the subject of the green, showing some claim of right. Very slight evidence of this character will probably be sufficient to induce the Courts to find in favour of the right claimed, where in fact the villagers have played on the green from time immemorial.

Rights of recreation have been established of recent years over Appes Quinton Green, Gloucestershire,* the Green of Walton in Gordano, Somersetshire,† and Stockbridge Common Down, Hants.‡

Each of these cases possesses considerable interest. In the Appes Quinton case the College claimed to inclose under an inclosure award a hundred years old, but they had not, in fact, inclosed until 1871. It was argued that the inclosure award was *ultra vires*, so far as related to the green, in consequence of the existence of rights of recreation in the inhabitants of the parish, and Mr. Manisty (afterwards Mr. Justice Manisty), who appeared for the College, did not argue the point.

* Magdalen College, Oxford, *v.* Hiatt, reported in "Times" of 26th January, 1876, and cited in Williams on Commons, 149.

† Virgo *v.* Harford; the case is reported on a subsidiary point in the "Times" of 30th March, 1893, but the language of the report would appear to be inaccurate.

‡ Lancashire *v.* Hunt, and Lancashire *v.* Maynard and Hunt, 10 Times Law Reports, 310, 448.

In the Walton in Gordano case the land over which the inhabitants of the parish were found to be entitled to rights of recreation extended to sixty-five acres, and was fine open land on the top of a hill. Mr. Justice Willes, who (with a special jury) tried the case, embodied in the formal judgment obtained by the plaintiff a declaration "that the said John Henry Virgo and all other the inhabitants resident in the parish of Walton in Gordano are justly entitled to use the village green mentioned in the statement of claim for recreation and for the playing of football, rounders, cricket, and all other lawful village sports, games, and pastimes."

In the Stockbridge case the land in question was known as the Stockbridge Common Down, and was of very considerable extent. The case was tried in the Chancery Division of the High Court by Mr. Justice Wright without a jury; and much of the discussion turned on a claim of trainers of racehorses to exercise their horses as a matter of business on the Downs. The learned judge held that such a claim was unreasonable, and that the usage on this point was too wide to prove a custom, as it was as much for the benefit of strangers, whose horses were taken in by the trainers, as of inhabitants. He finally made a declaration to the effect "that the inhabitants were entitled by custom to use the Downs for all useful and lawful games and recreation, including riding, and were entitled to erect such tents and other accessories as were necessary; but that such rights were not to include the right of exercising and training horses not belonging to such inhabitants but taken in by them, and should not include the right of carrying on the business of a trainer of horses by exercising or training horses on the Downs for profit."*

* There was an appeal on various points, but the Lord of the Manor or owner of the Downs did not at the bar contest the right of the inhabitants, as found in the Court below. See 11 Times Law Reports, 49.

In the case of Ratcliffe *v.* Jowers (Barnes Common, Surrey),* Mr. Justice Chitty mentioned incidentally that the evidence showed that Barnes Green, a portion of Barnes Common, containing two acres and a half, was subject to rights of recreation in the inhabitants of Barnes; but a decision on this point does not seem to have been strictly necessary to the case, which related to the powers of the Conservators under a scheme of management under the Metropolitan Commons Act.†

Such are some of the questions which arise with respect to a village green, when it is threatened with inclosure by the Lord of the Manor or other person claiming to be the owner of the soil of the green. Independently of the statutory remedies described below, it may be defended by the assertion of any right of common which may be proved to exist over it, or by the assertion of a right of recreation in the inhabitants of the village, parish, or other district.

There is no doubt that portions of village greens have often in the past been inclosed by way of copyhold grant. Small inclosures for cart-sheds or like purposes have been made by this means. But it is clear that no such grant can be valid against a right of recreation in the inhabitants. The inhabitants, enjoying their right by virtue of a custom or local law, would be entitled to remove any new inclosure which impeded its fair and reasonable exercise. However, as we have seen, in future no such inclosure can be made without the consent of the Board of Agriculture.‡

Similarly, no gravel-digging or other disturbance of the surface, which interferes with the enjoyment of a custom of

* 8 Times Law Reports, 6.

† See *post*, p. 231. In the case of Forbes *v.* the Ecclesiastical Commissioners for England, L.R. 15 Eq. 51, a right of recreation over Pear Tree Green, near Southampton, was recognised.

‡ See *ante*, p. 95.

recreation, can be supported. But such a custom would not, probably, prevent the felling of trees by the owner of the soil, unless such trees had been used by the inhabitants for the purpose of lawful recreation.

"Town greens" are frequently mentioned in Acts of Parliament in conjunction with village greens.* There is no distinction in law between the two species of green. But in corporate boroughs the soil of a town green is not infrequently vested in the Corporation, and thus practically belongs in all ways to the inhabitants.

No village green or town green can be inclosed under the Inclosure Acts.† On the contrary, these Acts contain provisions for their preservation as places of recreation. For the purpose of these enactments, a village green or town green means, it may be assumed, a green situate in a village or town and habitually used as the green of the place for recreation, air, and exercise; it would not be necessary to prove that a legal right of recreation in the inhabitants of the district existed. On the other hand, when a right of recreation is proved, the Board of Agriculture would no doubt hold, that the land over which it existed was a town or village green within the meaning of the Act, although the area might (as in the Walton in Gordano and Stockbridge cases) be large, and the land situate near, rather than in, the town or village.

Upon a Parliamentary inclosure the Inclosure Commissioners are authorised to allot a town green or village green to the churchwardens and overseers of the parish in trust, to allow the same to be used for the purpose of exercise and recreation;‡ and a green so allotted becomes subject to the

* Inclosure Act, 1845 (8 & 9 Vict. c. 118.), sec. 15; Commons Act, 1876 (39 & 40 Vict. c. 56.), sec. 29.

† Inclosure Act, 1845 (8 & 9 Vict. c. 118.), sec. 15.

‡ Inclosure Act, 1845, sec. 15. The effect of such an allotment would be to put an end to rights of common exerciseable over the green, but not to rights of recreation.

provisions of the Inclosure Acts as to allotments.* By the Local Government Act, 1894, the powers, duties, and liabilities of the churchwardens and overseers with respect to the holding and management of village greens or of allotments for recreation are transferred to the Parish Council,† and the property in such greens and allotments is vested in the Council.‡ Wherever, therefore, any village green has been allotted to churchwardens and overseers under old Inclosure Acts and awards, the Parish Council will henceforth be empowered to protect and improve such green; § and it is assumed that on any future inclosure, if a village green were allotted for exercise and recreation, it would be allotted to the Parish Council.

Upon an allotment of a village green for recreation under an Inclosure Act, the Inclosure Commissioners are directed either to fence off or to mark its limits by metes and bounds. ||

Any person injuring a town green or village green, or interrupting its use as a place for exercise and recreation, is liable upon summary conviction to a penalty of 40*s.* besides damages; and any matters deposited on the green may be sold by the Council, and the proceeds applied in aid of the highway rates.¶ The power of prosecuting for such an offence was originally conferred upon the churchwardens and overseers of the parish; and it may perhaps, therefore, pass to the Parish Council under the Local Government Act, 1894, as a power incidental to the management of the green.** Where the village green has a known and defined boundary,

---

* See *post*, Chap. XVII., p. 188. † Sec. 6 (1) (*c*) (iii). ‡ Sec. 5 (2) (*c*).

§ Local Government Act, 1894, sec. 8 (1) (*d*) and (*i*).

|| Inclosure Act, 1845, sec. 15; 15 & 16 Vict. c. 79. s. 14.

¶ Inclosure Act, 1857 (20 & 21 Vict. c. 31.), sec. 12, as extended by Commons Act, 1876, sec. 29.

** Local Government Act, 1894, sec. 6 (1) (*c*) (iii).

the prosecution may also be conducted in the name of any inhabitant of the parish.*

Further, an encroachment on, or inclosure of, a town or village green having a known and defined boundary, or any erection on, or disturbance or interference with, or occupation of, the soil of such green, made otherwise than with a view to the better enjoyment of such green, is a public nuisance.*

Anyone guilty of a public nuisance may be indicted for a misdemeanour. The obstruction of a public way is, in this manner, indictable as a public nuisance. The provision we have just quoted, therefore, puts encroachments on village greens (with defined boundaries) on the same footing as an obstruction of a highway.

It would seem that this procedure would not be applicable to a corner of a large common, usually called a green (*e.g.*, Barnes Green and Wimbledon Green, which are portions of Barnes Common and Wimbledon Common), unless some recognised and defined boundary line between the green and the rest of the common can be shown to exist.

All the above-quoted enactments would seem to apply to a green which is geographically a village or town green, and not merely to one over which a legal right of recreation has been established. Probably, therefore, in future, greens actually situated in towns or villages and lying open to general use may be more efficaciously protected by proceedings under these enactments than by asserting any legal right of recreation or any common right.

The Local Government Act, 1894, gives a Parish Council power to make bye-laws for the regulation of any village green for the time being under its control, and to provide by such bye-laws for the removal from the green of any person infringing any such bye-laws, by any officer of the Parish

* Commons Act, 1876, sec. 29.

Council or constable.* The Parish Council may also close any such green to the public on certain days (not exceeding twelve in one year, or four consecutive days on one occasion) for the purpose of a flower show or other entertainment or for any other public purpose, and may take or authorise the taking of money for admission on such occasions.† Bye-laws made under the provisions above noticed must, in order to take effect, be confirmed by the Local Government Board; penalties not exceeding £5 for each offence, or 40s. a day for a continuing offence, may be imposed by the bye-laws.‡

In a parish, where there is no Parish Council, village greens or recreation grounds allotted to churchwardens and overseers will pass to the Chairman of the Parish Meeting and the Overseers of the parish, as a body corporate, and will be held by them.§ Doubtless in such a case the County Council will, upon the application of the Parish Meeting, confer upon it the power of making bye-laws for the regulation of the green or recreation ground, which in a like case is given by the Act to the Parish Council.‖ It would seem, that a County Council might also confer upon a Parish Meeting power to acquire a village green or other land for purposes of recreation.¶

* Local Government Act, 1894, sec. 8 (1) (*d*), and Public Health Act, 1875 (38 & 39 Vict. c. 55.), sec. 164.

† Local Government Act, 1894, sec. 8 (1) (*d*), and Public Health Acts Amendment Act, 1890 (53 & 54 Vict. c. 59.), sec. 44.

‡ Local Government Act, 1894, sec. 8 (1) (*d*), and Public Health Act, 1875, secs. 183–186. Confirmation by the Local Government Board does not make a bye-law valid if it is beyond the power of the Parish Council (or other local authority) to make it. (Rex *v.* Wood and Rose, 5 E. & B. 49, 55; Elwood *v.* Bullock, 6 Q.B. 383.

§ Compare Local Government Act, 1894, sec. 19 (7) and sec. 5 (2) (*c*).

‖ Local Government Act, 1894. sec. 8 (1) (*d*) and sec. 19 (10).

¶ *Ib.* sec. 8 (1) (*b*) and sec. 19 (*d*).

CHAPTER XVII.

Of Fuel Allotments and Recreation Grounds.

UNDER the older Inclosure Acts, passed before 1845, it was not unusual to set out considerable tracts (not infrequently extending to a hundred acres or more, in one piece) for the purpose of supplying the poor of the parish with fuel. These tracts have in many cases been inclosed and built upon.* But in others they still exist. They are generally surrounded by a low bank, or traces of such a bank, and are seldom intersected by the main roads of the district after the manner of a common; yet in many respects they resemble common land. They are covered with turf and gorse, or heather; they lie rough, wild, and uncultivated; for practical purposes the public have free access to them; they are, in fact, open spaces, sometimes of the greatest value to the neighbourhood.

Their legal position is quite different from that of a common.

These allotments are usually vested, by the Acts and awards under which they are set out, in the parish authorities—the churchwardens and overseers, sometimes alone, and sometimes in conjunction with the minister of the parish. The trusts upon which they are held vary in different cases, but their main object is, as we have said, to supply

* At Croydon, on the south of London, very extensive allotments of this character were made on the inclosure of the woods and open lands of Norwood. The parishioners some years afterwards obtained a special Act authorising their sale, in order that with the proceeds a hall fit for the reception of Her Majesty's judges might be built. Croydon is now a large town, very poorly supplied with open spaces.

the poor, or the cottagers, of the parish with fuel. This may be effected either by allowing the cottagers to cut the furze or turf (heather with its roots) in certain quantities and according to certain regulations, or (the more usual course) by distributing the furze and turf among the cottagers, when cut by parish officers; or, again, by letting the land and applying the rent in purchasing fuel. The last course, however, has happily seldom been adopted.*

The counterpart of these fuel allotments, under inclosures since 1845, is to be found in allotments for recreation and for field gardens. We have already alluded to these in treating of Parliamentary inclosure, and, incidentally, in treating of village greens. A recreation ground is often of an unmistakeably artificial character, a square inclosure, useful for games, but not attractive in appearance; but sometimes it has the characteristics of a village green.

Under the Inclosure Act, 1845, allotments for recreation were usually awarded to the churchwardens and overseers of the parish.† The valuer, with the approval of the Commissioners, might, however, make the allotment to any person entitled to an allotment under the inclosure, upon condition, that he kept up the fences, preserved the surface in good condition, and permitted the land to be used at all times for exercise and recreation by the inhabitants of the parish and neighbourhood. Subject to these conditions, the herbage belonged to him.‡ This mode of allotment was obviously fraught with danger. It was the direct interest of the allottee to minimise the use of the land for recreation, as constant use obviously tended to impair the value of the herbage. If he were a landowner or farmer of influence

* For an instance of a fuel allotment, or "turf common," see Att.-Gen. *v.* Meyrick (Christ Church Inclosure Act), [1893] A.C. 1.

† Sec. 73.

‡ Inclosure Act, 1845, sec. 74.

in the neighbourhood, and not very scrupulous, he might, by making the use of the ground difficult, in time put an end entirely to such use, and establish an exclusive enjoyment of the land; and no doubt this has in fact sometimes been done. Accordingly, the Commons Act, 1876,* repealed so much of the Inclosure Acts as enabled a recreation ground to be thus allotted, and provided that every allotment for recreation thenceforth made should be vested in the churchwardens and overseers of the parish.

By the Local Government Act, 1894, it is provided† that, as from the day when the Act takes effect, "*the legal interest in all property vested either in the overseers, or in the churchwardens and overseers, of a rural parish, other than property connected with the affairs of the church, or held for an ecclesiastical charity, shall, if there is a Parish Council, vest in that Council, subject to all trusts and liabilities affecting the same; and all persons concerned are to make, or concur in making, such transfers, if any, as are requisite for giving effect to this enactment.*" And the same Act transfers to the Parish Council, upon its coming into office, "the powers, duties, and liabilities of the overseers, or of the churchwardens and overseers, of the parish with respect to the holding or management of allotments, whether for recreation grounds, or for gardens, or otherwise for the benefit of the inhabitants, or any of them."‡ Further, by another provision of the Act,§ "where trustees hold any property for the purposes of a public recreation ground or of allotments, whether under Inclosure Acts or otherwise, for the benefit of the inhabitants of a rural parish, or any of them, or for any public purpose connected with a rural parish, except for an ecclesiastical charity, they

* Sec. 25. † Sec. 5 (2) (*c*).
‡ Local Government Act, 1894, sec. 6 (1) (*c*) (iii).
§ *Ib.* sec. 14 (1).

may, with the approval of the Charity Commissioners, transfer the property to the Parish Council of the parish, or to persons appointed by that Council, and the Parish Council, if they accept the transfer, or their appointees, shall hold the property on the trusts and subject to the conditions on which the trustees held the same."*

Under these provisions nearly all recreation grounds set out under Inclosure Acts since 1845, and many of the fuel allotments previously set out, will, by operation of the recent Act, vest in, and come under the management of, Parish Councils or of their nominees;† while in other cases, where the allotments are vested in trustees other than the churchwardens and overseers, those trustees may, with the approval of the Charity Commissioners, transfer the allotments to the Parish Council.

It is useful, therefore, to examine what is the position of fuel allotments and recreation grounds, and what are the powers of the parish authorities in connection with them.

The churchwardens and overseers (*i.e.* for the future the Parish Council) are directed by the Inclosure Act to hold an allotment for a recreation ground "as a place of exercise and recreation for the inhabitants of the parish and neighbourhood."‡ It must be fenced,‡ or distinguished by marks and bounds,§ and drained and levelled where occasion requires,‡ and the fences and surface area are to be kept in order.‡ The grass and herbage may be let, and the rents applied in maintaining the ground.‡

The provisions already noticed in relation to village greens,

* For other provisions enabling a Parish Council to take part in the management of any local charity (fuel allotments and recreation grounds are charities), see sec. 14 of the Local Government Act, 1894, sub-secs. (2) to (9).

† Where there is no Parish Council, the Chairman of the Parish Meeting and the overseers of the parish take its place; see *ante*, p. 187.

‡ Inclosure Act, 1845, sec. 73.

§ Inclosure Act, 1852 (15 & 16 Vict. c. 79.), sec. 14.

making it an offence, upon summary conviction, to injure or damage the surface of the land by the deposit of rubbish, extend to recreation grounds.* It is an offence punishable in the same manner to lead or drive any cattle or animal on a recreation ground without lawful authority.†

With regard to the expense of maintaining a recreation ground, it was provided by the Inclosure Act, 1845, that if the herbage rents were not sufficient for the purpose, recourse should be had to the poor rate of the parish; while, on the other hand, if the herbage rents were more than sufficient to maintain the ground, the surplus should be applied in aid of the rates for the repair of the parish highways.‡ The Commons Act, 1876, however, provided that surplus rents arising from recreation grounds should thenceforth be applied in improving any like grounds in the same parish or neighbourhood, or maintaining the draining and fencing thereof, or in hiring or purchasing additional land for recreation grounds in the same parish or neighbourhood; § and the Commons Act, 1879,‖ enabled such sums to be also applied in the improvement of the field gardens in the same parish or neighbourhood.

The overseers and churchwardens of a parish, in whom a recreation ground is vested, are directed by the Commons Act, 1876,¶ to report to the Board of Agriculture, at such intervals of not less than three or more than five years as the Board may direct, in respect of the recreation ground under their management, with such particulars of the rents received by them as the Board may require. This duty will devolve upon the Parish Council.**

* Inclosure Act, 1857 (20 & 21 Vict. c. 31.), sec. 12; Commons Act, 1876 (39 & 40 Vict. c. 56.), sec. 29; and see *ante*, p. 185.

† Inclosure Act, 1857, sec. 12.

‡ Inclosure Act, 1845, sec. 73.

§ Commons Act, 1876, sec. 27.

‖ 42 & 43 Vict. c. 37.

¶ Sec. 28.

** Local Government Act, 1894, sec. 6 (1) (*c*) (iii).

If any allotment made under any Inclosure Act for the poor of a parish, or any class of such poor, or for any public or parochial purpose, is found to be unsuitable for the purpose for which it was set out, the Board of Agriculture may, upon the application of the churchwardens or overseers (*i.e.* in future of the Parish Council), and of the persons interested in any other land more convenient and suitable for the purpose, make an order exchanging such allotment for such other land; and the provisions of the Inclosure Acts relating to exchanges shall apply to any such exchange.* And any such order of exchange may declare new trusts in relation to the allotment if the same shall have been approved by a majority of the persons for whose benefit such allotment was set out, present at a meeting convened by the Commissioners for the purpose of considering the same.† The principle of an exchange effected by order of the Board of Agriculture is to shift the title and trusts affecting the one piece of land to the other, so that no question of title need be considered on the exchange, but merely the questions of expediency and of equality of value.

The provisions we have quoted as to exchanges apply, it will be seen, to fuel allotments set out under old Inclosure Acts as well as to allotments for recreation; and the provision enabling new trusts to be declared authorises such parochial allotments as those for the supply of gravel to be converted, partially or entirely, into recreation grounds, or to be otherwise charged with a distinct trust to secure their preservation as open spaces.

* Inclosure Act, 1845, sec. 149; Inclosure Act, 1852 (15 & 16 Vict. c. 79.), sec. 21: and for the provisions as to exchanges generally, see Inclosure Act, 1845, sec. 147; Inclosure Act, 1846, secs. 9 and 10; Inclosure Act, 1847, sec. 6; Inclosure Act, 1852, sec. 17; Inclosure Act, 1854, secs. 2 and 5; Inclosure Act, 1857, secs. 4–11; Inclosure Act, 1859, sec. 12.

† Inclosure Act, 1852, sec. 21. The operation of this section seems to be restricted by sec. 19 of the Commons Act, 1876; see p. 194.

A recreation ground may also, with the approval of the Board of Agriculture, be sold, and other fit and suitable land be bought with the proceeds. But the Board cannot sanction such a sale until they are satisfied that other and more suitable land will be bought.* This power of sale Parish Councils will, subject to the Board's sanction, be able to exercise in the future.

The Inclosure Act, 1845, declares † that allotments for recreation shall be held by the churchwardens and overseers, with the same legal powers and incidents as if the same allotments were lands belonging to the parish, but in trust, nevertheless, for the purposes for which the same were allotted. These words were construed to authorise the diversion of allotments for recreation from the use for which they were set out, and the inclosure of such allotments,—both under the School Sites Act ‡ (applied for the purposes of School Boards by the Elementary Education Act, 1870 §) and by the Charity Commissioners under the Charitable Trusts Acts.|| A like power was exercised by the Charity Commissioners with regard to fuel allotments under old Inclosure Acts.¶ But the Commons Act, 1876, freed fuel allotments and recreation grounds from these dangers. It declared ** that it should not be lawful (except as thereinafter mentioned) to authorise the use of or to use any such allotments or any part thereof for any other purpose than those declared concerning the same by the Act of Parliament and Award, or either of them, under which the same had been set out. It empowered the Charity Commissioners, however, in the exercise of their ordinary juris-

* Commons Act, 1876, sec. 27, 2nd par.

† Sec. 49.

‡ See 4 & 5 Vict. c. 38. s. 6.

§ 33 & 34 Vict. c. 75. ss. 20 and 21.

|| See 16 & 17 Vict. c. 137. ss. 24, 26; 18 & 19 Vict. c. 124. s. 38.

¶ In the recent case of Att.-Gen. *v.* Meyrick (Christchurch Inclosure), [1893 A.C. 1, a "turf common" was held to be a charity in favour of certain cottagers.

** Sec. 19.

diction under the Charitable Trusts Acts, upon the application of the trustees of any fuel allotment, to authorise its use as a recreation ground and field gardens or for either of these purposes, and to make an order under the provisions of the Charitable Trusts Act, 1860, for the establishment of a scheme for the administration of such fuel allotment accordingly. And it further empowered the Commissioners, on the like application, to authorise the exchange of any fuel allotment or any part thereof for land of equal value within the same parish or district, "if the Commissioners are of opinion that by reason of such exchange land better suited for the purpose for which the allotment was set out will be obtained."

By an order of the Charity Commissioners under the Charitable Trusts Acts, a fuel allotment, therefore, may, on the application of the Parish Council or of any trustees in whom it may be vested, be expressly dedicated to purposes of recreation.

The Inclosure Act, 1845, also contains provisions for the allotment of portions of the land to be inclosed—

(*a*) for a supply of stone, gravel, or other materials for the repair of the roads and ways within the parish, and

(*b*) for the formation or improvement of public ponds, wells, and watering places.

The allotments for road materials were directed to be vested in the surveyors of highways, who were authorised to let the herbage of the allotments and apply the rents in the repairs of the highways within the parish.

It is presumed that these allotments will in future be vested in and under the control of the District Councils.

The powers of exchange conferred by the Inclosure Acts noticed above* apply to such allotments; and the power to

* Inclosure Act, 1845, sec. 149; Inclosure Act, 1852, sec. 21.

declare new trusts of such lands, and consequently to devote them to purposes of recreation, will also apply.

Under the Sale of Exhausted Parish Lands Act, 1876,* allotments for the supply of road materials may be sold or exchanged with the consent of the majority of the rate-payers, and with the approval of the Local Government Board; and the proceeds of any sale may be applied in the repair or improvement of the highways of the parish, or in aid of the highway rate, as the Board may direct.†

It is not stated in the Act in whom public ponds are to be vested; if in the churchwardens and overseers, they will pass under the Local Government Act, 1894, to the Parish Council; or, where there is no Parish Council, to the Chairman of the Parish Meeting, and the Overseers of the Parish.

* 39 & 40 Vict. c. 62., referring to the Union and Parish Property Act, 1835 (5 & 6 Will. IV. c. 69.), sec. 3.

† See also the Highway Act, 1835 (5 & 6 Will. IV. c. 50.), sec. 48.

CHAPTER XVIII.

Of Exceptional Provisions as to Inclosure.

THERE are certain exceptional means of inclosure provided by statute, which, though obsolete in relation to the public opinion of the day, and therefore, one may hope, of little practical importance, nevertheless still form part of the law and should not, therefore, be overlooked by those interested in open spaces.

In the first place, there is still on the Statute Book an Act of Parliament of the last century* which enables a Lord of a Manor, with the consent of three-fourths of the commoners, to lease any portion of the wastes of his manor, not exceeding one-twelfth in area, for any period not exceeding four years, the rents derived from such letting being applied in draining, fencing, or otherwise improving the residue of the wastes. The consent of the commoners is to be given at a meeting, to be held after fourteen days' notice, given as directed by the Act, and the rent reserved is to be the best and most improved yearly rent that can be obtained by public auction. It is unlikely, that any inclosure under this statute would be practicable, or would be attempted at the present day.

There are also two Acts of more recent date designed to facilitate the inclosure of commons and arable fields. The first of these † gives power to the persons interested in such

---

* 13 Geo. III. c. 81.

† 6 & 7 Will. IV. c. 115.

fields to agree upon the inclosure thereof, so as to extinguish "the right of inter-commonage existing as well over as in respect of such lands." The inclosure is to be effected by means of Commissioners, and is made binding upon dissentients and upon persons under legal disability and not able to give a valid consent to the inclosure.

A subsequent Act * enabled the Commissioners to deal with questions of parochial and manorial boundaries, and extended the Act to such open and common arable fields as have common pastures adjacent thereto but not separated therefrom by any fence.

The Inclosure Act, 1845,† authorises the Board of Agriculture to remedy defects and omissions in awards under the last-mentioned Acts. And the Inclosure Acts, 1845 and 1849,‡ enable the Board to complete proceedings commenced under the same Acts. The Board will not, however, take such a course without a local enquiry; § and it is assumed that they would not proceed with any inclosure, unless they were satisfied that it would be for the public benefit. Local authorities and others interested would therefore have the same opportunities of objecting to the proposed inclosure as in an ordinary case. Moreover, the Board must, it would seem, submit any proposal for inclosure to Parliament for confirmation, as in the case of an inclosure commenced under the Inclosure Acts, 1845.‖ It is probable, therefore, that, if the Commissioners were requested to complete proceedings under the Acts upon which we are commenting, ¶ they would direct the applicants to make a fresh application under the Commons Act, 1876.

* 3 & 4 Vict. c. 31. † 8 & 9 Vict. c. 118. s. 152.

‡ 8 & 9 Vict. c. 118. ss. 153–4; 12 & 13 Vict. c. 83. s. 4.

§ Inclosure Act, 1847 (10 & 11 Vict. c. 111.), sec. 5.

‖ Inclosure Act, 1852 (15 & 16 Vict. c. 79.), sec. 1.

¶ 6 & 7 Will. IV. c. 115; 3 & 4 Vict. c. 31.

We have now to deal with inclosure for specific purposes.

GROWTH OF TIMBER.

In very early times an Act was passed "for inclosing of woods in forests, chases, and purlieus," in order to encourage the growth of timber.*

The Act seems to have aimed at giving the owners of lands subject to forest or chase laws relief as against the Crown and other owners of forests or chases. It authorised the inclosure of woods felled, by the licence of the Crown in royal forests, chases, or purlieus, or without such licence in other such places, for seven years, "for the preserving of the young spring." The inclosure was to be "with sufficient hedges able to keep out all manner of beasts and cattle." It was, nevertheless, held that the Act did not affect commoners in the forest, chase, or purlieu in which the wood lay, and that no inclosure made under the Act was good against such commoners.† The Act can, therefore, have little application at the present day.

In the reign of George II. two other Acts were passed to facilitate inclosure for the growth of timber. The first ‡ enables the owner of any waste, with the consent of the major part in number and value of the owners and occupiers of tenements to which a right of common over the waste belongs, to inclose and keep in severalty any part of the wastes for the growth and preservation of timber or under wood; or the inclosure for such purposes may be made by the commoners with the consent of the owner of the waste, or by a third party with the consent of commoners and owner. The commoners' compensation is to be paid to the overseers of the parish or township, to be applied for the relief of the

* 22 Edw. IV. c. 7.

† Sir Francis Barrington's case, 8 Rep. 136.

‡ 29 Geo. II. c. 36.

poor.* The second and amending Act † provides for the case where the right of common is enjoyed by a class more limited than the owners and occupiers of all the tenements within the parish or township, and directs that in such case the compensation shall be divided amongst the commoners in proportion to their interests.

These Acts appear to contemplate partial inclosures only, not the inclosure of the whole of a common.

Poor Law Administration.

Several Acts have been from time to time passed to facilitate the inclosure of waste lands for the supposed benefit of the poor.

The original Poor Law Act of Elizabeth (the Poor Relief Act, 1601‡) confers upon the churchwardens and overseers power to build houses for the poor upon manorial commons. The consent of the Lord of the Manor is necessary, but there is no reference to the consent of the commoners; and it is not quite clear whether or not a justices' order is necessary for the purpose. The following is the exact language of the enactment § :—

" *To the intent that necessary places of habitation may more conveniently be provided for poor impotent people, be it enacted that it shall be lawful for the churchwardens and overseers, or the greater part of them, by the leave of the lord or lords of the manor, whereof any waste or common within their parish is or shall be parcel, and upon agreement before with him or them in writing, under the hands and seals of the said lord or lords, or otherwise according to any order to be set down by the justices of the peace of the said county at their general quarter sessions, or the greater*

* Sec. 2. † 31 Geo. II. c. 41. ‡ 43 Eliz. c. 2. § Sec. 5.

part of them, by like leave and agreement of the said lord or lords, in writing under his or their hands and seals, to erect, build, and set up in fit and convenient places of habitation in such waste or common, at the general charges of the parish or otherwise of the hundred or county as aforesaid, to be taxed, rated, and gathered in manner before expressed, convenient houses or dwellings for the said impotent poor. And also to place inmates, or more families than one, in one cottage or house; which cottages and places for inmates are only to be used for the impotent and poor of the parish."

As few parishes now maintain their own poor and the enactment does not extend to guardians of poor law unions, it is probable that its power is practically spent.

By a statute of William IV.* poor law authorities† are authorised to inclose any area of waste land, not exceeding fifty acres, and to cultivate it for the benefit of the poor, or to let it to the industrious poor. In this case the consent of the Lord of the Manor and that of the major part in value of the commoners, signified under their respective hands and seals, is necessary.

In the same year another statute‡ was passed authorising the poor law authorities to take, with the consent of the Treasury, part, not exceeding the same maximum area (fifty acres), of any forest or waste belonging to the Crown. Nothing is said in this enactment of common rights, and it seems doubtful, if the statute was intended to have any effect

* 2 Will. IV. c. 42.

† That is, the churchwardens and overseers of a parish maintaining its own poor, the overseers of any township or other district in a parish separately maintaining its poor, and the guardians of any poor law union. The writer remembers that under the enactment in question inclosures of some size had been made on Plumstead Common, near Woolwich, the common which was the subject of the case of Warrick *v.* Queen's College, Oxford, L.R. 6 Ch. App. 716.

‡ 1 & 2 Will. IV. c. 59.

except by way of authority to the Crown to alienate its lands.

By a subsequent enactment (the Union and Parish Property Act, 1835*) it was provided that the powers given by the two statutes last mentioned should be exercised by the overseers of the poor and by guardians of poor law unions, as the case may be, "under the control of the Poor Law Board" (*i.e.*, now, of the Local Government Board), and should extend to sites for workhouses and other purposes of poor law administration.

There are, therefore, it will be seen, two checks upon the powers of taking common land thus conferred upon poor law authorities. They cannot be exercised save (1) with the consent of the majority in value of the commoners, and (2) with the consent of the Local Government Board. The latter body, being a branch of the Government, can be questioned as to its proceedings in the House of Commons; and it is not likely that it would at the present day authorise any inclosure of common land.

Ecclesiastical Purposes.

There are several statutes authorising small inclosures of common land for sites for churches and parsonages.

By an early Act of George III. (the Clergy Residence Repair Act, 1776†) any archbishop, bishop, or ecclesiastical corporation, whether sole or aggreeate, being lord of any manor,‡ is authorised to grant waste of his manor for a house or buildings for the use of the clergy of the parish, provides he leaves sufficient common for the commoners.

---

* 5 & 6 Will. IV. c. 69. s. 4.

† 17 Geo. III. c. 53. s. 21.

‡ This would include the case of the rector or vicar of the parish who as such was Lord of a Manor, but not the case where the rector or vicar of a parish owned a manor in his private capacity.

This enactment is little more than a repetition of the Statute of Merton as applied to the particular case.

A more important enactment is that of the Church Building Act, 1810,* which authorises the grant by any person seized in fee of a manor of any part of the waste, not exceeding five acres, for—

(*a*) a church or chapel;

(*b*) a churchyard or burial ground;

(*c*) the site of a house or conveniences for the minister of the parish.

The land so granted is to be freed from all rights of common.

It has been held that this statute does not extend to rights of recreation claimed by the inhabitants of a parish or hamlet, but only to "rights of common and manorial rights of a like nature."†

By another statute, the Church Building Act, 1818,‡ passed a few years later, the Church Building Commissioners (now the Ecclesiastical Commissioners) were empowered to require parishes to find sites for churches, where church accommodation was needed. And it was provided,§ that where there shall be occasion to take part of any common or waste for the purposes of the Act, the conveyance of such portion by the Lord of the Manor shall be a good and sufficient conveyance, as if every commoner had joined in it. Compensation for injury to the rights of common was in this case to be paid to the churchwardens of the parish, and to be applied by them as directed by the vestry of the parish. By an amending Act ‖ it was made

* 51 Geo. III. c. 115. s. 2.

† Per Chitty, J. Forbes *v.* the Ecclesiastical Commissioners for England, L.R. 15 Eq. 51. The case related to Pear Tree Green, near Southampton.

‡ 58 Geo. III. c. 45. ss. 35–8.

§ Sec. 38.

‖ 19 & 20 Vict. c. 104. s. 28.

compulsory on the churchwardens to accept such compensation.

Sites for Schools.

By the School Sites Act it was provided, that, where a Lord of a Manor granted gratuitously any portion, not exceeding one acre, of waste or commonable land as a site for a school for the education of poor persons or for the residence of a school-master or school-mistress, the rights and interests of all persons should be barred and divested by such conveyance. But the land so granted is to revert on its ceasing to be used for the purposes of the Act.*

The powers conferred by this Act may be exercised by School Boards under the Elementary Education Act, 1870;† they have thus a somewhat wide application.

Sites for Museums.

Similar provisions to those existing in relation to school sites apply to sites for museums and institutions for the promotion of science, literature, and art. If waste land for any of these purposes is granted by a Lord of a Manor gratuitously, the rights of all commoners over such land are barred, but the area granted must not exceed one acre.‡

The Defence of the Realm.

By the series of Acts known as the Defence Acts, large powers of acquiring land for the service of the Ordnance Department or the defence of the realm are conferred upon the Secretary of State for the War Department.§ And in particular by the Defence Act, 1854,‖ he is authorised, where he

* 4 & 5 Vict. c. 38. s. 2. † 33 & 34 Vict. c. 75.; see secs. 20, 21.

‡ 17 & 18 Vict. c. 112. § 5 & 6 Vict. c. 94. s. 16, and following sections.

‖ 17 & 18 Vict. c. 67., made applicable with the other earlier Defence Acts to the Secretary for War by the Ordnance Board Transfer Act, 1855, 18 & 19 Vict. c. 117. ss. 1, 4.

has purchased lands under the Defence Acts, to avail himself of the provisions of the Lands Clauses Acts, 1845, for the purpose of ascertaining and extinguishing the common rights over such lands. By this enactment the Secretary of State is put in the position, so far as regards common rights, of a railway company authorised by Parliament to acquire lands under the provisions of the Lands Clauses Acts. What these provisions are, and how they affect common rights, we shall see when, in the next chapter, we deal with the appropriation of common lands by authority of Parliament for industrial undertakings. It is important, however, to bear in mind that the Defence Acts thus enable the Secretary of State, without applying to Parliament, to extinguish common rights over any land he may think it necessary to take for the purpose of building a fort or otherwise providing for the defence of the country.

MILITARY PURPOSES GENERALLY.

The powers we have just mentioned, however, are confined to the acquisition of land for purposes of actual defence. Until recently the Secretary of State for War possessed similar, though not identical, powers in relation to the acquisition of land for camps, rifle ranges, or other similar purposes. But the law on this subject was recently recast, and is now contained in the Military Lands Act, 1892.*

* *55 & 56* Vict. c. 43. The alteration of the law embodied in this Act was brought about by an attempt of the Secretary of State for War in Lord Salisbury's Government to take a large tract of the New Forest for a camp, drill-ground, and rifle-ranges. The New Forest Association, the Commons Preservation Society, and other bodies interested in open spaces, opposed the project, and pointed out the unsatisfactory state of the law. In the result the scheme was abandoned, and a Bill consolidating the various Acts on the subject, introduced by the Secretary for War, was referred to a Select Committee, where, at the instance of Mr. Shaw Lefevre, the law was made to assume its present form.

By that measure,* if the Secretary of State desires to acquire land compulsorily for military purposes, he must proceed by way of provisional order made by him, after notice to all concerned, and a local enquiry.† Such provisional order has no effect till confirmed by Parliament, and, if opposed by petition in Parliament by any persons (such as commoners) legally interested in the land, will be referred to a Select Committee, before which witnesses and agents or counsel will be heard, as in the case of a private Bill. Moreover, such a Bill may, like any other public Bill, be opposed in the House of Commons; and an appeal may be made to the Government, by deputation, questions in the House, and otherwise, to abandon the scheme. In any such case, however, it would be most desirable that, if the interests of the commoners of the district or of the general public are prejudicially affected, a strong representation to this effect should be made at the local enquiry. The Parish and District Councils of the neighbourhood, though not probably entitled to formal notice, will doubtless hear of the project, and should take it into their most serious consideration at the earliest possible stage.

If the Bill confirming the provisional order becomes law, the Secretary of State will possess the same powers of compulsory acquisition as are conferred by private Act upon a railway company or the promoters of other industrial undertakings, and his proceedings will be regulated by the provisions of the Lands Clauses Acts.‡

* Secs. 1 and 2.

† The Secretary of State may also make a provisional order, after the same preliminaries, for the acquisition of land for military purposes by a volunteer corps or the Council of a county or borough. In this case the corps or Council must petition the Secretary of State; see secs. 1 and 2.

‡ See *post*, p. 211.

Military purposes (*i.e.* the purposes for which the land may be acquired) are defined by the Act* to be—

Rifle or artillery practice.

The building or enlarging of barracks and camps.

The erection of butts, targets, batteries, and other accommodation.

The stowing of arms.

Military drill, and

Any other purpose connected with military matters approved by the Secretary of State.

When the Secretary of State has purchased common lands for military purposes, and extinguished the common rights, he may frame bye-laws regulating the use of such lands by the public, the object being so far to exclude the public as may be necessary for their safety, and to enable the lands to be used freely for the purposes for which they were acquired.†

* Sec. 23. † Secs. 14–17.

CHAPTER XIX.

Of the Appropriation of Common Lands for the Purposes of Industrial Undertakings.

WE have in the previous chapter referred more than once to the power of acquiring common lands conferred by private Act of Parliament upon the promoters of industrial undertakings. Serious inroads were at one time made upon the common lands of the country by railway companies acting under the powers thus conferred. Common land, lying uncultivated, and therefore being, as a rule, of less value than inclosed fields or woods, was considered by the engineers and promoters of new lines to furnish peculiarly appropriate sites for railways and works; and they consequently laid out their lines through as much common land as possible. It was not only the cheapness of the land in itself which attracted them; there was little chance of opposition to the scheme from those interested in such land. For the Lord of the Manor was usually only too glad to make something out of land which was perhaps wholly unproductive to him; while the commoners were not allowed by the rules of Parliament to appear individually in opposition to the Bill. They could only oppose through a committee representing a majority in number and value; and it is not easy to get a number of persons to agree in spending money in law, with perhaps but slight chance of success.

Moreover, when the Act was passed, owing to the acquisition of the land piecemeal, so to speak, in the manner presently described, less even than the full value of the land as uncultivated waste was not unlikely to be paid. There was every inducement, therefore, to railway promoters to take their line through common lands, and they were not slow to do so.

On the other hand, the injury to a common arising from its intersection by a line of railway is peculiarly serious. Not only is a piece of the common appropriated, but there is a severance of one part of the open waste from another. The value of a large waste for purposes of pasturage often depends upon the freedom of the cattle to range from part to part. To one spot they resort at one time of the day, or at one season; to another, at another. A railway, acting like a fence, destroys this freedom of range, and may indefinitely deteriorate the value of the common for grazing purposes.

Again, the public were completely ignored in the whole transaction. A common might have been of peculiar value as a place of resort and recreation. But no local authority, no member of the public, was heard on the proposal to destroy the common before the Select Committee which virtually decided the fate of the Bill; and no compensation was paid in any form to the public, or to any body representing the public, when the Act passed and the common was appropriated.

We will describe briefly the manner in which common land is obtained for the purposes of an industrial undertaking.

A railway company * seeking power to make a new line advertises in November its intention to apply to Parliament in the ensuing session for an Act to authorise the formation of the railway. It then, before the 30th of November, deposits in the Private Bill Office of each House of Parlia-

* We take a railway company as the type of a private Bill promoter; the proceedings are the same in the case of a corporation or company seeking to construct waterworks, or the promoters of any other industrial undertaking seeking compulsory power to acquire land.

ment a plan showing the route of the line and the lands the company desires to acquire in order to make it, and a book of reference showing the owners, lessees, and occupiers of such lands. In the case of an ordinary manorial common, the Lord of the Manor would be scheduled as the owner of the common, and the Lord of the Manor and the commoners as the occupiers. In the case of a common field or meadow, the owners of the several strips would be entered as owners, and they and the class entitled to depasture the field or meadow during the open season as the occupiers. Shortly afterwards the Bill of the company is deposited, and becomes public property. This document contains a clause empowering the company to "enter upon, take, and use the lands shown on the deposited plans and books of reference," and another clause incorporating with the Bill the Lands Clauses Acts.* When Parliament meets, the Bill is read a first time, on the petition of the company; it is ascertained whether the Standing Orders of Parliament in relation to private Bills have been complied with, and, if so, the Bill is read a second time and referred to a Select Committee. The detailed examination of the Bill on its merits takes place before this tribunal. If any person whose land is taken, or whose property is otherwise affected,† presents (within a certain time) a petition praying to be heard against the Bill, the Select Committee hears the case for and against the Bill by agents or counsel and witnesses, after the manner of the trial of an action in a court of law.‡ The Bill may be

* The principal of these is the Lands Clauses Act, 1845, 8 & 9 Vict. c. 18.

† A single Commoner is not, according to the usual practice of Private Bill Committees, heard against a Bill. The Commoners must form a Committee in order to be heard on Petition.

‡ Where no one petitions against a Bill it is referred for examination in the House of Commons to a Committee consisting of one or two members and some of the principal officers of the House, and in the House of Lords to the Lord Chairman of Committees, who examines it with the aid of his Counsel.

thrown out by the Committee, passed as it is, or amended. It then goes back to the House for third reading, and goes through the same process in all respects in the Second House. When passed, the railway company proceeds to purchase the lands shown on the deposited plans and books of reference in accordance with the provisions of the Lands Clauses Acts, which, as we have seen, are incorporated in the special Act.

Now the provisions of the Lands Clauses Acts as to the purchase of common lands are of a special character.* They deal separately with the purchase of the soil and with that of the common rights. The soil is purchased from the owner in the same way as though the common were private land, though of course the existence of common rights is taken into account to reduce the amount of purchase money paid. In the case of a manorial common the company must first treat with the Lord of the Manor, and settle † the price to be paid to him for his interest in the soil. The Lord of the Manor then conveys to the company the part of the common to be taken, and this conveyance under the terms of the Act ‡ vests the land in the company and entitles it to possession, subject, however, to the common rights, until they are extinguished by payment or deposit of compensation. For the purpose of ascertaining the compensation to be paid to the commoners, a meeting is called by the company, by advertisement in the local papers, and by notice on the church doors. The object of this meeting is to appoint a committee to treat with the company; and the decision of the majority at the meeting binds the minority and all absentees. The compensation payable to the com-

* See Lands Clauses Act, 1845 (8 & 9 Vict. c. 18.), secs. 99–107.

† By agreement, or by the verdict of a jury or award of an arbitrator, as in the case of other lands.

‡ Sec. 100.

moners is such amount as may be agreed between this committee and the railway company, or, in default of agreement, may be determined by the verdict of a jury or the award of an arbitrator.* The receipt of the committee for the compensation thus ascertained is a good receipt on behalf of the commoners; and the committee is left to apportion the compensation money amongst the several commoners.† If no committee is appointed at the meeting, or the proceedings are otherwise rendered abortive by the default of the commoners, the compensation may be determined, at the instance of the railway company, by a surveyor appointed by two justices of the peace.‡ And if a duly appointed committee fails to give a receipt for the compensation money, the railway company may deposit the money in the Bank of England in the name of the committee. Upon payment of the compensation money to the committee or its deposit in the Bank, the common rights are extinguished, and the company may use the common land for the purposes of their works.§ But it has been held, that the company has no right to enter upon the land and use it for its works, until the commoners' compensation has been ascertained and paid, or deposited.||

It will be seen from this description of the process of acquiring common land, that it is not likely to be favour-

* See secs. 101–3.

† Sec. 104.

‡ Sec. 106.

§ Sec. 107.

|| Stoneham v. The London, Brighton, and South Coast Railway Company, L.R. 7 Q.B. 1. (Tooting Beck Common, near London.)

All the provisions of the Lands Clauses Acts which we have described apply to the case, where the soil of the common land belongs to the commoners (*i.e.* to certain descriptions of common fields, meadows, and pastures), with this exception, that there being no separate owner of the soil, the first step to be taken by the company is the summoning of the commoners' meeting to appoint a committee, and the committee, in giving a receipt for the compensation money, also convey the land.

able to the commoners. Instead of buying the whole land at its full market value and leaving the money to be apportioned amongst the parties, the company first puts itself in possession of the soil, which it gets for very little on the ground that the common rights prevent its full use, and then, being in possession as owner of the soil, buys up the common rights as a mere burden on the land. Moreover, the poorer commoners, to whom the common is of most value, may have little voice in the appointment of the committee, and commoners' rights may be questioned and negatived in a summary manner, and the number of commoners and the compensation payable may by this means be much reduced.

Thus, from every point of view, it is in the interests of a railway company, or of any other persons desiring to obtain land compulsorily, to appropriate common land, and it is against the interests of the commoners and the public, that it should be appropriated, where any other land can be found to answer the purpose.

It has accordingly been for many years past the policy of the Commons Preservation Society to prevent such appropriation, or, where it cannot be avoided, to make special terms for the commoners and the public.

We have pointed out, that the public have no means of opposing a railway or other private Bill before the Select Committee, where its merits are discussed, and that commoners can only be heard before such a Committee under very disadvantageous conditions.

The only effectual means, therefore, of protecting common land from such appropriation and compelling Parliament to consider both sides of the question, is to oppose the Bill on second reading in the House of Commons. This is the course which has been adopted of recent years, and with marked success.* Sometimes the Bill is thrown out on second reading, sometimes terms are made in the House, and sometimes, though those interested in open spaces have been beaten in the House, the Select Committee to which the Bill has been referred,† having had its attention called to the matter, has interfered to protect the public. Indeed, so clearly is it now recognised by the promoters of private Bills, and particularly by railway companies, that common land is not lightly to be scheduled amongst the lands to be acquired, that Bills making serious inroads on commons have become rare,‡ and where some appropriation is proposed, negotiations between the Commons Society and the promoters, before the second reading, usually result in terms satisfactory to the public.

These results could not, however, have been achieved but for a slight alteration in the Standing Orders of Parliament, made at the instance of Mr. Shaw Lefevre some ten years ago. The Bill by which authority to appropriate lands is sought contains no indication on the face of it that common land is to be taken; it is only by an examination of the plans and books of reference, or from local information, that this can be ascertained. The first process is very laborious, when perhaps 150 or 200 Bills are introduced in one session; the second source of information is untrustworthy.

* The late Mr. Fawcett and Mr. Shaw Lefevre may be said to have originated this procedure, and have undoubtedly been foremost in resisting the unconsidered destruction of commons by private Bill legislation. For some account of the history of the struggle, see Mr. Lefevre's "English Commons and Forests," Cassell & Co., Limited, 1894.

† It is the ordinary rule, we believe, when there has been a division on second reading, to put on the Committee some member who has voted against the Bill.

‡ The most serious attacks of late years have proceeded from local authorities promoting schemes of water supply, or (in one or two cases) seeking to enlarge cemeteries.

The Standing Orders of each House of Parliament now, however, require that in the notice of the Bills advertised in the *Gazette* and in other papers in November, the promoters shall state the particulars of any common land which they propose to acquire by means of the Bill. Thus, by perusing the *Gazette* notices of Bills each November, any person interested in open spaces is able to ascertain what common lands are threatened. The Commons Preservation Society always performs this duty. Every Bill found to affect common land is carefully scrutinised, communications are opened with the local authorities of the districts in question, and such steps as may be thought necessary are taken.*

Something has also been done for the protection of the public and the commoners in relation to the application of the compensation money paid to commoners,† where common lands are compulsorily taken.

We have seen that the duty of apportioning the compensation money amongst the individual commoners is imposed by the Lands Clauses Acts upon the committee appointed to receive the money. It may well be imagined that this is

* These negotiations are in practice conducted by Mr. Percival Birkett, the hon. solicitor to the Commons Preservation Society (under the directions of the Committee), and the public is much indebted to Mr. Birkett for the pains and ability which he devotes to the subject. The general policy of the Society is to secure, where a case is made out for the appropriation of common land, that an equivalent area shall, where possible, be substituted, as common, for that taken. In some cases, where large tracts are required not for inclosure, but as a collecting ground for water, the Society procures clauses preserving free access to the public and protecting common rights, and thus avoiding any disturbance of the rural economy of the district; see, *e.g.*, the Birmingham Corporation Water Act of a few years since.

† For convenience we refer in the following pages to "commoners" as the parties interested in compensation moneys, but the enactments apply equally where money has been paid to a committee of persons interested in the soil of common lands (or of lands of that nature).

often a very difficult task, and it was not long before the Legislature found it necessary to come to the aid of the committee.

By the Inclosure Act, 1852, it was provided that in any such case, upon the application of the committee, the Inclosure Commissioners (now the Board of Agriculture) might call a meeting of the commoners, with the object of securing the appointment of trustees of the compensation money, the investment of such money, and the application of the interest to such purposes, for the benefit of the commoners, as the Commissioners should approve. At such meeting the majority in number and the majority in respect of interest were to bind the minority and all absent parties. If no instructions as to the compensation money were resolved upon, or the Commissioners deemed them unjust or unreasonable, they were empowered by an order under their seal to give instructions for the investment of the money and the application of the income, and to provide for the appointment of new trustees from time to time. Upon payment of the compensation money to the trustees under any such resolution or order, the committee were discharged from all liability in respect thereof.*

By the Inclosure Act, 1854, the powers of the Inclosure Commissioners (now the Board of Agriculture) were further extended. The Commissioners were authorised, upon the application of the commoners' committee, to call a meeting of the commoners to determine whether or not the compensation money should be apportioned under the following provisions of the Act. If the majority in number and interest so resolved, the money was to be paid into the Bank of England to the credit of an account to be named by the Commissioners, and the committee was thereupon discharged of liability.

* Inclosure Act, 1852 (15 & 16 Vict. c. 79.), sec. 22.

The Commissioners were then authorised to proceed by themselves or an Assistant Commissioner* to ascertain who were the persons interested in the compensation money, and in what proportions. For this purpose they were empowered to hold meetings, call for documents, examine witnesses on oath, and employ surveyors and valuers; and the award of the Commissioners or an Assistant Commissioner was made binding on all parties. The Commissioners' expenses of the enquiry were to be deducted from the compensation money, and the balance divided amongst the parties interested as directed by the award.†

The powers thus conferred upon the Inclosure Commissioners were fraught with danger to common lands. They afforded a cheap and summary mode of obtaining a register of commoners; and the Lord of the Manor, being in possession of such a register, has sometimes proceeded to buy up the commoners one by one with a view to enclosing the common. This was the case at Banstead, where Mr. Nathan Wetherell, an experienced Assistant Commissioner, compiled a schedule of commoners for the purpose of distributing the compensation money paid by the London, Brighton, and South Coast Railway Company on passing through Banstead Downs. The Lord of the Manor (a subsequent purchaser), relying on this list as exhaustive, made a determined attempt to buy up and extinguish all the rights indicated by it. But when his inclosures were challenged, it was proved to the satisfaction of the Courts, that there were many rights not accounted for by the award, and the attempt to inclose, after long and costly litigation, failed.‡

* In practice they always appoint an Assistant Commissioner for any such purpose.

† Inclosure Act, 1854 (17 & 18 Vict. c. 97.), secs. 15–20.

‡ Robertson *v.* Hartopp, 43 Ch. Div. 484, 516.

On the other hand, the powers of application and apportionment given by the Inclosure Acts, 1852 and 1854, were not found to meet all cases, and compensation moneys were often left in the hands of a committee or of trustees without being of the slightest benefit to the commoners. Accordingly in 1882, further powers were conferred upon the Commissioners—powers now enjoyed by the Board of Agriculture.

By the Commonable Rights Compensation Act, 1882,* the Board of Agriculture is empowered, upon the application of the commoners' committee, or, after the expiration of twelve months from the payment of the compensation money to such committee, of any three persons claiming to be interested in the compensation money, to call a meeting to consider generally the application thereof.

At any such meeting the majority in respect of numbers, and the majority in respect of interest, of the persons present may decide by resolution, that the money shall be applied—

(*a*) In the improvement of the remainder of the common land in respect of a portion of which the money has been paid;

(*b*) In defraying the expense of proceedings for the management and regulation of the common under the Metropolitan Commons Acts, or the Inclosure Acts, or by way of private Bill, or otherwise;

(*c*) In defraying the expense of legal proceedings for the protection of the common land or the commoners' rights over the same;

(*d*) In the purchase of additional land to be used as common land;

(*e*) In the purchase of land to be used as a recreation ground for the neighbourhood.

* 45 Vict. c. 15.

The resolution is to bind the minority and all absent parties, and the Board is to give effect to it by an order under their seal. Upon service of this order upon the persons in possession of the compensation money, they are to pay and apply such money as directed by the order.*

The Act further provides that any land purchased to be used as common land shall be vested in trustees upon trust for the persons interested, such trustees to be appointed and trusts to be declared, with all proper provisions, by an order under the seal of the Commissioners pursuant to resolutions to be passed at special meetings to be convened by the Commissioners;† and that any land purchased for a recreation ground shall be conveyed to, and vest in, the local authority, and be held and managed by such authority in accordance with the provisions of the Inclosure Acts relating to recreation grounds.‡ By the conjoint operation of this Act and the later Acts relating to local management, the local authority to take charge of such recreation grounds will be—in the County of London, the County Council; in urban districts, the Corporation or the Urban District Council; and in rural districts, the Parish Council.§

The calling and conduct of meetings under the Act is to be regulated by the Board of Agriculture, and they may direct an Assistant Commissioner to preside at any meeting.‖

The Act is retrospective in its operation, and enables an irregular application of compensation money for any of the purposes mentioned in the Act to be legalised.¶

The Act further contains a provision, that compensation paid under an Act of Parliament by a railway company or

* 45 Vict. c. 15. s. 2 (1). † See sec. 2 (2) and (3) ‡ Sec. 2 (5).

§ Compare sec. 2 (5) and the Schedule of the Commonable Rights Compensation Act, 1882, with the Local Government Act, 1888, sec. 40 (8), and the Local Government Act, 1894, secs. 21 (1), 5 (2) (*c*), and 6 (1) (*c*) (iii).

‖ Sec. 2 (4). ¶ Sec. 4.

other promoters of an undertaking, for the acquisition of a recreation ground or allotment for field gardens, shall be applied in manner provided by the Inclosure Acts with respect to the surplus rents of recreation grounds and field gardens respectively.*

At the present day, therefore, it rests with the commoners, where common land is compulsorily taken, to apply the compensation money in acquiring other land to be used as common in substitution for that taken, or to apply it in providing for the regulation of the residue of the common as an open space, or in providing a recreation ground. Such an application is that which is most conducive to the interests of the public, and the injury arising from the taking of the land is thus minimised.

* Sec. 3; and see *ante*, p. 192.

CHAPTER XX.

Of the Regulation of Commons as Open Spaces.

I.—Under the Metropolitan Commons Acts.

We have seen that the proper person to preserve order on an ordinary manorial common, and to protect it from injury, is the Lord of the Manor, as he alone has a right to bring an action for trespass, or to put in force any provisions of the criminal law applicable to the case. But this duty, especially in the case of commons near towns, which have little value for pasturage or wood, is an onerous and thankless one, and Lords of Manors cannot be relied upon to perform it. On the contrary, they have sometimes thought it their interest to connive at disorder and nuisances, foreseeing that the state to which the common was thus reduced would be urged as a reason for its inclosure.

It was the perception of this serious danger to commons which led to the passing of the Metropolitan Commons Act, 1866,* an Act which for the first time made provision for the preservation of commons as open spaces under the management of public bodies.

This Act has been since amended by the Metropolitan Commons Amendment Act, 1869,† and the Metropolitan Commons Act, 1878,‡ and these three Acts form, under the

* 29 & 30 Vict. c. 122. The public owe this Act, under which most of the metropolitan commons have been placed under local management, to the late Mr. Philip Lawrence, formerly hon. solicitor to the Commons Preservation Society, and subsequently Solicitor to H.M. Office of Works. Mr. Lawrence not only urged upon Parliament the necessity of legislation of this character, but gave shape to the Act.

† 32 & 33 Vict. c. 107.

‡ 41 & 42 Vict. c. 71.

name of the Metropolitan Commons Acts,* a code for the regulation of metropolitan commons. They apply only to commons the whole or any part of which is situate within the Metropolitan Police District, as defined at the passing of the Act.†

Under the Metropolitan Commons Acts a scheme for the establishment of local management with a view to the expenditure of money on the drainage, levelling, and improvement of a metropolitan common, and to the making of bye-laws and regulations for the prevention of nuisances and the preservation of order thereon, may be made on a memorial in that behalf presented to the Board of Agriculture by—

(*a*) the Lord of the Manor;

(*b*) any commoners;

(*c*) the local authority for the district into which any part of the common extends;

(*d*) any twelve or more ratepayers, inhabitants of the parish or parishes in which the common is situate.‡

The local authority thus authorised to initiate proceedings is—

(*a*) in the case of a common the whole or any part of which is situate within the County of London, the County Council;§

(*b*) in the case of a common the whole or part of which is within an urban district, and no part of which is within the County of London, the Corporation or Urban District Council; ||

(*c*) in the case of any other common, the Parish Council.¶

---

* Short Titles Act.

† The Greater London of the Registrar-General; see *ante*, p. 108. There has been no alteration in the boundary of this district since 1866.

‡ Metropolitan Commons Act, 1866, sec. 6; Metropolitan Commons Amendment Act, 1869, sec. 3.

§ *Ib.* sec. 2 and first schedule; Local Government Act, 1888, sec. 40 (8).

|| *Ib.* sec. 2 and first schedule; Public Health Act, 1875, sec. 6; Local Government Act, 1894, sec. 21.

¶ *Ib.* sec. 2 and first schedule; Local Government Act, 1894, sec. 6 (1) (*a*).

The procedure of the Board of Agriculture under the Metropolitan Commons Acts differs in form from that under the Inclosure Acts.

Upon the presentation of a memorial, the Board, after such examination and enquiry as they think fit, may prepare the draft of a scheme respecting the common or any part thereof.* This draft scheme is printed and delivered to the memorialists, the Lord of the Manor, and the local authority (whether or not the local authority are the memorialists), and the scheme or an abstract of it is published and circulated in such manner as the Board direct.† Two months must elapse, during which written objections and suggestions may be made to the Board.‡ At the end of this time, if the Board decide to proceed with the scheme, they may, and in practice always do, hold a local enquiry by means of an Assistant Commissioner.§ This enquiry, though not the subject of such detailed statutory provisions as the corresponding enquiry upon an application to enclose a common,‖ is practically conducted in much the same manner, ample notice (fourteen days is the minimum time prescribed) being given of the sittings of the Assistant Commissioner, and the fullest opportunity afforded to all persons to express their views on the proposed scheme.

The Assistant Commissioner reports the result of the enquiry to the Board of Agriculture, with his opinion upon the scheme, and the Board then, if they think fit, finally settle and approve the scheme in such form as they think expedient,¶ and certify it and seal it with their common seal,**

* Metropolitan Commons Act, 1866, secs. 7, 8. In practice it is usual for the memorialists to prepare a draft and submit it with their memorial. The Board then examine it, and adopt it with such alterations or additions as they think fit.

† Sec. 9. ‡ Sec. 10. § Sec. 11.

‖ See *ante*, pp. ¶ Secs. 12, 13. ** Sec. 16.

delivering copies (as before) to the memorialists, the Lord of the Manor, and the local authority, and publishing and circulating the scheme or an abstract thereof in such manner as they think sufficient to give information to all parties interested.*

In February in every year the Board report to Parliament all proceedings under the Metropolitan Commons Acts during the preceding calendar year, setting forth in full every scheme certified by them, with the grounds of their approval, and a statement of the proceedings taken.† A scheme has no operation of itself, but has full operation when confirmed by Parliament, with or without modification.‡

The practice is that the Home Secretary introduces a Bill to confirm each scheme certified under the Metropolitan Commons Acts. This Bill is treated in all respects as a public Bill, unless a petition is presented against it, when it is referred to a Select Committee, before which the petitioners may appear and oppose, as in the case of a private Bill.§ Schemes under the Metropolitan Commons Acts are not referred to a Select Committee of the House of Commons before the introduction of the confirming Bills, as in the case of provisional orders for inclosure or regulation under the Inclosure Acts.||

When discussing the Parliamentary inclosure of a common, we saw that the consent of the persons legally interested in the soil and in the rights of common over such common played an important part in the procedure. No application for an inclosure can be entertained by the Board of Agriculture unless persons representing one third in value concur in the application; and no provisional order for inclo-

* Sec. 19.

† Secs. 20, 21.

‡ Sec. 22.

§ Sec. 23.

|| The confirming Bill is promoted by the Government without cost to the persons interested, unless the Bill is opposed before a Select Committee.

sure can be certified to Parliament unless persons representing two thirds in value consent to the order. Most important of all, in the case of a manorial common the Lord of the Manor has an absolute veto upon inclosure.

There are no such provisions in the case of a scheme for the local management of a metropolitan common. This difference is one of principle, and should be carefully borne in mind.

The provisions of the Metropolitan Commons Acts affecting legal interests in a common which is the subject of an application to the Board are as follows :—

"*Every scheme shall state what rights (if any) claimed by any person or class of persons are affected by the scheme, and in what manner and to what extent they are affected thereby, and whether or not the scheme has been in relation thereto consented to by that person or class of persons, or any of them.**

"*No estate, interest, or right of a profitable or beneficial nature in, over, or affecting a common shall, except with the consent of the person entitled thereto, be taken away or injuriously affected by any scheme, without compensation being made or provided for the same, and such compensation shall, in case of difference, be ascertained and provided in the same manner as if the same compensation were for the compulsory purchase and taking or the injurious affecting of lands under the provisions of the Lands Clauses Consolidation Act,* 1845, *and the Lands Clauses Consolidation Acts Amendment Act,* 1860.†

"*If any person claiming any estate, interest, or right in, over, or affecting the common to which any scheme relates is dissatisfied with any determination made or implied by the Commissioners, or by the scheme concerning any estate,*

* Metropolitan Commons Act, 1866, sec. 14. † *Ib.* sec. 15.

interest, or right in, over, or affecting the common, every such person may obtain a decision thereon in an action at law in the manner provided by sec. 56 of the general Act to facilitate the inclosure and improvement of commons, passed in the session of the 8th and 9th years of the reign of her present Majesty, cap. 118."*

In construing these sections we have the advantage of a careful judicial decision of the late Master of the Rolls (Sir George Jessel) in the case of the Hackney commons.

The Hackney commons (which were for the most part lammas lands) were placed under the management of the Metropolitan Board of Works by the Metropolitan Commons Supplemental Act, 1872, which confirmed a scheme for the local management of the commons made by the Inclosure Commissioners under the Metropolitan Commons Acts. This scheme conferred upon the Board powers of preserving and managing the commons, with a view to good order and the prevention of nuisances and to the improvement of the commons. It contained, as required by sec. 14 of the Act, a statement of the rights claimed by the Lord of the Manor, the owners of the lammas lands and the commoners, and then added: "This scheme affects the rights so claimed as aforesaid only so far as is absolutely necessary for the purpose contemplated by the scheme." It contained no clause providing (in the words of sec. 15) for the compensation of the Lord of the Manor or other persons "in respect of any estate or right of a profitable or beneficial nature in, over, or affecting the commons taken away or injuriously affected by the scheme." But it contained a saving clause, "saving to all persons all such estates, interests, and rights of a profitable or beneficial nature in, over, or affecting the commons, or any

* Metropolitan Commons Act, 1866, sec. 16.

part thereof, as they or any of them had before the confirmation of the scheme by Act of Parliament, or could or might have enjoyed, if the scheme had not been confirmed by Act of Parliament."

The Act * confirming the scheme was in the usual form. It did not modify the scheme, but confirmed it, and then enacted that—

"*From and after the passing of this Act, the scheme shall be deemed to be a public general Act of Parliament, of like form and effect as if the provisions of the same had been enacted in the body of this Act.*"

Subsequently to the passing of the Act of 1872, the Lord of the Manor dug gravel on Hackney Downs (one of the lammas lands included in the scheme). He was admitted to be also the owner of certain portions of the Downs. The Metropolitan Board filed an information against the lord (Mr. Tyssen-Amherst), in the name of the Attorney-General, and also brought an action against him in the name of the Board. They claimed that his acts were inconsistent with the provisions of the scheme and with the rights conferred by it upon the public, and they claimed an injunction to restrain such acts.

The Master of the Rolls held, in the first place, that the public obtained under the scheme no rights which could be enforced in any court of law, and he therefore dismissed the information of the Attorney-General, which could only be warranted by the existence of such rights.

He held, however, that the provisions of the scheme as confirmed by Act of Parliament gave the Metropolitan Board such rights in the commons as entitled the Board to bring an action against any person infringing those rights. He pointed

* The Metropolitan Commons Supplemental Act, 1872.

out that the rights specified in the scheme extended to the "right of entering upon the common and taking care of it," the right of draining, levelling, fencing, and improving the common, the right of preserving the turf and trees and of planting, the right of preventing trespass and encroachments (which he held to mean illegal encroachments) on the common, and of making and enforcing bye-laws to preserve order and prevent nuisances. He considered that these rights amounted to more than an easement, to a modified right of possession, which entitled the Board to sue a wrong-doer.

He held, however, that it could not be assumed that the Legislature intended to take away any right of a profitable or beneficial nature without compensation; and that, there being no compensation clause in the scheme, sec. 15 of the Metropolitan Commons Act, 1866, did not in itself give compensation, and, consequently, no compensation was provided.

He considered that the Act of 1872 took away, or modified, without compensation, certain rights of the Lord of the Manor, but not any profitable or beneficial right. "The right of keeping order" (said the learned Judge) "remains (to the Board), and the lord has no legal right to interfere with the officers of the Board and the persons appointed by them to keep order and keep off bad characters, and so on. Then, again, he could not interfere with them for improving the grass and the turf, and so forth, merely because he had the right of the ownership. All that is saved is his beneficial ownership. If, therefore, before the Act of Parliament passed, he might have brought trespass against anybody who interfered to level his common, or to make it more beautiful, he has lost that right, because it does not affect his beneficial interest."

The right to take gravel, however,—if any such right existed before the Act passed—being a beneficial interest, the

Master of the Rolls considered to be saved by the Act; and he therefore declined to grant an injunction against the lord, unless it could be proved that he had not, before the Act passed, any right to dig and take gravel. He held, in fact, that the scheme and the confirming Act of Parliament in no way affected any claim of the lord to make a profit out of the common, but that such claim must be tested by its effect upon other rights, such as those of the other owners of the lammas lands and of the commoners. All that the scheme did as against the persons legally interested in the common was to enable order to be preserved and the common improved.*

In a recent case, that of the Banstead Commons, the question was raised before the Board of Agriculture, whether a scheme could be made without the consent of the Lord of the Manor, unless his interest in the common was first purchased. The Board, after a lengthy and expensive enquiry, decided against this contention and made a scheme without the lord's consent, and without any provision for his compensation, except so far as any profitable or beneficial right was taken away or injuriously affected.

The Lord of the Manor subsequently petitioned against the Bill introduced by the Home Office to confirm the scheme of the Board of Agriculture, and his case was heard by a Select Committee, both in the House of Commons and in the

* Attorney-General *v.* Amhurst (5th April, 1879), 23 Solicitors' Journal, 443. The case is only very shortly reported in this paper. It is of such importance as a decision on the Metropolitan Commons Acts that it has been thought well to print in the Appendix, p. 353, a full note of the judgment transcribed from shorthand notes, furnished to the Commons Preservation Society by the solicitor to the late Metropolitan Board of Works.

It may be added that the construction put by Sir George Jessel upon the Metropolitan Commons Act and the schemes made under it, is precisely that intended by those who framed the Act and passed it through Parliament. The object was to protect a common from wrong-doers, leaving as they were the rights of all persons legally interested.

House of Lords. In the latter House a slight amendment of detail was made, and, subject to this, the Act was passed.*

It is now, therefore, clearly established that a scheme may be made and confirmed by Parliament under the Metropolitan Commons Acts for the local management of a metropolitan common, not only without the consent, but in spite of the opposition, of the Lord of the Manor and, *à fortiori*, of the commoners. Such a scheme is in fact a measure of police, upon which the judgment of the inhabitants and the local authority is all important.

We shall see, when we come to consider the regulation of commons under the Inclosure Acts, that a contrary principle unfortunately prevails in these cases.

The main provisions of a scheme under the Metropolitan Commons Acts have been already alluded to in discussing the judgment in the Hackney case, and will be seen more at length in the specimen of a scheme given in the Appendix.

The scheme opens with a declaration that the common shall henceforth be managed † by the local authority or other body specified in the scheme. For this purpose they are authorised to appoint common keepers and other servants, who are empowered to remove wrong-doers from the common. The managing body is further authorised to execute any works of drainage, raising, levelling, and fencing, for the general improvement of the common. They are to preserve the turf, shrubs, trees, plants, and grass, and for this purpose may inclose portions by fences for short periods, and may plant and otherwise beautify the common, but not in a way to vary or alter its natural aspect or features. They are also em-

* The Act and scheme as thus approved are set forth in the Appendix, p. 367.

† Sir George Jessel considered that the body to which the management is entrusted is compelled to manage. It has the duty, as well as the power, of management. (See Appendix, p. 357.)

powered to set apart portions of the common for games, and to form cricket grounds, and to temporarily inclose such grounds with an open fence to prevent cattle straying thereon. Further, they are to maintain the common free from encroachments, and to permit no trespass on, or partial or other inclosure of, any part thereof.

They are authorised to make bye-laws, subject to confirmation by the Local Government Board, for the preservation of order and the protection of the common, persons offending against these bye-laws being liable to penalties to be enforced upon summary conviction.

In this last power lies the gist of a scheme under the Metropolitan Commons Acts. A civil action for damages is quite ineffective to prevent nuisances and depredations on a common, and this is the only remedy possessed, even by the lord, for most offences committed to the injury of a common by outsiders. The power, reposed in some responsible body, of summoning wrong-doers before a magistrate, at once enables order to be enforced and property to be protected upon an open space.

The kind of power possessed by a managing body under a scheme is illustrated by a recent case relating to Barnes Common.* The conservators of Barnes Common, under the power conferred upon them to form cricket grounds and to temporarily inclose the same with an open fence to prevent cattle straying thereon, erected posts and rails along one side of Barnes Green (a part of Barnes Common) between a cricket ground and an approach road to the house of a commoner. The commoner took down the fence, and the conservators brought an action claiming an injunction to prevent a repetition of the act. The posts and rails were about three

* Ratcliffe *v.* Jowers, 8 Times Law Reports, 6.

feet high, and there were two open places for foot-passengers and a moveable bar to admit a cricket-roller. This bar was opened at suitable times to admit cattle and horses. The commoner had never applied for the admission of his commonable cattle before breaking down the fence. On the other hand, the conservators admitted that the fence was to be permanently maintained.

Mr. Justice Chitty held that the conservators had not, as against the commoner, exceeded their powers in erecting the posts and rails in question, but must undertake to allow the commoner access to the green for his commonable cattle at all suitable times and seasons.*

The managing bodies appointed under schemes sanctioned in pursuance of the Metropolitan Commons Acts vary in different cases.

Although by these Acts a local authority for each class of Metropolitan Commons is specified, this is only for the purpose of initiating schemes and defraying, or contributing towards (as the case may be), the expenses of providing and carrying out schemes.†

Where, however, the local authority defined by the Metropolitan Commons Acts ‡ memorialise the Board of Agriculture, the management of the common is almost as a matter of course confided to that body. Thus, commons within the County of London which are the subject of schemes are, without exception, placed under the management of the

* It has also been held that a bye-law prohibiting public meetings, unless held with the permission of the managing body, is a good bye-law; see De Morgan *v.* The Metropolitan Board of Works (Clapham Common, 1880), 5 Q.B.D. 155. But a bye-law cannot prejudicially affect a beneficial interest saved by the scheme; see Hoare *v.* The Metropolitan Board of Works (Blackheath, 1874), L.R. 9 Q.B. 296.

† Metropolitan Commons Act, 1866, secs. 6, 24, 25; and see Metropolitan Commons Act, 1878, sec. 2.

‡ Act of 1866, sec. 2, and first schedule.

London County Council, the authority specified in the Metropolitan Commons Act of 1866. Again, when, outside the County of London, local boards have memorialised the Board of Agriculture, they have been appointed the managing body.*

But there are other cases in which the Board have been memorialised by commoners or inhabitants, and in which a special managing body, under the name of conservators, has been appointed.†

There is this difference between the two cases. The Board of Agriculture have held, that they cannot by a scheme give power to any managing body to levy a new rate for the maintenance of a common put under local management. Rating powers, they hold, must be derived solely from the Metropolitan Commons Acts themselves. Now these Acts give power to the local authority entitled to memorialise the Board in respect of a common, to defray the expenses incurred by the Board in connection with a scheme,‡ and to contribute such an amount as they think fit (in a gross sum or by annual payments or otherwise) towards the expenses of executing any scheme, including the payment of the compensation (for the taking away or injurious affecting of profitable or beneficial rights), if any, to be paid in pursuance thereof.§ All expenditure thus incurred by a local authority is to be paid out of the local rates as defined by the Act, *i.e.*, in the case of the County Council, the rate leviable for defraying the expenses of the Council under the Metropolitan

* *E.g.*, the Local Board of Ealing for the Ealing Commons, the Local Board of Staines for the Staines Common, and the Local Board of Tottenham for the Tottenham Commons. These bodies are now District Councils.

† *E.g.*, in the cases of Hayes Common, Barnes Common, the Mitcham Commons, Chislehurst Common, and the Banstead Commons. The conservators are constituted a quasi-corporation, with a common seal, and power to sue and be sued by their clerk.

‡ Metropolitan Commons Act, 1866, sec. 24.

§ *Ib.* sec. 25.

Management Acts; in the case of a Corporation or Urban District Council, the general district rate; and in the case of a Parish Council, the poor rate.*

Where, therefore, the local authority, as defined by the Act of 1866, is the managing body under a scheme, it can charge upon the rates all expenses of carrying out such scheme. But when a body of conservators, specially created, is the managing body, it must depend for the means of defraying such expenses upon voluntary subscriptions and donations, and upon contributions by the local authority, or by the London County Council under the special powers which we shall notice directly. In other words, it has no rating powers, but must depend upon the good will of the constituted authorities and of private donors.

The London County Council has exceptional powers of contributing towards the expense of carrying out schemes for the management of metropolitan commons. It may, in relation to any metropolitan common (although not one for which it is the local authority as defined by the Metropolitan Commons Act, 1866), contribute towards such expenses such amount as it thinks fit (in a gross sum or by annual payments or otherwise), and defray such expenses out of the rate leviable for defraying its general expenses.†

Thus, the County Council may, if it thinks fit, defray the expenses of a body of conservators managing a common wholly outside the County of London, or may join with any local board or vestry in defraying the expenses of managing such a common. Probably in such a case it would ask to have the right to appoint one or more members of the managing body. It is assumed that the board might provide for such an appointment in a scheme, or might, indeed, give

* Metropolitan Commons Act, 1866, sec. 26.

† *Ib.* secs. 25, 26.

the whole management of a common outside the County of London to the County Council.

Although it is the principle of the Metropolitan Commons Acts, that commons may be placed under local management without the acquisition by the managing body of the legal interest of the Lord of the Manor, or of any owner of the soil, or of any commoner, and even in spite of the opposition of the persons possessing such legal interests, still it is quite consistent with the Acts that the Lord of the Manor or a commoner should convey his interest to the managing body, and in many cases the interest of the lord has been thus conveyed.* That this is contemplated by the Act is shown by the provision,† that "where any estate, interest, or right in, over, or affecting a common is by deed conveyed for the purposes of a scheme under the Act, with the approval of the Commissioners (*i.e.* the Board of Agriculture), the provisions of the Act 'to restrain the disposition of lands, whereby the same became inalienable,' ‡ shall not apply to the conveyance."

The London County Council can also, in respect of any common within the County of London, purchase and hold, with a view to prevent the extinction of the rights of common, any saleable rights in common or any tenement of a commoner having annexed thereto rights of common.§ This power may be exercised irrespective of the management of the common under any scheme; but, united with the power of management, it may become exceptionally valuable.

* *E.g.*, in the case of Clapham Common and Tooting Beck Common.

† Metropolitan Commons Act, 1866, sec. 31.

‡ 9 Geo. II. c. 36, commonly called the Mortmain Act. The object of this Act was to prevent the accumulation of land in the hands of corporations.

§ Metropolitan Commons Act, 1878 (41 & 42 Vict. c. 71.), sec. 2. See *ante*, p. 83, as to this power in the case of District Councils.

Hitherto, as we have seen, it has not been the practice outside the County of London and the districts of urban authorities, to constitute the Vestry of a parish the managing body under schemes for the management of metropolitan commons. This has been due mainly to the fact that an open Vestry is an inconvenient executive body. Now, however, that Parish Councils of convenient size and definite powers have taken the place of Vestries, it may be anticipated, that in the case of such commons the Parish Council will in future naturally be appointed the managing body. It is assumed that in such case the Council will be able to charge on the poor rate the expenses of managing the common, irrespectively of the maximum rate of 6*d.* prescribed by the Local Government Act, 1894.*

Where metropolitan commons are already under the management of conservators, and it is desired to transfer the management to the Parish Council, this may be done by an amending scheme, certified by the Board of Agriculture † and confirmed by Parliament.

Although many commons within the Metropolitan Police District have been placed under local management (notably those within the County of London), there are still 3,355 acres of such commons not so dealt with. Particulars of these commons will be found in the report of the Commons Preservation Society for the years 1888–1892.‡ Amongst them are Epsom Downs and the other commons of Epsom, and the group of commons in the parish of Thames Ditton, close to the populous neighbourhood of Kingston and Surbiton.

* 56 & 57 Vict. c. 73; see sec. 11.

† Metropolitan Commons Act, 1866, sec. 27. Probably, also, a transfer might be made under sec. 14 of the Local Government Act, 1894.

‡ To be had on application to the secretary, 1, Great College Street, Westminster.

CHAPTER XXI.

Of the Regulation of Commons as Open Spaces.

II.—Under the Commons Act, 1876.

The Metropolitan Commons Act, 1866, as we have seen, prohibited the Parliamentary inclosure of commons within the Metropolitan Police District, and provided means for their regulation as open spaces, subject to the maintenance of all profitable and beneficial rights of the lord and commoners, and, consequently, without the consent of those persons. Ten years later Parliament legislated in the same direction with regard to the commons of the whole country outside the Metropolitan Police District; but it did not go so far.

The Commons Act, 1876,* does not prohibit inclosure at the instance of the Inclosure Commission (*i.e.* now the Board of Agriculture), but it declares "that it is desirable that inclosure in severalty as opposed to regulation of commons should not be hereafter made, unless it can be proved to the satisfaction of the Commissioners and of Parliament that such inclosure will be of benefit to the neighbourhood as well as to private interests, and to those who are legally interested in any such commons."

While thus declaring in favour of regulation, the Act does not, like the Metropolitan Commons Acts, enable regulation to be carried out without the consent of the parties legally

* 39 & 40 Vict. c. 56. This Act does not apply to metropolitan commons; see sec. 35.

interested.* On the contrary, it places regulation on precisely the same footing as inclosure in this respect. It requires the consent of persons representing two thirds in value of the legal interests in the common,† and gives the Lord of the Manor, in the case of a manorial common, a veto upon regulation.‡

This is the salient distinction between the two Acts. Metropolitan commons—commons within Greater London§—may be regulated as open spaces as a measure of police, subject to the maintenance *in statu quo* of all profitable and beneficial rights of the parties legally interested. Commons outside the Metropolitan Police District, or Greater London, can only be regulated as open spaces with the consent of the specified proportion of the parties legally interested, and especially with the consent of the Lord of the Manor in the case of a manorial common. Subject to these consents, the rights of the parties may be adjusted—that is, definitely ascertained—and, in some cases, extinguished on compensation.||

The Commons Act, 1876, declares that the Inclosure Commission (now the Board of Agriculture ¶) may entertain an application for a provisional order—

(1) for the regulation of a common, or

(2) for the inclosure of a common, or part of a common;

and further that an application may be made, as respects the same common, for the regulation of part, and the inclosure of the residue.** In the latter case, the application is dealt with, as respects such parts, as if they were separate commons, "with this exception, that the boundaries, as proposed

* Preamble; see also sec. 10 (4), 2nd par. † Sec. 12 (5).

‡ Sec. 12 (5). § See *ante*, p. 108. || Sec. 4.

¶ For convenience we shall refer to the Board of Agriculture throughout, as though they were mentioned in the Commons Act.

** Sec. 2. From this it would seem that an application may not relate to the regulation of part of a common, unless it also proposes the inclosure of the rest.

in the application, of the part to be regulated and the part to be inclosed may be modified by the provisional order."*

A provisional order for the regulation of a common may provide, generally or otherwise, and in the order, or through the machinery of subsequent proceedings, for the adjustment of rights in respect of the common, and for the improvement of the common, or for either of these purposes, or for any of the things by the Act comprised under the expression "adjustment of rights" or "improvement of a common."†

The adjustment of rights, as defined by the Act, comprises—

(1.) As regards a manorial common, or a common of that nature,‡ the determination of the persons entitled to rights of common, the regulation of the exercise of such rights, and the restriction, modification, or abolition of any of such rights (except common of pasture) which may permanently injure the common, upon compensation, by a grant of an equal right, or, with the consent in writing of the person affected, in money.

(2.) As regards other common land (*i.e.*, substantially, common fields, meadows, and pastures), the stinting or determination and regulation of the rights of common, and the restriction, modification, or abolition (on the same terms as in the case of a manorial common) of any of such rights which may be in-

* Sec. 2.

† Sec. 3.

‡ The words of the Act are "waste land of a manor," and that expression is defined as including—

(*a*) waste land of a manor on which the tenants of such manor have rights of common;

(*b*) any land subject to any rights of common which may be exercised at all times of the year for cattle levant and couchant, or to any rights of common which may be exercised at all times of the year, and are not limited by number or stints. (Sec. 37.)

jurious to the general body of the commoners or the proper cultivation of the land.

(3.) As regards any common, whether a manorial common or not, the determination of the rights and obligations of the persons legally interested in the soil (as distinguished from commoners), and the restriction, modification, or abolition (on the same terms as in the case of rights of common) of such rights.

(4.) Generally, as regards any common, the determination of any rights, and settlement of any disputes, between the parties legally interested, so as to conduce to the interests of all or any class of persons interested in the common.*

The improvement of a common, as defined by the Act, comprises—

(1.) Draining, manuring, or levelling.

(2.) Planting, or otherwise improving or adding to the beauty of the common.

(3.) The making of bye-laws for the prevention of nuisances and the preservation of order.

(4.) General management.

(5.) The appointment of conservators of the common for the above purposes.†

From the above provisions we see that the regulation of a common under the Commons Act, 1876, while comprising the same objects (under the name of an improvement) as regulation under the Metropolitan Commons Act, also extends to the regulation between themselves of the rights of the parties legally interested,—the owners of the soil and the commoners—but subject to these two provisos :—

(*a*) That no right of any kind can be taken away or injuriously affected without either the grant of a

* Sec. 4.

† Sec. 5.

right of equal value, or the consent of the owner; and

(*b*) That no right of common of pasture on a manorial common can be taken away or injuriously affected at all.

The procedure for the regulation of a common is the same, save where the object in view itself occasions differences, as that for the inclosure of a common. The description of the last-mentioned procedure contained in Chapter XIII. therefore applies, and we shall only in the following pages notice points which arise particularly in relation to regulation.

As in the case of inclosure, it is desirable, that any persons, or a local authority, contemplating the regulation of a common should communicate in the first instance informally with the Board of Agriculture. This informal communication is followed by advertisements and by notice to the local authorities,* and by an application, in the form specified by the Board, accompanied by a map of the common. In this application it must be stated whether the whole or only certain specified provisions of the Act are to be applied to the common, and whether to the whole of the common or to part.† Thus, in some cases, the adjustment of rights only, and that only on some particular point, may be applied for; while in others the object of the application may be to place the common under proper management, leaving all rights as they are. The application may, in fact, in the latter case, be assimilated to an application under the Metropolitan Commons Acts.

Throughout the proceedings applicants for regulation are in one respect in a different position from applicants for inclosure. As regulation is favoured, and inclosure discouraged, by the Commons Act, by the Board of Agriculture,

* See *post*, p. 246. † Sec. 10 (2).

and by Parliament, the burden of proof thrown on the applicants is much lighter.* Nevertheless, where the adjustment of rights is contemplated, and even in other cases, it will be necessary to prove, both generally in the initial application, and in detail at the meeting held by the Assistant Commissioner, that the proposal will benefit the public, and not injure the persons legally interested in the common. It is not beyond the ingenuity of man to devise a species of regulation which would, in its practical results, be equivalent to inclosure.† A local authority, and all persons interested in an open space, should therefore look very narrowly at any proposal for its regulation under the Commons Act, 1876.

We have seen that on an inclosure provisions of two kinds for the benefit of the public are made, viz.:—

(*a*) Allotments for recreation and for field gardens for the labouring poor; and

(*b*) "Statutory provisions for the benefit of the neighbourhood"—that is, provisions relating to the preservation of particular objects of interest, the setting out of roads, and other steps of a like character tending to preserve the amenities of the neighbourhood.

Upon the regulation of a common it is obviously unnecessary to set out an allotment for recreation, since the whole

* See sec. 10 (4), 2nd par.

† The writer remembers a case in which it was proposed, first to inclose, and then to regulate, a common in the neighbourhood of the New Forest. The Inclosure Commission, upon the written representation of opponents of the first proposal, considered that no *primâ facie* case was made out for inclosure. The substituted application for regulation they referred to an Assistant Commissioner, who held a local enquiry. At this enquiry it appeared that the main feature of the so-called regulation was the fencing off of the common from adjoining commons with which it lay in one tract. It was proved, that this step would inflict great injury upon the commoners of the whole district, and would, except as to a very small class, amount to an inclosure; the Commission therefore declined to proceed upon the application.

common will remain open as before; and it seems doubtful whether it is within the intention of the Act that the Board should provide for such an allotment in a provisional order for regulation.*

The Board is, however, expressly authorised to set out by their provisional order an allotment for field gardens if it should think fit.†

The insertion in the provisional order of the statutory provisions for the benefit of the neighbourhood,‡ so far as they are applicable to the case, is, however, equally obligatory upon the Board upon a regulation and upon an inclosure.§ Perhaps the most important of these provisions, in the case of regulation, is the reservation of "a privilege of playing games or enjoying other species of recreation" on the common or on specified parts thereof; and this privilege has usually been reserved in relation to the whole common in provisional orders for regulation made by the Board in recent years.‖

There are certain provisions relating to private interests which are of importance in cases of regulation. Where valuable mineral rights exist under a common, it is obvious, that their unrestrained exercise may be inconsistent with the good order of the common, while, on the other hand, it would be unfair to deprive the owner of the power of exercising such rights without compensation. The Commons Act, therefore, provides, that, when such rights are affected by a pro-

* See sec. 12 (2).

† Commons (Expenses) Act, 1878 (41 & 42 Vict. c. 56), sec. 4.

‡ Commons Act, 1876, sec. 7. § Sec. 12 (2).

‖ See, for example, the Provisional Orders set out in the Appendix, pp. 378, 382, for the regulation of High Road Well Moor, in the Borough of Halifax, and Bexhill Down, in the County of Sussex (House of Commons Papers, 1895, Nos. 255 and 256), confirmed by the Commons Regulation (Halifax) Provisional Order Confirmation Act, 1895, and the Commons Regulation (Bexhill), Provisional Order Confirmation Act, 1895.

visional order (whether for regulation or inclosure), proper provision (in accordance with the Inclosure Acts, 1845 to 1868) shall be made in relation to such rights.*

The question of expense in connection with the regulation of a common is one which requires to be dealt with. In the case of inclosure, it is the almost invariable practice to sell a portion of the common to pay the expenses of carrying out the inclosure; and, of course, subsequently to the inclosure there are no permanent expenses of a general nature to be provided for. In the case of regulation, not only have the expenses of obtaining the Provisional Order, Act of Parliament, and subsequent Award to be provided for, but also the expense of the future care and management of the common.

With regard to the costs of the Order and subsequent proceedings, the Board of Agriculture may insert in the Provisional Order a provision for the raising and payment of these expenses, either wholly or partly, by a sale of a portion of the common; but they must, in such case, specify in the Provisional Order the situation and maximum area to be sold.† The expenses will then be raised and paid in manner provided by the Inclosure Acts in the case of an inclosure.‡

The permanent expenses of management may be provided for in two ways, either (*a*) by a rate "to be levied on the persons and in respect of the property who and which respectively will be benefited, or principally benefited, by such improvement or regulation," or (*b*) "by the sale of any outlying or other small portion of the common, not exceeding in the whole one fortieth part of the total area."§ There seems

* Sec. 12 (3). See on this subject the Inclosure Act, 1845 (8 & 9 Vict. c. 118), secs. 76, 98, and amending provisions in subsequent Inclosure Acts.

† Commons (Expenses) Act, 1878 (41 & 42 Vict. c. 56.), sec. 2.

‡ Sec. 77.

§ Commons Act, 1876, sec. 14.

to be no reason why both these methods of defraying the permanent expenses of regulation should not be combined; and it is assumed that any casual profits of the common, such as fees for marking the commoners' cattle, or the proceeds of any wood or bushes cut in the due and husbandlike management of the common, may be also applied to pay such expenses. But it would probably be deemed to be contrary to the spirit of the Act to provide in a provisional order for the management of a common with a view to profit, where such management would impair the maintenance of the common as an open space.

When the provisional order of the Board contemplates the sale of any portion of the common to defray permanent expenses of management, the situation and maximum area to be sold must be specified in the order;* and the Board may also insert in the order a provision for the investment of the proceeds of the sale or any part of such proceeds, and for the application of the annual income towards the improvement or protection of the common, and for the sale of the investment or any part thereof from time to time, and the application of the proceeds of such sale towards such improvement or protection.†

Not infrequently the application for the regulation of a common comes from the local authority, and with the wide diffusion of effective local government now sanctioned, this may be expected to be still more often the case. In such cases—and even where it is not the initiating party—the local authority often charges itself with all the expenses of obtaining the order and of the permanent management of the common, and it is not necessary to resort to a rate on the

* Commons (Expenses) Act, 1878 (41 & 42 Vict. c. 56.), sec. 3.
† *Ib.*

parties interested, or to a sale of any part of the common, The powers of local authorities in relation to regulation are as follows:—

Every Urban District Council for a district of more than 5,000 inhabitants (such Councils we may call for convenience "large Urban District Councils") is entitled to notice of every application for the regulation of any common wholly or partly within its district or within six miles of the centre of its district.*

Every District Council, whether urban or rural, is entitled to notice of any application for the regulation of any common within its district,† and every Parish Council to notice of any application for the regulation of any common, any part of which is within its district.‡

Large Urban District Councils § and (with the consent of the County Council) small Urban District Councils and Rural District Councils || may, with the sanction of the Board of Agriculture,—

(*a*) "enter into an undertaking to contribute out of their funds for or towards the maintenance of recreation grounds, or of paths or roads, or the doing any other matter or thing for the benefit of their town or district in relation to the common to which the application relates;"

(*b*) "enter into an undertaking to pay compensation in respect to the rights of commoners for the purpose

---

* Commons Act, 1876, sec. 8, 1st par. See *ante*, p. 81, for mode of measurement. When part only of a common comes within the requisite distance, that part is to be considered a separate common in relation to the powers of the Urban Council (Commons Act, 1876, sec. 8, last par.).

† Local Government Act, 1894, sec. 26 (2).

‡ *Ib.* sec. 8 (4).

§ Commons Act, 1876, sec. 8.

|| Local Government Act, 1894, sec. 26 (2).

of securing greater privileges for the benefit of their town."*

These powers are of a somewhat limited and special character, but the second may sometimes be of use in combination with other powers.

Any District Council † may also, with the consent of persons representing at least one third in value of the interests in a common proposed to be affected by a provisional order, make an application to the Board of Agriculture for the regulation of the common with a view to the benefit of their town and the improvement of the common.‡

When a Council takes any one of the steps above mentioned, or "makes any other payment out of its funds in respect of a common," it may, "if the Board of Agriculture deem it advisable, having regard to the benefit of the neighbourhood as well as to private interests, be invested with such powers of management or other powers as may be expedient."§

All expenses incurred by an Urban Council in the execution of the powers thus specified may be defrayed out of any rate applicable to the payment of expenses incurred by such authority in the execution of the Public Health Act, 1875, and not otherwise provided for.‖

All similar expenses incurred by a Rural District Council will be defrayed in manner directed by the Public Health Act, 1875, with respect to expenses incurred in the execution of that Act by a rural sanitary authority.¶ The expenses

* Commons Act, 1876, sec. 8, 2nd and 3rd pars.

† In the case of a small Urban Council or a Rural Council, with the consent of the County Council.

‡ Commons Act, 1876, sec. 8, 6th par.

§ *Ib.* sec. 8, 7th par.

‖ *Ib.* sec. 8, 8th par., and see Local Government Act, 1894, sec. 28.

¶ Local Government Act, 1894, sec. 29.

incurred by a rural sanitary authority are divided into general and special expenses, and special expenses include "all expenses incurred or payable by the rural authority in or in respect of any contributory place within the district, and defined by the Local Government Board to be special expenses." It would seem, therefore, that the expenses of obtaining an order for regulation, and of managing a common under such order, would be special expenses, and would therefore be payable by the parish in which the common is situate. Where the common extends into two parishes in the same rural district, the Rural Council may apportion the expenses between the two.*

The Council of a county borough (*i.e.* a borough which is a county of itself) is entitled to exercise all the powers in relation to commons conferred upon District Councils by the Local Government Act, 1894.† Such a body, therefore, has all the powers conferred not only by the Commons Act, 1876,‡ but by the Local Government Act, 1894,§ if in any point the one Act gives larger powers than the other; and as it is itself a County Council, it can of course act under the second statute without obtaining the consent of any other County Council.

The powers of a Parish Council with respect to the initiation of proceedings for the regulation of a common are not very clear. The Local Government Act, 1894,‖ gives power to such a Council "to apply to the Board of Agriculture under sec. 9 of the Commons Act, 1876." But the section referred to relates merely to procedure, providing that the Board of Agriculture shall direct from time to time the mode in which applications for inclosure and regulation shall be made to them by the persons interested in the common. Possibly, however, it may be held that the words of the Act

* See Public Health Act, 1875 (38 & 39 Vict. c. 55.), secs. 229, 230.

† Sec. 26 (7). ‡ Sec. 8. § Sec. 26 (2). ‖ Sec. 8.

of 1894 are sufficient to empower a Parish Council to initiate proceedings for regulation, with the consent of persons representing one third in value of the legal interests in the common. It does not seem to be contemplated that a Parish Council should be entrusted by a provisional order with the management of a common under the Act of 1876; though we have seen that they may obtain such powers of management in relation to a metropolitan common under the Act of 1866.

Speaking generally, therefore, it would seem to be the result of present legislation, that in rural districts the District Council will be the local authority to manage a common, while the expenses will be charged upon the parish in which the common is situate. Where, however, it is not an object to throw the expense of management on the rates, a special board of conservators may be constituted with power to raise the expenses from the persons legally interested in the common.

The Commons Act provides that "the Board of Agriculture may insert in any provisional order for the regulation of a common any provisions they may deem necessary for the purpose of carrying such order into effect; but that, subject as aforesaid, when an Act of Parliament has been passed enacting that the regulation of a common shall be proceeded with, the subsequent proceedings for carrying into effect the regulation of the common shall be the same, so far as practicable, as they would be in case the common were to be enclosed instead of being regulated."*

We have already seen, generally,† the nature of the proceedings for inclosure subsequent to the confirmation of the provisional order of the Board of Agriculture by Parliament. The machinery consists in the appointment of a valuer, who works out in detail the directions of the order of

* Sec. 13.

† See *ante*, p. 123.

the Board, and makes an Award which is confirmed by the Board. The same machinery is applied to regulation; and in this respect, again, the Commons Act of 1876 differs from the Metropolitan Commons Act of 1866. Under the last mentioned Act, the Board makes a complete scheme for the management of the common, and this scheme when confirmed by Parliament immediately places the common under local management. Under the Act of 1876 the Order and Act of Parliament in themselves do nothing; effect must be given to them by an Award of a valuer confirmed by the Board of Agriculture. This machinery may be well adapted to the case where an elaborate adjustment of legal rights is proposed, but for the placing of a common under local management it is cumbrous and inappropriate. It would seem, however, that the Board may, if they choose, provide for management and for the general improvement of the common at once by their provisional order, since the opening words of the section just quoted are very wide.* Although in rural districts the adjustment of rights may sometimes be of importance, in the neighbourhood of towns the placing of a common under local management is usually the step most to be desired, and the machinery for so doing should be as simple and inexpensive as possible.

* The practice seems to be to make an Award in all cases. See the Provisional Orders for the Regulation of High Road Well Moor, and Bexhill Down, before mentioned, both of which have for their sole object the placing of the Commons under local management, and are of the simplest character.

PART II.

OF FOOTPATHS, AND OTHER RIGHTS OF WAY.

CHAPTER I.

Of the Nature of a Footpath.

A FOOTPATH is one variety of a public way or highway; and a highway has been defined to be "a passage which is open to all the Queen's subjects."*

There are three kinds of public way, a foot-way, a bridle-way, and a carriage or cart way.

A foot-way, or footpath, is a way for passage on foot only. A person riding or endeavouring to take a horse and cart along a footpath would be a trespasser.

A bridle-way is a way for men and horses, but not for wheeled vehicles. It is sometimes called a foot-way and horse-way, and, in early days, a "packe and prime way," because, Lord Coke tells us,† it is both a foot-way, which was the first or prime way, and a pack or drift way also. Before good roads became common in England,—and this was hardly the case before the beginning of this century,—a large amount of the carrying trade of the country was effected by means of pack-horses, and many of the oldest tracks are pack-horse ways. In modern times, however, such ways tend to develop into cart-ways, or to degenerate into footpaths.

A cart-way or carriage-way is, as the name implies, a way not only for foot passengers and horses, but for carts and carriages.

---

* 2 Smith's Leading Cases, 159.

† Co. Litt. 56*a*; and see as to the three kinds of highway per Holt, C.J., in Reg. *v.* Saintiff, 6 Mod. 255.

As a rule, every cart-way is also a bridle-way and footpath; and every bridle-way is also a footpath; the greater, so to speak, includes the less.*

A footpath, then, is a highway for passengers on foot. Every subject of the Queen, every member of the community, has an equal right to use such a path; and no one person or class of persons can have a better right to use it than another. So absolute is this legal doctrine, that if it be proved that a certain class of persons, *e.g.* the inhabitants of a parish, have used a path, while other persons have been turned back or forbidden, the conclusion is drawn, that the path is not a public way. Even if it be proved that the owner intended to give, or, to use the legal phrase, to dedicate, a path or other way to a limited class of persons, it is held that the intended gift or dedication is void and of no effect, and that there has been no dedication at all.† The only dedication of a highway possible is that of a way open to all alike, and this will not be inferred from any evidence of an intention to effect a partial dedication.

In this respect the right to a footpath (or to any other kind of highway) differs radically from the rights of common and rights of recreation of which we have treated in the earlier part of this work. For whereas rights of common and rights of recreation cannot be claimed by the public at large, but only by specific persons or classes of persons, highways, on the other hand, can only be claimed by the public, and cannot be enjoyed by any one section of the public as distinguished from others.

* See, *e.g.*, per Lord Denman in Davies *v.* Stephen, 7 C. & P. 570. The case of a towing-path is an exception to this rule; such a path may be a way for towing only, and not a footpath. See per Bayley, J., in Rex *v.* Severn and Wye Railway Co., 2 B. & Ald. 648; Winch *v.* Conservators of Thames, L.R. 7 C.P. 471.

† Poole *v.* Huskinson, 11 M. & W. 827; Vestry of Bermondsey *v.* Brown, L.R. 1 Eq. 204, 215.

There may, indeed, be a private right of way, which is to some extent analogous, in law, to a right of common; but this is essentially different in its nature from a public footpath or any other kind of highway.

The owner (A) of a house or field may have a right to pass over the land of another man (B), in order to reach his (A's) property. This is a right or easement attached to the house or field of A, and belongs to the successive owners and occupiers of that house or field, and to them alone. It may, like a right of common, have its origin in an express grant by B or his predecessors in title, or in user extending over a long series of years, and thus raising the presumption of a grant. It is a piece of private property, in which the public have no interest.*

One species of private way is very common in rural districts, viz., cart-ways, known as "occupation roads." These roads sometimes pass merely from field to field of the same owner, and in this case no separate right of way exists at all. In other cases they pass over the land of one owner to reach the land of another; and here they are examples of those private rights of way which we have just mentioned. In neither case have the public any right of way over them.

But it may be, and very often is, the case, that along a private occupation road there is a public footpath. The public have no right to use the way with carts, or even

* It is true that rights of common which are also, viewed individually, rights of property, are nevertheless of great importance to the public. This arises from the fact, that they are mostly owned by many persons or classes of persons, and exercised over a wide tract of land, which in effect they preserve as an open space accessible to the public. Private rights of way, on the other hand, are usually enjoyed, not by classes of persons, but by the owner of a particular house or piece of land, while at the same time it is perfectly easy to restrict the enjoyment of the right (as by locked gates or bars) to the persons entitled to it. As a rule, therefore, a private right of way is of no practical use to the public; and even if by permission the public use a private road for a time, it can be easily shut against them.

horses; for such purposes the road is only used to give access to a particular farm. But on foot they have a right to traverse the road from end to end. In these cases there is very often a stile by the side of the farm gate which gives access from field to field.

When a public footpath passes along a private occupation road, the road may, so far as the public are concerned, be stopped at any time; but in that case sufficient facilities for the use of the way by the public on foot must be left.

The right of the public in relation to a footpath (or any other kind of highway) is the right to pass over the soil, not to use it in any other way.* Subject to the right of passage, the owner of the soil retains all his interest in it, and is entitled by virtue of his occupation to bring an action of trespass against any member of the public who does more than pass over the land in accordance with the right of way claimed. For example, riding along a footpath, or digging up the soil of a public way, or damaging trees or shrubs adjoining a footpath, or even standing and loitering upon a way to the annoyance of the owner of the soil, and in such a manner as to indicate some other intention than that of using the way to go from point to point, would render the person committing the act liable to an action of trespass.

A footpath can be created only in one of two ways:—

(*a*) by Act of Parliament;

(*b*) by the dedication, express or presumed, by the owner of the land of a right of passage over it to the public at large.†

* See the observations of the Judges in Reg. *v.* Pratt, 4 E. & B. 860, where a conviction for trespassing on a road in search of game was upheld. See also the reasoning of the Court in Dovaston *v* Payne, 2 H:Bl. 527.

† See per Parke, B., in Poole *v.* Huskinson, 11 M. & W. 830; and see a clear statement of the general law by Wills, J., in Eyre *v.* the New Forest Highway Board, 56 J. P. 517.

The creation of footpaths and other highways by Act of Parliament is by no means unusual.

Upon the inclosure of a common by Parliamentary sanction,* public roads are almost invariably set out, and sometimes footpaths. The particulars of such ways are to be found in the Awards made by special commissioners or valuers under the Inclosure Acts; and these Awards, or copies, are usually to be found with the Clerk of the Peace for the county and the churchwardens of the parish (in future the Clerk to the Parish Council).† Again, the private Acts of railway companies often throw upon a company the duty of making new footpaths and other highways, generally in substitution for old highways stopped up. In former times Turnpike Acts and Acts of that nature authorised the construction of new roads, or gave Parliamentary recognition to old ones; ‡ and in towns new streets are constantly being made under special Acts of Parliament.

But the highways of the country, and particularly the footpaths, have, as a rule, originated not in Acts of Parliament, but in dedication by the owner of the soil. And most of the questions which arise in relation to footpaths turn upon the circumstances under which dedication will be presumed, and the results which flow from a presumed dedication. In the common case, for example, where a path, which has been open to the public for some time, is blocked up, the legality or illegality of the obstruction

* See *ante*, Part I., Chap. XIII.

† Inclosure Act, 1845 (8 & 9 Vict. c. 118.) sec. 146; Local Government Act, 1894 (56 & 57 Vict. c. 73.), secs. 6 (1) (*b*) and 17 (7) and (8).

‡ See for example the Acts authorising the Finchley Road and the long road known, in different sections, as the New Road, the Euston Road, and the Marylebone Road.

depends, in the last resort, upon the question whether such circumstances can be shown as will establish the inference of "a dedication to the public of the occupation of the surface of the land for the purpose of passing and repassing."*

With the rules of law relating to dedication we shall deal more at length in treating of the obstruction of footpaths.

As a footpath (or other highway) can only originate, so also it can only be destroyed, in one of two methods, either—

(*a*) by Act of Parliament, or

(*b*) by an Order of Justices, enrolled in Quarter Sessions, pursuant to the provisions of the Highway Acts.†

A footpath once existing cannot be lost by mere non-user; "once a highway always a highway" is an established maxim of law.‡

* Lord Cairns' definition of a highway; see Rangeley *v.* the Midland Railway Company, L.R. 3 Ch. App. 311.

† A highway may be extinguished by the destruction of the land over which it passes; and a way may cease to be a highway where access to it at either end has become impossible by means of the legal stoppage of ways leading to it (Baily *v.* Jamieson, 1876, 1 C. P. Div. 329). But these cases scarcely qualify the general proposition of law we have laid down.

There is also an old process for the stopping of a footpath by licence of the Crown, granted after an inquiry by the sheriff and a jury, held pursuant to a writ of "*ad quod damnum*" issued by the Court of Chancery. But this process is now absolutely disused, having been superseded by the proceedings under the Highway Acts.

‡ See per Byles, J., in Dawes *v.* Hawkins, 29 L.J. C.P. 347, and in Gerring *v.* Barfield, 16 C.B. (N.S.) 603. See also per Gibbs, J., in Rex *v.* St. James's, Taunton, quoted in Selwyn's "Law of Nisi Prius," 1264; and per Cockburn, C.J., in Berridge *v.* Ward, 2 F. & F. 212; and see the remarkable case of Reg. *v.* Edwards, before Williams, J., at the Wilts Summer Assizes, 1847, 11 J.P. 602, where encroachments on a highway eighty feet wide, proved to have existed for forty years and upwards, were held to constitute an indictable nuisance. See also Young *v.* Cuthbertson, 1 Macq. 455. In Queen *v.* Lordsmere, 19 L.J. (N.S.), Mag. Cas. 220, Lord Campbell, C.J., said: "Dedication amounts to an irrevocable licence granted to the public, who are to have the right of travelling along the road at their free will and pleasure."

Private Acts of Parliament authorising the construction of works not infrequently empower the promoters of such works to close or stop up footpaths and other public ways. All such Acts of Parliament are preceded (in the month of November) by notices in the local papers describing the provisions which it is proposed to ask Parliament to sanction, and several weeks before Parliament assembles (towards the end of December) the Bill which it is sought to pass into an Act is deposited in the Private Bill Office of each House of Parliament. The Bill, a print of which may easily be obtained, sets out in detail the footpaths and other public rights of way which it is proposed to stop up or divert. The road authority of the district, that is, in future the District Council, has a right to petition against the Bill, and to be heard by counsel or agents and witnesses before the Select Committee of each House to which the Bill is referred. Probably, also, the Parish Council, looking at the position with respect to public ways, and especially to footpaths, assigned to it by the Local Government Act, 1894, would be entitled to be similarly heard. And, apart from opposition of this character, the Bill may be opposed on second reading in the House of Commons, through the Member for the Division or any Member interested in public rights. If proper vigilance is exercised, therefore, no public ways of importance should be stopped, without at least a full discussion in Parliament.* But vigilance is necessary, for there is no doubt that in past times railway companies have destroyed many valuable footpaths and other public ways without giving any adequate equiva-

* The Commons Preservation Society (Secretary, E. W. Fithian, Esq.), 1, Great College Street, Westminster, would probably in most cases be able to render valuable advice and assistance.

lent, merely because no one took action to protect the public.*

Public ways can only be stopped up by an Order of Justices, enrolled in Quarter Sessions, on the ground that they are unnecessary; † and no such stoppage can take place without the consent of the Parish Council, and full notice to the inhabitants of the parish, who have a veto on the stoppage.‡ The consent of the District Council is also necessary.§ Public ways may also be diverted by similar procedure, and sometimes the diversion is equivalent to a stopping up. In this case the ground of diversion must be, that the new way is nearer or more commodious to the public than the old one.‖ The Parish Council, the Parish Meeting, and the District Council are, by the recent Act,¶ placed in the same position with respect to the diversion as with respect to the stopping up of a public way.

The exact procedure in case of stopping up and diversion, and the considerations which arise, will be dealt with subsequently.

* By the Railways Clauses Consolidation Act, 1845 (8 & 9 Vict. c. 20.), sec. 46, if a railway crosses any public highway (except where otherwise provided by the special Act), the road must be carried over the railway, or the railway over the road, by a bridge, unless it is otherwise ordered by two Justices. The company must give fourteen days' public notice by advertisement of their intention to apply to the Justices for leave to cross a bridle-way or foot-way on the level, and an appeal lies from the Justices to Quarter Sessions (secs. 59 & 60). When a bridle-way or foot-way is crossed on the level, the company must maintain convenient ascents, descents, and approaches, with hand-rails, or other fences, and good and sufficient gates or stiles (sec. 61); and the Justices in Petty Sessions may make an order on the company to provide such accommodation under penalties (sec. 62).

† Highway Act, 1835 (5 & 6 Will. IV. c. 50.), sec. 84.

‡ Local Government Act, 1894, sec. 13 (1).

§ *Ibid.*

‖ Highway Act, 1835, sec. 84.

¶ Local Government Act, 1894, sec. 13 (1).

CHAPTER II.

Of the Obstruction of Footpaths; and herein, of their Dedication.

WE have seen from the foregoing remarks that a public footpath, once existing, cannot be lost through disuse, or through the obstruction of the owners of the land over which it passes.

Nevertheless, in rural districts, it is not uncommon to find a path, obviously more or less used, but obstructed by locked gates, barricaded stiles, or other similar impediments; while it is yet more common to see by the side of a path a notice to the following effect—" No thoroughfare. Trespassers will be prosecuted."

It is desirable, then, to consider in some detail the questions which arise under such circumstances.

As the obstruction of a footpath is unquestionably illegal, if it be once admitted, or proved, that a public right of way along it ever existed, where the owner of the soil blocks a footpath, or forbids its use, he must defend his act, on the ground, not that the footpath has fallen into disuse, or been otherwise destroyed, but that no legal footpath ever existed.

In reply to this challenge it must be proved on behalf of the public, either that an Act of Parliament has created the footpath, or that the circumstances are such as to show, that there must at some time have been an intention on the part of the owner of the soil to dedicate the footpath to the public.

Footpaths created by Act of Parliament are exceptional, and it is not often that they are obstructed. When, however, the footpath or other track obstructed passes over land formerly common, but inclosed by Act of Parliament, the Inclosure Act and Award should always be examined. A map is usually attached to the Award, which is to be found, as a rule, in the office of the Clerk of the Peace for the county, and with the churchwardens of the parish, or the Clerk to the Parish Council.* If the path be set out by the Award as a public path, there can be no further question on the subject.

In ordinary cases, however, the question turns upon evidence of dedication by the owner of the land over which the path passes.

Now, it is important to bear in mind, that what it is necessary to prove is not any actual grant of the path to the public, but an intention on the part of the owner of the soil, that the public should have a right of way over his land. "In order to constitute a valid dedication to the public of a highway by the owner of the soil, it is clearly settled, that there must be an *intention* to dedicate—there must be an *animus dedicandi*, of which the user by the public is *evidence*, and no more."† This intention may be shown by overt acts on the part of the owner, and in such cases there may be an immediate dedication of the way. Thus, it has been judicially declared, that "if a man builds a double row of houses opening into an ancient street at each end, making a street, and sells or lets the houses, that is instantly a highway."‡ Acts of this sort may even, it has been said, prevail over a contemporaneous declaration to the opposite

* Inclosure Act, 1845 (8 & 9 Vict. c. 118.), sec. 146; Local Government Act, 1894 (56 & 57 Vict. c. 73.), secs. 6 (1) (*b*), and 17 (7) and (8).

† Per Parke, B., in Poole *v.* Huskinson, 11 M. & W. 830; and see Lord Campbell's definition of dedication in note ‡ on p. 258 *ante*.

‡ Per Chambre, J., in Woodyer *v.* Hadden, 5 Taunt. 124. See also per Lord Ellenborough in Rex. *v.* Lloyd, 1 Campb. 262, quoted *post*, p. 301.

effect.* But, as a rule, and especially in the case of footpaths, no evidence of any actual intention is forthcoming. In such cases an intention to dedicate the path is presumed from the actual use of it by the public; and it is a question of fact, to be determined by the jury before whom the case is tried, whether this use and other circumstances prove a dedication.

Evidence of the repair of a way by a public authority is the strongest kind of evidence which can be produced; but such evidence in the case of disputed footpaths is very rare. Isolated acts of repair at long intervals may occasionally be found, and are very valuable.

But, as a rule, the evidence of dedication in the case of a disputed footpath must turn upon its use and enjoyment by the public. If free and uninterrupted use by the public for a considerable period can be shown, this, it has been held, is such strong evidence of an intention on the part of the owner of the soil to dedicate, that dedication ought to be found as a fact, unless there is evidence that such dedication is impossible. In such a case it has been said by a learned judge, "We ought not to enquire very nicely into the ownership of the soil or into the evidence of any precise intention to dedicate." †

On the other hand, there is no rule, as is often supposed, that twenty years' user, or user for any other defined period, in itself establishes a public right of way. In some cases a very short enjoyment of the path, if under circumstances

* Per Littledale, J., in Barraclough *v.* Johnson, 8 A. & E. 105; in this case, however, a cotemporaneous agreement and the acts consequent upon it were held to override mere user by the public and to negative a dedication.

† Reg. *v.* East Mark, 11 Q.B. 877, 882. In this case the road in question was set out as a *private* road on an inclosure, but it was held that 50 years uninterrupted user by the public established a public right of way over it. See also similar circumstances in Rex *v.* Wright, 3 B. & Ad. 681.

which make it difficult to account for the user on any other supposition than an intention to dedicate on the part of the owner, will establish the public right. In other cases a comparatively long user may be explained consistently with an absence of any dedication, and may fail to establish a footpath. As much depends on the character of the user as on its duration. If it has been confined to few persons, and those mostly connected with the occupation of the land over which the path passes, or to which it leads, and if persons have from time to time been turned back by the owner of the soil, or bars have been erected, though not continually maintained,* even though the path may have been used for some years, it may be held to be no highway. The existence of stiles, swing-gates, or other arrangements to facilitate the use of a path by the public, is, in the absence of special explanation, an important piece of evidence in favour of the right of the public. For a stile, or swing-gate without a lock, indicates that the owner of the soil has taken steps to assist, not any particular class of persons (such as might be supplied with keys), but all persons who may wish to use the path, in passing over the hedges and fences which would otherwise form obstacles in the way. On the other hand, farm-gates across an occupation road, along which the public claim a way on foot, do not assist the claim, since they are necessary for the passage of the carts of the owner of the soil from field to field.

While, however, length of user is not the only consideration in determining whether the public have a right to a disputed footpath, it is a consideration of the utmost importance. For, it must be remembered, a footpath cannot in the view of the law be gained by adverse use, *i.e.* use against the

* See cases quoted in note to Rex. *v.* Lloyd, 1 Campb. 260.

wish of the owner of the soil. On the contrary, it must be possible to draw the inference, or, in legal phrase, the presumption must be raised, that at some time or other the owner intended that the public should have free passage over his land. Now, if the user of the path can be carried back indefinitely, so that no point of time can be cited at which there was certainly no path, then there is a wide scope for the act of dedication. It may have taken place at any time since landowners existed in England. But if the user can only be shown for a comparatively short period, and there is no evidence of the existence of a path before that period, then the dedication must have taken place within that period, and evidence of interruption or adverse acts on the part of the owner of the soil may be held sufficient to show, that during the time of user he did not intend to give the public any right of way.

Where use of a path by the public of any considerable age is shown, the inference of dedication thus raised has been held to prevail over a subsequent obstruction of many years, complained of but not removed.*

And, speaking generally, long user will prove a public right over a path, unless facts can be proved incompatible with a dedication.†

Moreover, it is not necessary, in claiming a footpath at law, to state the points from and to which the way leads, or when it became a highway.‡

User of the way claimed being shown, it then rests upon the person who has obstructed the path to show, that this

* Reg. *v.* Petrie, 4 E. & B. 737.

† Same case, and Reg. *v.* East Mark, 11 Q.B. 877; see also Young *v.* Cuthbertson, 1 Macq. 455.

‡ Rouse *v.* Bardin, 1 Hy. Bl. 351; Aspinall *v.* Brown, 3 T.R. 265; and see the point mentioned in Davies *v.* Stephen, 7 C. & P. 570.

user is not of a character to give rise to the presumption of a dedication; in other words, he must rebut the presumption.

This he can do by proving interruption of the user, as, for example, by the turning back of persons attempting to use the path, or by previous obstructions of the path for some time, acquiesced in by the public. Even if the obstruction finally removed or complained of has been allowed to exist for some time, it would afford some, though by no means conclusive, evidence of the absence of a public right. On the other hand, an unsuccessful attempt to turn back the public or to obstruct the path, though it would show that at the particular time the then owner had no intention to dedicate, would be no evidence against a former dedication, but would tend to strengthen the presumption, that there had been such a dedication.

It has been held, that the character of the place over which the path is claimed may be used as evidence against the probability of any dedication of a highway. Thus, where mere tracks varying from time to time and impassable in bad weather run over open land, such as a common or the waste of a forest, where persons can roam as they like, user of such tracks has been held not to prove a highway.* It is not of course to be assumed from this, that a footpath cannot be established across a common; † but in such cases abundant and definite user, and that from point to point, and not by way of mere roaming, must be shown.

Again, the presumption of a dedication may be rebutted by proof, that during the whole time of the use of the path the land has never been in the hands of any owner who had power to dedicate.‡ Much-used paths have occasionally

* Chapman *v*, Cripps, 2 F. & F. 864; Schwinge *v*. Dowell, 2 F. & F. 845.

† See on this point, Rex *v*. Marquis of Downshire, 4 A. & E. 720.

‡ Reg. *v*. Petrie, 4 E. & B. 737.

been lost through this doctrine. Where land is in settlement, so that the owner for the time being has only an estate for life or in tail, such owner has no power to dedicate a footpath or other right of way to the public, since he has himself only a limited interest in the land and cannot prejudice his successor.* Consequently, if it can be conclusively proved, that as far back as the evidence of the use of the path extends, the land over which it passes has been in the possession of limited owners, then, in order to establish a highway, some prior dedication must be relied on. There is no reason, however, why such a dedication should not be presumed, if the evidence goes to prove an ancient path.

In such a case the persons disputing the path must prove from abstracts of the title to the land that a dedication was at no time possible.† The burden of so proving rests upon them, and must be strictly discharged.

Thus, in one of the leading cases on this subject, the public had freely used a road between 1828 and 1836; in that year the road was blocked, and though complaints were made, the obstruction was not removed; the case was tried in 1855. There was evidence of such a state of title as made dedication impossible during considerable periods, but this evidence did not cover the whole time between 1828 and 1836. It was held that the use of the road between the years in question raised a presumption of dedication, and that, when this is once done, the onus lies on the person who seeks to deny the inference from such user to show negatively, that the state of the title was such, that dedication was impossible, and that no one capable of dedicating existed.‡

* There is a statutory exemption to this rule in the case of roads and ways laid out by a tenant for life, in connection with the development of a building estate, Settled Land Act, 1882, ss. 16, 21, 25.

† Reg. *v.* Petrie, 4 E. & B. 737; Powers *v.* Bathurst, 49 L.J. Ch. 294.

‡ Reg. *v.* Petrie, *ubi supra.*

The fact that the land over which a footpath is claimed belongs to the Crown, does not rebut the presumption of a dedication, as the Crown may dedicate a way.*

So also trustees, or a corporation, may dedicate, if the dedication is not incompatible with the purpose for which the land is vested in them.†

On the other hand, a copyholder cannot dedicate a way over his land without the consent of the Lord of the Manor. But this consent will be presumed where the user extends over a long period.‡

It follows, also, that a tenant for life,§ or a mere lessee, or tenant, of land for a term of years‖ cannot dedicate without the consent of his landlord. Nevertheless, when land has been let to successive tenants, and uninterrupted use of the footpath is shown during the successive tenancies, a dedication will be presumed.¶ And when the use of the path goes back as far as living memory will extend—say sixty or seventy years—even though the land has been in lease all the time, the Court will presume an anterior dedication.**

No formal acceptance of a right of way on the part of the public is necessary to constitute the public right, or to throw the burden of repair upon the parish. The mere user of the way shows acceptance.†† And a way may (since the passing of the Highway Act, 1835 ‡‡) be dedicated to the public,

* Turner *v.* Walsh, 6 App. Cas. 636 ; and see Harper *v.* Charlesworth, 4 B. & C. 574, where it is inferentially recognised, that the Crown can dedicate.

† Rex *v.* Leake, 5 B. & Ad. 469 ; Grand Junction Canal Co. *v.* Petty, 21 Q.B. Div. 273.

‡ Powers *v.* Bathurst, 49 L.J. Ch. 294.

§ Eyre *v.* New Forest Highway Board, 56 J.P. 517.

‖ Wood *v.* Veal, 5 B. & A. 454.

¶ Rex *v.* Barr, 4 Campb. 16.

** Winterbotham *v.* Lord Derby, L.R. 2 Exch. 316 ; see also Davies *v.* Stephens, 7 C. & P. 570.

†† Rex *v.* Leake, 5 B. & Ad. 469.

‡‡ 5 & 6 Will. IV. c. 50.

although no notice of dedication under sec. 23 has been given, and although the way has not been made up, and the highway authority is consequently not bound to repair it.*

We have already stated † that it is of the essence of every kind of highway, from a footpath to a main county road, that it should be open to the use of all Her Majesty's subjects alike. There cannot be a dedication of a footpath to part only of the public; any such dedication, even if it appears to have been intended, is void.‡ Consequently, proof that only a certain class of persons, as the inhabitants of a particular village or parish, have used a way, is proof that the way is not a public way.

But, though there can be no dedication to a part only of the public, conditions of many kinds may be attached to a dedication, or, in other words, a footpath or other highway may be dedicated subject to conditions.§ Thus, to take an instance of constant occurrence, a footpath may be dedicated subject to the right of the owner of the soil to plough it up in the regular course of cultivation.|| As such a right can only exist as a condition of the original dedication of the path, it follows that, to establish such a right, the evidence must show that the path has been ploughed up as long as it has existed; a path which had been used for many years without any such interruption cannot lawfully be ploughed up for the first time.¶ When, therefore, any such new ploughing takes place, steps should at once be taken to prevent such an obstruction of the way.

---

* Roberts *v.* Hunt, 15 Q.B. 17.

† *Ante*, p. 254.

‡ Poole *v.* Huskinson, 11 M. & W. 827; Vestry of Bermondsey *v.* Brown, L.R. 1 Eq. 204, 215.

§ Fisher *v.* Prowse, 2 B. & S. 770; Mercer *v.* Woodgate L.R. 5 Q.B. 26, 31.

|| Mercer *v.* Woodgate; Arnold *v.* Blaker, L.R. 6 Q.B. 433.

¶ Harrison *v.* Danby, 34 J.P. 759.

In like manner a highway may exist subject to the right to put up gates across it to prevent cattle straying.* In the case of a footpath, gates and stiles between field and field are a matter of course. Nevertheless, it has been held that the owner of the soil has no right to put up a new gate where there was none before, or to replace a stile by a more difficult one. For instance, it was held illegal to remove a stone stile two feet high and to put up a high five-barred gate with a step on it;† and the existence of gates in other places was held to afford no justification of such an act.‡

Another case of a footpath dedicated subject to conditions is that of a towing-path. It has been held, that a footpath along a towing-path must be enjoyed subject to the main use of the path for towing, so that a foot passenger must protect himself from any risk arising from the towing.§

So, also, a highway may be enjoyed subject to the existence of locks,|| or of steps projecting into the way in certain places, or of low bridges over the way, or of water inconveniently near to the highway (as in a tidal ditch).

Further, a highway may be dedicated for use at certain times only. For instance, a bridge which was used for carriages only in times of floods and frosts, when an adjacent

* Davies *v.* Stephens, 7 C. & P. 570. Note, that in Davies *v.* Stephens the gate was sometimes locked; but this fact does not seem to have been considered by Lord Denman as fatal even to a public carriage-way.

† Bateman *v.* Burge, 6 C. & P. 391.

‡ Same case, per Parke, J. The remarks of Lord Hatherley in Orr-Ewing *v.* Colquhoun, 2 App. Cas. 846, do not seem to be consistent with this decision, but his Lordship's remarks were made only by way of illustration, and were probably more in accordance with Scotch law. See same Case, 871.

§ Grand Junction Canal Co. *v.* Petty, L.R. 21 Q.B. Div. 273, 276. It is not every towing-path which is a public footpath.

|| See Davies *v.* Stephens, *ubi. sup.*

ford used in ordinary weather became dangerous, was held to be a highway.*

Hence, evidence of the qualification, so to speak, of the right of the public, by the existence of any such acts or circumstances as we have indicated, does not rebut the inference of dedication from the use of a path by the public, or prevent the existence of a public right of way along the path.

It is also important to bear in mind that, if part of a road or path has been legally closed, as by an Inclosure Act, a Railway Act, or some other Act of Parliament, so that the remainder becomes a cul-de-sac, the public right over the remainder is not destroyed.†

Such are the principal rules relating to the circumstances under which a highway may be dedicated. The evidence of the enjoyment of the way by the public which is put forward to vindicate the public right against an obstruction must be consistent with these rules.

Assuming a public path to exist, not only is it illegal to block all passage by it, but also to render its use in any way less convenient. Thus, as we have seen, ploughing up a path which has never been ploughed before is an illegal obstruction; ‡ and the substitution of less, for more, convenient gates.§ So any act by which a path is thrown into disorder, such as digging holes in it, or placing manure or rubbish upon it, is an obstruction.

Indeed, it has been held in a series of cases, that any unreasonable use of a highway, though not amounting to

---

* Reg. *v.* Northants, 2 M. & S. 262; Rex *v.* Marquis of Buckingham, 4 Campb. 189.

† Reg. *v.* Downshire, 4 A. & E. 698, and see especially per Patteson, J., 713; Gwyn *v.* Hardwicke, 25 L J. Mag. Cas. 97, 99; Reg. *v.* Burney, 31 L.T. 828.

‡ Harrison *v.* Danby, 34 J.P. 759.

§ Bateman *v.* Burge, 6 C. & P. 391.

a permanent obstruction, is an indictable nuisance, and cannot be legalized by lapse of time. Thus it is unlawful for stage coaches to stand in the public street for an unreasonable time to collect passengers ("the King's highway is not to be turned into a stable-yard" *), for a timber merchant to cut up logs of timber on the street adjoining his timber yard, for a farmer of adjoining land to leave an agricultural implement on the side of a highway so as to terrify horses, and for the lessee of a theatre to collect a crowd in a highway in connection with his entertainment.†

The late Sir Geo. Jessel (Master of the Rolls), in a Case relating to the use of two contiguous wharves on a river, explained, with his usual perspicuity, the conditions under which a highway may be reasonably used by the owners of the premises abutting upon it. For example, in the case of two adjoining houses, the occupier of each has a right to draw up at his own door, even though his carriage may temporarily stand in front of his neighbour's door. But he must make way for his neighbour if necessary; and there must be no systematic obstruction of the thoroughfare, so as to incommode a neighbour or the public.‡

* Per Lord Ellenborough, Rex. *v.* Cross, 3 Campb. 224.

† Rex *v.* Cross, 3 Campb. 224; Rex. *v.* Jones, 3 Campb. 230; Harris *v.* Mobbs 3 Ex. Div. 268; Wilkins *v.* Day, 12 Q.B. Div. 110; Barber *v.* Penley (1893), 2 Ch. 447. In the last-mentioned case Mr. Justice North reviews the earlier decisions.

‡ Original Hartlepool Collieries Co. *v.* Gibb (1877), 5 Ch. Div. 713.

CHAPTER III.

Of the Remedies for the Obstruction of Footpaths.

THE obstruction of a public footpath is a public nuisance,* and the author of the obstruction may be indicted for a misdemeanour at the Assizes or Quarter Sessions, and punished by fine or imprisonment, or both. No length of time will legalize a nuisance.† Therefore, upon such an indictment, the only defence of the person obstructing a path must be that the path is not a public path, and the only question to be tried will be, whether or not the path is a highway. This question will be tried by a jury.

It will thus be seen that the obstruction of a public way is a criminal offence.‡

Another course of action in the case of an obstructed footpath is to remove the obstruction, and leave the landowner who disputes the path to bring an action of trespass. The defence to such an action will be, that there is a public right of way along the path, and the question of the public right will be tried by a jury.

If this course be taken, however, great care must be observed not to remove more of the obstruction than is necessary to enable the persons using the path to pass by. For it is now clearly established law, that a private person

* 2 Rolle's Abr. 137; 1 Hawkins' Pleas of the Crown, 700.

† See the remarks of Lord Ellenborough in Rex *v.* Cross, 3 Campb. 224; and see Reg. *v.* Edwards, 11 J.P. 602.

‡ It is a practical drawback to this method of proceeding in respect of an obstruction that costs are not (save in certain special cases) awarded to the successful party.

has no right to abate a public nuisance, except so far as he sustains special damage by reason of it. If he is using the path and finds an obstruction he is specially damaged, and may thereupon remove the obstruction so far as is necessary to let him pass, but he has no right to go further, and to constitute himself the officer of the public to put down with his own hand what is a crime against good order and the public welfare.*

The law on the subject is thus clearly laid down by the Court of Queen's Bench :—" It is very important for the sake of the public peace, and to prevent oppression even on wrong-doers, not to confound common with private nuisances in this respect [*i.e.* in relation to the mode in which they may be lawfully abated]. In the case of the latter the individual aggrieved may abate (3 Blackstone's Commentaries, 5) so as he commits no riot in doing it; and a public nuisance becomes a private one to him who is specially and in some particular way inconvenienced thereby, as in the case of a gate across a highway which prevents a traveller from passing, and which he may therefore throw down; but the ordinary remedy for a public nuisance is, itself public, that of indictment; and each individual who is only injured as one of the public can no more proceed to abate than he can bring an action."†

In one decided case it was held, that when the back entrance of a house was in a public court, which was a cul-de-sac, and owing to an obstruction in this court the access to the house from it was interfered with, the owner of the house was, nevertheless, guilty of a trespass in throwing

* Arnold *v.* Holbrook, L.R. 8 Q.B. 96; Mayor of Colchester *v.* Brooke, 7 Q.B. 339, 377; Dimes *v.* Petley, 15 Q.B. 276, 283. Some of these cases relate to the navigation of a river; but the principle involved is the same, a navigable river being a highway.

† Mayor, &c. of Colchester *v.* Brooke, 7 Q.B. 377.

down the obstruction, because he did not allege in his pleadings that the removal of the obstruction was necessary to enable him to reach his house by the back entrance.*

Great care, therefore, must be taken to remove no more of an obstruction than is necessary to enable the footpath to be used, and to remove the obstruction for the purpose of using the footpath. But, assuming these precautions to be observed, the removal of an obstruction is often the most convenient remedy to adopt. The forms of civil procedure are better adapted than those of criminal for trying what is really a question of legal right, and in a civil action, such as an action of trespass brought by a landowner to justify an obstruction on a path, the successful party will, as a matter of course, recover costs, whereas on an indictment no costs are, as a rule, awarded.

There is a third remedy (not often noticed in the textbooks) for the obstruction of a highway. With the permission of the Attorney-General, an Information may be filed in his name, on the relation of the authority, or persons, complaining of the obstruction, in the High Court of Justice informing the Court of the obstruction and asking for an order (technically called a mandatory injunction) to prohibit its continuance. This proceeding has, within the writer's experience, been used with great convenience and success in several cases of encroachments on roadside waste, and there seems to be no reason, why it should not be used in the case of any important footpath. The first step is to prepare the necessary Information, a document (similar to the Chancery Bill of former days) which fully sets out the facts, and to send a print to the Attorney-General of the day with a request for his fiat to file it. The Attorney-General may use

* Bateman *v.* Bluck, 18 Q.B. 870.

his discretion in granting such fiat. When granted, the proceedings are conducted by the "relators" named in the Information, *i.e.* the authority or persons upon whose relation of the facts the Attorney-General takes action. The relators will be responsible for the costs, if the Court, being of opinion that no footpath exists, discharges the Information; and, on the other hand, will recover their costs, if an obstruction of a public footpath is proved. In this case the Court will make an order forbidding the defendant from suffering the obstruction to remain, and, if he does not then remove the obstruction, he is guilty of a contempt of Court, and may be committed to prison.

It is one advantage of this course of procedure, that the persons complaining of the obstruction can shape their case as they think best in the first instance, and have the right to begin and to reply at the trial.

It is a hardship upon private persons to have to bear the burden of asserting and maintaining public rights, and the public have always naturally looked to the authority responsible for the repair of footpaths to prevent their obstruction and to take the necessary legal proceedings for that purpose.

Originally each parish was responsible for the repair of all its highways, and, therefore, of its footpaths. The inhabitants of the parish in Vestry assembled elected a surveyor of highways,* and the duty of supervising the highways was cast upon this officer. Subsequently Highway Boards, on which several parishes were represented, were constituted in most parts of the country, and made responsible for the repair of all the highways in the district comprising such parishes. These Highway Boards have now given place to the District Councils constituted by the Local

* An officer first constituted by the statute 2 & 3 Ph. & Mary, c. 8.

Government Act, 1894,* which † transfers to the District Council of all rural districts all the powers, duties, and liabilities of any highway authority in the district.‡

Unfortunately the authority responsible for the care and repair of highways has not always been eager to protect the rights of the public to footpaths; and from the passing of the Highway Act, 1835,§ until the passing of the Local Government Act, 1894,|| no statutory duty was cast upon such authority to prevent the obstruction of footpaths,¶ though it was within their province to prevent such obstruction, if willing to do so.

The Local Government Act, however, contains a clear and stringent enactment on the subject. It declares, that ** "*it shall be the duty of every District Council to protect all public rights of way, and to prevent as far as possible the stopping or obstruction of any such right of way, whether within the district or in an adjoining district, in the county or counties in which the district is situate, where the stoppage or obstruction thereof would in their opinion be prejudicial to the interests of their district.*" A District Council may, for the purpose of performing this duty, institute or defend any legal proceedings and generally take such steps as they deem expedient.††

This enactment, it will be observed, affects not only Rural but Urban District Councils, and, therefore, extends to the

* 56 & 57 Vict. c. 73. † Sec. 25.

‡ This transfer of powers may be postponed by the order of the County Council for any period not exceeding three years from the day when the District Council assumes office, or for such further period as the Local Government Board, on the application of the County Council, may allow (sec. 25 (1)).

§ 5 & 6 Will. IV. c. 50. || 56 & 57 Vict. c. 73.

¶ Before 1835 there were provisions enforcing such a duty upon the surveyor of highways; see 7 Geo. III. c. 42. s. 8, repealed, and re-enacted by 13 Geo. III. c. 78. s. 12, and enforced by sec. 17 of the first-cited Act.

** Sec. 26 (1). †† Sec. 26 (3.)

Town Councils of Corporate Boroughs as well as to those numerous bodies, which, until lately, were designated Local or District Boards, or, more rarely, Improvement Commissioners.* Thus throughout the country, except, perhaps, in the County of London, and in County Boroughs,† there is now a constituted body directed by Act of Parliament to protect footpaths and prevent their obstruction.

Further, the Parish Council of any rural parish may compel the District Council to take action or to justify their refusal to do so.

"*Where a Parish Council have represented to the District Council that any public right of way within the district or an adjoining district in the county or counties in which the district is situate has been unlawfully stopped or obstructed, it shall be the duty of the District Council, unless satisfied that the allegations of such representations are incorrect, to take proper proceedings accordingly; and if the District Council refuse or fail to take any proceedings in consequence of such representation, the Parish Council may petition the County Council for the county within which the way is situate, and if that Council so resolve, the powers and duties of the District Council under this section shall be transferred to the County Council.*"‡

When, therefore, a Parish Council becomes aware of the obstruction of a footpath in which it is interested (whether the obstruction be in its own or an adjoining parish), it should at once make a representation on the subject to the District Council.

Inasmuch as the Act declares that "it shall be the duty" of the District Council to take action for the abatement of an

* See sec. 21, and compare with Public Health Act, 1875, 38 & 39 Vict. c. 55. s. 6.

† See Local Government Act, 1894, sec. 35. ‡ *Ibid.* sec. 26 (4).

obstruction to a footpath, when the obstruction is brought to its notice by a Parish Council, unless satisfied that the statements of the Parish Council are incorrect (*i.e.* either that there has been no obstruction or that there is no public right of way along the footpath), it would appear that upon the refusal of the District Council, the Parish Council (or any private person interested in maintaining the path) may apply to the High Court of Justice for a mandamus (or order) to the District Council to take the necessary proceedings. Upon any such application, the question for the Court would probably be, whether the District Council could have been reasonably satisfied, upon information before it, that no right of way existed (the fact of the obstruction could hardly be in serious dispute). If the Parish Council could prove the right of way beyond question, the Court would, it is assumed, grant the mandamus. But if any reasonable doubt existed, the Court would probably decline to interfere with the decision of a deliberative body. Except in an abundantly clear case, therefore, it will probably be better to appeal to the County Council.

It appears to be optional with a County Council to take action for the abatement of an obstruction. The powers and duties of the District Council are transferred to the County Council, if the latter body "so resolve."*

So, in a County Borough, where (speaking generally) the Town Council acts as both District and County Council, though the powers conferred upon a District Council by the section under consideration are entrusted to the Council of the County Borough, no statutory duty to prevent obstructions is cast upon them.†

A District Council or County Council acting in pursuance of the powers conferred by the enactment under

* Sec. 26 (4). † Sec. 26 (7).

consideration is protected from any risk of a charge of acting *ultra vires*, in case it should ultimately be determined in any legal proceedings undertaken by the Council, that no right of way exists.

"*Any proceedings or steps taken by a District Council or County Council in relation to any alleged right of way shall not be deemed to be unauthorised by reason only of such right of way not being found to exist.*" *

We need not particularize the mode of proceeding open to a District Council to prevent the obstruction of footpaths. All the methods open to any private person are open to the Council. They may proceed by indictment, or with the permission of the Attorney-General by Information, or they may remove the obstruction so far as such removal is necessary for the purpose of passage, and may defend any action brought against them or their agents. † Probably, in the latter case, they would give previous notice to the person responsible for the obstruction, requiring him to remove it, and informing him, that in default they would proceed to do so. This is the course recommended by the Local Government Board in its Circular to District Councils on the subject.‡

In a rural parish where there is no Parish Council, a Parish Meeting may make a representation to the District Council as to the obstruction of a footpath, and may complain to the County Council, if the District Council take no action on the representation.§ Any action by way of mandamus open to a Parish Council, would in such case also be open to a Parish Meeting. Although for certain purposes a Parish

* Sec. 26 (5).

† See *ante*, pp. 273–6, for remarks on the several modes of procedure.

‡ See Appendix, p. 386. As to the right of a District Council to abate an obstruction which does not wholly prevent passage, see p. 312.

§ Local Government Act, 1894, sec. 19 (8).

where there is no Parish Council is represented by the Chairman of the Parish Meeting and the Overseer of the Parish, it seems clear that these officers could not make a representation or complaint with respect to a footpath, except in pursuance of a Resolution on the subject passed at an assembly of the Parish Meeting.*

In an urban parish, as there is no Parish Council or Parish Meeting, no representation can be made under the Act to the District Council. Such a Council, therefore, is only governed by the first sub-section of the enactment under consideration,† and, having regard to the qualifying words, which require the Council to take action only "where the stoppage or obstruction of the way would, in the opinion of the Council, be prejudicial to the interests of their district," it would probably be difficult to obtain a mandamus against such a Council. Nor does any appeal lie to the County Council.

Footpaths, however, are much less in need of protection in urban than in rural districts.

The provisions of the Local Government Act expressly apply to all highways, whether footpaths, bridle-ways, or cart and carriage roads. Cart and carriage roads are seldom entirely stopped up save by process of law. But bridle-ways (*i.e.* ways for foot-passengers and horses, but not for carts or carriages) are not infrequently lost through obstruction; or the right of way for horses may be disputed, while that for foot-passengers is admitted. The foregoing remarks apply to any such case.

* Compare s-s. (8) & (6) of sec. 19.

† Sec. 26 (1).

CHAPTER IV.

Of the Stoppage or Diversion of a Footpath by an Order of Quarter Sessions.

We have seen that a public footpath once existing can never be lost to the public by mere disuse or by obstruction. There are cases, however, in which, owing to changes in a neighbourhood, it may be in the public interest, either to stop up a footpath, or to divert it, throughout the whole or part of its course, a nearer or more commodious way being substituted.

Accordingly a legal process for extinguishing the public right has always existed; and an essential feature of such process has always been the ascertaining by a proper enquiry whether the opinion of those more particularly interested in the path (the local public) is in favour of the stoppage or diversion. This was formerly done through an enquiry by the sheriff and a jury, what damage would result to the Crown or to other persons, if the way were stopped or diverted. If the verdict of the jury were favourable to the proposed change, a licence from the Crown to effect it might be granted.

In modern times there was substituted for this enquiry,—first, a vote of the inhabitants of the parish; secondly, a decision of two Justices of the Peace upon a view of the path; and thirdly, a trial by jury at Quarter Sessions, if any person interested challenged the decision of the justices.

One blot upon this process was, that the vote of the inhabitants being taken according to the laws governing proceedings in Vestries, a ratepayer assessed for a considerable property might give as many as six votes, while the cottager could give only one. Thus the wishes of the bulk of the inhabitants, and probably of those to whom the footpath was of most importance, might be overruled by the desire of a few wealthy ratepayers; and those who were opposed to the stoppage or diversion might be put to the expense of an appeal to Quarter Sessions, with the weight of a vote of the Vestry and a decision of justices against them.

This has now been altered by the Local Government Act, 1894, which forbids the stoppage or diversion of any public way without the consent of the popular representative bodies created by the Act. The present procedure for stopping or diverting a footpath in a rural parish is as follows.

The first step is to obtain the consent of the Parish Council.*

If the desire to stop or divert the footpath originates with the Parish Council, they may, after public notice, at once proceed to the consideration of the question. But if any private person desires such stoppage or diversion, the proper course is that he should require the District Council, as the highway authority fulfilling the duties formerly discharged by the surveyor of highways, to give notice to the Parish Council to consider his desire.†

In either case the Parish Council cannot give a consent to the stoppage or diversion of a footpath, except after public notice.‡

* Highway Act, 1835 (5 & 6 Will. IV. c. 50.), sec. 84, and Local Government Act, 1894 (56 & 57 Vict. c. 73.), secs. 6 (1) (*a*) and 13 (1). For procedure in rural parishes having no Council and in urban districts, see p. 290.

† Highway Act, 1835, sec. 84; Local Government Act, 1894, secs. 25 and 6 (1) (*a*) and (*b*).

‡ It would seem that, where the desire to stop or divert a path proceeds from a private person, there must be a preliminary meeting to consider his desire, and subsequently, if any member of the Council is prepared to move that the consent of the Council be given, a meeting after public notice. The Act says: "A Parish Council shall give public notice of a resolution to give such consent" (sec. 13 (1))

A public notice given by a Parish Council must be given in manner required for giving notice of Vestry meetings (*i.e.* by affixing the notice for three clear days before the meeting on the principal door of the church or chapel of the parish), and by posting the notice in some conspicuous place or places within the parish, as well as in any other manner which may appear desirable to the Council or to the persons convening the meeting.*

The notice must specify not only the day, hour, and place of holding the meeting, but also the proposed resolution to consent to the stoppage or diversion of the footpath, and must be signed by or on behalf of the Chairman of the Parish Council or persons convening the meeting.†

If after such notice a resolution is passed, this resolution will not operate

"(*a*) *unless it is confirmed by the Parish Council at a meeting held not less than two months after the public notice is given;* ‡ *nor*

"(*b*) *if a Parish Meeting, held before the confirmation, resolve that a consent ought not to be given.*" §

Thus the Parish Meeting—the whole assembly of the parishioners entitled to vote either for county or parliamentary purposes‖—has a veto upon the closing or diversion of a path, even if the Parish Council consents thereto.

A Parish Meeting can be convened at any time by the Chairman of the Parish Council, or any two Parish Coun-

---

and it is difficult to see, how any such notice can be given, upon the requirement of the District Council, that a meeting shall be held to consider the applicant's desire.

* Local Government Act, 1894, sec. 51, and 58 Geo. III. c. 69. s. 1, as amended by 7 Will. IV. and 1 Vict. c. 45. s. 2.

† Same enactments, and see Local Government Act, 1894, sec. 13 (1), and as to notices of ordinary Parish Meetings, First Sched., Part II., Rule 5.

‡ That is, apparently, after the notice of the meeting at which the resolution was passed.

§ Local Government Act, 1894, sec. 13 (1).

‖ *Ibid.* sec. 2.

cillors, or any six parochial electors.* The question will be decided in the first instance by the majority of those present and voting, *i.e.* by a show of hands, or any other convenient method of counting votes.† But a poll may be demanded by any one parochial elector at any time before the close of the meeting; ‡ and such poll will be taken by ballot.§ On any such poll each member of the parish meeting will have one vote and no more.

Before the passing of the recent Act the duty of the highway authority, or surveyor of highways, in relation to the stoppage and diversion of footpaths, appears to have been purely ministerial, and not to have given rise to any exercise of discretion. But it is now expressly provided, that the consent of the District Council shall be required for the stoppage or diversion of a public right of way.‖ This consent may apparently be given at any time before the justices are called upon to view the way. The District Council may therefore refuse its consent to the stoppage or diversion of a footpath even after the Parish Council has consented.

If the Parish Council and District Council both consent to the stoppage or diversion, two justices will, on the request of the District Council, acting by the surveyor of highways, view the path. The justices must, on such view, form their own conclusion, if the proposal is to stop a way without providing a substitute, whether or not, the path is unnecessary, or, if the proposal is to divert a footpath, whether or not, the new path is nearer or more commodious. This conclusion must be formed exclusively from the justices' own

* Local Government Act, 1894, sec. 45 (3).

† *Ibid.* First Sched., Part I., Rule (5).

‡ *Ibid.* Rules (6) and (7) (g).

§ *Ibid.* sec. 2 (5); and see sec. 48, especially sub-secs. (3) and (8).

‖ *Ibid.* sec. 13 (1).

inspection of the path, and not from statements made to them.* And the justices' certificate must be so framed as to leave no doubt on this point. Where the proposal is one for diversion, the new path must be nearer *or* more commodious, but need not satisfy both conditions, and the addition of fresh land to an old highway, so as to widen it and make it a more commodious road, is a sufficient substitution of a "new highway."† And the word "nearer" means nearer between the point from which the old and new lines of footpath diverge and the point where the old line reaches a road leading to various places, and not nearer between any two selected places between which the path runs, even though such places may be those between which there is most traffic.‡

If satisfied that the path is unnecessary, or, where the case is one of diversion, that the new way is nearer or more commodious, and that the owner of the land, through which the new way is to be taken, consents to the alteration, the justices will direct the District Council to publish a notice of the intended application to Quarter Sessions to stop or divert the path. This notice must be posted at *each* end of the path which it is proposed to stop or divert, and on the door of the church of every parish in which the footpath proposed to be stopped up or diverted lies. It must also be advertised in a local newspaper for four successive weeks. After proof of the posting and publication of the notice, the justices will give their certificate, which, if the proposal is to stop a path, must show why, in the opinion of the justices, the path is unnecessary, or, if the proposal is to divert a path, must state that

* Reg. *v.* Sir Richard Wallace, 4 Q.B. Div. 641; and see also Rex *v.* Worcestershire Justices, 8 B. & C. 254; Rex *v.* Downshire (Marquis), 4 A. & E. 698; Reg. *v.* Jones, 12 A. & E. 684.

† Queen *v.* Phillips, L.R. 1 Q.B. 648; half a highway longitudinally cannot be stopped, Rex *v.* Milverton, 5 A. & E. 841.

‡ Reg. *v.* Shiles, 1 Q.B. 919.

the new highway is nearer or more commodious to the public. This certificate, with an appropriate plan, is lodged with the Clerk of the Peace, and read in open court at the Quarter Sessions held next after the expiration of four weeks from the day when the certificate is lodged. In the meantime the certificate may be inspected, and any person considering himself injured or aggrieved may, upon giving fourteen clear days' notice to the District Council, appeal to the Quarter Sessions against the finding of the justices' certificate. The person appealing must, it would seem, be a person who has sustained some special injury.* But any person living in the neighbourhood and in the habit of using the path who is obliged to take a more circuitous route would be held to have a special grievance entitling him to appeal.† The injury or grievance should be stated in the notice of appeal, which should also state the grounds of appeal. The District Council must within forty-eight hours after its receipt deliver a copy of the notice of appeal to the party who required the Council to bring the matter before the Parish Council, in order that such party may support the justices' certificate. But when the Parish Council itself initiates the proceedings, apparently the District Council is expected to defend the justices' certificate.

Assuming proper notice of appeal to have been given, the question whether or not the path should be stopped as unnecessary, or, as the case may be, whether the new way

* Rex *v.* Essex Justices, 5 B. & C. 431.

† Rex *v.* Adey, 4 Nev. & M. 365; and see Rex *v.* Taunton, 3 M. & S. 472; Rex *v.* Williamson, 7 T.R. 32. In the two cases last-mentioned, the question arose upon Indictments, with reference to the right of the prosecutor to costs; but in both the Court held that a person who had used a highway, and was compelled, upon its obstruction or non-repair, to take a more circuitous route was a party aggrieved within the meaning of the Statute 5 & 6 W. & M. c. 11. sec. 3.

is nearer or more commodious, will then be tried by a jury at the Sessions.*

On an appeal, any substantial defects in the form of the certificate afford a good ground of objection to the stoppage or diversion of the path, apart from the question referred to the jury.† And the Court may even without an appeal refuse to make an order on the ground of defects in the certificate; indeed, it has been said, that it is their duty to be satisfied that the certificate comes before them correct in its form, and accompanied by plans and proof such as the Statute requires.‡

If the certificate is found by the Court to be bad on the face of it, or if the jury find against the stopping up or diversion of the path, the Court of Quarter Sessions will make no order, and the path will be saved. If, on the other hand, no one appeals, and the certificate is not found by the Court to be defective in form, or if the jury on the appeal confirm the finding of the justices' certificate, the Court will make an order for the stoppage or diversion of the path.

The costs of the appeal follow success. If the appellant wins and the path is preserved, the appellant will receive his costs from the District Council, if the proceedings for stoppage or diversion commenced with the Parish Council, or, in any other case, from the party who desired to stop or divert the path and put the District Council in motion. If, on the other hand, the appeal fails, the appellant will pay to the District Council, or, as the case may be, to the private

* See, for the procedure above indicated, the Highway Act, 1835 (5 & 6 Will. IV. c. 50.), secs. 84 to 92, as amended by the Local Government Act, 1894. But it must be remembered that the notice of appeal to Quarter Sessions is now (as stated in the text), fourteen days, and not ten days as stated in sec. 88. This change is due to the operation of the Quarter Sessions Act, 1849 (12 & 13 Vict. c. 45.), sec. 1; see Reg. *v.* Maule, 41 Law J., Mag. Cas. 47.

† Reg. *v.* Worcestershire Justices, 23 L.J., Mag. Cas. 113.

‡ Same case, 120.

party initiating the stoppage or diversion, the costs incurred by such Council or party.*

When the order is for diversion, the old highway is not to be stopped until the new highway is completed and put into good condition and repair, and so certified by the justices of the peace upon view thereof.† Until the new way is completed, therefore, the old way remains a highway; but as soon as the diversion is established by the completion of the new highway to the satisfaction of the justices, the old way ceases to be a highway, "and the land reverts unencumbered by any covenant to the original owner of the soil." ‡ Such owner can therefore stop the old way.

It is not necessary in order to extinguish the old highway, that there should be an actual stoppage.§ As, however, the owner of the soil may re-dedicate it, if he should leave it open and allow it to be used for any length of time, it might be presumed that such re-dedication had taken place.

After the order of Quarter Sessions has been made, the High Court of Justice may quash it, on the ground that the justices' certificate is not in accordance with the Statute, and that the Court of Quarter Sessions had therefore no jurisdiction to make the order. And, in such case, the Court may issue a mandamus to remove an obstruction on the old highway.‖

And if any member of the public considers, after the order has been made, that the justices have not complied with the Statute, and have thus exceeded their power, he may remove any obstruction on the path stopped up or diverted, so far as is necessary to enable him to pass, and

* Highway Act, 1835, sec. 90; Quarter Sessions Act, 1849, sec. 5.

† Highway Act, 1835, sec. 91.

‡ Per Cockburn, C.J., Reg. *v.* Wallace, L.R. 4 Q.B.D. 644.

§ Per Denman, C.J., and Coleridge, J., in Rex *v.* Milverton, 5 A. & E. 841, 847.

‖ Reg. *v.* Newmarket Railway Co., 19 L.J., Mag. Cas. 241.

may contest the validity of the order in the action of trespass which will be brought against him.*

In any such action, however, the defendant would be confined to showing, that the order of Quarter Sessions was bad ; he could not re-open the substantial question, whether the path was necessary to the public, or whether, in case of diversion, the new way was nearer or more commodious than the old.

We have described the above proceedings as they would take place in a parish where there is a Parish Council.† In other parishes the Parish Meeting takes the place of the Parish Council.‡ The Parish Meeting may initiate proceedings for the stoppage or diversion of a path ; or, when some other party initiates such proceedings, the District Council, as the highway authority, will, at the request of such party, bring his proposal before the Parish Meeting. This will be done by notice to the Chairman,§ who holds office for the year.‖ Seven clear days' notice of a Parish Meeting to consider the proposal must be given ;¶ and any resolution for the stoppage or diversion must be confirmed at another Parish Meeting held not less than two months after notice of the first meeting.**

The proceedings subsequent to the confirmed vote of the Parish Meeting will be the same as in the case of a Parish which has a Parish Council.

* Welch *v.* Nash, 8 East 394, confirmed on this point (though overruled on another) by the Queen *v.* Phillips, L.R. 1 Q.B. 648, 658.

† *i.e.* in all parishes of 300 inhabitants, and in other parishes where an order of the County Council has established a Parish Council (Local Government Act, 1894, sec. 1).

‡ Local Government Act, 1894, sec. 19 (8).

§ *Ibid.* First Sched., Part I., Rule 2.

‖ *Ibid.* sec. 19 (1).

¶ *Ibid.* First Sched., Part I., Rule 2.

** *Ibid.* sec. 13 (1).

In an Urban District, the District Council is, by the Public Health Act, 1875, endowed with all the powers both of the Surveyor of Highways and of the inhabitants in vestry assembled of any parish within their district.* Consequently the Council may resolve, that a footpath should be stopped up or diverted without consulting the ratepayers. But the view and certificate of two Justices and the appeal to Quarter Sessions above described apply to footpaths in urban districts as to footpaths elsewhere.

* 38 & 39 Vict. c. 55. s. 144.

CHAPTER V.

Of the Repair of Footpaths.

THE repair of highways is a subject which has frequently employed both the Legislature and the Courts, and volumes have been written on the legal questions to which it has given rise.* But, as may be supposed, the questions considered have almost always related to the repair of carriage-ways, and there is little decided law in relation to the repair of footpaths.

As a rule, footpaths are not repaired. They are mere beaten tracks, passing from point to point across fields and woods, and to make them up with hard materials would not only be unnecessary, but would deprive them of the informal character which is so pleasant to the walker.

Occasionally, of course, the case is quite different. A footpath passes from street to street in a town between walls. Here proper maintenance in a reasonably hard condition is as necessary as in the case of a carriage-road, and not infrequently such paths are asphalted, or even paved.

Again, rural footpaths usually pass from field to field over stiles or through gates. The condition and maintenance of these stiles and gates is a question closely analogous to that of repair of the way itself.

The principle of law governing all questions of this sort appears to be, that nothing can be done to a footpath which, on the one hand, will enlarge the right of the public against

* See, for example, the numerous references to the subject in Glen's exhaustive work on "The Law relating to Highways," Butterworth, Knight & Co.

the landowner, or, on the other, impair the facilities for the use of the path which the public have enjoyed from time immemorial. Thus, in one of the few reported cases, a footway crossed a brook by fourteen stepping-stones. The surveyors of highways replaced these stones by eight higher stones, and connected them by some means of passage so as to form a rough bridge. It was held that they had no right to do so, as such an act amounted to an enlargement of the public right against the landowner. Such repairs as were done must, it was said, be confined to maintaining the way as of old.* And similarly, as between the parish authorities and the public, it was laid down in an old case that "the parish is not bound to put a footpath in a better condition than has been time out of mind, but as it has usually been at the best."†

On the other hand, it would seem, that a footpath must be kept in such a condition, that one may pass along it without unusual exertion. Thus, where a footpath crossed a brook which an active, agile person might easily jump, and there had never been a bridge or stepping-stones, it was ruled, on an indictment for non-repair, that the parish authorities were bound so to keep the path that persons might walk along it dry-shod, and that, if a bridge was necessary for this purpose, a bridge must be made.‡

In the somewhat analogous case of soft cart-roads, it has been held that the parish is bound to make the road "reasonably passable for the ordinary traffic of the neighbourhood at all seasons of the year." In the case in which the law was so declared to the jury (by a distinguished judge, Mr. Justice Blackburn), the road in question was an old *soft*

* Sutcliffe *v.* Surveyor of Highways of Sowerby, 1 L.T. (N.S.) 7.

† Reg. *v.* the Inhabitants of Cluworth (*temp.* 3 Anne), 1 Salk. 359.

‡ Reg. *v.* Healaugh, "Times" newspaper, 18 April 1863.

road formed of Weald of Kent clay, and had never been repaired with hard substances. The parish contended that it was not bound to make the road into a hard road. But Mr. Justice Blackburn charged the jury that, in some way, the road was to be made passable, and, if necessary, stone or other hard substances must be laid down for the purpose.*

By analogy it may perhaps be assumed that the highway authorities are bound, at the instance of the public, to keep any footpath passable, putting down, if necessary, a few stones in bad places, but not essentially changing the character of the path. And, if bound so to act, it follows, that they must have the right so to act as against the landowner.

There is one case which is an exception even to this modified rule. We have seen that a footpath is sometimes dedicated subject to the right of the owner to plough it up in the regular course of husbandry. In such cases the highway authority cannot make a hard path which would prevent ploughing.†

Not only a passable condition under foot, but stiles, gates, and bridges of a reasonably easy character are of great importance to the preservation of a path. For, if the path cannot be used in comfort, it will fall out of use, and it will then be far easier to the landowner to obstruct it. Moreover, anything like the blocking of a path through a barricaded stile, a locked gate, or a broken bridge, tends to show that there is no dedication of the path. It is, therefore, most advisable, that stiles and gates should be kept in good repair.

---

* Reg. *v.* High Halden (Kent), 1 F. & F. 678; and see the decision of the Court of Queen's Bench to the same effect in Reg. *v.* Claxby (Lincolnshire), 24 L.J. Q.B. 223.

† Arnold *v.* Blaker, L.R. 6 Q.B. 433.

Now, it seems clear that the owner of any hedge, wall, or brook which crosses the path is bound to maintain in good order such means of crossing his property as have existed from time immemorial, otherwise the hedge, wall, or brook becomes an obstruction to the path, and the owner would be indictable. The District Council, as the surveyor of highways, or any member of the public, might, therefore, it would seem, indict the owner for not keeping gates, stiles, and bridges * in good condition as heretofore.

But it would be often much more simple and convenient were a public authority to assume the care of arrangements which are so obviously for the public convenience. In such case the rule would seem to be, even more strictly than in the case of the repair of the way itself, that no substantial change should be made.† But, on the other hand, the landowner must not enlarge his right against the public by substituting less for more convenient stiles and gates. Thus it has been held to be illegal to remove a stone stile two feet high and to substitute for it a high five-bar gate with a step on it. And the learned judge, who so held, emphasized his view by saying, that the existence of twenty gates at other places on the path would not justify the erection of a gate at a new place.‡ The highway authority may, therefore, insist on the maintenance in perpetuity of every facility once enjoyed by the public for the use of a path.

* The liability to repair public bridges rests by common law upon the county; and this liability may apply to a foot-bridge (Rex *v.* Middlesex, 3 B. & Ad. 201; per Lord Ellenborough, in Rex *v.* Salop, 13 East 95). But it would seem not to extend to the slight structures which are sufficient to carry a rural footpath over a brook or stream, but to be confined to works of more solidity and importance (Reg. *v.* the Inhabitants of the County of Southampton (Tinker's Bridge Case), 21 L.J. Mag. Cas. 205). Moreover, by the County Bridges Act, 1803, no bridge built after the passing of that Act is repairable by the county unless built to the satisfaction of the county authorities (43 Geo. III. c. 59. s. 5).

† See Sutcliffe *v.* Surveyor of Highways of Sowerby above cited.

‡ Bateman *v.* Burge, 6 C. & P. 391.

The District Council, as we have seen, is the highway authority for its district,* and is therefore the authority responsible for the repair (within the limits we have already described) of the footpaths, as of all other highways, within the district. It is also bound to protect all public rights of way within its district, and to prevent, as far as possible, the obstruction of any such right of way.†

A Parish Council is, however, empowered by the Local Government Act, 1894,‡ to undertake the repair and maintenance of any public footpaths within the parish, not being footpaths at the side of a public road; but the possession or exercise of this power is not to relieve any other authority or person of any liability to repair. In respect of footpaths, therefore, the District and Parish Councils will have a concurrent power to repair; but the District Council alone, as the highway authority, would be indictable for any neglect of duty with respect to repairs.

As against the owner of the land over which a footpath passes, the powers of repair exercisable by the Parish Council would, it is assumed, be the same as those of the District Council. It may be suggested, however, that a special power conferred by an Act of Parliament to repair footpaths, raises a necessary implication that, as against the landowner, the Council may lawfully exercise some right of repair. The enactment, therefore, confirms the view above expressed, that sufficient repairs to render a way passable are, as against the landowner, within the competence of the authorities representing the public.

The remedy for the non-repair of any public way is to indict the body responsible for its repair for the commission of a public nuisance.

* Local Government Act, 1894, sec. 25 (1).

† *Ibid.* sec. 26 (1).

‡ Sec. 13 (2).

CHAPTER VI.

Of Highways of an Exceptional Kind.

Bridges and Fords.

A BRIDGE dedicated to and used by the public is in the same position as a road as regards the right of the public to pass over it.* It may be a foot-way, a bridle-way, or a carriage-way.

We have already seen,† that the liability to repair bridges, at common law, rests upon the county and not upon the parish, but that this liability does not, as a rule, attach to slight structures connected with footpaths.

A highway not infrequently passes through a stream or fordable river. In such case the ford is part of the highway; and this may be the case even though the ford is sometimes impassable. Thus, there may be a highway which passes through a ford in ordinary weather, but in times of frost or flood over a bridge, which, save at such times, is locked.‡ The water through which the highway passes may be tidal, and the wash of the tide such as to preclude effectual repair; this does not affect the public character of the way, though it may limit the liability of the parish to repair.§

* Coke, Second Institute, 700, 701.

† *Ante*, p. 295, note.

‡ Reg. *v.* Inhabitants of Northants, 2 M. & S. 262.

§ See Rex *v.* Landulph, 1 Moo. & Rob. 393, where, however, the jury found the parish liable.

Where a public road passes through a stream by a ford there is usually a foot-bridge for passengers on foot.*

The analogy to a ford in a public road is supplied by the stepping-stones across a brook or stream in the course of a footpath, and these are part of the footpath.†

FERRIES.

A ferry is not an uncommon incident in a highway. It is as much a part of the highway as the approaches on either side, and the public have a right to embark and disembark at the landing places, provided they are using the highways on either side.‡ A public ferry is a public highway of a special description, and its termini must be in places where the public have rights, as towns or vills or highways leading to towns or vills.§

The owner of the ferry need not be the owner of the land on either side, provided he has the right to land and embark passengers there.|| The right of ferry originates in a grant from the Crown, either express, or presumed from usage from time immemorial, and consists in the right to have a boat upon the river for the conveyance of passengers (and it may be of horses and carriages) from side to side for a reasonable toll.¶ Every ferry ought to be provided with expert and able ferrymen, and to give frequent passage. The person enjoying the ferry may be indicted if he does not provide proper boats, with competent boatmen and all things necessary for the

* See such a case mentioned in Rex *v.* York, W.R., 5 Burr. 259.

† See incidentally the cases previously referred to of Sutcliffe *v.* Surveyor of Highways of Sowerby (Linc.), 1 L.T. (N.S.) 7; Reg. *v.* Healaugh, "Times" newspaper, 18 April 1863.

‡ Newton *v.* Cubitt, 12 C.B. (N.S.) 58; and see Huzzey *v.* Field, 2 C.M. & R. 442; Wellbeloved on Highways, 32 *et seq.*

§ Huzzey *v.* Field, 2 C.M. & R. 442.

|| Peter *v.* Kendal, 6 B. & C. 703.

¶ Letton *v.* Goodden, L.R. 2 Eq. 130; and see Hopkins *v.* Great Northern Railway Co., 2 Q.B. Div. 224, 230, where the nature of a ferry is discussed.

maintenance of the ferry in an efficient state and condition for the use of the public.*

On the other hand, the right of ferry is exclusive within reasonable limits. The owner of a ferry may bring an action for the disturbance of his right by the establishment of another ferry so near as to draw away custom.† But if persons wish to go to other points on the river, and it would be unreasonable to make them travel out of their way to use the ferry, carrying persons to another point would not be deemed to be a disturbance of the ferry.‡ And a ferry cannot be taken to control the approach to a whole district, such as the Isle of Dogs on the Thames.§ And so the opening of a railway across the river near a ferry will not give the owner of the ferry any ground of complaint. Indeed, the Court deciding this question stongly inclined to the opinion, that an action for disturbance of an ancient ferry will lie only where the disturbance is caused by another ferry.‖

The obstruction of a public ferry is indictable, like the obstruction of any other highway.¶ The owner cannot suppress it and put up a bridge in its place.¶

A highway may, however, properly lead to the side of a navigable river, though there is no ferry, ford, or bridge to carry passengers over the river. Such a highway is not a cul-de-sac, because it terminates on the bank of the river, the river itself being a highway.**

* Payne *v.* Partridge, 1 Showers, 255; Letton *v.* Goodden, L.R. 2 Eq. 131.

† 2 Rolles' Abr. 140, tit. Nuisance (G); Blissett *v.* Hart, Willes, 508; Huzzey *v.* Field, 2 C.M. & R. 440.

‡ Tripp *v.* Frank, 4 T.R. 666; Huzzey *v.* Field, 2 C.M. & R. 432; Newton *v.* Cubitt, 12 C.B. (N.S.) 32.

§ Newton *v.* Cubitt, *ubi. supra.*

‖ Hopkins *v.* Great Northern Railway Co., L.R. 2 Q.B.D. 224.

¶ Payne *v.* Partridge, 1 Show. 255, 1 Salk. 12.

** See, amongst other authorities, per Eyre, J., in Payne *v.* Partridge, 1 Show. 256.

TOWPATHS.

A towpath, or towing-path, is a way on the banks of a navigable river dedicated to the public for the purpose of towing boats, with or without horses, only. It does not exist by the side of every river, that is to say, there is no public right to a towing-path on the banks of every navigable river merely because the river is navigable. The existence of the towing-path, like any other highway, rests upon the doctrine of dedication.* Where there is a towing-path, it will include so much of the banks of the river as is necessary and proper for the towing of barges.†

A towing-path may or may not be also a public footpath, or a public bridle-way or carriage-way. There is not necessarily any right of way along it except for towing.‡ And where there is a right of foot-way along a towing-path, the use as a foot-way may be subject to the use for towing, so that foot passengers must look out for themselves, and cannot complain of any injury they may sustain from the reasonable use of the path for towing.§

CULS-DE-SAC.

We have seen that a highway terminating on the bank of a navigable river is not a cul-de-sac. But a cul-de-sac may be a highway. It is a question of fact in each case whether it is a highway or not.||

A noted case, and perhaps the earliest reported decision

* Ball *v.* Herbert, 3 T.R. 253; Winch *v.* Conservators of the River Thames, L.R. 7 C.P. 471.

† Winch *v.* Conservators of the Thames, L.R. 7 C.P. 459, 468.

‡ See per Bayley, J., in Rex *v.* Severn and Wye Railway Co., 2 B. & A. 648; Winch *v.* Conservators of Thames, L.R. 7 C.P. 471.

§ Grand Junction Canal Co. *v.* Petty, 21 Q.B.D. 273, 276.

|| Bateman *v.* Bluck, 18 Q.B. 870.

on the question of a cul-de-sac, is that relating to Lamb's Conduit Street.* In this case Lord Kenyon held that the street was dedicated to the public, though it had only been used eight years, and in answer to the objection that it was not a thoroughfare, he said: "As to this not being a thoroughfare, that can make no difference. If it were otherwise, in such a great town as this it would be a trap to make people trespassers."

And in another London case, Lord Ellenborough held, that it was no defence to an indictment for obstructing a way, that it led out of and into the same thoroughfare, and was thus only a circuitous and longer way of passing between two points already connected by a public way. His Lordship said: "If the owner of the soil throws open a passage, and neither marks by any visible distinction, that he means to preserve all his rights over it, nor excludes persons from passing through it by positive prohibition, he shall be presumed to have dedicated it to the public." †

And consistently with these decisions it has been held, that, if part of a highway be legally closed, so that the remainder becomes a cul-de-sac, the right of the public along the cul-de-sac thus created is not destroyed.‡ This consideration is important with reference to highways stopped by railway companies. The Act of Parliament commonly stops the way only between the boundaries of the company's land, and thus leaves a cul-de-sac on each side. Sometimes the

* The Trustees of the Rugby Charity *v.* Merryweather, 11 East 375, note, 10 R.R. 528.

† Rex *v.* Lloyd, 1 Campb. 260, 262, 10 R.R. 676; see also per Lord Cranworth, L.C., in Young *v.* Cuthbertson, 1 Macq. 456; the remarks of Cockburn, C.J., in Reg. *v.* Hawkhurst, 7 L.T. (N.S.) 268, 26 J.P. 724; Souch *v.* East London Railway Co., L.R. 16 Eq. 108, 110.

‡ Rex *v.* Downshire, 4 A. & E. 698; Gwyn *v.* Hardwicke, 25 L.J. Mag. Cas. 97, 99; Reg. *v.* Burney, 31 L.T. 828; Wood *v.* Veal, 5 B. & Ald. 454.

way thus left affords a pleasant walk, and sometimes it may enable the public to secure a substituted thoroughfare.

But in the converse case, where both ends of a highway are legally closed, but the intermediate portion remains untouched by the Acts of Parliament or orders of justices which effected the stoppage,—or, to state the case another way, where through the legal stoppage of other highways a highway is left without access at either end—it has been held that the way thus isolated ceases to be a highway, on the ground that "there cannot be a public highway, public access to which has lawfully been stopped at either end."*

* Bailey *v.* Jamieson (1876), 1 C.P. Div. 329, 333.

CHAPTER VII.

Of Roadside Waste.

It is almost the rule with country roads and lanes that the hedges or fences do not immediately border upon the metalled way. Sometimes on each side of a high road a broad strip of green sward runs for miles. In other cases waste land of irregular width, and often carrying bushes and trees, continually occurs. Such margins to the roads are of inestimable value to the wayfarer. They furnish soft ground for riding and walking, and they give relief to the eye and a pleasant sense of space and freedom.

Unfortunately, such wayside waste has been very largely inclosed in past times. No one passing through a rural district can fail to observe many spots where there is a double hedge by the roadside. The present hedge is close to the metalled road or footpath. But some twenty or thirty feet inside will be seen clear traces of another boundary line, which evidently at one time marked the limit of the inclosed property. Sometimes the whole of the old hedge remains, sometimes it can be identified by a ditch, by trees or remnants of fencing; and often the added strip comes suddenly to an end, one of two neighbours having enlarged his borders, while the other has left the roadside waste intact. The growth of fields and woods under the system of inclosure we have indicated must throughout the country have deprived the public of hundreds, even thousands, of acres.

Happily, however, much roadside waste still remains, and Parliament has now declared that it shall be jealously guarded.

The inclosures in past times have proceeded partly from a mistaken view of the law,* and partly from absence of effective opposition.

Now, in dealing with the law of the subject, there are two quite distinct questions which are often confused. One is the ownership of the land; the other is the right of passage over it.

It is a well-known rule of law that, in the absence of evidence to the contrary, the owners of the land on either side of a highway own the soil of the highway up to the middle of the way, *usque ad medium filum viæ.*†

It follows from this doctrine, that any roadside waste between the metalled way and the hedge or fence is presumed, till the contrary be shown, to belong to the owner of the adjoining land, whether such owner be a freeholder, leaseholder, or copyholder.‡ The origin of such strips is suggested by Chief Justice Abbott to have lain in the law, that the public might deviate from the road on to the adjoining land, when the road was out of repair. This right ceased, if the owner fenced against the road, but in that case the liability of the parish to repair the road was transferred to the owner, who by his act deprived the public of the right of deviation. In order, therefore, to avoid the burden of repair, the owner took care to leave an ample margin for deviation outside his fences.§ Hence there is a *primâ facie*

* See note to p. 311.

† See this principle recognised in Salisbury (Marquis of) *v.* Great Northern Railway Co., 5 C.B. (N.S.) 174, 208, 213; Rex *v.* Edmonton, 1 Moo. & Rob. 32.

‡ Steel *v.* Prickett (1819), 2 Stark. N.P.C. 463, 20 R.R. 717, where C.J. Abbott explains the law at length; see also Doe d. Pring *v.* Pearsey, 7 B. & C. 304; Grose *v.* West, 7 Taunt. 39; and see as to the right to deviate, per Buller, J., in Ball *v.* Herbert, 3 T.R. 262.

§ See per Abbott, C.J., in Steel *v.* Prickett.

presumption in every case that such strips, where found, belong to the adjoining owner.

This presumption may, however, be rebutted by evidence tending to show, that the soil of the strip is in some other person.* In some cases there may be evidence of the original setting out of the road, or of an intention not to convey the soil of the road, which may show conclusively that the road belongs to one of the two adjoining owners, or to a third party.† But the fact that a close is conveyed as bounded by the road in question does not in itself rebut the presumption,‡ nor does the fact that the conveyance describes the land conveyed by precise description, plan, and measurements, and that the acreage is made up without reckoning any part of the road.§ Many roads in the country are set out under Inclosure Awards. In such cases the soil, unless specially allotted (and even if the herbage of the road is vested in the adjoining proprietor), remains in the Lord of the Manor or other previous owner of the soil of the common.‖

In the case of roads not set out under an Inclosure Award, the wayside strips sometimes belong to the Lord of the Manor. This is mostly the case, where such strips communicate with open commons or larger portions of land undoubtedly waste of the manor. In this instance the "evidence of ownership which applies to the larger portions applies also to the narrow

* Doe d. Harrison *v.* Hampson, 4 C.B. 267.

† See Salisbury (Marquis of) *v.* Great Northern Railway Co., 5 C.B. (N.S.) 174, 209–10, 214; Plumstead Board of Works *v.* British Land Co., L.R. 10 Q.B. 16.

‡ Simpson *v.* Dendy, 8 C.B. (N.S.) 433; Lord *v.* Commissioners for the City of Sydney, 12 Moore's P.C. 473.

§ Berridge *v.* Ward, 10 C.B. (N.S.) 400.

‖ Poole *v.* Huskinson, 11 Mee. & W. 827, 830; Rex *v.* Hatfield, 4 A. & E. 164. But see the recent case of Haigh *v.* West, 1893, 2 Q.B. 19, where evidence of acts of ownership on the sides of a road set out under an Inclosure Act ousted the claim of the Lord of the Manor; *ante*, p. 70.

strip which communicates with them."* Sometimes it may be a very nice question, whether the lord or the adjoining owner is the owner of the waste, and here acts of ownership on the strip, such as cutting trees and bushes or depasturing cattle, are all-important. In other cases, the general character of the neighbourhood may in itself tend to rebut the usual presumption. For instance, in Epping Forest all roadside strips, though at some distance from the open forest, were in the proceedings before the Epping Forest Commissioners adjudged without contest to be waste of the forest and not to belong to the adjoining owners. In a reported case it was held, that to prove ownership in the Lord of the Manor, evidence might be received of acts of ownership by the lord on similar strips of land, not adjoining his own freehold, in various parts of the manor.† But such acts of ownership will not rebut the ordinary presumption of ownership, when acts of ownership in the particular strip claimed have been exercised by the adjoining owner.‡ And, speaking generally, while the presumption is always in favour of the adjoining owner, the amount of evidence necessary to rebut this presumption varies greatly in different cases, and it is for the jury to say in each case whether it is rebutted.§

But the question of the ownership of the soil of roadside waste is quite distinct from that of the right of the public over them. In whomsoever the soil is vested, the presumption of law is, that the public have a right of way over the whole road from hedge to hedge. This question has repeatedly been discussed by the Courts, and has been decided

* Grose *v.* West, per Gibbs, C.J., 7 Taunt. 40.

† Doe d. Barrett *v.* Kemp, 7 Bing. 332.

‡ Simpson *v.* Dendy, 8 C.B. (N.S.) 433.

§ Doe d. Harrison *v.* Hampson, 4 C.B. 267; and see Scoones *v.* Morrell, 1 Beav. 251.

beyond question. In a noted modern case a telegraph company had, with the consent of the highway authority, placed posts on the green margin of a road. The company was indicted for obstructing the highway, and at the trial Baron Martin directed the jury as follows :—

"(1.) In the case of an ordinary highway, although it may be of a varying and unequal width, running between fences on each side, the right of passage or way *primâ facie*, and unless there be evidence to the contrary, extends to the whole space between the fences, and the public are entitled to the use of the entire of it as the highway, and are not confined to the parts which may be metalled or kept in repair for the more convenient use of carriages or foot-passengers.

"(2.) A permanent obstruction erected on a highway, and placed there without lawful authority, which renders the way less commodious than before to the public, is an unlawful act and a public nuisance at common law; and if the jury believed the defendants placed, for the purpose of profit to themselves, posts, with the object and intention of keeping them permanently there, in order to make a telegraphic communication between distant places, and did permanently keep them there and the posts were of such size and dimensions and solidity as to obstruct and prevent the passage of carriages and horses or foot-passengers upon parts of the highway where they stood, the jury ought to find the defendants guilty on this indictment; and the circumstances that the posts were not placed upon the hard or metalled part of the highway, or upon a footpath artificially formed upon it, or that the jury might think that sufficient space for the public traffic remained, are immaterial circumstances as regards the legal right, and do not affect the right of the Crown to the verdict."*

* Reg. *v.* the United Kingdom Electric Telegraph Co., Limited, 2 F. & F. 73.

This ruling was confirmed by the Court of Queen's Bench, which refused a new trial.*

In a much older case, Lord Tenterden laid down the same doctrine with equal emphasis. Under an Inclosure Act, commissioners appointed to carry out the inclosure were authorised to set out public and private roads, the public roads to be sixty feet wide between the fences. The road in question was described in the Award as a private road, eight yards (or twenty-four feet) wide, but in setting it out a space of sixty feet was left between the fences. The commissioners also directed both public and private roads to be repaired by the township. The centre of the road in question had been repaired by the township for eighteen years, and used by the public as a carriage-road. At the end of this time an encroachment was made on the margin of the road within the sixty feet space, but outside the metalled way. On an indictment against the adjoining landowner for obstructing the highway by the encroachment, the jury found a verdict of guilty on the ground that the road had been dedicated to the public subsequently to the Award, and extended to the whole sixty feet. A new trial was refused, and Lord Tenterden, C.J., stated his view of the law as follows:—

"I think the case was for the jury, and they found a right verdict. I am strongly of opinion, when I see a space of fifty or sixty feet through which a road passes between inclosures set out under an Act of Parliament, that, unless the contrary be shown, the public are entitled to the whole of that space, though perhaps from economy the whole may not have been kept in repair. . . . The space at the sides is also necessary to afford the benefit of sun and air. If trees and

* 6 L.T. (N.S.) 378; 31 L.J. Mag. Cas. 166; 26 J.P. 324. The last-mentioned report shows that the consent of the highway authorities to the erection of the poles had been obtained by the company.

hedges might be brought up to the part actually used as the road, it could not be kept sound." *

There are other reported cases in which the same doctrine has been enforced under somewhat remarkable circumstances. In one case a roadway had been set out under an Inclosure Award of fifty feet. Trees had, however, been allowed to grow up for twenty-five years on the sides of the road, so that it was practically reduced to a width of twenty-five feet. At the end of this time the highway authority cut down the trees growing on the roadside waste, and the adjoining owner thereupon took action in the Court of Chancery to restrain the Highway Board. The Court held, that the public was clearly entitled to a right of way over the whole fifty feet, notwithstanding the condition of the sides of the road, and that the Highway Board was justified in cutting down the trees, but not in converting them to their own use, the property in the trees being in the adjoining owner. †

In another case, the obstruction which was the subject of the indictment, and which was one of several on the same highway, was a fence surrounding a garden plot which had been inclosed for many years, but had been originally taken in from the side of the road. It was proved that some of the encroachments had existed for forty years and upwards. On the other hand, it was proved that the ancient width of the way was eighty feet, the stoned part running along the centre being but nine feet wide and the remainder being grass. Fifty years before the indictment the whole width of the way from hedge to hedge had been used by the public for waggons, horses, sheep, and cattle, the grass sides being of great importance for the passage of flocks and herds. It was ruled, that under these circumstances the public had a clear

* Reg. *v.* Wright, 3 B. & Ad. 681, 683.

† Turner *v.* Ringwood Highway Board, L.R. 9 Eq. 418.

right to resume the use of the whole of the old highway, no period of modern enjoyment being of any avail to deprive the public of the right they had once enjoyed. "Once a highway always a highway," whatever the width.*

It will be noticed that the public right of way over roadside wastes is confined in all the reported decisions to roads passing between fences, hedges, or other defined boundaries. When a road passes over an open common or green, it is obvious that the same considerations do not apply. The common or green has been left open for other reasons, and not to give the public a right of way. The extent of the right of way in such a case must therefore depend upon the actual user and all the circumstances relating to such user. In a reported case a road crossed a village green of five or six acres. The road was metalled to the width of eight feet. The Lord of the Manor, the owner of the soil of the green, built a wall on each side of the road, the distance from wall to wall being sixteen feet. The Highway Board summoned him under the Highway Act, 1864,† for encroaching on the sides of a cart-way within fifteen feet of the centre. A case was submitted by the justices who tried the summons for the opinion of a Superior Court, and in this Case it was found, that the grass on which the walls were built had not been dedicated to the public for purposes of passage to any greater extent than the whole green. The Court held, that no offence had been committed under the Statute, as it must be deemed that the expression "sides of a carriage-way or cart-way" meant land dedicated to the public as part

* Reg. *v.* Edwards, 11 J.P. 602. Amongst other cases on the subject of road-side waste, see per Denman, C.J., (incidentally) in Williams *v.* Wilcox, 8 A. & E. 329; the remarks of the Court (Denman, C.J., Patteson, Williams, and Coleridge, JJ.) in Elwood *v.* Bullock, 6 Q.B. 409; and per Blackburn, J., in Easton *v.* the Richmond Highway Board, L.R. 7 Q.B. 69.

† 27 & 28 Vict. c. 101. s. 51.

of the highway, though not metalled, and there was in the case before the Court no evidence of any dedication outside the land within the walls.*

It will be seen from the case last quoted, that when an encroachment is within fifteen feet from the centre of a highway, and on land which has been dedicated to the public, the author of the encroachment may be summoned before justices, who may fine him, and also order the encroachment to be removed.†

This remedy, however, is only available if the encroachment is within the prescribed distance; and even in that case the jurisdiction of the justices may be ousted, if (as in the Richmond case) it is *bonâ fide* disputed, that the land on which the encroachment is made has ever been dedicated to the public.‡

The usual remedy, therefore, for the obstruction of roadside waste is the same as that for the obstruction of a footpath or any other kind of highway, viz., indictment for a misdemeanour, on the ground that the encroachment is a public nuisance.

The alternative remedy of an Information by the Attorney-General, praying for an order for the removal of an encroachment, is also available, if the Attorney-General's fiat can be obtained. The Information will be laid on the relation of the persons applying for the fiat, and at their expense.

This form of procedure is very apt and convenient in the case of a highway on the sides of which many encroachments have taken place, perhaps at different dates and of various characters. In such a case all the parties may be

* Easton *v.* the Richmond Highway Board, L.R. 7 Q.B. 69.

† Highway Act, 1864, 27 & 28 Vict. c. 101. s. 51.

‡ The summary remedy for encroachments within fifteen feet of the crown of the road has in one way been prejudicial to roadside strips, for it has produced an erroneous impression, that inclosures outside this distance are lawful, although there is no foundation whatever for such a doctrine.

brought before the Court in one proceeding, and the expense and annoyance of a number of indictments is saved.*

In the case of the blocking of a footpath, as we have seen, the obstruction, if and so far as it prevents passage, may be removed, and the question of the public right may be tried in an action of trespass by the landowner.

It would not be safe, however, for any private person to remove an encroachment on roadside waste, if he can pass along the highway without interfering with the obstruction. The act of encroachment being a criminal act, should be dealt with by the constituted authorities, and not by private persons.†

With respect to the right of a highway authority to remove an encroachment on roadside waste, which does not block passage along the highway, the late Master of the Rolls (Sir Geo. Jessel) held that a Local Board was entitled to remove such an obstruction, when it had been judicially decided to be illegal; and the observations of the learned judge seem to support the right of the highway authority to remove any illegal obstruction, though not judicially so pronounced.‡

By two recent cases § it has been established beyond doubt that an Urban Council may safely remove an encroachment on a highway (including in that expression roadside waste) without first obtaining a judicial decision, although in doubtful cases it would be better they should obtain such a deci-

* This course was taken with excellent effect in the case of the high road from Ascot to Bracknell, which had been set out, on the inclosure of Windsor Forest, of a great width, but was gradually being narrowed by successive encroachments. For an account of the case see Mr. Shaw-Lefevre's "English Commons and Forests," Cassell & Co., 1894.

† Arnold *v.* Holbrook, L.R. 8 Q.B. 96; Mayor, &c. of Colchester *v.* Brooke, 7 Q.B. 377; Dimes *v.* Petley, 15 Q.B. 276, 283; Bateman *v.* Bluck, 18 Q.B. 870.

‡ Bagshaw *v.* Buxton Local Board of Health, L.R. 1 Ch. Div. 220; see also Turner *v.* Ringwood Highway Board, L.R. 9 Eq. 418.

§ Reynolds *v.* Urban District Council of Presteign, 1896, 1 Q.B. 604; Louth District Council *v.* West, 40 Solicitors' Journal 602, *Times* of 18th June 1896.

sion. In one of these cases considerable stress was laid on the fact that highways are vested in Urban Councils. In the other, however, the statutory duty cast upon all District Councils to protect highways and roadside waste was the ground of the decision, and this consideration applies equally to Urban and Rural Councils. In the later case it was decided, that an Urban Council might sue the person who had encroached for the expense of removing the encroachment, such expense being special damage. There seems now, therefore, to be little doubt that, under section 26 of the Local Government Act, 1894, any District Council, whether Urban or Rural, may abate an encroachment on a highway, though, if it should turn out subsequently, that they were wrong in considering an encroachment to have taken place, they will become liable to pay damages for trespass.

The Local Government Act, 1894,* throws upon District Councils the duty of preventing encroachments on roadside wastes. "*It shall be the duty,*" the Act declares,† "*of every District Council to prevent any unlawful encroachment on any roadside waste within their district.*" For the purpose of performing this duty the Council may "*institute or defend any legal proceedings, and generally take such steps as they deem expedient.*"‡

Moreover, the Parish Council may set the District Council in motion, and if they decline to take effective steps may appeal to the County Council.

"*Where a Parish Council have represented to the District Council, that an unlawful encroachment has taken place on any roadside waste within the district, it shall be the duty of the District Council, unless satisfied that the allegations of such representations are incorrect, to take proper proceedings accordingly; and, if the District Council refuse or fail to*

* 56 & 57 Vict. c. 73. † Sec. 26 (1). ‡ Sec. 26 (3).

take any proceedings in consequence of such representation, the Parish Council may petition the County Council for the county within which the waste is situate, and if that Council so resolve the powers and duties of the District Council under this section shall be transferred to the County Council."*

Where, then, a Parish Council becomes aware that an encroachment on roadside waste has taken place within the parish,† the proper course is to make a representation on the subject to the District Council.‡

The District Council can take action by way of indictment, or, with the permission of the Attorney-General, of Information. And, as we have seen, the Council will be justified in removing the encroachment, where it is clearly illegal, after reasonable notice to the person responsible for it.§

The provision of the Local Government Act which we have quoted expressly enacts, that "nothing in the section shall affect the powers of the County Council in relation to roadside wastes." || This provision refers to a section of the Local Government Act, 1888, which authorises County Councils to prevent encroachments on such wastes by the side of main roads maintained by the County Council, and to assert the right of the public to the use and enjoyment of such strips.¶

* Sec. 26 (4).

† A Parish Council may make representations as to any encroachments within the district of the District Council; but will usually be most interested in those in its own parish.

‡ See Chapter III., p. 278, as to the possibility of compelling the District Council to act by mandamus. The obstruction of a footpath and encroachments on roadside waste are in the same position in this respect.

§ See *ante*, p. 312.

|| Local Government Act, 1894, sec. 26 (6).

¶ Local Government Act, 1888, 51 & 52 Vict. c. 41. s. 11; and see as to the nature of the interest of the County Council in roadside waste, Curtis *v.* Kesteven County Council, 45 Ch. Div. 504.

In the case of main roads, therefore, there appears to be a concurrent jurisdiction in the District and in the County Council. Either Council may prevent such encroachments, while it is distinctly declared to be the duty of the District Council to do so. But in practice, as there is an appeal from the District Council to the County Council on questions of roadside waste, the District Council will, where it is disinclined to act, probably seek to leave it to the County Council, as the road authority, to deal with encroachments on the sides of roads under their care.

The Council of a borough which is a county of itself acts within its district as both County and District Council. The Act of 1894 expressly provides, that such a Council shall have the powers conferred upon a District Council by the section we have quoted.* In such case there can be no appeal to any County Council.

Nor in the case of any Urban District Council can there be any representation by a Parish Council, since Parish Councils exist only in rural parishes, that is parishes within the district of a Rural District Council.†

It will be noticed, however, that the Act casts absolutely upon every District Council the duty of preventing any unlawful encroachment on roadside waste within their district.‡ The duty is not, as in the case of a right of way, made conditional upon the opinion of the Council that the interests of the district are affected. Probably, therefore, a mandamus could be obtained by a Parish Council in a rural district, and, in any place, by any person interested in preserving the roadside waste in question, if, in a clear case, the District Council refused to act.§

* Sec. 26 (7).

† Local Government Act, 1894, sec. 1 (1) and (2).

‡ Sec. 26 (1).

§ See on this subject the remarks in Chapter III., p. 278.

Where, in a rural parish, there is no Parish Council, the Parish Meeting may make a representation to the District Council of an encroachment on roadside waste, and may complain to the County Council, if the District Council take no action on their representation.* A resolution of the Parish Meeting would be necessary either for a representation or a complaint.†

It is sometimes asserted by persons who have made encroachments on roadside waste, that they have occasioned no injury to the public, but have even in some manner improved the road. Any such allegation is no answer to an indictment, though it may properly be urged in mitigation of the sentence, after the verdict of guilty has been found.‡ The measure of public inconvenience caused by an obstruction of a highway can be considered only with regard to the punishment of the person causing it.

In the United Kingdom Electric Telegraph Company's case it was argued, that the interference with the public was but slight, and in another case in which a tramway for the use of the public was laid along a public road with the consent of the road authority, it was argued that the public would be absolutely benefited; but in both cases the Court held, that such considerations could not be taken into account in considering, whether a nuisance had been committed.§

In reference to this question there is a reported case which should, perhaps, be noticed. Upon an indictment for obstructing a highway, the jury found that " a portion of the

* Sec. 19 (8).

† See sec. 19 (6).

‡ See the principle laid down in Reg. *v.* Burney, 31 L.T. (N.S.) 828, which related to the obstruction of a cul-de-sac.

§ Reg. *v.* the United Kingdom Electric Telegraph Co., Limited, 2 F. & F. 73, 6 L.T. (N.S) 378, 31 L.J. Mag. Cas. 166, 26 J.P. 324; Reg. *v.* Train, 31 L.J. Mag. Cas. 169.

site of the chapel mentioned in the indictment and of the land inclosed by iron railings to the extent in the whole of 187 feet was part of the parish highway, but that the obstruction was inappreciable." Upon this finding a verdict of "Not Guilty" was entered, and upon a motion for a new trial, on the ground of misdirection, the Court refused to disturb the verdict.*

This case seems to amount to little more than a decision, that the Court will not interfere, when they understand it to have been the intention of the jury to acquit the defendant. An indictment for obstructing a highway is a criminal proceeding, and it has been laid down in a more recent case, that inasmuch as the defendant in such a case "stands in danger of imprisonment," it is contrary to the principles of English law to grant a new trial in any such case, "if the prisoner or defendant having stood in that danger has been acquitted."† The principle of law, that an indictment cannot be answered by showing, that the obstruction is trifling, or even for the benefit of the public, is not affected by these decisions.

It should also be distinctly borne in mind, that no highway authority can legalize an encroachment on roadside waste, or any other obstruction of a highway. Both in the United Kingdom Electric Telegraph Company's case, and in that of Train, the consent of the highway authority—to the erection of the poles in the one case, and the laying of the tramway in the other—had been obtained; but such consent did not justify the acts for which the indictment was laid.‡

* Reg. *v.* Lepine or Leprue, L.T. (N.S.) 158, 30 J.P. 723.

† Reg. *v.* Duncan, 7 Q.B. Div. 198.

‡ Reg. *v.* the United Kingdom Electric Telegraph Co., 26 J.P. 324; Reg. *v.* Train, 31 L.J. Mag. Cas. 169.

CHAPTER VIII.

Of Fore-shore and Cliffs.

THE public enjoyment of the sea-shore, either by way of the fore-shore or of the bordering cliffs, is an interest of considerable importance, and one with respect to which questions often arise.

The name fore-shore is given to the land lying between high and low water mark, *i.e.* the land which is covered with water at high tide and uncovered at low. And, speaking generally, the soil of this land belongs to the Crown by virtue of its prerogative.

It is obvious, however, that the limits of the fore-shore vary greatly, as they are computed with reference to spring or to neap tides.

The civil law held that the title of the Crown extended to all land covered by the highest natural tide in the year. But it has been held, after elaborate argument, that this is not the principle of the English common law. That principle is, that the Crown's title shall not extend to land which is cultivable, and land covered only by the highest spring tides may be cultivable. It has accordingly been ruled that the right of the Crown extends only to "the line reached by the average of the medium high tides between the spring and the neap in each quarter of a lunar revolution during the whole year."*

* See Attorney-General *v.* Chambers. Attorney-General *v.* Rees, 23 L.J. (N.S.) Ch. 662; and see, for the general principles governing the Crown's right, the authorities there cited.

The title of the Crown rests on a *primâ facie* presumption. In the absence of evidence to the contrary, the fore-shore, limited as above described, belongs to the Crown. But the fore-shore may belong to the owner of the adjoining manor, by virtue of an actual grant from the Crown, or by virtue of acts of ownership exercised from time immemorial and giving rise to the presumption of a grant. A noted case on this subject related to the fore-shore of the river Irwell, which was claimed as part of the port of Ipswich by virtue of the royal charter creating the port, but was held to belong to the Lord of the Manor of Walton-cum-Trimley by reason of acts of ownership extending over a long period.*

The fore-shores of the Crown are now under the management of the Board of Trade, except where they are adjacent to Crown manors, where they are controlled by the Commissioners of H.M. Woods and Forests, or by the Duchy of Lancaster, as the case may be.†

As a rule the public are not obstructed in passing over the fore-shore. But it has been decided, that, in England, there is no common law right of bathing in the sea from the shore, or of passing over the sea-shore to bathe, or (according to the reasoning of the Court) for any other purpose.‡

The case in which this was decided arose at a place called Great Crosby, on the banks of the Mersey. The fore-shore and the adjoining land were the property of the lord of the adjoining manor, not of the Crown, and the Lord of the Manor also had a private and exclusive right of fishing with stake nets.§ The proprietor of a neighbouring hotel, by the

* See *Re* the Manor of Walton-cum-Trimley, *Ex parte* Tomline, 28 L.T. (N.S.) 12.

† Crown Lands Act, 1866 (29 & 30 Vict. c. 62.), secs. 7--25. Notice the language of sec. 7 as to public rights.

‡ Blundell *v.* Catterell, 5 B. & A. 268.

§ *Ibid.* 304 *et al.*

licence of the Lord of the Manor, let out bathing machines, which passed to and fro over the fore-shore for the purpose of enabling persons to bathe in the sea. The plaintiff endeavoured to set up rival bathing machines, and also claimed generally the right to bathe off the fore-shore; and the action was brought to test the exclusive right of the hotel proprietor to authorise and facilitate bathing.* The case was very elaborately argued, not only at the Bar, but on the Bench, for Mr. Justice Best dissented from the rest of the Court (Lord Chief Justice Abbott and Justices Holroyd and Bailey). It was admitted, that, when the fore-shore was covered with water, the public had by the common law a right to use this as well as all other parts of the sea for the purposes of passage to and fro and for fishing. Incidental to this right was a right to get on to and off the water "at such places only as necessity or usage have appropriated for those purposes." But it was held that there was no general right of landing or embarking at any part of the shore, except in case of peril or necessity.† "When," it was remarked, "the fore-shore and adjoining soil are the King's, and no mischief or injury is likely to arise from such a practice as bathing, it is not to be supposed that unnecessary and injurious restrictions upon the subjects would be imposed by the King, who is *parens patriæ*.‡ In other words, where the fore-shore is the Crown's, as in most places, the public, though not exercising a right which can be pleaded in law, will not practically be interfered with in passing over it; and this will doubtless be the same in most cases, where the fore-shore is in private hands. But the enjoyment of the public cannot be set up to prevent some other use of the fore-shore inconsistent with such enjoyment; and such inconsistent use is more likely

* Blundell *v.* Catterell, 5 B. & A. 269, 316.

† *Ibid.* 302. ‡ *Ibid.* 300.

to arise, where the fore-shore is in private hands. In fact, the position of the public with regard to the fore-shore is very much that which it occupies with respect to a common. Practically, while a common is open the public wander over it at will, there is no criminal procedure for trespass, and no damage upon which to found a civil action can be shown; but the public cannot set up a right of wandering to prevent inclosure. So it is with the fore-shore.

This decision must, however, be understood to apply only to a general right existing by virtue of the common law. The learned Judges were most careful to say, that they in no way prejudiced any special local or personal right. Thus, Mr. Justice Holroyd stated, "My opinion will not affect any right gained by prescription or custom, either by individuals or by either the permanent or the temporary inhabitants of any vill, parish, or district."* And in another passage the Court said, "Where any benefit or urgency from the systematic use of the fore-shore existed, then usage or custom would no doubt be found to justify it."

But though the public have no legal right in or over the fore-shore, which can be asserted to prevent the owner making a profit therefrom, yet, in Scotland at least, the Crown will interfere to prevent an encroachment on the fore-shore by a person having no title.† Near Edinburgh are the sands of Portobello, much resorted to for purposes of recreation. A proprietor of adjoining ground, which was described by his title as of a specified extent and as bounded by the sea-shore, erected a wall thirty feet below the high water mark of spring tides. There being no evidence before the Court, that such proprietor had any legal interest in the soil

* Blundell *v.* Catterell, 5 B. & A. 289.

† Smith *v.* Earl of Stair and others, Officers of State for Scotland, 6 Ball's Appeal Cases, 487, and see especially pp. 497, 500.

below high spring-tide water mark, the Court considered that he was a wrong-doer. This being so, they held, that he had no right to encroach upon the enjoyment of the sea-shore by the lieges (*i.e.* the public) for the purposes of passage or of recreation by bathing, riding, golf-playing, or otherwise. And the Court further held that the Crown, though not proving its title to the soil of the fore-shore (which might in the particular case have been granted to the Marquis of Abercorn with the adjoining barony), had a title to prevent the encroachment by application for an interdict.

This decision, though not exactly establishing in the public such a right to use the sea-shore for purposes of passage and recreation as would enable them to prevent inclosure by the owner of the soil, shows that, in Scotland at least, there is such a quasi-easement as will justify interference by the representatives of the Crown to prevent encroachments by wrong-doers.

Such a doctrine strengthens the view previously expressed, that the public, so long as the fore-shore is not inclosed or obstructed by the lawful owner, are at liberty to enjoy it for passage and recreation.

It is of course clear that there may be a right of way ending on the sea-shore. There is a reported case in which the evidence showed that fishermen had occasionally carried up fish by the way claimed, that other persons had come up the way, when driven in by stress of weather, or had gone down it to bathe, while wreck, sand, stones, and sea-weed had been hauled up along the way; the jury found on this evidence, despite some adverse circumstances, in favour of a foot-way.* In another case the road under consideration was set out under an Inclosure Award, and connected a Yorkshire

* Davies *v.* Stephens, 7 C. & P. 570.

village with the sea-shore; at the end of the road was a landing-place, also set out under the Award.*

In many parts of the coast of England cliffs rise immediately above the fore-shore, and there are few more delightful walks anywhere than those along the edge of such cliffs. There is no special law relating either to the soil or to the right of access to such cliffs. The soil of the cliff may belong to the Crown or to a private owner. It may be common land subject to rights of common, or purely private property. There is not, as a matter of course, any right of way along the edge of the cliff, and everyone will recall instances in which private inclosures cut off all access to the cliff edge. There is, however, very commonly a walk used by the coastguard, and, where this is clearly defined, leads from point to point, and, is freely used by the public, it may be assumed that such walk is a public footpath. The erection of stiles and gates across the path, where it passes through walls or hedges, is strong evidence of public right.

Sometimes, also, there are public carriage roads along the cliff edge, and some curious questions have arisen, where the cliff has fallen and the portion over which the path ran has thus disappeared. It has been held, that, where, by the encroachment of the waves, the road and the land over which, it passed are swept away, the highway authorities are not bound to restore the road,† nor is a landowner, bound to repair a road by reason of his tenure of the land over which it passes, obliged, in such a case, to make up the road or to give an easement over his adjoining land.‡ "To restore the road, as he is required to do, he must create a part of the

* Reg. *v.* Hornsea, Dearsley Cr. Cas. 291.

† Reg. *v.* Hornsea, Dearsley Cr. Cas. 291; see also Worthing Local Board *v.* Lancing Parish, "Times" of 9 Dec. 1879.

‡ Reg. *v.* Bamber, 5 Q.B. 279.

earth anew. . . Under these circumstances, can the defendant be liable for not repairing the road?"* But there may be cases where the road has not entirely disappeared, but has only been rendered less commodious by the falling or slipping of the land, and in such cases the parish is bound to restore the road, though at considerable expense. In a reported case, a road on the side of a hill had been carried away and overlaid by a landslip for 252 yards. The road on either side remained, and it was possible, in dry weather, to pass over the *débris* on the interrupted part. It was practicable to form a permanent and passable road along the old track, of a similar character to the adjoining parts of the old road, for £341. There were other roads between the points connected by the interrupted road, but such other roads were circuitous. The Court (Blackburn and Quain, JJ.), on an indictment of the parish for non-repair, held, that the line of the road being known, and the expense of repair not being more than the subject-matter of the repair was reasonably worth, the parish was liable to restore and repair the road.†

The public may also have a right of way along a sea-wall or quay. There is nothing inconsistent in the use of the sea-wall as a thoroughfare and its main use to prevent the incursion of the sea. Evidence which would raise a presumption of the dedication of a public way over ordinary land will raise it also in the case of a sea-wall.‡ But if the sea-wall is washed away, the highway authorities are not bound to restore it.§

* Per Lord Denman, C.J., in Reg. *v.* Bamber, 5 Q.B., 287.

† Reg. *v.* Inhabitants of Greenlaw, 1 Q,B. Div. 703.

‡ Greenwich District Board of Works *v.* Maudslay, L.R. 5 Q.B. 397; and see as to the principle upon which a dedication of a way may be presumed over lands or water held for specific purposes, Rex *v.* Leake, 5 B. & Ad. 469; Grand Junction Canal Co. *v.* Petty, 21 Q.B. Div. 273.

§ Reg. *v.* Inhabitants of Paul, 2 Moo. & Rob. 307.

CHAPTER IX.

Of Rivers and Lakes.

THE use by the public of rivers and lakes for purposes of enjoyment is so nearly allied to the questions of which this volume treats that it may be convenient to give an outline of the law on the subject. Rights of fishing—which have given rise to a distinct set of legal questions—will not, however, be alluded to except incidentally.

The leading principle to be apprehended in relation to the use of rivers and lakes is, that where there is a right to go upon such waters in vessels and boats, such right is a right of way, the river or lake being a public highway. "A common river is as a common street."* "It cannot be disputed that the channel of a public navigable river is a king's highway and properly so described."† "Again, there be other rivers, as well fresh as salt, that are of common or public use for carriage of boats and lighters, and these, whether fresh or salt, whether they flow and reflow or not, are, *primâ facie, publici juris*, common highways for men or goods, or both, from one inland town to another."‡

---

* 13 Rep. 33.

† Per Lord Denman, C.J., in Williams *v.* Wilcox (1838), 8 A. & E. 329, and see an almost identical dictum of the same learned judge in Mayor of Colchester *v.* Brooke (1845), 7 Q.B., 373.

‡ Lord Hale, De Jure Maris, ch. 3, quoted by Whiteside, C.J., in Bristow *v.* Cormican, Ir. Rep. 10 C. L. 436.

The public, as such, cannot enjoy a right of recreation, as distinguished from a right of way, on a river or lake; such a right is not known to the law.* But there would seem to be no reason why a limited class of persons (*e.g.*, the inhabitants of a parish or other defined district, or possibly the riparian owners on a stream or lake) should not enjoy such a right on the same principle and on the same conditions as apply to rights of recreation on land.†

All running streams are not common highways. In this relation rivers may be divided into three classes—

(1) Public navigable rivers where the tide ebbs and flows.

(2) Public rivers, above the ebb and flow of the tide.

(3) Private rivers.

There is probably no substantial difference in the right of way of the public over the rivers coming under the first two categories, but it is enjoyed under somewhat different conditions.

In public tidal navigable‡ rivers the soil is in the Crown, and is held by the Crown for the benefit of its subjects for the purposes of navigation.§ And any grant of the soil by the Crown must be taken to be made subject to the right of navigation, which is not in any way prejudiced by such

* Bourke v. Davis (River Mole, Surrey, 1889), 44 Ch. Div. 110.

† Bourke *v.* Davis, 44 Ch. Div. 120 125; and see as to rights of recreation on land, *ante*, pp. 177 to 182.

‡ In Murphy *v.* Ryan the Court came to the conclusion that the word navigable as applied to a river in a legal sense imported, that the river was tidal, but this restricted and non-natural use of the word does not seem to have been since consistently observed (see, *e.g.*, the judgment in Orr-Ewing *v.* Colquhoun, 2 App. Cas. 874, which declared the River Leven, a non-tidal river, to be "a navigable river, free and open to the public").

§ Per Lord Denman, C.J., in Williams *v.* Wilcox (River Severn, 1838), 8 A & E. 333; Mayor of Colchester *v.* Brooke (1845), 7 Q.B. 339, 374; Gann *v.* The Free Fishers of Whitstable, 11 H. L. Cas. 192, and see especially per Lord Westbury, 207.

grant.* In all such waters, *primâ facie* the public have the right of fishing, and such right cannot be ousted by any grant made since the commencement of the reign of Henry II., all grants since that time being made illegal by Magna Charta.

A grant of a several fishery to the exclusion of the public may, however, have been granted to a subject before the reign of Henry II., and such a grant will be presumed from long enjoyment.†

The ebb and flow of the tide is not in itself conclusive evidence that the place in question (river or creek) is subject to a public right of navigation; but it furnishes strong *primâ facie* evidence of such a right.‡ "How does it appear that this is a navigable river? The flowing and reflowing of the tide does not make it so, for there are many places into which the tide flows, that are not navigable rivers; and the place in question [a creek in the neighbourhood of Lynn Regis called Dowshill Fleet] may be a creek in their own private estate." § "The flowing of the tide, though not absolutely inconsistent with rights of private property in the creek [Rainham Creek communicating with the Thames], is *primâ facie* evidence of its being a navigable river."||

The test of the tidal character of a river is whether the water flows and reflows, and not whether it is salt or fresh. Where the flow and reflow takes place, there *primâ facie* the

* Gann *v.* The Free Fishers of Whitstable, 11 H. L. Cas. 192.

† Malcolmson *v.* O'Dea (River Shannon, 1862), 10 H. L. Cas. 618; Neill *v.* Duke of Devonshire (River Blackwater), 8 App. Cas. 135. It would appear that evidence of actual possession and enjoyment is necessary in such a case as well as a paper title; evidence of fishing by the public is admissible as against the claim.

‡ Mayor of Lynn *v.* Turner (1774), 1 Cowp. 86; Miles *v.* Rose (1814), 5 Taunt. 705; King *v.* Montague (1825), 4 B. & C. 598.

§ Per Lord Mansfield in Mayor of Lynn *v.* Turner, *ubi supra.*

|| Per Gibbs, C.J., in Miles *v.* Rose, *ubi supra.*

soil is in the Crown.* "And it seems that, although the water be fresh at high water, yet the denomination of an arm of the sea continues, if it flows and reflows, as in the Thames above the Bridge."†

In rivers of the second class, public rivers where the tide does not ebb and flow, there is no *primâ facie* presumption that the soil is in the Crown.‡ The soil may be in the Crown by special title, or may be held by a subject under a grant from the Crown.§ But as a rule the presumption, as in the case of a highway on land, is that the soil up to the half of the river bed (*ad medium filum viæ*) belongs to the riparian owners on each side. The river, in fact, belongs to them, subject to the right of passage of the public.‖ In such rivers the public have no right to fish; such a right is unknown to the law, and cannot be presumed from user, however long and uninterrupted.¶ And this is the case even

* Murphy *v.* Ryan, Ir. Rep. 2 C. L. 150, 151.

† Lord Hale, De Jure Maris, p. 12, quoted in Murphy *v.* Ryan, *ubi supra.*

‡ See per Lord Denman, C.J., in Williams *v.* Wilcox (River Severn, 1838), 8 A & E. 333; Murphy *v.* Ryan (River Barrow, 1867), Ir. Rep. 2 C. L. 143, 151; Malcolmson *v.* O'Dea (1862), 10 H. L. Cas. 618 (the opinion of the judges delivered by Wills, J.).

§ See Bourke *v.* Davis (River Mole, 1889), 44 Ch. Div. 110.

‖ See this very emphatically stated by Lord Blackburn in the modern case of Orr-Ewing *v.* Colquhoun (River Leven, between Loch Lomond and Clyde, 1877) 2 App. Cas. 839.

¶ Murphy *v.* Ryan (River Barrow, 1867), Ir. Rep. 2 C. L. 143; Hargreaves *v.* Diddams (River Itchen, 1875), L. R. 10 Q. B. 582; Mussett *v.* Birch (River Stour, Essex, 1876), 35 L. T. (N. S.) 486; Blount *v.* Layard (Thames at Maple Durham), [1891] 1 Ch. 681 *n.*; Smith *v.* Andrews (Thames near Maidenhead), [1891] 1 Ch. 678; and see the observations of Lord Selborne as to a claim to fish by the public in Neill *v.* Duke of Devonshire, 8 App. Cas. 154. See also Micklethwayt *v.* Vincent (Hickling Broad, Norfolk, 1892), 67 L. T. (N. S.) 225. Blount *v.* Layard and Smith *v.* Andrews related to different parts of the same several fishery; in both cases it was held, that, though long and uninterrupted acts of fishing by the public could never establish a right in the public to fish, yet evidence of such acts was admissible, by way of defence to an action of trespass, to discredit the title of the claimant to the several fishery, and to show that his title cannot really be so good as he says, but must have some infirmity in it, or he never would have allowed such acts to be done constantly and openly. See Smith *v.* Andrews, 707.

when a river has been made navigable for commerce by Act of Parliament, with or without payment of tolls, and by means of locks or otherwise.*

With regard to the right of passage, however, there seems to be no difference between a tidal river and a non-tidal river which is in fact used for purposes of navigation. Lord Hale, in a passage already partially quoted,† says: "Some streams or rivers are private not only in property but in use, as little streams and rivers not a common passage for the King's people. Again, there be other rivers, as well fresh as salt, that are of common or public use for the carriage of boats and lighters, and these, whether fresh or salt, whether they flow and reflow or not, are, *primâ facie, publici juris,* common highways for men or goods, or both, from one inland town to another." Again, in a case relating to the River Severn, Lord Denman said: "It is clear that the channels of public navigable rivers were always highways; up to the point reached by the flow of the tide the soil was presumably in the Crown, and above that point, whether the soil at common law was in the Crown or in the owner of the adjacent lands (a point perhaps not free from doubt),‡ there was at least a jurisdiction in the Crown, according to Sir Matthew Hale (De Jure Maris, Part I. ch. 2. p. 8.), to reform and punish nuisances in all rivers, whether fresh or salt, that are a common passage, not only for ships and greater vessels, but also for smaller, as barges or boats. In either case the right of the subject to pass up and down was complete."§ And his Lordship concluded, that neither in tidal nor in non-tidal

* See Hargreaves *v.* Diddams, Mussett *v.* Birch, *ubi supra.*

† De Jure Maris, ch. 3. Cited with approval by Whiteside, C.J., in Bristow *v.* Cormican, Ir. Rep. 10 C. L. 436.

‡ It is now settled law that the Crown has no *primâ facie* right to the soil above the tide. Bristow *v.* Cormican (1878), 3 App. Cas. 641, 652, 665–7.

§ Williams *v.* Wilcox (1838), 8 A. & E. 314.

rivers had the Crown any power at common law to obstruct the river, or to grant to any subject the power to obstruct.

The character of the public right of way on a non-tidal river came incidentally under the consideration of the House of Lords in the case of the River Leven, by which the waters of Loch Lomond pass to the Clyde.* This river is tidal to a certain point, but not throughout. At a point of its course, where it was unaffected by the tide, a bridge had been erected across the stream by a trading firm which owned the land at the point in question on both sides. The bridge was erected on piers placed on the bed of the stream. It was not questioned, that the bed of the stream belonged to the persons who had erected the bridge. The river was navigated throughout by steamers, as well as by barges and smaller boats. The Scotch Courts held, that, though the piers of the bridge might not be an actual obstruction to the navigation (as to which they appear to have been doubtful), their erection, as it might possibly hereafter, through a change in the flow of the stream, or other action of the water, cause some inconvenience to the navigation, was in itself illegal. Against this decision the persons responsible for the bridge appealed to the House of Lords, and that tribunal justified them in their act on the ground, that no actual injury to the right of way had been shown. It was emphatically laid down by all the noble Lords that the right of the public in such a river is a right of way, and not a right of property (this is clearly the case also in a tidal river); that consequently an erection in the bed of the river by the owner of the soil was not illegal *per se;* and that, unless there is a present interference with the right of the public to navigate, or it can be shown, that what is done

* Orr-Ewing *v.* Colquhoun (1877), 2 App. Cas. 839.

will necessarily produce effects which will interfere with that right, there is no *injuria;* and if there is no *injuria,* the right to have the thing erected removed, fails.* Upon the evidence, the House found that, having regard to the character of the water-way, and the conditions under which the navigation had previously been carried on, the piers of the bridge did not interfere with the navigation. And in their formal judgment, the House pronounced that the Leven was "a navigable river free and open to the public"; that "the appellants (the persons erecting the bridge) had no right to execute any works which will interfere with or obstruct navigation or the free use of the towing path along the banks of the river for purposes of navigation"; but that the appellants had not executed any such works.†

In tidal navigable waters the erection of a pier on the bed of the river would undoubtedly be illegal, as an intrusion on the property of the Crown. But this fact does not seem to create any distinction in the right enjoyed by the public as such over tidal and over non-tidal waters.

The use of a river, not only by the larger kind of craft and for commercial purposes, but by small boats, affords evidence towards the establishment of a public right. Reference to the smaller class of boats is made by Lord Hale in some of the passages which we have quoted; and in the case of Rainham Creek ‡ the fact, that the creek had been used by pleasure boats, was held by the Court to constitute material

* See per Lord Blackburn, 853, 854.

† 874. The remark of Lord Hatherley in this case, that gates may be put across a highway on land, if they can be opened, and thus do not obstruct passage, does not seem to be in accordance with established decisions in English law (Bateman *v.* Burge, 6 C. & P. 391), though it is supported by Scotch law; see the case of Sutherland *v.* Thomson, 3 Court of Sessions Cases, 4th Series, 489. quoted by Lord Gordon, p. 871.

‡ Miles *v.* Rose (1814), 5 Taunt. 705.

evidence of the right of navigation. It was proved, that the creek had been used very slightly for commercial purposes, except by the person who claimed it as his private property. But the Court, in delivering judgment, said: "Even as to pleasure boats, if a person wishes to protect his exclusive possession, he must keep the evidence of his right by guarding it against intruders."*

A right of navigation, however, is under all circumstances a right of way. Consequently, where there is no access to a stream from public highways, and the stream does not itself constitute a highway from one public place to another, it seems that the public at large cannot claim as of right to take boats upon it for pleasure. This question was recently discussed with reference to the River Mole in Surrey (a tributary of the Thames).† The passage into the Mole from the Thames is blocked at a short distance above the confluence of the two streams; and it was not alleged, that this obstruction was unlawful. Higher up the stream, however, there is a considerable stretch of the river—from a mill-dam a little below Esher Bridge upwards to Cobham Bridge—where small boats can be rowed or paddled. It was proved that there was no public access to the river at Cobham Bridge, and the Judge (who tried the case without a jury) was not satisfied that there was any such access either at Esher Bridge, or at the mill-dam which constituted the lower limit of the navigation. At one or two places highways approached the stream, but the stream was not used in connection with them; nor was the river itself used as a thoroughfare from one place to another. There had for some time been considerable boating for pleasure, but it had

* Per Gibb, C.J.

† Bourke *v.* Davis (1889), 44 Ch. Div. 110.

originated with the riparian proprietors, and so far as the public were concerned had grown gradually, and more or less secretly. Those who let out boats had at first only lent them for what the borrower liked to give, and had no fixed scale of charges. There was also some evidence of objection, though not effective, on the part of the riparian owners; and a notice against trespassers had been placed at one point of the river from 1864 downwards. The bed of the river was in the Crown (by special title) till 1820; it was then granted to certain trustees, and had been in settlement from that time till the date of the action, so that since 1820 there had been no one able to dedicate any right of way to the public. Under these circumstances the Court * held, that on the evidence there was no highway along the piece of river in question.† A right of recreation in the public, as distinguished from a right of way, was held, following the cases relating to Village Greens,‡ to be impossible; but it was intimated, that the riparian proprietors might as a class be entitled to a private right of way, or to a customary right of boating for pleasure for themselves and their friends.

The River Mole may therefore be taken as a specimen of the third class of rivers—those which, to use Lord Hale's words, are private, "not only in property, but in use."

Whether a non-tidal river is or is not "a common passage for the King's people" would appear to depend, as in the case of a highway on land, upon the question, whether such a user can be shown as will raise a presumption of

* Mr. Justice Kay.

† It is believed that, notwithstanding this decision, the barrier complained of in the action was soon afterwards removed, and the river is now used for boating by the public.

‡ *Ante*, pp. 177–182.

dedication; and in connection with the user the character of the river will naturally be taken into account: its capacity to bear vessels and boats, and to furnish a thoroughfare from one public place to another.

The same considerations, indeed, apply to a tidal river, with this difference, that in such case there is always a presumption that the river is navigable.

Inland lakes, not subject to the flow and reflow of the tide, seem to stand in the same position, with reference to the right of navigation by the public, as non-tidal rivers. It has been decided by the House of Lords, that there is no presumption, that the soil of such waters is in the Crown.* Lord Blackburn stated, that he knew of "no case or book of authority to show, that the Crown is of common right entitled to land covered by water, when the water is not running water forming a river, but still water forming a lake."† It has also been decided, by a series of Irish cases, that the public have not, of common right, a right to fish in large inland waters in which the tide does not flow and reflow, although such waters are navigable.‡ One of these cases related to Lough Erne, 45 miles long, and another to Lough Neagh, 24 miles long and 10 or 12 broad. In the latter case two eminent Irish judges (Whiteside, C.J., and Baron Dowse) seemed to think, that the previous decisions had gone too far in treating a great inland sea on the same principle as an ordinary river; and though they felt bound by these decisions, they hoped that the House of Lords would deal afresh with the whole subject. Owing to the state of the pleadings when the case went to the House of Lords,

* Bristow *v.* Cormican (Lough Neagh, 1878), 3 App. Cas. 641.

† Bristow *v.* Cormican, 665–7.

‡ Murphy *v.* Ryan (River Barrow, 1867), Ir. Rep. 2 C.L. 143; Bloomfield *v.* Johnson (Lough Erne, 1868), Ir. Rep. 8 C.L. 68; Bristow *v.* Cormican (Lough Neagh, 1894), Ir. Rep. 10 C.L. 398.

the question of the public right to fish was not considered there. Neither was it decided, whether the soil was to be presumed to be in the adjoining proprietors, Lord Blackburn even stating, that such a presumption would seem to be rather inconvenient in the case of a large lake. All that was decided was, that the soil was not, of common right, in the Crown.*

With regard to the right of navigation, it was, however, admitted in all these cases, that the right to navigate existed in the public, the lakes being, in fact, common highways. A similar conclusion was arrived at in the case of Lake Ulleswater, in the North of England. This lake was the subject of two actions, in 1860 and 1871.† In the first action it was proved at the trial, ‡ that as far back as human memory went all persons having property on the lake, or having lawful access to it, were accustomed to use the privilege of going and being conveyed on the lake in boats, with or without goods, and of landing "where they might." And in the second action, in a special case stated for the opinion of the Court, it was found as a fact, that the right of the public had been established in the first action; and the judgment of the Court on the particular point at issue (which related to an obstruction), was based on the view, that the lake was a public highway. A learned Judge has indeed doubted, whether, if an inland lake were touched by a highway only at one point, all the other banks being private property, the public would be entitled to any right of navigation upon it.§ Resort to so extreme a supposition to negative the public

* Bristow *v.* Cormican, 665–7.

† Marshall *v.* Ulleswater Steam Navigation Co. (1860), 3 B. & S. 732; Marshall *v.* Ulleswater Steam Navigation Co. (1871), L.R. 7 Q.B. 166.

‡ *Ubi supra* 739.

§ Per Kay, J., in Bourke *v.* Davis, 44 Ch. Div. 110.

right tends to show, that a public right of way may be expected to be found on most lakes of any size. Whether there is or is not such a right, would appear to depend on user, as proving dedication, just as in the case of a non-tidal river, or a highway on land.

In a recent case * relating to the largest of the Norfolk Broads, Hickling Broad,—a shallow water covering 600 acres and extending into three parishes,—the plaintiff, who claimed to be the owner, sought to restrain the defendant from shooting and fishing on the Broad, and from entering upon any part of the Broad except the channel or waterway between two points known as Hickling Staithe and Deep-Go Dyke. The defendant claimed to fish and shoot as one of the public; and, besides disputing the plaintiff's title on other grounds, claimed that the Broad was tidal. The Court † held, that it was not, that the plaintiff had made out his title as owner, and that the defendant could not set up, as one of the public, a right to shoot and fish. But the Court declined to limit the right of way of the public to the channel between the points named.

As in the case of a highway on land, the right of passage of the public extends to the whole of a river. "Those who use the river are entitled to say they have a right to the whole space." ‡

It follows from this, that no kind of obstruction to the navigation of the river is justifiable. Thus oysters thrown into the bed of a navigable river (the Colne) were held to be a nuisance.§ And a dummy or landing-stage, moored alongside a wharf on a river, so as to rise and fall with the tide,

* Micklethwayt *v.* Vincent (1892), 67 L.T. (N.S.) 225.

† Romer, J.

‡ Per Mellish, L.J., Att-Gen. *v.* Terry, L.R. 9 Ch. App. 423.

§ Mayor of Colchester *v.* Brooke (1845), 7 Q.B. 339.

or a pier projecting into a lake, is an obstruction, if it prevents a person navigating the river or lake from landing at the wharf, or on the bank of the lake, as he otherwise would.* In the case of the Ulleswater Lake (a non-tidal body of water), it was laid down very distinctly by the Court, † that, where there is a public highway, the owners of adjoining land have the right to go on the highway from any spot on their own land, and the same right exists in the case of a river or lake which is a highway. The necessary incidents of such a right follow. Steamers or other boats can be taken as close as possible to the shore, and landing may be effected either by wading, by the use of smaller boats, or by planks laid from the vessel to the shore. Where, however, in a non-tidal water, the soil of the river or lake does not belong to the owner of the shore where landing takes place, there must be no disturbance of the soil, as by casting an anchor. A pier projecting into the river or lake prevents landing in the way in which it would otherwise be effected, and therefore is an obstruction to the rights of navigating and landing. Consequently, those who have the right to land can either remove it or "put foot on it and get across."‡

Again, the construction of works for the extension of a wharf, and the consequent narrowing, even to a very slight extent, of the navigable area of a river, is illegal.§ In the River Stour at Sandwich—a tidal river at this point—a wharf-owner drove piles into the bed of the river to extend his wharf, occupying in this way 3 feet out of a total breadth of 60 feet. The Corporation of Sandwich were endowed

* Eastern Counties Railway Co. *v.* Dorling (River Orwell, 1859), 5 C.B. (N.S.) 821, 837; Marshall *v.* Ulleswater Steam Navigation Co. (Ulleswater Lake, 1871), L.R. 7 Q.B. 166.

† Blackburn, Mellor, and Lush, JJ.

‡ Marshall *v.* Ulleswater, *ubi supra* 172, 173.

§ Att.-Gen. *v.* Terry (River Stour at Sandwich, 1874), L.R. 9 Ch. App. 423.

with statutory powers of maintaining the navigation of the Stour, and at their relation the Attorney-General moved the Court for a mandatory injunction for the removal of the piles. The late Sir George Jessel (Master of the Rolls) held, that an indictable obstruction to the navigation of the river had been caused; and he laid down, that no man has a right to put an obstruction in the bed of a navigable river, which may become a nuisance in the future, even if it is not actually one at the time.* The learned judge examined at some length an earlier case † in which an enlargement of a wharf had been allowed on the ground, that there was a countervailing benefit to the public in greater facilities for the shipment of coal, and a consequent reduction in its price at other places. Sir George Jessel held that this case could not be supported. The only advantage, which it is lawful to consider by way of set-off to an encroachment on a navigable river, must be of a similar nature to the obstruction, so that there is a balance of advantage to the public at the particular place where the obstruction is caused.‡ If, for example, at the same time that a wharf was extended in one place, it was thrown back in another, and by this or other means the navigation of the river were improved; or even if a bridge for the convenience of the public of the locality were built by means of piers placed in the bed of the stream which did not in fact impede the navigation,§ the benefit might perhaps be set off against the obstruction, and the jury might find that there was no nuisance. But, where the obstruction was caused in the mere pursuit of private gain, no facilities offered to trade could be properly taken into account.

* Att.-Gen. *v.* Terry, *ubi supra* 429.

† Reg. *v.* Russell, 6 B. & C. 566.

‡ Att.-Gen. *v.* Terry, *ubi supra* 428.

§ Queen *v.* Betts (River Witham, Linc. 1850), 16 Q.B. 1022.

And with this view the Court of Appeal seems to have agreed, Lord Justice Mellish remarking: * "Those who use the river are entitled to say they have a right to the whole space; and in my opinion it is no answer that any obstruction only occurs at certain times of the tide, and that in some respects the alteration would be advantageous."

The River Stour was a tidal river; and the rule as to obstructions requires some qualification in its application to a non-tidal river. In the case of the River Leven, between Loch Lomond and the Clyde, we have already seen, that the placing of the piers of a bridge in the bed of the stream was held not to be illegal, where no interference with the navigation was in fact caused; and in this case it is clear, that the bridge was erected merely for private gain and not for public traffic.† The correct rule in relation to a non-tidal river appears to be, that nothing must be done "which will interfere with or obstruct the navigation."‡ In tidal rivers, where the bed of the river belongs to the Crown, the rule may be taken to be that laid down by Sir Geo. Jessel.

Length of time alone is no justification of an obstruction in a navigable river, whether tidal or non-tidal. Thus a mill-owner, who had had a mill in a river for twenty years, was held to have no right to the maintenance of the water at a given level, if the river was a public navigable river.§ Indeed, it is obvious that, a navigable river being a highway, the maxim "once a highway, always a highway," applies.|| But, in the case of a highway on land, the right of way may

* Att.-Gen. *v.* Terry, L.R. 9 Ch. App. 423.

† Orr-Ewing *v.* Colquhoun (1877), 2 App. Cas. 839.

‡ See formal judgment pronounced by the House, p. 874.

§ Vooght *v.* Winch (1819), 2 B. & A. 662. This case related to a stream called the Channel Sea River at West Ham, and the injury complained of was the diversion of the water by means of Potter's Ditch, which flowed into the Water-works River and so into the Lea.

|| *Ante*, p. 258.

have been dedicated subject to conditions (*e.g.*, the existence of gates, or a right of ploughing); and similar conditions may be assumed in the case of rivers. Consequently, in a non-tidal stream, it is probable, that the existence of obstructions for any considerable length of time might be held to afford ground for a presumption of the dedication of the river subject to the right to maintain works of the kind in question. It is therefore undoubtedly important, especially in a non-tidal river, to take action against obstructions without delay.

A public navigable river or lake, like a highway on land, is open to reasonable use by all Her Majesty's subjects for a reasonable purpose.

The analogy between a public river and a highway on land in this respect was forcibly illustrated by an incident which occurred on the Thames at Ratcliffe.* There existed, side by side, two wharves, one of which was used in the ordinary way for the landing and embarking of goods, and the other as a dry-dock, with an entrance available at certain states of the tide. The owner of the landing wharf possessed a steamer, the length of which was greater than the frontage of the wharf, so that, when the steamer was lying alongside the wharf, she overlapped the neighbouring wharf. The owner of the wharf, conceiving, that his rights were infringed by this overlapping, placed logs in the water opposite his wharf in such a manner as to prevent the steamer lying alongside her own wharf. It was held (by the late Sir Geo. Jessel, M.R.) that the placing of these logs in the river was an illegal act, and a mandatory injunction for their removal was granted. The learned judge laid down, that all Her Majesty's subjects had a right to use a navigable river in a reasonable manner and for reasonable purposes; and so, any

* Original Hartlepool Collieries Co. *v.* Gibb (1877), 5 Ch. Div. 713.

riparian owner had a right, in a reasonable course of business, to bring alongside his wharf a steamer which overlapped his neighbour's wharf, provided that by so doing he did not interfere with the access to his neighbour's wharf in the reasonable use of that wharf according to the business actually carried on there. In this particular case, the neighbouring wharf being used as a dry-dock, the steamer offered no obstruction, except at certain states of the tide, and then only, if it was desired to float vessels into or out of the dock. The case was likened to that of two householders in an ordinary thoroughfare (*e.g.*, the occupiers of two houses in Portland Place, where the doors actually adjoin); each has a right to draw up at his own door (either with his own carriages or those of his friends), even though in so doing he should temporarily stand in front of his neighbour's door. But, if his neighbour wishes to bring a carriage up to his own door, the obstructing carriage must move away. And there must be no systematic obstruction of the thoroughfare, so as to incommode a neighbour, or the public using the highway.

Such is the close analogy between a river and a highway on land. There are one or two points in which the analogy fails. There is no right, in the case of a river, to pass along the adjoining land *extra viam*, as there is in the case of a foundrous way on land; and there is no obligation at common law upon the inhabitants of any district, or upon any person, to maintain the river in good order for purposes of traffic, as by cleansing and scouring it.*

Public navigable rivers do in fact sometimes become closed to navigation by the silting up of sand, or by the retirement of the sea. In such cases the right of way enjoyed by the public is extinguished with the cessation of

* See per Lord Denman, C.J., in Mayor of Colchester *v.* Brooke, 7 Q.B. 339.

the actual use of the river.* And when by the working of natural agencies a river shifts its course, making a new channel, the highway is transferred to the new channel. "If a water be a high street, which water by its own force changes its course upon another soil, yet it shall have the same high street as it had before in its ancient course, so that the lord of the soil cannot disturb the new course."†

The highway along a river may also be extinguished, as in the case of a highway on land, by Act of Parliament.‡ Commissioners of Sewers and Conservators of rivers may be endowed with statutory power to alter the course of rivers and stop particular channels;§ this is in fact merely a variety of extinguishment by Act of Parliament. And a river may also, in theory, be stopped by a writ of *ad quod damnum* addressed to the sheriff, and an inquisition found thereon by a jury.‖ This procedure we have seen ¶ also in ancient times applied to highways on land. If the inhabitants of the county or district upon such a proceeding found, that it would be no injury to the Crown or other persons, if the highway, whether by land or water, were stopped, the Crown granted a licence for the stoppage of the way. This procedure has been superseded as to highways on land by the process established by the Highway Acts; ** and it may be doubted whether it would in fact be used at the present day for the stoppage of a highway by water. But when a water-way has in fact been stopped for many years, the possibility of a

* King *v.* Montague (Yantlet Creek connecting the Thames and the Medway on the west side of the Isle of Grain, 1825), 4 B. & C. 598.

† Dictum of Thorp, J., in Year Book, 23 Edw. 3. c. 93., quoted by Holroyd, J., in King *v.* Montague, 4 B. & C. 598, 603, 604; and see Mayor of Carlisle *v.* Graham, L.R. 4 Ex. 367, 371.

‡ Rex *v.* Montague, 603, 604; and see *ante*, p. 258–9.

§ Rex *v.* Montague, 603, 604.

‖ *Ib.* 282.

¶ *Ante*, p. 282.

** See *ante*, pp. 282–290.

stoppage under a writ of *ad quod damnum* is one of the grounds on which the Court may presume that the way has been legally extinguished.* As regards rivers actually navigable at the present day, it would appear that there are only two means by which the right of way can be extinguished—(1) by the obstruction of the way from natural causes, and (2) by an Act of Parliament. No disuse or obstruction for any length of time will in itself extinguish the public right of navigation.

With regard to the remedies for the obstruction of a public water-way, the law seems to be precisely the same as in the case of the obstruction of a highway over land. The author of the obstruction may be indicted for the nuisance he has caused,† or an information may be filed in the name of the Attorney-General, praying for an injunction against the continuance of the obstruction.‡ A private person cannot bring an action for the obstruction of a public water-way, unless he can show special damage.§ A private person may remove an obstruction in a public water-way, if he cannot pass without doing so, as in that case he is specially damaged.‖ If, however, he can pass without such removal, he has no right to abate the obstruction, as he is thus taking the punishment of a public nuisance into his own hands. One of the leading cases on this subject relates to a navigable tidal river, the Colne, where a person navigating a vessel was held bound to exercise care not to injure oysters belonging to

* King *v.* Montague, 4 B. & C. 598, 603, 604. Littledale, J., said, however, that he would not presume a stoppage by legal process without some evidence to warrant such a presumption.

† See for examples of Indictments, King *v.* Montague (1825), 4 B. & C. 598; Queen *v.* Betts, 16 Q.B. 1022; and see *ante*, p. 273.

‡ See Att.-Gen. *v.* Terry, L.R. 9 Ch. App. 423; and see *ante*, p. 275.

§ See Mayor of Lynn *v.* Turner (1774), 1 Cowp. 86; and for a case of an action by persons specially damaged, see Original Hartlepool Collieries Co. *v.* Gibb (1877), 5 Ch. Div. 713.

‖ See *ante*, pp. 273, 274.

the Corporation, and placed in the bed of the river, although it was at the same time held, that the oysters were an indictable nuisance.* In the case in question, it was proved, that the vessel might have been navigated so as to reach Colchester without damaging the oysters. Had it been otherwise, there would have been a private injury, and the right to abate would have arisen.

The provisions of the Local Government Act, 1894, in relation to the protection of rights of way † may possibly apply to public water-ways, though there is no distinct reference to that variety of highway. A series of recent decisions establish, that a highway authority, upon which is cast the duty of protecting public rights of way and preventing encroachments on roadside wastes, may abate an obstruction and charge the expense on the author of it.‡ There seems to be no reason, why the principle of these decisions should not apply to any local authority upon which is cast the duty of preserving the navigation on a river. But probably, in most such cases, the authority would have special statutory powers of abating obstructions.

Most rivers of importance are the subject of special Acts of Parliament, which provide for the maintenance of navigation by some constituted body under proper conditions. In particular, the traffic on the Thames has been regulated by a long series of Acts, which have recently been superseded and consolidated by the Thames Conservancy Act, 1894. This Act distinctly recognises the use of the river for purposes of pleasure under suitable conditions.

---

* Mayor of Colchester *v.* Brooke (1845), 7 Q.B. 339; see *ante*, p. 274, for a quotation of the judgment of the Court upon the question of procedure.

† See *ante*, p. 277.

‡ Reynolds *v.* Urban District Council of Presteign (1896), 1 Q.B. 604; Louth Rural District Council *v.* West, *Times*, 18 June 1896, 40 Sol. Journal, 602.

APPENDICES.

APPENDIX I.

Note as to Close and Open Times in Common Fields and Pastures.

In the borough of Nottingham, the Burgesses, claiming through the Corporation, enjoyed sole pasturage over "The Meadows" from Old Midsummer Day to Old Lammas Day, and from the 3rd of October to Candlemas, and over two other tracts called Sand Field and Clay Field, from Old Lammas Day to Old Martinmas Day; see Rex *v.* Churchill, 4 B. & C. 750.

In the borough of Colchester the Burgesses, claiming through the Corporation, enjoyed sole pasturage in certain scattered lands lying round the walls of the town from Lammas to Candlemas, except when the lands were under crop, when the rights commenced after harvest; see Johnson *v.* Barnes, L. R. 7 C. P. 592, 594.

In Derby, the Corporation claimed common (probably really sole pasturage) in a common field called Littlefield, for two years, between harvest and sowing; and the third year, when the field was fallow, for the whole year; see Mellor *v.* Spateman, 1 Wms. Saund. 343, 346*d.*

In several old Reported Cases the time of commoning upon arable common fields is stated generally to be from harvest "until the land is sowed again"; see Sir Miles Corbet's case, 7 Rep. 5; How *v.* Strode, 2 Wils. 296; Cheeseman *v.* Hardham, 1 B. & A. 706. In Whiteman *v.* King, 2 H. Bl. 4, the open time seems to have been substantially the same.

APPENDIX II.

Extract from the Register of the Decision of Claims of Rights of Common and other Rights in and over the New Forest, pursuant to an Act of Parliament passed in the year of Our Lord 1854, for the Settlement of Claims upon and over the said Forest.

Whereas I, Charles James Gale, the Judge of the County Court of Southampton, was appointed one of the Commissioners for the settlement of claims upon and over the New Forest, by an Act of Parliament passed in the year of our Lord 1854; and we, James Barstow and John Duke Coleridge, Barristers-at-Law, were appointed in writing by the Lord Chief Justice of Her Majesty's Court of Queen's Bench at Westminster, within two months from the passing of the said Act, to be the two other Commissioners for the purposes of the said Act:

And whereas each of us, before entering upon the execution of his office, made and subscribed the Declaration directed by Section 3 of the said Act; and each such Declaration was deposited in the Office of Land Revenue Records and Inrolments:

And whereas after the making of such Declaration we held divers meetings for the purposes of the said Act at divers places in or in the vicinity of the said Forest, as appeared to us most convenient, of which several meetings notice was given by advertisement in a newspaper usually published and circulated in the County of Southampton, and such notice of each such meeting was given at least 28 days before the holding of any such meeting; and in every case, when such meeting was for the purpose of hearing claims and objections, a list shewing what particular claims and objections were to be heard was prepared, and was also in like manner advertised 28 days at least before the holding of any such meeting:

And whereas at some of such meetings applications were made to us by and on behalf of divers persons for leave to make new claims, some of which applications were by us refused, and the others were by us allowed and leave given; and in the cases last mentioned the claims so allowed to be made were made and delivered to our Clerk, as directed by us, and within six months from the passing of the said Act, and such new claims were duly registered by the said Clerk, and an abstract thereof was published in the "London Gazette" of Tuesday the 27th day of March in the year of our Lord 1855; and such publication was a publication of all claims which had not been already published in the "London Gazette":

And whereas all claims and objections made previous to the passing of the said Act, together with the Entry Book or Register thereof, were, pursuant to Section 16 of the said Act, delivered by the Verderers to us:

And whereas the claims were objected to on behalf of Her Majesty, and no other objection to any claim was made, and the objections made after the passing of the said Act were made and delivered as directed by the said Act:

And whereas every claim not wholly disallowed was amended, and each claim wholly or in part allowed was entered, in accordance with our decision, on the Registry of Claims:

And whereas we, in the manner directed by the said Act, did decide the several questions arising on the said claims, and we caused our decisions to be reduced into writing, and the same were signed by us:

And whereas, in one of the cases, No. 603 in the list of claims, there being a difference of opinion on a point of law brought before us, a case was in pursuance of the said Act submitted to Her Majesty's Court of Common Pleas, and by that Court decided, and the judgment of the Court thereon has been by us treated as our judgment:

And whereas, having decided on and determined all the claims, this our present Register thereof, as by us amended or altered, has been prepared to be signed and sealed by us in duplicate, and to be deposited as by the said Act is directed, each sheet being signed in initials by each of us:

Now we, the said Charles James Gale, James Barstow, and John Duke Coleridge, to avoid unnecessary repetitions in each case, do hereby declare that each allowance of any right is made subject to, and that the same is to be exercised and enjoyed according to, the laws and assize of the said Forest, and that in all cases wherein a right is allowed subject to a payment, such payment is to be made to our Lady the Queen, and that every right of common of pasture may be exercised and enjoyed at all times of the year, except during the fence month, that is to say, the 20th day of June to the 20th day of July yearly, and the time of the winter hayning, that is to say, the 22nd day of November to the 4th day of May yearly, during which times we declare there is no right in all the unenclosed waste lands of our Lady the Queen within the said Forest for all their commonable cattle, levant and couchant, in and upon the lands in respect of which the allowance is made.

And we do hereby declare that common of pasture for sheep is allowed only in cases where it is expressly mentioned.

And we do hereby also declare that every right of common of mast is to be exercised only in time of pannage, that is to say, on and from the 25th day of September, up to and on the 22nd day of November yearly, in all the open and unenclosed woods and woody lands of our Lady the Queen in the said Forest, for all their hogs and pigs, ringed, levant, and couchant, in and upon the lands in respect of which the allowance is made, upon payment, unless otherwise expressed, yearly, to or for the use of our Lady the Queen, for every hog or pig, exceeding the age of one year, 4*d.*, and for every hog or pig under that age, 2*d.*

And we do hereby also declare that every allowance of turbary is of the liberty of having, digging, cutting, and taking turf, in and upon the open wastes of our Lady the Queen within the said Forest by the view and allowance of the Foresters of the said Forest, and of carrying away the same turf from the said places to and into the messuages mentioned and described in this our Register for the necessary fuel of the said messuages, to be therein burnt and expended. And that every allowance of fuel and fuel wood is an allowance of the quantity described of good fuel wood yearly from the open and unenclosed parts of the said Forest by the view and allowance of the Foresters of the said Forest as reasonable and necessary estovers for the necessary firewood of the messuages mentioned and described in this our Register, to be burnt and expended therein.

And we do hereby also declare that every allowance of a claim of marl is of a right to have, dig, take, and carry away from the open and accustomed marl pits in the said Forest, a Schedule whereof is set forth at the end of this Register, by the view and allowance of the

Foresters of the said Forest, sufficient marl for the necessary marling of the lands in respect whereof the said marl is allotted and adjudged to be exclusively used thereon.

And we do hereby also declare that, save as aforesaid, no payment or render is to be made to Her Majesty or her successors in respect of any of the said rights, or in respect of the allowance thereof, except such as is herein mentioned.

Charles James Gale.
James Barstow.
John Duke Coleridge.

NEW FOREST REGISTER OF DECISIONS ON CLAIMS of Forest Rights by the Commissioners acting under the Act of 17th and 18th Victoria, Chapter 49.

Number of Claim.	Name, place of abode, profession, trade, &c., of claimant.	Whether claim allowed, disallowed, or amended.	Date of allowance, disallowance, or amendment.	Nature, extent, and particulars of claim as finally allowed or amended after having been objected to.	Lands or Tenements in respect of which claim has been allowed or amended.
1	William Woolridge, South Baddesley, Boldre; Beer retailer.	Amended	31st December 1855.	Common of turbary (paying yearly sixpence).	An ancient messuage, situate at South Baddesley, in the Parish of Boldre, in the County of Southampton, formerly called Teeling's Cottage, and numbered 1465 on the Tithe Map of Boldre aforesaid.
2	Samuel Shrimpton, Lymington, Hants; Saddler.	Amended	31st December 1855.	Common of turbary -	An ancient messuage, called Portmore and Jordans, situate in the Parish of Boldre, in the County of Southampton, and numbered 1132 on the Tithe Map of Boldre.
				Common of pasture, common of mast, and the right to dig and take marl (paying yearly three shillings).	76 a. 3 r. 14 p. of land in the Parish of Boldre aforesaid, and numbered on the Tithe Map of that Parish 1075, 1076, 1077, 1094, 1114, 1115, 1116, 1117, 1118, 1119, 1120, 1122, 1123, 1124, 1125, 1130, 1131, 1132, and 1032.
3	Ellen Susan Jones, Lymington, Hants; Spinster.	Amended	31st December 1855.	Common of turbary and three loads of fuel wood.	An ancient messuage situate at Pilley, in the Parish of Boldre, in the County of Southampton, called Elgars, and num- on the Tithe Map of that Parish 987.
				Common of pasture, common of mast, and the right to dig and take marl (paying yearly 2*s.* 7*d.*)	34 a. 2 r. 20 p. of land situate in the said Parish of Boldre, formerly called Walls, Wheelers, and Harmons, and now "Elgars," and numbered on the Tithe Map of that Parish 859, 860, 862, 863, 972*b*, 974, 978, 979, 987, 998, and 999.

NEW FOREST REGISTER, &c.—*Cont.*

Number of Claim.	Name, place of abode, profession, trade, &c., of claimant.	Whether claim allowed, disallowed, or amended.	Date of allowance, disallowance, or amendment.	Nature, extent, and particulars of claim as finally allowed or amended after having been objected to.	Lands or Tenements in respect of which claim has been allowed or amended.
4	Joseph Weld, Lulworth Castle, Dorset; Esquire. And Edward Joseph Weld, Tavistock, Devon; Esquire.	Amended	31st December 1855.	Common of turbary -	An ancient messuage, called Lisle Court, situate in the Parish of Boldre, in the County of Southampton, and numbered on the Tithe Map of that Parish 1280.
				Common of pasture, common of mast, and the right to dig and take marl (paying yearly 1s. 9½*d.* and one bushel of oats, imperial measure).	61 a. 0 r. 28 p. of land situate in the said Parish of Boldre, and numbered on the Tithe Map of that Parish 1271, 1272, 1273, 1274, 1275, 1276, 1277, 1278, 1279, 1280, 1281, 1282, 1283, 1284, 1285, 1286, 1486, 1488, 1489, 1490, 1491, 1492, 1493, and 1494.
	* *	*	* *	* *	* * *

NOTE.—The total number of claims scheduled is 1311, of which 448 were disallowed. Of the allowed claims (863), 102 were in respect of property in Wilts, and 10 of property in Dorset.

SCHEDULE of open and accustomed Marl Pits and places within the New Forest.

Description.	Name of Walk.
The open and accustomed marl pits and places at Lyndhurst Hill.	Iron's Hill.
The like at Bank - - - - - - - -	Iron's Hill.
The like, called Oslemsley Ford, near the Christchurch Road railway station.	Holmesley.
The like, called Old Hole, near Levett's Gate - -	Holmesley and Wilverley.
The like at Hinchelsea - - - - - - -	Rhinefield.
The like at or near the Marl Pit Oak - - -	Rhinefield.
The like near the New Inn, Battramsley - - -	Rhinefield.
The like at Blackhamsley Hill - - -	Rhinefield.
The like near Sway - - - - - - -	Wilverley.
The like at Broadley - - - - - - -	Wilverley.
The like at Crockford - - - - - -	Lady Cross.
The like at Two Bridges - - - - - -	Lady Cross.
The like at Monkey Hornhand Sheepwash - -	Lady Cross.
The like near Dilton - - - - - - -	Lady Cross.
The like at Frogmoor - - - - - - -	Lady Cross.
The like at Greenmoor - - - - - - -	Lady Cross.
The like at Hatchett's Pond - - - - - -	Lady Cross.
The like at Holland's Wood - - - - - -	Whitley Ridge.
The like at Pignell - - - - - - -	Whitley Ridge.
The like at Sandydown opposite Hayward Mill -	Whitley Ridge.
The like near Brockenhurst Mill - - - - -	Whitley Ridge.
The like at Winding Shoot - - - - - -	Boldrewood.
The like at Acre's Down - - - - - -	Boldrewood.
The like at Ferney Crofts - - - - - -	Denny.

CHARLES JAMES GALE. (L.S.)
JAMES BARSTOW. (L.S.)
JOHN DUKE COLERIDGE. (L.S.)

Signed and sealed by the said James Barstow and John Duke Coleridge the 5th day of November 1857, and by the said Charles James Gale on the 11th day of the same month, in the presence of

WILLIAM STEAD,
Clerk to the said Commissioners.

Received into the Office of Land Revenue Records and Inrolments, the 14th day of November, 1857.

T. R. FEARNSIDE,
Keeper of the Records.

APPENDIX III.

IN THE HIGH COURT OF JUSTICE, CHANCERY DIVISION, 1st April 1879.

Before the Master of the Rolls (Sir Geo. Jessel).

The Attorney-General *v.* Amhurst.

JUDGMENT ON PRELIMINARY POINTS.

The Master of the Rolls :—The questions raised by this suit are novel, and though I do not consider them very difficult as far as I am concerned, that is merely my individual opinion. It by no means follows that other judges will take the same view as I do of the construction of these very curious instruments called Acts of Parliament.

The first question I have to decide is whether the information can be maintained. Inasmuch as the main portion of it has been given up by the foremost Counsel at the Bar, I have not to consider the information as it stands actually, but as it stands with that portion omitted. The information, as originally framed, is an information at the relation of the Metropolitan Board of Works. It alleged that the public had certain rights of recreation over certain commons at Hackney, which were shortly called Hackney Commons; that the defendant in alleged exercise of a right of enclosure, rights for digging gravel, and other things, was interfering with the rights of recreation exercised and enjoyed by the public at large; and it claimed an injunction on that ground. Indeed, the rights of recreation were stated by the information to be both in the inhabitants of Hackney and in the public at large; and, to show the way in which it was framed by the very experienced Counsel whose name is to it, you could see at once that the defendants could not demur to the information. The 43rd paragraph of the information charges "that as well the " rights of the said inhabitants of Hackney in respect of such custom

" of recreation as aforesaid, as also the rights of the public under the " provisions of the said Scheme, have been and will be materially " injured, diminished, and interfered with by the acts and proceedings " of the defendant already done and threatened by him to be done, in " exercise of his alleged rights, and that they will be deprived of their " respective rights, and of the benefit of the said Scheme so confirmed " by the said Act of Parliament as aforesaid, and also of the " customary rights exercised and enjoyed by the inhabitants of " Hackney as aforesaid, and also of the rights heretofore exercised " and enjoyed by the public previous to and irrespective of the said " Scheme, and in respect of such rights, as well as for the purpose " of maintaining and enforcing the provisions of the said Scheme as " confirmed by the said Act of Parliament, the informant, on behalf " of the public, claims to be entitled to such relief as hereinafter " prayed."

Now, I am not going to read the portions of the information which state what the rights were. They were admitted to be substantial rights of recreation and walking over the place. All that has been given up at the Bar by the Counsel for the informants, so that they cannot maintain any such rights; so that the question of the maintenance of the information no longer depends upon the allegation of public rights specifically described, simply on the allegation that what is about to be done or threatened to be done by the defendant is inconsistent with the purposes of the Scheme. Therefore, in considering whether or not the information as such can be maintained, I am bound to look at the Scheme to see if any rights are thereby conferred upon the public, it being admitted that the public have no rights independent of the Scheme.

Now, when I come to look at it, I confess that I am utterly at a loss to discover where the rights of the public are. I asked both the learned Counsel who so ably represent the informant to show me where they were, and the only answer that I could get was that they expected to find them there, but they did not say that they had found them; and I must say that, before I looked at the Scheme, I entertained the same expectation, and after looking at it, I have arrived at the same result. There are two Acts of Parliament necessary to be referred to, but the first is a general Act. Now, as I understand that Act of Parliament, it provides for enquiry and for the framing of a Scheme, but it does not do anything more. It does not make anything obligatory on anyone when you have got the Scheme framed. In other words, I read all the directions of the Act of Parliament to have reference to the contents of the Scheme, leaving the Scheme to be dealt with by a subsequent Act of Parliament.

It will be necessary to consider for a moment that question as regards compensation, which I will do presently more in detail, but for the present it will be necessary to say that under the 22nd Section of this Act of Parliament the Scheme certified by the Commissioners shall not of itself have any operation, but the same shall have full operation when and as confirmed by Act of Parliament, with such modifications, if any, as Parliament may see fit. So that it is nothing at all till Parliament interferes; and then when Parliament interferes, it only operates as Parliament directs it to operate, and in no other way. I therefore dismiss the first Act of Parliament and come to the second.

Now the second Act of Parliament, which is the Act of 1872, confirmed the Scheme, but it did a great deal more. Of course an Act of Parliament may do anything almost, with some few exceptions, and we must look to see what the Act of Parliament did. Now it first of all confirmed the Scheme, and then it went on to say this :—

"From and after the passing of this Act the Scheme shall be "deemed to be a public general Act of Parliament, of like force and "effect as if the provisions of the same had been enacted in the body "of this Act."

Therefore the Scheme becomes a public general Act of Parliament.

Now the Scheme, as a Scheme with respect to Hackney Downs, first of all says in the 1st paragraph, that it shall henceforth, for the purposes of this Scheme, be regulated and managed by the Metropolitan Board of Works—not "generally," but for the purposes of this Scheme. Then there are certain powers given to the Board by the 2nd paragraph for management; and then by the 3rd for executing certain works of drainage so far only as may be required for the purposes of the Metropolitan Commons Act. And then there are powers of preservation and so on, which I shall have to read presently. Then the 4th is, that they shall maintain the commons from all encroachment. The 5th is, that they make bye-laws, which are referred to further in the 6th and and 7th clauses. Then there are certain provisions in the 8th clause, and certain prohibitions in the 9th clause, a power for an amended scheme by the 10th clause, certain powers of borrowing by the 11th clause, a formal provision or a provision as to form by the 12th clause, a saving clause in the 13th, a statement of claims in the 14th, an enactment as to printing copies of the Act in the 15th, and that is all. From the beginning to the end of the Scheme I find no rights conferred either on the public at large or on the inhabitants of Hackney, or on the inhabitants of the Metropolis. That being so, the public appear to me to have no rights under the Scheme, and if the public have no rights under the Scheme (and it is now admitted at the bar that the public have no rights independently of the Scheme), it follows that the public have no rights at all as far as this matter is concerned, and therefore the Attorney-General has no right to inform the Court on behalf of the public, and the information must be dismissed. That is the first question which I have to decide.

The next point is a different one. That is, can the Metropolitan Board of Works sue? Now I must state what has occurred, because my position cannot be fully understood without a reference to the history of the cause. The Metropolitan Board of Works has powers of management, but it has also imposed upon it certain duties—Parliamentary duties and obligations—of which it cannot free itself. It is not merely management, but, if I may coin an expression, it is a compulsory management—it is compelled to manage, and, as I read the Act of Parliament—and I will go a little more into detail presently—in order to enable the Board to perform the duty which it is compelled to do, it has certain legal rights conferred upon it, which amount at least to an easement, and to a certain extent, to a right of possession—a modified right of possession. These are legal rights in respect of which the Board, like any other owner of legal rights, it appears to me must be entitled to sue if those rights are infringed. Whether you look upon this Court, as it is now, both as a Court of Law and a Court of Equity, or as a Court of Law, if these legal rights are infringed, and the Corporation entitled to the rights sues, it is in a proper case entitled to ask for and obtain an injunction to restrain either the threatened interference with the rights, or the continued interference with the rights, when such interference has already taken place.

But it might have been said, and, I think, would have been said in that case, that where the beneficial ownership of the land is divided in some way or other between the commoners and the Lord of the Manor, so that they between them have the whole beneficial ownership, and where the question raised by the Bill is a question in which a commoner as well as the lord has an interest, it is impossible that that suit can proceed in the absence of parties claiming such beneficial interest. If those persons are not plaintiffs they must be defendants. But in the course of proceedings in this case the plaintiffs desired at a late stage to bring the commoners before the Court. The defendants objected on the ground of the lateness of the proceedings, and the increase of expense, and the uselessness of the result. When it was before me in Chambers, I put it to the defendant that he was not to be entitled, if I disallowed the amendment, to object at the trial that the commoners were not before the Court, and that the plaintiff was to bring his suit to trial in the same way as if they were before the Court. That offer was accepted by the defendant and by the plaintiff, and on that I refused their application to amend; and the cause, therefore, now comes on for trial subject to those conditions. But that being so, I must take it exactly either as if the commoners were represented by the Metropolitan Board of Works, or, at all events, as if they were sufficiently represented by an adequate number of defendants. It does not matter, I think, in the view I take of the case, which way I treat it; but that being so, and having, therefore, for this purpose, the commoners here, what is the question I have to decide? It is this,—that persons, or a body corporate, having legal rights amounting, as I said before, at least to an easement, but I think to something more, those legal rights being improperly interfered with, they come to prevent that improper interference, because I am now deciding the case on the assumption that the defendant was wrong. If they are in any sense trustees—and I am by no means prepared to say that they are; that is, the Metropolitan Board of Works—they are trustees for all parties interested in the land. But I think they have something which is beyond a mere trust. They have undertaken these duties which are imposed upon them by Parliament at the expense of the Metropolis, and it is quite plain that they are not mere bare trustees in the sense of acting only and entirely for the commoners and the lord. They also act for the Metropolitan Board of Works, which, as a corporation, has been willing to pay, or to have imposed upon it the obligation to pay, for some of these improvements; and I suppose they consider, therefore, that they get an equivalent for their constituents in some shape or other for the payment. And this is quite intelligible, because the mere fact of keeping these open spaces still open may be in some sense, though not in a direct sense, a benefit to the public, a benefit to the Metropolis, of which the Board is, for certain purposes, the governor and the manager. Therefore, I conceive that there is something more than a trust for the commoners and for the lord. There is, in some sense, a kind of trust —it cannot be called a strict, theoretical trust—for the ratepayers of the Metropolis who contribute the funds which are to be applied, amongst other things, to the keeping open of these breathing places, in a sense, for the benefit of all the ratepayers. I do not look upon them, therefore, as what I would call bare trustees—that is, bare trustees for the commoners and the lord. But I think, independently of that, that where there is a statutory power and duty conferred and imposed on a body, whether a corporation or a number of individuals, and they have a legal right commensurate with the exercise of the powers and the fulfilment of the obligation, the right to sue must follow as a matter of necessity as against any person unduly interfering with the exercise of the powers or the performance of the obligation; and I do not think that the cases cited have any direct bearing on that proposition. They are cases in which the Attorney-General had an undoubted right to sue on behalf of the public, and it was considered that that being so, the nature of the powers conferred on that particular body was not such as either to give the body a co-ordinate right of suing or an exclusive right of suing. Now here, when you come to look at their powers and duties, you will see that they must, at least, have an easement, and, I think, as I said before, possession to a certain extent. You find that, for the purposes of the Scheme, the commons are to be regulated and managed. Well now, how? They are to appoint common keepers, and other officers and servants, and to make rules for regulating the duties and conduct the several officers; and they are to pay the costs, which are to be raised under the powers of the Metropolis Local Management Act. Now then, that being so, these servants must have the right to perform their duties by having care of the common; the right, therefore, to enter upon the common and to take care of it; and that right, therefore, must be in the Board which appoints them.

Then the next is this. They may execute any works of drainage, raising, levelling, fencing, and improvements of the commons so far only as may be required for the purposes of the Metropolitan Commons Act. Now, when we turn to these purposes, we find that the 6th section says:—

"With a view to the expenditure of money on the drainage, level-"ling and improvement of a Metropolitan common."

So that you find that they may do these things. And how are they to do them? They can only do them by having a right to come upon the common and perform the work. As I said before, that right is, at least, an easement. I think it is more. I think it is a modified right of possession. Then they have something more:—

"They shall preserve the turf, shrubs, trees, plants, and grass, and
" for this purpose may enclose by fences for short periods such portions
" as may require rest to revive the same, and may plant or otherwise
" beautify the commons, but shall do nothing that shall otherwise
" vary or alter the natural aspect or features of the said commons.

"Fourth: The Board shall maintain the commons respectively
" as delineated in the plan deposited with the Inclosure Commis-
" sioners free of all encroachments, and shall permit no trespass
" on or partial or other inclosure of any part thereof, and no
" fences, posts, rails or matters or other things shall be maintained,
" fixed, or erected thereon without the consent of the Board."

How can they do this? They shall commit no trespass. They must have some kind of possession to prevent trespass. How can you object and say that a body shall permit no trespass unless it has some means of preventing? It appears to me that, when you look at these sections, it is plain that there is some kind of possession authorised to be taken by the Board, and, consequently, that they not only have an easement, but they have, as I said before, a modified right of possession, modified in this way. It is a possession for certain purposes, but not a general possession for all purposes. But possession it is, whether a possession in common with the commoners and the lord or not, it is not material to inquire, but it is possession, and a right of possession.

But then the bye-laws point the same way. They are obviously bye-laws which are intended to be enforced by the officers of the Board, and I think it all points the same way, to a right of possession. I have myself, therefore, no difficulty in saying that the Metropolitan Board of Works is entitled to sue a wrong-doer.

But I go further in this particular instance, and I say that, having regard to what has occurred at Chambers, the defendants have no right to object that the commoners are not co-plaintiffs. They are not to take objection for want of parties, because of the absence of the commoners. If it were necessary, which I do not think it is, I consider that the defendant has precluded himself from raising that objection before us.

Well, that being so, I now come to the next point. The defendant says that, assuming that he has any rights—and I am not now deciding that question—his rights are not to be taken away for nothing. When I say "rights," he is the owner of the manor, he is the owner of the Lammas lands; and, therefore, as regards the manor, he has the fee simple of the waste. As regards the Lammas lands, he has the peculiar rights of those persons who have the right of pasturage for something like half a year over those Lammas lands.

Mr. *Chitty*:—It is not material, my Lord, in this particular instance. He only claims to be the owner of a portion of the Lammas lands; not the whole of the Lammas lands.

The Master of the Rolls:—Oh, no; I know perfectly well.

Mr. *Chitty*:—There are 30 acres in one field, and he says that he is entitled to 10.

The Master of the Rolls:—Yes, he does not claim ownership to all the Lammas lands. I am speaking of those of which he claims to be the owner.

Mr. *Davey*:—They are partly copyhold, and partly freehold.

The Master of the Rolls:—Well, partly copyhold and partly freehold—there is an absolute fee simple of one, and a modified fee simple of the other. He says: "In respect to my lordship of the "manor, I am entitled not only to the actual soil—to take away "portions of the soil for gravel, minerals, and so on—and that, not-"withstanding that I may interfere to a certain extent with the right "of pasturage on the Common." And he also claims certain rights of enclosure, according to the custom of the manor, to exclude the commoners, therefore, in two ways—to a limited extent by taking away portions of the soil, and to a larger extent by absolute enclosure. He says that these are rights of property which certainly it is not in the habit of the legislature of this country to take away without adequate compensation; and he says that in approaching the construction of this Act of Parliament, I ought, as a Judge, to bear this in mind, that rights of property, rights of ownership especially, are respected by legislature, and that I ought not to anticipate, and that I ought not without the clearest words to decide that these rights of property are taken away without compensation. Now I agree to that. Of course, the legislature may, contrary to its usual habit and custom, in some particular instance have taken away a man's property without any compensation; but if so, it must be shown by clear and legal expressions.

The next point, therefore, which arises is, whether or not the legislature have given compensation in this particular instance; and a point of no inconsiderable difficulty as regards the construction of these Acts of Parliament is to be decided.

The plaintiff says that the right of compensation is given in respect to the rights of the defendant taken away. The defendant says that they are not. Now it is necessary, as I said before, to decide this before I consider, as I am going to consider next, the meaning of the several clauses,—not that it necessarily decides it, but it throws some light on what I would call the reasonableness of the construction which I am about to give to that proposition.

The 15th section of the Act of Parliament must not be read without looking at what the Act enacts before you come to that. Let me begin at the 6th section. After excluding, by the 5th, the authority of the Enclosure Commissioners over these Commons, the 6th provides that there shall be a Scheme under the Act. "A Scheme," it says, "may be made under this Act." Then the 7th directs what enquiry there shall be. The 8th directs the Commissioners to prepare a draft scheme. The 9th directs the printing and publication of the draft scheme. The 10th allows people to object. The 11th directs how a Commissioner shall enquire into the objections at a Public Sitting. The 12th makes the Assistant Commissioner make a report of the result of the enquiry before him. The 13th directs the final settlement and approval of the Scheme. Now it is to be observed that from the 6th to the 13th the whole of the enactment refers to the preparation of the Scheme. Then we come to the 14th, and as I read the 14th and 15th also, they refer to the contents of the Scheme. The 14th is express: —

"Every Scheme shall state what rights (if any) claimed by any " person or class of persons are affected by the Scheme, and in what " manner and to what extent they are affected thereby."

In my opinion, when I come to look at the Scheme, this has not been complied with by the Scheme in question.

" And whether or not the Scheme has been in relation thereto " consented to by that person or class of persons or any of them."

Now comes the 15th :—" No estate, interest, or right of a profitable " or beneficial nature in, over, or affecting a Common shall, except " with the consent of the person entitled thereto, be taken away or " injuriously affected by any scheme without compensation being " made or provided for the same, and such compensation shall, in " case of difference, be ascertained, according to the Lands Clauses " Consolidation Acts."

Now to my mind it is tolerably clear that it refers merely to what has been put in the Scheme. Now why? It does not say "shall be " taken or injuriously affected," but "shall be taken or injuriously " affected by any scheme."

Now the Scheme itself does not injuriously affect. The injurious affecting applies to the lands: the lands are injuriously affected. The

Scheme must, therefore, only empower you to injuriously affect. Well, we know very well what that means in the Lands Clauses Act. You come for compensation after the injury is done. You cannot tell beforehand what compensation you will be entitled to. It is not like a compulsory purchase or anything of that kind, and, therefore, when it says it is taken or injuriously affected by this Scheme, it must be that the Scheme did not authorise it to be injuriously affected without compensation (and it shows it more clearly in these words):

"Without compensation being made or provided for the same—"
"made or provided for in the Scheme."

How could it be provided for without a provision being inserted in the Scheme? And as to the words "such compensation shall be ascertained," how can it be ascertained in the manner required by the Lands Clauses Act, except by a provision in the Scheme? If the lands are injuriously affected, then you may get compensation, but not until then. I am, as I said before, of opinion that that is the true meaning of the 15th section.

The other meaning would be this, that the lands themselves should not be injuriously affected. Then you strike out the words "by the "Scheme" and put "in consequence of any scheme." But how could that be? How can you say that it shall not be injuriously affected without compensation when you cannot get the compensation until after the injury has taken place? It is impossible to read it in that way. It would be exactly the contrary of what occurs in the Lands Clauses Consolidation Act. The Lands Clauses Consolidation Act gives you the right to compensation for the injury which has taken place, but this is a prohibition of injury, and, therefore, it could never take place according to that theory. It appears to me that that section, like the 14th, is a provision which is to be inserted in the Scheme, and not an independent provision at all. There is another reason for saying that. The Scheme itself is only to have operation when and as confirmed by Act of Parliament; not only "when" but "as," therefore it has operation only according to that mode, showing clearly to my mind that that is a provision in the Scheme and nothing else.

Now you will find that there is an appeal given by the 16th section against "any determination made or implied by the Commissioners "or by the Scheme concerning any estate," because the Scheme must state what his claims are, and whether he has consented or not, and it must also state whether he is to be compensated or not, as I read it; and, consequently, you find the 16th section applies to the contents of this Scheme, and the 17th section does so plainly. "Every Scheme shall contain a provision for the sale at all times of "printed copies thereof to all persons desiring to buy the same at "a price not exceeding a reasonable sum to be fixed by the Scheme." It does not say that copies shall be sold, but it is again a provision of the Scheme, showing to my mind that it is in the Scheme. The 18th is that when the Scheme is finished, it is to be certified and sealed, and then it is to be printed and published under the 19th. Now that makes all those clauses consistent from the 14th to the 19th inclusive. You are dealing with the contents of the Scheme itself, and not with independent enactments. Well, that being so, when I turn to the Scheme, I find no provision or power for compensating people whose lands are injuriously affected.

And now I come to another section of the original Act, the 24th. All expenses of the Commissioners will be defrayed as the 24th section enacts. Then, under the 25th, we have the local authority coming in: and the local authority, the Metropolitan Board of Works, may contribute such amount as they think fit. Now it is to be remembered that there is no obligation on them to contribute one farthing;

"Such amount as they think fit towards the expenses of executing "any scheme under this Act, when confirmed by Act of Parliament, "including the payment of the compensation, if any, to be paid in "pursuance thereof."

Therefore, there is no provision in the general Act of Parliament for payment of compensation. There is a simple authority given to the Board which they may or may not exercise according as they think fit to raise money required for compensation. Here again it is plain that you must have a provision in the Scheme, because if you have not, you have no means of getting the money. Even if the Scheme said that you were to have it, there is no means of getting payment of anybody, and, therefore, you must look into the Scheme to find the raising of the money. Now you will find that the Scheme does provide this as regards the carrying into execution, and it is in the second section of the Scheme—

"all costs and expenses incurred by the Board in reference to this "Scheme and its execution from time to time shall be deemed to be "expenses of the Board, and be raised accordingly."

But it is only "incurred by the Board." It is not "incurred," but, incurred by the "Board." And, therefore, unless you can show an obligation somewhere on the Board to make the compensation, it is not an expense incurred by the Board, and you are thrown back to the 25th section of the first Act of Parliament, which is merely permissive and not obligatory.

Well, that being so, it seems to me that there is no provision for giving compensation, and there is no obligation on anybody to pay the compensation.

Now, before I part with the Scheme I must say that in my opinion the Scheme does not follow the provisions of the 14th section of the Act of Parliament. This Act of Parliament requires the Scheme to state what rights, if any, claimed by any person or class of persons, are affected by the Scheme, and in what manner and to what extent they are affected thereby. This is the way the Scheme complies with that direction:—

"This Scheme affects the rights so claimed as aforesaid only so far "as is absolutely necessary for the purpose contemplated by this "Scheme."

I cannot find out from that whether it affects them at all or not. The Act of Parliament says it is to state what rights are affected—exactly what it does not state; nor does it tell me to what extent they are affected. They are affected so far as they may be affected. It appears to me pretty clear that it is an illusory compliance, using the word illusory in the proper sense of making game of this enactment, to put such a clause as that into the Scheme.

Well then, passing from that, arriving as I do at the conclusion that there is no compensation provided for land injuriously affected to be paid to anybody, and no liability on anybody to pay such compensation, I now come to the saving clause, which is all-important. The saving clause is in number 15. It is in the common form, "and "saving always all persons," and so forth, "all such estates, interests," and so forth,—

"of a profitable or beneficial nature, in, over, or affecting the commons, "or any part thereof, as they or any of them had before the confirma- "tion of this Scheme by Act of Parliament, or could or might have en- "joyed if this Scheme had not been confirmed by Act of Parliament."

The only variation is that it only refers to interests of a profitable or beneficial nature, and in this respect it is not unimportant; because it is plain, for instance, that the right of the lord to exclude all persons from trespassing would not be of a profitable or beneficial nature,—to keep the police off, for instance, or the officers of the Metropolitan Board of Works, who keep order; nor would it be of a beneficial nature to let the ground to gipsies and vagrants, and card sharpers, and other persons mentioned, or to prevent them being

driven off. It has some sense. Again, the lord might have an abstract right to keep everybody off, but he gets no benefit from that, the commoners taking the herbage that is not reserved to him. Therefore, right of keeping order remains, and he has no legal right to interfere with the officers of the Board, and the persons appointed by them to keep order, and keep off bad characters, and so on. Then, again, he could not interfere with them for improving the grass, and the turf, and so forth, merely because he had the right of the ownership. He would have that right independently. All that is saved is his beneficial ownership. If, therefore, before the Act of Parliament passed, he might have brought trespass against anybody who interfered to level his common, or to make it more beautiful by preserving the turf or the trees, he has lost that right, because it does not affect his beneficial interest. Well, if before the Act of Parliament he had a right to the gravel, and if the improving of the common is to interfere with that right, then his beneficial right is affected, and in my opinion this would be the saving clause. It is, therefore, not true to say that the saving clause makes the whole of the Scheme nugatory. It does not appear to me to do so at all, except to the extent that the beneficial right is actually interfered with. The result is that the Board of Works may enclose the common, they may preserve it, they may level it, they may improve it to any extent, they may do all the good they like to do, and neither the commoners nor the lord can interfere, unless and until you interfere with some beneficial ownership, which may be of a very limited character. Of course the extent of it depends on their rights, irrespectively of the Act of Parliament. Nothing can be plainer to my mind than this clause. It is as clear as can be, the rights that they—
"could or might have enjoyed before the confirmation of this Scheme
" by Act of Parliament, or if this Scheme had not been confirmed."

But it is said to be cut down. Well, cut down by what? Of course you might have a proviso even on a saving clause, but in the ordinary state of the Acts of Parliament you have never an exception to saving clauses, and the cutting down clause would simply be the 14th, because it says:—

"This Scheme affects the rights so claimed as aforesaid, only so far as
" is absolutely necessary for the purpose contemplated by this Scheme."

Now there are two things to be considered. The first is, that where there is no compensation you are to give the saving clause its full effect, or otherwise you take the rights away for nothing. The next is, even supposing that rule did not apply, still you must have clear words. Now what are the clear words? This Scheme affects him [*i.e.* the lord]—

"so far as is absolutely necessary for the purpose contemplated by "this Scheme."

How am I to find out what is absolutely necessary? As far as I understand it, all that is absolutely necessary is to keep the commons open and in good order—that is the main point; and to keep bad characters off. That is the substance of it, and that is the main object of the regulation and management. I do not find that it is absolutely necessary for the purpose of the Scheme to interfere with any rights of the lord, unless, indeed, it may be said, the words "free "from all encroachment, and shall commit no trespass," and so forth, are absolutely necessary to be carried beyond this, that "encroachment" must be illegal encroachment. And then if you put that in you make the whole thing clear enough. They are to keep that open as a common which is a common. If by law the lord has a right to make it cease to be a common, I see nothing here which says that that is an encroachment within the meaning of that section. I do not think, therefore, that there is any difficulty in seeing that even if these words were to be looked upon as controlling words, they would control the effect of the saving clause. In my opinion they are not controlling words at all. They simply refer to the direction, though, as I said, in an illusory way, which is required by the 14th section of the first Act to be inserted in the Scheme, and if we are to take the word Scheme to mean the whole, that is, the whole of the clauses numbered 1 to 15 inclusive, then the 13th is as much a part of the Scheme as the rest of them, and therefore nothing is absolutely necessary for the section which comes before the 13th; but if you take the meaning to be the Scheme without the saving clause, then the answer is that the Scheme is subject to the saving clause, and to that extent the rights of persons are excepted from the Scheme. Therefore, taking it in either way, it appears to me that the owners of the rights as they existed, of beneficial rights as they existed before the passing of the second Act of Parliament, still remain. The result of what I have said is that the only questions remaining to be decided are, what are the rights of the lord in respect to enclosure, that is, whether what he is about to do is an enclosure or not, or is legal or not, and whether what he threatens to do about gravel and interfering with the herbage was authorised before the passing of the Act. To these two questions I think the rest of the argument must apply.

APPENDIX IV.

Act and Scheme under the Metropolitan Commons Acts for the Management of the Banstead Commons.

[56 & 57 Vict. c. cvii.]

An Act to confirm a Scheme under the Metropolitan Commons Acts, 1866 to 1878, relating to Banstead Downs, Banstead Heath, Burgh Heath, and Park Downs, in the parish of Banstead, Surrey. [29th June 1893.]

Whereas the Board of Agriculture have in pursuance of the Metropolitan Commons Acts, 1866 to 1878,* duly certified a scheme for the establishment of local management with respect to Banstead Downs, Banstead Heath, Burgh Heath, and Park Downs, situate in the parish of Banstead, in the county of Surrey:

And whereas the said scheme is set forth in full in the report which was made by the said Board for the year ending the thirty-first day of December one thousand eight hundred and ninety-two, and which was duly laid before both Houses of Parliament:

And whereas by the said Metropolitan Commons Acts it is provided that any such scheme shall not of itself have any operation, but shall have full operation when and as confirmed by Act of Parliament, with such modifications, if any, as to Parliament seem fit:

And whereas it is expedient that the said scheme should be confirmed, subject to certain modifications:

Be it therefore enacted by the Queen's Most Excellent Majesty, by and with the advice and consent of the Lords Spiritual and Temporal, and Commons, in this present Parliament assembled, and by the authority of the same, as follows:—

1. The scheme for the establishment of local management with respect to Banstead Downs, Banstead Heath, Burgh Heath, and Park Downs, situate in the parish of Banstead, in the county of Surrey, certified by the Board of Agriculture, under their seal, on the

* 29 & 30 Vict. c. 122.; 32 & 33 Vict. c. 107.; 41 & 42 Vict. c. 71.

thirteenth day of December one thousand eight hundred and ninety-two, shall be modified so as to be in the terms specified in the schedule hereunto annexed, and so modified is hereby confirmed.

2. This Act may be cited for all purposes as the Metropolitan Commons (Banstead) Supplemental Act, 1893.

SCHEDULE.

THE METROPOLITAN COMMONS ACTS, 1866 to 1878.

Scheme with respect to Banstead Downs, Banstead Heath, Burgh Heath, and Park Downs.

1. The pieces of land with the ponds and roads thereon, commonly called or known by the names of Banstead Downs, Banstead Heath, Burgh Heath, and Park Downs, and the small piece of waste, with the Jubilee Tree planted thereon, all situate in the parish of Banstead, in the county of Surrey, as the same are delineated in a plan deposited with the Board of Agriculture, and thereon coloured green, and are herein-after collectively referred to as "The Commons," shall henceforth, for all the purposes of this scheme, be regulated and managed by a body of Conservators to be styled "the Banstead Commons Conservators."

2. The first Conservators shall be the following persons, namely:—Two persons to be nominated (if they think fit) by the owners for the time being of the soil of the commons, if they can agree upon two persons to be so nominated, or in default of agreement, by the owners for the time being of the largest extent in area of the commons, such nomination to be in writing under the hands or seals of the owners so appointing, and the following six persons, that is to say: the Hon. Francis Henry Baring, Walter Samuel James Brown, William Hodson, Peter Robertson Rodger, Sir Charles Russell, Q.C., M.P., and Thomas Claye Shaw.

3. The first and all succeeding Conservators nominated by the owners of the soil of the commons as aforesaid shall hold office until their nominations are revoked or other persons are nominated in their place by such owners of the soil as aforesaid. As to the other six of the first Conservators, two of them shall go out of office in the month

of April next following the confirmation of this scheme by Act of Parliament, and two in the month of April in each of the two succeeding years.

4. At some meeting of the Conservators held before the month of April next following the confirmation of this scheme by Act of Parliament, it shall be determined by lot which two of the last-mentioned first Conservators shall go out of office in the said month of April, and which in the month of April in each of the two succeeding years.

5. The Conservators other then the first shall consist of two persons nominated as aforesaid by the owners of the soil of the commons, and of six persons to be elected by the vestry of the parish of Banstead, which six persons are herein-after referred to as "the elected Conservators." The term of office of the elected Conservators shall be three years, and the two elected Conservators who have been longest in office without re-election shall go out of office each year.

6. Election of Conservators in the place of those going out of office shall be made by the vestry of the parish of Banstead at a meeting to be held in the month of March or April.

7. Any elected Conservator after going of office, resigning, or otherwise ceasing to be a Conservator may be again elected a Conservator. Should any vacancy in the number of Conservators arise by death, resignation, or otherwise, between the times fixed for election as aforesaid, or if at any time there shall not be a full number of Conservators, the Conservators for the time being shall continue to be as competent to act as if no such vacancy or deficiency in number had occurred. Provided that in the case of any vacancy occurring in the number of elected Conservators, the vestry shall, as soon as conveniently may be, elect some proper person as a Conservator to supply such vacancy, but the person so elected shall retain his office so long only as the vacating Conservator would have retained the same if no vacancy had occurred.

8. No bankrupt or person who has compounded with his creditors shall be capable of being or continuing a Conservator.

9. No Conservator shall receive any remuneration or hold any office of profit under this scheme.

10. Any act of the Conservators shall not be invalidated or be illegal by reason of there being any vacancy among the Conservators, or by reason of any person not qualified, or ceasing to be qualified, acting as a Conservator, or by reason of any irregularity, failure, or

omission whatsoever in or about any election, or in or about any matter preliminary or incidental thereto.

11. The Conservators shall hold meetings for transacting business under this scheme twice at least in every year, and at such other times as may be necessary, for properly executing their powers and duties under this scheme, and shall from time to time make regulations with respect to the summoning, notice, place, management, and adjournment of such meetings, and generally with respect to the transaction and management of business by the Conservators under this scheme. Provided always, that no business shall be transacted at any such meeting unless three Conservators at least are present thereat, and all questions shall be decided by a majority of votes, and the names of the Conservators present shall be recorded; and the Conservators shall annually appoint one of their number to be chairman for one year at all meetings at which he is present, and in case the chairman so appointed be absent from any meeting at the time appointed for holding the same, the Conservators present shall appoint one of their number to act as chairman thereat, and in case the chairman appointed as first aforesaid shall die, resign, or become incapable of acting, another Conservator shall be appointed to be chairman for the period during which the person so dying, resigning, or becoming incapable, would have been entitled to continue in office, and the chairman at any meeting shall have a second or casting vote in case of an equality of votes.

12. The Conservators may from time to time provide and maintain such offices as may be necessary for transacting their business and that of their officers and servants under this scheme. The Conservators shall be a body corporate, with perpetual succession, and shall have a common seal. Documents or copies of documents purporting to proceed from the Conservators, and to be sealed or stamped with their seal, shall be received as primâ facie evidence in all courts and places whatsoever.

13. The Conservators shall cause entries of all proceedings of the Conservators, and of every committee appointed by them, with the names of the Conservators who shall attend each meeting, to be duly made from time to time in books to be provided for the purpose, which shall be kept by the clerk under the superintendence of the Conservators, and every such entry shall be signed by the chairman of the meeting at which the proceedings took place, and such entry so signed shall be received as evidence in every court and before all judges, justices, and others, without proof of such meeting having

been duly convened and held, or of the persons attending such meeting having been or being Conservators or members of committees respectively, or of the signature of the chairman, or of the fact of his having been chairman, all of which last-mentioned matters shall be presumed until the contrary is proved, and such book shall at all reasonable times be open to the inspection of any of the Conservators.

14. The Conservators may from time to time appoint and employ a clerk, treasurer, common-keepers, collectors, and other officers and servants as may be necessary and proper for the preservation of order on, and the enforcement of bye-laws with respect to, the commons, and otherwise for the purposes of this scheme, and may make rules for regulating the duties and conduct of the several officers and servants so appointed and employed (altering such rules as occasion may require), and the Conservators may pay out of the moneys to be received under this scheme to such officers and servants such reasonable wages, salaries, or allowance, as they may think proper, and every such officer and servant shall be removable by the Conservators at their pleasure.

15. The Conservators may execute any works of drainage, raising, levelling, or fencing, for the protection and improvement of the commons, so far only as may be required for the purposes of the Metropolitan Commons Acts, 1866 to 1878, and may do any work necessary for the proper cleansing of the ponds on the commons, and shall preserve the turf, shrubs, trees, plants, and grass thereon, and for this purpose may enclose by fences for short periods such portions as may require rest to revive the same, and may plant trees and shrubs for shelter or ornament, but shall do nothing that may otherwise vary or alter the natural features or aspect of the commons, or interfere with free access to every part thereof.

16. The Conservators shall maintain the commons, as delineated in the plan deposited with the Board of Agriculture, free of all encroachment, and shall not permit any trespass on, or partial or other enclosure of, any part thereof, and no fences, rails, sheds, or buildings, whether used in connexion with the playing of games or not, or other matters or things, shall be maintained, fixed, or erected thereon, nor shall ice be taken off the ponds on the commons without the consent in writing of the Conservators.

17. The Conservators may set apart such portion or portions of the commons as they may consider expedient for games, and may form any cricket ground or grounds, and may allow the same to be temporarily enclosed with posts and chains or other open fence, so as

to prevent cattle and horses straying thereon. Provided that the Conservators shall not so exercise their powers under this scheme as to interfere without consent or the payment of compensation with the rights, if any, of the lord of the manor or owners of the soil to let the shooting on the commons or to let places on the commons for the playing of games or the training of horses.

18. The Conservators shall frame bye-laws and regulations for the prevention of nuisances and the preservation of order upon the commons. The bye-laws may include any of the following purposes, viz. :—

The prevention of encroachments, and of the deposit of road-sand, materials for the repair of the roads, dung, rubbish, flints, wood, or other matter on, and of the illegal taking, cutting, digging, and selling the turf, sods, gravel, sand, or other substances from, the commons, and of the illegal cutting, felling, or injuring the gorse, heather, timber, or other trees, shrubs, brushwood, or other plants for the time being growing thereon, and of the removal of ice from the ponds.

The prevention of injury to or the defacing or removal of seats, fences, or barriers, or notice boards, or other things put up or maintained by the Conservators on the commons.

The prevention of injury to or disfigurement of fences or trees on the commons by the posting of bills, placards, or notices.

The prevention of bird-catching, illegal setting of traps, gins, or nets, or liming trees, or laying snares of any description for birds or other animals, taking of birds' eggs or nests, and illegal shooting or chasing of game or other animals on the commons or brought there for the purpose of being shot or chased.

The regulation, subject to clause 17, of games to be played and other means of recreation on the commons, and of assemblages of persons thereon.

The prevention or regulation of vehicles being driven or horses being exercised by grooms or others on or across the commons.

The exclusion, removal, and apprehension, if necessary, of gamblers, card sharpers, gipsies, squatters, vagrants, sellers and exhibitors of infamous books, prints, photographs, or pictures, or persons guilty of brawling, fighting, or quarrelling, or using indecent and improper language, or any idle or disorderly person, so that all such persons may be dealt with according to law.

The regulation as to place and mode of digging and taking gravel, sand, or other substances from, and of cutting and felling of trees and underwood growing upon, the commons, in exercise of any right of common or other right over or upon the commons.

The prevention of unauthorised persons from turning out or knowingly permitting cattle, sheep, or other animals to graze or feed or remain upon the commons, and generally for the prevention or restraint of any act or thing tending to the injury or disfigurement of the commons, or to interfere with the use thereof by the public for the purposes of exercise and recreation.

Provided that all bye-laws made by the Conservators shall be in writing under their seal, and the Conservators may by such bye-laws impose upon offenders against the same such reasonable penalties, to be recovered on summary conviction, as they shall think fit, not exceeding the sum of five pounds for each offence, and in the case of a continuing offence a further penalty not exceeding the sum of forty shillings for each day on which the offence is continued after conviction therefor; and the Conservators may alter or repeal any bye-laws by other bye-laws sealed as aforesaid, and may make other bye-laws as they may from time to time think fit. Provided always, that all bye-laws imposing any penalty shall be so framed as to allow of the recovery of any sum less than the full amount of the penalty. Provided always, that no bye-laws shall be repugnant to the laws of England or the provisions of this scheme, and no bye-laws, or any alteration or repeal of any bye-laws, shall be of any force or effect unless and until the same be confirmed by the Local Government Board. Provided that a copy of any bye-laws, signed and certified by the clerk of the Conservators to be a true copy, and to have been duly confirmed, shall be evidence, until the contrary is proved, in all legal proceedings of the due making, confirmation, and existence of such bye-laws without further proof. Provided also, that no bye-laws shall be confirmed unless notice of intention to apply for confirmation thereof shall have been given in one or more of the London daily morning newspapers, and a newspaper circulating in the parish of Banstead, one calendar month at least before any such application. A copy of the proposed bye-laws shall be kept at the office of the Conservators, and be open during office hours thereat to the inspection of the ratepayers of the parish of Banstead, and other persons interested, without fee or reward; and the Conservators shall furnish every such person applying for the same with a copy thereof, or of any part thereof, on payment of sixpence for every one hundred words contained in such copy.

19. All bye-laws made by the Conservators in pursuance of this

scheme shall be printed, and shall be sold to any person who may apply for the same at such price, not exceeding one shilling per copy, as the Conservators may determine; and all bye-laws shall be legibly written or printed at length on boards of suitable size, and placed on such parts of the commons (not less than four) as to the Conservators may appear desirable.

20. Except for the Conservators for the purposes of this scheme, and for the owner or owners of the soil, it shall not be lawful for any person or persons without the consent in writing of such owner or owners and the consent in writing of the Conservators to form, build, or lay any sewer, drain, pipe, waterway, or other matter of a like nature, in, into, or under any part or parts of the commons.

21. Except for those persons who now are entitled to do so, it shall not be lawful to turn out on the commons, or any part thereof, for grazing, any cattle, sheep, or other animal.

22. The Conservators shall be at liberty to receive and apply for the purposes of this scheme, or any of them, any subscriptions or donations applicable thereto that may come to their hands.

23. The Conservators shall cause books to be provided and kept, and true and regular accounts to be entered therein of all sums of money received and paid for and on account of this scheme, and of the several purposes for which such sums of money shall have been received and paid, which books shall at all reasonable times be open to the inspection of any of the Conservators, and of any ratepayer of the parish of Banstead, without fee or reward, and the Conservators and ratepayers, or any of them, may take copies of, or extracts from, such books without paying anything for the same.

24. The Conservators shall cause their accounts to be balanced in each year to the thirty-first day of December, or to some other day to be fixed by them from time to time.

25. An auditor of the accounts, not being a Conservator, shall be from time to time appointed by the chairman of quarter sessions for the county of Surrey, who shall fix his remuneration.

26. The auditor shall attend, within one month after the day to which the accounts have been balanced, at the office of the Conservators, or at some other convenient place to be appointed by the Conservators, and from time to time shall, in the presence of the clerk of the Conservators if he desire to be present, proceed to audit the accounts of the Conservators for the year preceding such day, and the Conservators shall, by their clerk or otherwise, produce and lay before the auditor the Conservators' accounts, accompanied

with proper vouchers, and all books, papers, and writings in their custody or power relating thereto, and any person interested in the accounts, either as a creditor of the Conservators or otherwise, may be present at the audit of the accounts by himself or his agent, and may make any objection to any part of the accounts, and if the accounts be found correct the auditor shall sign the same in token of his allowance thereof, but if the auditor thinks there is just cause to disapprove of any part of the accounts he, or any other person interested in the accounts, may appeal against any parts of the accounts which shall be disapproved of to one of the two next quarter sessions for the county of Surrey, notice in writing of such appeal being given to the clerk of the Conservators fourteen days at least before the hearing of such appeal.

27. Upon the hearing of such appeal, the justices may make such order as they think fit respecting the payment of the costs of the appellant out of the moneys coming to the hands of the Conservators, or otherwise, as they think fit, and such order shall be final.

28. For purposes of police the commons shall be deemed a place of public resort, and the powers and duties of police constables in relation to public safety and preservation of order and protection of property shall extend thereto.

29. Any constable, or any officer of the Conservators, being in uniform or authorised by the Conservators in writing, which authority he shall produce on demand, and any person called by such constable or officer to his assistance, may, without any other warrant than this scheme, seize and detain any person offending, or having offended, against any bye-law of the Conservators, whose name and residence shall be unknown to and cannot be ascertained by such constable or officer, and such constable or officer shall convey him with all convenient despatch before a justice to be dealt with according to law.

30. Proceedings with a view to the summary conviction of offenders under this scheme or under any bye-laws of the Conservators, or to the recovery of any money or expenses authorised to be recovered summarily, or to any other order to be made by justices under this scheme or any such bye-law, shall be taken before a court of summary jurisdiction according to the provisions of the Summary Jurisdiction Acts. Any pecuniary penalty, expenses, or costs, or other money recovered by the Conservators shall, notwithstanding anything in any other Act, be paid to the Conservators, and shall be applied by them for the purposes of this scheme.

31. A person shall not be disabled from acting as a justice or

otherwise in any matter arising under or in relation to this scheme by reason of his being an elector under this scheme.

32. No proceeding to be had touching the conviction of any offender under this scheme, nor any order or other matter or thing whatsoever made, done, or transacted in or relating to the execution of this scheme shall be vacated, quashed, or set aside for want of form.

33. The clauses of the Commissioners Clauses Act, 1847, with respect to contracts to be entered into and the deeds to be executed by commissioners, and with respect to giving notices and orders, proof of debt in bankruptcy, and tender of amends (as far as the same are applicable for the purposes of and not inconsistent with this scheme) are hereby incorporated with this scheme.

34. The Conservators may at any time apply for an amended or a new scheme.

35. Saving always to all persons and bodies, politic and corporate, and their respective heirs, successors, executors, and administrators, all such estates, interests, or rights of a profitable or beneficial nature in, over, or affecting the commons, or any part thereof, as they or any of them had before the confirmation of this scheme by Act of Parliament, or could or might have enjoyed if this scheme had not been confirmed by Act of Parliament, except only so far as any such estates, interests, or rights shall be purchased or acquired or otherwise compensated for by the Conservators, whether by agreement or compulsorily.

36. The lord of the manor of Banstead, or persons deriving title under him, claim the soil and freehold of the commons and the minerals under the same. The Right Honourable the Earl of Abingdon and the Reverend the Honourable Alberic Edward Bertie claim an estate in fee simple, and all the rights of the lord of the manor, subject only to the rights of common of the tenants of the manor of Banstead entitled thereto in those portions of the commons called Banstead Heath and Banstead Downs. Charles Ellis Bird and George Henderson, as trustees of the will of John Lambert, deceased, claim an estate in fee simple, subject only to the rights of common, if any, of the tenants of the manor of Banstead entitled thereto in that portion of the commons called Park Downs. The lord of the manor of Tadworth claims to be owner in fee of portions of the commons, and claims rights over other portions. The owners and occupiers of a large area of lands and tenements in the parish of Banstead claim rights of common of pasture and estovers, and other rights over the commons.

37. This scheme affects the estates, interests, or rights in, over, or affecting the commons so claimed as aforesaid, only so far as is absolutely necessary for the purposes of this scheme, that is to say, by conferring on the Conservators such powers of management, improvement, and control as herein before provided; and for such purpose the power of taking, restricting, diminishing, or extinguishing any such estate, interest, or right whenever it shall appear to the Conservators that the continuance of such estates, interests, or rights will interfere with the control, preservation, or improvement of the commons by the Conservators, or with any of the purposes of this scheme. So far as such estates, interests, or rights are of a profitable or beneficial nature, and are taken away or injuriously affected by this scheme, compensation in respect thereof shall be made by the Conservators to the bodies or persons entitled thereto. The amount of such compensation shall, in case of difference, be ascertained and provided in the same manner as if the same compensation were for the compulsory purchase and taking or the injuriously affecting of lands under the provisions of the Lands Clauses Acts. Provided always, that, in the event of any compensation which may be agreed upon or awarded not being paid by the Conservators within six months after the date of such agreement or award, nothing in this scheme contained shall affect such estates, interests, or rights, or shall prevent the enjoyment or exercise of the same estates, interests, or rights in respect of which compensation shall have been agreed upon or awarded, as the owner or owners thereof would have been entitled to enjoy or exercise in case this scheme had not been confirmed by Act of Parliament, but without prejudice to the recovery from the Conservators by such owner or owners of any costs or damages which, in the meantime, he or they may have been put to or have sustained in relation to any such agreement or award, or any such estate, interest, or right as aforesaid.

38.—(*a.*) Upon the Conservators taking any proceedings under the provisions of the Lands Clauses Acts, with respect to any estate, interest, or right of a profitable or beneficial nature in, over, or affecting the commons or any part thereof, they shall, if required, give security to the owner or owners of such estate, interest, or right, to the satisfaction of the Board of Agriculture, for the costs to which he or they would be entitled under the same Acts.

(*b.*) Upon the Conservators commencing, or being made defendants to, any action in a court of law against the owner of any part of the commons, they shall, if and when required, give such security for costs as the court shall prescribe, in the manner provided by the rules of such court for the time being in force.

39. The lord of the manor of Banstead, and the persons deriving title under him, and, in particular, the Earl of Abingdon and the Reverend the Honourable Alberic Edward Bertie and the trustees of the will of the said John Lambert have not consented, and the lord of the manor of Tadworth has consented, and some of the owners and occupiers of lands and tenements in the parish of Banstead have consented, and others have not consented, to their rights being affected in the manner and to the extent herein expressed.

40. Printed copies of this scheme shall at all times be sold at the office of the Conservators to all persons desiring to buy the same at a price not exceeding sixpence each.

41. The costs, charges, and expenses preliminary to, and of and incidental to the preparing, applying for, obtaining, and confirming of this scheme by Act of Parliament, and the expenses incurred by the Conservators in the carrying out of this scheme, including the payment of compensation (if any) as herein-before mentioned, may be paid by the Conservators out of any moneys coming to their hands under the provisions or for the purposes of this scheme.

The Board of Agriculture, pursuant to the Board of Agriculture Act, 1889, and the Metropolitan Commons Acts, 1866 to 1878, hereby certify the foregoing scheme.

In witness whereof they have hereunto set their official seal this thirteenth day of December, one thousand eight hundred and ninety-two.

T. H. Elliott,
Secretary.

APPENDIX V.

COMMONS ACT, 1876.

(HIGH ROAD WELL MOOR, HALIFAX.)

Provisional Order for the Regulation of High Road Well Moor, Halifax.

Whereas the Mayor Aldermen and Burgesses of the Borough of Halifax with the consent of persons representing at least one-third in value of the interests in certain lands called or known as High Road Well Moor situate in the said Borough of Halifax in the County of York such lands being a Common within the meaning of "The Inclosure Acts 1845 to 1882" and hereinafter referred to as "the Common" have made application to the Board of Agriculture to issue a Provisional Order for the regulation of the Common and to certify that it is expedient that such Provisional Order should be confirmed by Parliament:

And whereas the said Board having taken the said application into consideration were satisfied that a *primâ facie* case had been made out and that regard being had to the benefit of the neighbourhood as well as to private interests it was expedient to proceed further in the matter and accordingly ordered a local inquiry to be held by an officer of the Board:

And whereas the said officer having caused public notice to be given as required by the said Acts held pursuant to the said notice public meetings at the Town Hall Halifax on the 7th and 8th January 1895 at the respective hours of 11 in the forenoon and 8.30 in the evening to hear all persons desirous of being heard on the subject-matter of the said application and any information or evidence which might be offered in relation thereto and inquired into the correctness of the statements in the said application and otherwise into the expediency of making the Provisional Order applied for and into the nature of the provisions to be inserted in such Provisional Order:

And whereas the said officer inspected the Common as required by the said Acts:

And whereas the said officer duly reported in writing to the said Board the result of the local inquiry and of the public meetings held by him together with the information obtained by him as to the several particulars in the said application and all other information required by the said Acts and annexed to his report a sketch map of the Common a copy of which map is deposited in the office of the said Board:

And whereas the Common is waste land of the Manor of Skircoat of which manor the Right Honourable John Savile Baron Savile is the Lord:

And whereas the Corporation of the Borough of Halifax to which borough the Common is suburban within the meaning of the said Acts have with the sanction of the said Board entered into an undertaking to contribute such sums as may from time to time be necessary for the maintenance and management of the Common:

Now therefore in pursuance of the powers given to them by the Board of Agriculture Act 1889 and the said Acts the Board of Agriculture being satisfied that having regard to the benefit of the neighbourhood as well as to private interests the Regulation of the Common is desirable have framed for the consideration of the persons interested this Draft Provisional Order specifying the provisions for the benefit of the neighbourhood and the improvement of the Common which are to be put in force and the terms and conditions on which provided the necessary consents are given thereto they are prepared to certify that it is expedient the Provisional Order should be confirmed by Parliament that is to say:

That there be reserved to the inhabitants of Halifax and the neighbourhood a right of free access to the Common and a privilege of enjoying lawful recreation thereon subject to such bye-laws as may from time to time be made by the said Corporation.

That such roads and paths be set out and made to the satisfaction of the Board of Agriculture as may be convenient for public use.

That in consideration of the said Corporation having undertaken to contribute such sums as may from time to time be necessary for the maintenance and the management of the Common the general management of the Common be vested in the said Corporation who shall have power for the improvement of the Common to drain manure level fence plant or in any other way improve or add to the beauty of the Common and to make bye-laws and regulations for the prevention of and protection from nuisances and for keeping order on the Common.

That for the purpose of giving complete effect to this Provisional Order there shall be inserted in the Award to be made in pursuance of the said Acts such provisions not inconsistent with such Acts as the said Board shall think desirable and proper.

In witness whereof the Board of Agriculture have hereunto set their Official Seal this Thirtieth day of April One Thousand Eight Hundred and Ninety-five.

(Signed) RICHARD DAWSON,
Authorised by the President.

APPENDIX VI.

COMMONS ACT, 1876. (BEXHILL DOWN.)

Provisional Order for the Regulation of Bexhill Down.

Whereas persons interested in certain lands called or known as Bexhill Down situate in the parish of Bexhill in the county of Sussex such lands being a Common within the meaning of "The Inclosure Acts 1845 to 1882" have made application to the Board of Agriculture to issue a Provisional Order for the regulation of the Down and to certify that it is expedient that such Provisional Order should be confirmed by Parliament:

And whereas it has been made to appear to the said Board that the persons making the said application represent at least one-third in value of such interests in the Down as are proposed to be affected by the Provisional Order:

And whereas the said Board having taken the said application into consideration were satisfied that a *primâ facie* case had been made out and that regard being had to the benefit of the neighbourhood as well as to private interests it was expedient to proceed further in the matter and accordingly ordered a local inquiry to be held by an officer of the Board:

And whereas the said officer having caused public notice to be given as required by the said Acts held pursuant to the said notice public meetings at the Bexhill Institute at Bexhill on the 18th and 19th days of January 1895 at the respective hours of eleven in the morning and seven in the evening to hear all persons desirous of being heard on the subject-matter of the said application and any information or evidence which might be offered in relation thereto and inquired into the correctness of the statements in the said application and otherwise into the expediency of making the Provisional Order applied for and into the nature of the provisions to be inserted in such Provisional Order.

And whereas the said officer inspected the Down as required by the said Acts:

And whereas the said officer duly reported in writing to the said Board the result of the local inquiry and of the public meetings held by him together with the information obtained by him as to the several particulars in the said application and all other information required by the said Acts and annexed to his report a sketch map of the Down a copy of which map is deposited in the office of the said Board:

And whereas the Bexhill Urban District Council as the Urban Sanitary Authority of a town to which the Down is suburban within the meaning of the said Acts have with the sanction of the said Board entered into an undertaking to contribute out of their funds such sums as may from time to time be necessary for the maintenance of the Down:

Now therefore the Board of Agriculture in pursuance of the powers given to them by the Board of Agriculture Act 1889 and the said Acts and being satisfied that having regard to the benefit of the neighbourhood as well as to private interests the regulation of the Down is desirable have framed for the consideration of the persons interested this Draft Provisional Order specifying the provisions for the benefit of the neighbourhood and for improvement which are to be put in force and the terms and conditions on which provided the necessary consents are given thereto they are prepared to certify that it is expedient the Provisional Order should be confirmed by Parliament that is to say:

That there be reserved to the inhabitants of Bexhill and the neighbourhood a right of free access to the Down and a privilege of playing cricket and other games and enjoying reasonable recreation thereon subject to such bye-laws as may from time to time be made by the Bexhill Urban District Council.

That in consideration of the said Council having undertaken to contribute out of their funds such sums as may from time to time be necessary for the maintenance of the Down the general management of the Down be vested in the said Council who shall have power for the improvement of the Down to drain manure level fence plant or in any other way improve or add to the beauty of the Down to lay out and preserve any cricket ground or grounds thereon to lay out and make with the consent in writing of the Lord of the Manor any new roads or paths over the Down and to make bye-laws and regulations for the prevention of and protection from nuisances and for keeping order upon the Down including the regulation of the exercise of lawful rights of common subsisting over or on the Down.

That this Provisional Order be without prejudice to the rights of the Lord of the Manor in the mines minerals stone and other substrata under the Down.

That the expenses incurred by the said Council under or in pursuance of this Provisional Order shall be defrayed by means of any moneys applicable to the purpose that may come into their hands and subject thereto in manner provided by the said Acts and that the receipts and expenditure of the said Council under or in pursuance of this Provisional Order shall for the purposes of Sections 245 247 (except so much thereof as is repealed by the District Auditors Act 1879) 249 and 250 of the Public Health Act 1875 be deemed to be receipts and expenditure under the last-mentioned Act.

That for the purpose of giving complete effect to this Provisional Order there shall be inserted in the award to be made in pursuance of the said Acts such provisions not inconsistent with such Acts as the Board of Agriculture shall think desirable and proper.

In witness whereof the Board of Agriculture have hereunto set their Official Seal this Twenty-ninth day of April One Thousand Eight Hundred and Ninety-five.

(Signed) RICHARD DAWSON,
Authorised by the President.

APPENDIX VII.

Memorandum as to the Powers and Duties of Rural District Councils under the Local Government Act, 1894, with respect to Rights of Way, Roadside Wastes, and Commons.

1.—*Rights of Way.*

It is the duty of a District Council, whether they be the Highway Authority or not, under Section 26 (1) of the Local Government Act, 1894, to protect all public rights of way and to prevent, as far as possible, the stopping or obstruction of any such right of way, whether within their district or in an adjoining district in the county or counties in which the district is situate, where the stoppage or obstruction thereof would, in their opinion, be prejudicial to the interests of their district; and under sub-section 3 of the same section they may, for the purpose of carrying into effect the section, institute or defend any legal proceedings, and generally take such steps as they deem expedient.

This section applies not merely to future obstructions or stoppages of rights of way, but to any past obstructions or stoppages which have been effected in recent times; and where there is clear evidence that the public have in past times enjoyed such rights, the District Council will be entitled to take proceedings for the purpose of recovering them, or of putting an end to the obstructions. It is not necessary, however, to point out that it will not be expedient to rake up cases which have long been allowed to pass unquestioned, for although there is no limit of time to the enforcement of public rights, there may be difficulty of proof in respect of rights which in fact have ont been exercised for a length of time.

The Act, by Section 26 (4), provides that where a Parish Council have represented to the District Council that any public right of way within the district, or an adjoining district in the county or counties in which the district is situate, has been unlawfully stopped or obstructed, it shall be the duty of the District Council, unless satisfied that the allegations of such representation are incorrect, to take proper proceedings accordingly.

If the District Council refuse or fail to take proceedings in consequence of such representation, the Parish Council may petition the County Council of the county within which the way is situate, who are then empowered to take such proceedings as the District Council might have done. In view of this provision it will be necessary for the District Council carefully to inquire into any such case of obstruction or stoppage which is brought before them by a Parish Council, and to take action upon it, if it should be clear to them that the right of the public has been infringed. It may, however, be pointed out that the duties of a District Council are not limited to cases where they are set in motion by a Parish Council, but that, in any case where it is brought to their notice from any quarter that a footpath has been obstructed or stopped, it will be their duty to take steps to vindicate the right of the public, if fully satisfied of the validity of the claim.

These observations apply equally to bridleways as to footpaths. It not infrequently happens that the right of the public to use a way for horses is questioned, while that of its use for foot passengers is admitted. In cases of bridleways it will be the duty of the District Council to assert the right of the public to use the way for horses.

With respect to the proceedings to be adopted by the District Council where they are clearly of opinion that a footway or bridleway has been obstructed or stopped, there appear to be three courses open to them :—

(1.) To direct the removal of the obstruction.

(2.) To indict the person who has caused the obstruction for a misdemeanour.

(3.) To proceed by way of action in the name of the Attorney-General, for which his "fiat" must be obtained in the usual way.

The last of these courses will, in many cases, be found preferable to that of indictment. As a general rule, however, where the public right appears to be quite clear, it will be better for the District Council to direct their surveyor to remove the obstruction to a footpath, leaving it to the person who has placed it there, if he wishes to raise a question of law, to do so by bringing an action of trespass.

This course should be adopted only after due notice to the parties concerned.

With respect to the legal diversion or stoppage of footpaths, it is to be observed that under the Local Government Act, 1894, Section 13, sub-section (1), the consent of both the Parish Council (or of the Parish Meeting where there is no Parish Council) and the District Council is necessary before Justices in Quarter Sessions can give their sanction to such a course. The only ground on which a footpath can be wholly stopped without the substitution of another is that it is unnecessary, and this question will be for the consideration of both the Parish and the District Council. Where it is proposed to divert a footpath the question for consideration will be whether the proposed footpath is more commodious for the public than the existing footway. (*See* Highway Act, 1835, 5 & 6 Will. 4. c. 50. Sections 84–92.)

The District Council may refuse their consent to the stoppage or diversion of a footpath even after the Parish Council has given consent.

The owner of the land over which a public footpath lies has the right to maintain existing stiles or swing gates across it, provided they are of a reasonable kind, and are such that the public are not debarred from the use of the footway. But it will be the duty of the District Council to see that the use by the public of a footpath is not hindered by the erection of stiles or gates which are substantially less convenient than have existed in the past.

2.—*Roadside Wastes.*

Where on either side of a public road strips of land exist, open to the public, between the metalled road and the fences beyond, *primâ facie*, the public right of way extends, unless there be evidence to the contrary, over such strips or roadside wastes, and they cannot lawfully be enclosed by the owner of the adjoining land or by the lord of the manor, or by any other person. Such strips may be of varying width, and the adjoining owner has no right to straighten the line of his fences by taking in any part of the roadside waste. It is not uncommonly believed that there is a right to enclose up to 15 feet from the centre of the road. This is not so; the public, unless it can be proved to the contrary, have the right to the roadside waste beyond this limit, and between the fences and the road, and, moreover, the District Council have no power to authorise the enclosure of any portion of such roadside waste. The fact that trees or shrubs have been allowed to grow up on these roadside wastes, so as to interfere with their use by the public, does not necessarily destroy such right or justify their enclosure.

The Local Government Act, 1894, by Section 26 (1) and (3) makes it obligatory on the part of District Councils to enforce the law for the protection of such roadside wastes. "It shall be the duty," the Act says, "of every District Council to prevent any unlawful encroachment on any roadside waste within their district," and they may, for the purpose of performing this duty, "institute or defend any legal proceedings, and generally take such steps as they deem expedient." As in the case of footpaths, a Parish Council may make representation on this subject to the District Council, and if the District Council neglect or refuse to act, the Parish Council may appeal to the County Council, who may then, if they think fit, take action in the matter at the expense of the District Council. The District Council, however, are not limited in their action to cases where representation is made under the section referred to. They should at once take into consideration any information which they may receive that encroachments have been made on a roadside waste, from whatever source the information may come. The power of appealing to the County Council conferred on the Parish Council may be exercised by a Parish Meeting where there is no Parish Council. (Section 19, sub-section 8.)

It should be recollected that this right of the public to the maintenance of the roadside waste in rural districts does not mean that the soil of the land belongs to the public. As a general rule the ownership of the land of the roadside waste in rural districts is vested in the owner of the adjoining land, subject to the right of passage by the public. In some cases, however, it is part of the waste of a manor and belongs to the lord of the manor subject to any manorial rights, and in some few cases the roadside waste belongs to the highway authority, where the road has been laid out under an Enclosure Act or other private Act. As in the case of footpaths, the powers of the District Council are not limited to future encroachments or enclosures of roadside wastes. There is no limit of time to the assertion of the right of the public to the use of roadside wastes. The District Council should therefore consider all encroachments which have been made within recent times.

The legal remedies in the hands of the District Council, where encroachments on roadside wastes have been made, are the same as in the case of stoppage of footpaths, and need not be repeated. In the case of all future encroachments where there is no doubt as to the public right, it will, as a general rule, be advisable to assert the right of the public by removing the obstruction, after due notice to the person who has made the encroachment, leaving it to the person claiming the right to obstruct to assert it by an action of trespass.

It will be borne in mind that as regards main roads the Local Government Act, 1888, confers on County Councils the necessary powers for preventing and removing obstructions, and for asserting the right of the public to the use and enjoyment of the roadside wastes. The District Council should therefore, in the case of a main road, bring under the attention of the County Council any such obstruction or interference with the public rights in respect of roadside wastes within their district which may come to their knowledge.

3.—*Commons.*

The Local Government Act, 1894, contains very important provisions framed with the object of keeping open, in the interest of the public, any existing commons or open lands subject to common rights, of preventing their enclosure, and enabling District Councils to propose Schemes for their maintenance and regulation. These must be considered in connexion with the provisions of other Acts passed in late years.

With a view to prevent the enclosure of commons, the Law of Commons Amendment Act, 1893, 56 & 57 Vict. c. 57., has provided that no enclosure under the Statute of Merton should thenceforward be valid unless made with the consent of the Board of Agriculture, and further, that the Board should not consent to any such enclosure unless satisfied that it would be for the benefit of the neighbourhood. In combination with this it should also be noticed that the Commons Act, 1876, by Section 31, provides that any person intending to enclose a common or part of a common must publish a statement of his intention at least three months beforehand, three times in two or more of the principal local newspapers; and the Local Government Act, 1894, by Sections 8 (4) and 26 (2) requires that notice of any application to the Board of Agriculture in relation to a common shall be served upon the District Council and upon the Council of any parish in which any part of the common is situate.

In future, therefore, it is clear that where any lord of a manor or other person attempts to make an enclosure of a common or any part of it, without the previous consent of the Board of Agriculture, he will commit an illegal act and proceedings may be taken by the

District Council to restrain him. Where, however, he applies to the Board of Agriculture for their consent to the enclosure the Parish Council and the District Council will have due notice, and they should at once make representations to the Board of Agriculture in any case where they are satisfied that the enclosure will not be for the public benefit.

With the view of affording means of preventing the complete extinction of all rights of common which might entitle the owner of the soil to claim that the common no longer exists as such, the Local Government Act, 1894, by Section 26, sub-section 2, empowers a District Council, with the consent of the County Council, to exercise the powers conferred by Section 8 of the Commons Act of 1876 on certain urban sanitary authorities, and thus to acquire by gift or by purchase any land or houses having common rights annexed thereto. Where they have done this, the District Council will be in the position in the future to claim that the land in question remains at law a common, and cannot be lawfully enclosed under the Statute of Merton, or otherwise, without the consent of the Board of Agriculture, who are bound by the Statute above referred to to refuse their consent if it be not proved to their satisfaction that the enclosure is for the benefit of the neighbourhood.

In view of these provisions, the Council of any district within whose area any common land now exists will probably deem it right to consider whether they should not purchase one or more cottages or a small plot of land having a right of common annexed. The transaction need not be a costly one to the Council, for the house or land thus purchased may be let on lease, or otherwise, for its full value without risk to the Council of losing their *locus standi.*

It will be obvious that the proceedings under the Law of Commons Amendment Act, 1893, on the part of a local authority who have acquired an interest in a common to prevent the enclosure will be simple and inexpensive, as compared with a suit previous to that Act to prove that rights of common still exist, and that sufficiency of common has not been left as provided by the Statute of Merton.

The Local Government Act further vests in District Councils important functions with respect to the regulation of commons. It often happens that, in the case of commons in populous districts or near to large towns, which are largely resorted to for recreation, it is desirable that regulations should be made for the preservation of order, for the prevention of nuisances, and for maintaining the surface and natural features of the common. In such cases a District Council may, under Section 26 (2) of the Local Government Act, 1894, with the consent of persons representing one-third in value of the legal interests in a common, and with the consent of the County Council, apply to the Board of Agriculture for a Provisional Order for regulation of the common, which will then be proceeded with in accordance with the provisions of the Commons Act, 1876. Where a regulation Scheme has been confirmed by Parliament, the common cannot afterwards be enclosed.

If application is made by any other person or persons to the Board of Agriculture for the regulation of a common, the District Council and the Parish Council within whose area the common is situate are entitled to notice of the same, with a view to their making any representation they may deem necessary to the Board upon the subject. (Local Government Act, 1894, Sections 8 (4) and 26 (2).)

In the case of commons within the Metropolitan Police District, application for a regulation Scheme must be made in accordance with the Metropolitan Commons Acts, 1866–69, and no consent of the commoners is required.

As the protection of the rights of the public in the matters above referred to, and the processes to be adopted in their assertion, will often involve difficult questions of fact and law, it will be well that District Councils should consult their legal adviser before taking action in such cases.

Local Government Board,
January 1895.

APPENDIX VIII.

Memorandum as to Powers and Duties of Parish Councils and Parish Meetings, under the Local Government Act, 1894, with respect to Rights of Way, Roadside Wastes, Commons, Village Greens, and Recreation Grounds.

1.—*Rights of Way.*

It is the duty of a District Council, whether they are the Highway Authority or not, under Section 26 (1) of the Local Government Act, 1894, to protect all public rights of way, and to prevent, as far as possible, the stopping or obstruction of any such right of way, whether within their district or in an adjoining district in the county or counties in which the district is situate, where the stoppage or obstruction thereof would, in their opinion, be prejudicial to the interests of their district; and under sub-section (3) of the same section they may, for the purpose of carrying into effect the section, institute or defend any legal proceedings, and generally take such steps as they deem expedient.

If, however, a Parish Council are satisfied that any right of way within the district in which their parish is comprised, or an adjoining district in the county or counties in which such district is situate, has been unlawfully stopped or obstructed, they are empowered by sub-section (4) of Section 26 to make a representation to that effect to the District Council, and thereupon it becomes the duty of the District Council, unless satisfied that the allegations of such representations are incorrect, to take proper proceedings accordingly. If the District Council refuse or fail to take proceedings in consequence of such representation, the Parish Council may petition the County Council for the county in which the way is situate, who are then empowered to take such proceedings as the District Council might have taken in respect to the stoppage or obstruction of the right of way. These provisions apply equally to bridleways as to footpaths.

The powers referred to apply to cases where footways or bridleways have been unlawfully stopped or obstructed before the constitution of the Parish Council or Parish Meeting, and not merely to cases which have occurred subsequent to such constitution. Where, therefore, the Parish Council are satisfied that a right of way has been stopped or obstructed within recent times before the passing of the Local Government Act, it will be within their competency to make a representation to the District Council on the subject.

In a parish where there is no Parish Council the Parish Meeting have, under Section 19 (8) of the Act, the same powers as a Parish Council as regards making a representation to the District Council with respect to the unlawful stoppage or obstruction of a right of way and of appealing to the County Council.

No public right of way in a rural parish can in future be lawfully stopped in whole or in part or diverted without the previous consent of the Parish Council (Section 13 (1)), or of the Parish Meeting where there is no Council (Section 19, sub-section (8)), of the parish in which it is situate. The only ground on which a public footpath can be wholly stopped without the substitution of another is that it is unnecessary. The question, therefore, whether it is unnecessary will be a subject for the consideration of the Parish Council or Parish Meeting. The only ground on which a public footpath can be diverted is that the proposed footpath is more commodious for the public than the existing footway (Highway Act, 1835, 5 & 6 Will. IV., cap. 50, Sections 84–92). This also will be for the consideration and determination of the Parish Council or Parish Meeting.

The consent of the District Council in whose district the right of way is situate must also be obtained before a public footpath is stopped or diverted, and as the District Council will in most cases be the Highway Authority, it may be presumed that their consent will first be obtained, and that they will communicate their views to the Parish Council or Parish Meeting in whose parish the footway is situate.

In a parish which has a Parish Council the Parish Council must give "public notice" of any resolution passed by them giving consent to the stoppage or diversion of a footpath, and the resolution will not operate—

(*a*) unless it is confirmed by the Parish Council at a meeting held not less than two months after the public notice is given; nor

(*b*) if a Parish Meeting held before the confirmation resolve that the consent ought not to be given.

A Parish Meeting may be summoned by the Chairman of the Parish Council or by any two Parish Councillors, or by the Chairman of the Parish Meeting, or by any six parochial electors. A poll must be taken on the question if it is demanded by one parochial elector present at the meeting. The question for the electors at the poll will be whether the assent of the parish should be given to the stopping or diversion of the footpath.

In a parish where there is no Parish Council the resolution of the Parish Meeting in favour of the stopping or diversion of a footpath must be confirmed at a subsequent meeting of the parish not less than two months after public notice has been given of the resolution passed at the first meeting.

A Parish Council may, subject to the provisions of the Act with respect to limitations on expenditure, acquire by agreement any right of way, whether within their parish or an adjoining parish, the acquisition of which is beneficial to the inhabitants of the parish or any part thereof (Section 8 (1) (*g*)).

The Parish Council may also, subject to the like limitations on expenditure, undertake the repair and maintenance of all or any of the public footpaths within their parish, not being footpaths at the side of a public road (Section 13 (2)).

2.—*Roadside Wastes.*

Where on either side of a public road strips of land exist open to the public, between the metalled road and the fences beyond, *primâ facie*, the public right of way extends, unless there is evidence to the contrary, over such strips or roadside wastes, and they cannot lawfully be enclosed by the owner of the adjoining land or by the Lord of the Manor or by any other person.

Such strips may be of varying width, and the adjoining owner has no right to straighten the line of his fences by taking in any part of the roadside waste. It is not uncommonly believed that there is a right to enclose up to 15 feet from the centre of the road. This is not so. The public, unless it can be proved to the contrary, have the right to the whole of the road-side waste between the fences and the road. The fact that trees or shrubs have been allowed to grow up on these roadside wastes so as to interfere with their use by the public does not necessarily destroy such right or justify their enclosure.

The Local Government Act, 1894, places such roadside wastes under the protection of District Councils. By Section 26 it is provided that it shall be the duty of every District Council to prevent any unlawful encroachment on any roadside waste within their District, and they may for the purpose of performing this duty institute or defend any legal proceedings, and generally take such steps as they deem expedient.

As in the case of footpaths, a Parish Council, when satisfied that a roadside waste has been unlawfully encroached on, are empowered to make representation on the subject to the District Council, and if the District Council neglect or refuse to take proceedings, the Parish Council may appeal to the County Council, who are then authorised to take such proceedings as the District Council might have taken. The powers of the Parish Council and the District Council are not limited by the Local Government Act to cases where the encroachment on a roadside waste has been made after the passing of the Act or after the constitution of such Councils. The Parish Council, therefore, will be justified in making representations to the District Council, where they are satisfied that unlawful encroachments on roadside wastes have been made before the Council came into existence, though it may not be expedient on their part to do so in cases where such encroachments have been of long date.

Where no Parish Council exists the Parish Meeting have the same power as a Parish Council of making representations to the District Council and County Council on the subject.

3.—*Commons.*

The Local Government Act, 1894, contains very important provisions with the object of preventing the unlawful enclosure of commons. Powers for this purpose are conferred on District Councils. In order that these powers may be properly carried out it will be well that a Parish Council should keep a careful watch on any commons within the parish and make representations to the District Council when any enclosure is threatened or has taken place.

Before any proceedings are taken by a Lord of a Manor to enclose any common or part of a common under the Statute of Merton, the consent of the Board of Agriculture must be obtained under the Law of Commons Amendment Act, 1893, and that Act provides that the Board shall not give their consent to any such enclosure unless satisfied that it will be for the benefit of the neighbourhood. Notice of any such application to the Board of Agriculture must be served upon the Council of any parish in which such common or any part of it is situate (Local Government Act, 1894, section 8 (4)). The

Parish Council, therefore, in such case will have the opportunity of stating their objections to the enclosure.

With a view also of affording means of preventing the complete extinction of all rights of common, which might entitle the holder of the soil to claim that the common no longer exists as such, power is given to District Councils, with the consent of the County Council, to purchase any house or land having common rights annexed thereto (Section 26 (2)). It would be well for a Parish Council where a common exists within the parish to make any representation to the District Council which they may deem desirable on the subject, and to bring under their attention any opportunity which may occur of effecting such a purchase.

The Parish Council are not themselves invested with any such power of purchasing. They may, however, acquire, by gift, any land with rights of common attached, and they may purchase for purposes of recreation any land, and if such land should have a right of common attached to it this will be a great security against the enclosure of the common.

Power is given by the Local Government Act, Section 26 (2), to District Councils to apply to the Board of Agriculture for a scheme for regulating any common within their district, with the consent of the County Council and of persons representing one-third in value of the legal interests in the common. Such a scheme must be confirmed by Parliament. A Parish Council within whose parish such commons are situate are entitled to notice of any application for schemes of regulation, and may make such representations to the Board of Agriculture as they may think fit.

4.—*Village Greens and Recreation Grounds.*

Where on any open land the inhabitants of a village or parish have from time immemorial been accustomed to play games, such custom practically constitutes the land a village green, and the inhabitants cannot lawfully be deprived, by enclosure or otherwise, of their right so to use it. In such a case, where any attempt is made to injure the green, or to interrupt its use as a place of exercise and recreation, the Parish Council may proceed against the person committing such act before the justices; and such person, if convicted, is liable to damages and penalties. See Inclosure Act, 1857, Section 12, extended by Commons Act, 1876, Section 29, and applied to Parish Councils by the Local Government Act, 1894, Section 6 (1) (*c*) (iii).

Not unfrequently a village green, a recreation ground, or a fuel allotment has been allotted under some enclosure award to the Churchwardens and Overseers of a Parish. Where this has been the case, such land will henceforth be vested in and managed by the Parish Council (Local Government Act, 1894, Sections 5 (2) (*c*), and 6 (1) (*c*) (iii)).

Where there is no Parish Council the village green or other recreation ground vests in the Chairman of the Parish Meeting and the Overseers (Section 19 (7)), and the County Council have the power of conferring on the Parish Meeting the right to make bye-laws in respect of it (Section 19 (10)).

A fuel allotment may be made available for purposes of recreation by a scheme of the Charity Commissioners, on the application of a Parish Council, when they are the trustees of the allotment, under the provisions of the Commons Act, 1876, Section 19.

A Parish Council is empowered to purchase or acquire land for a recreation ground, and for public walks.

With respect to any village green, recreation ground, open space, or public walk for the time being under the control of the Parish Council, the Council may make bye-laws for its regulation (Local Government Act, 1894, Section 8 (1) (*d*); and Public Health Act, 1875, Sections 164 and 183–6).

Local Government Board,
March 1895.

INDEX.

Eyre & Spottiswoode, *Her Majesty's Printers*, Downs Park Road, Hackney, N.E.

For EU product safety concerns, contact us at Calle de José Abascal, 56–1°, 28003 Madrid, Spain or eugpsr@cambridge.org.

www.ingramcontent.com/pod-product-compliance
Ingram Content Group UK Ltd.
Pitfield, Milton Keynes, MK11 3LW, UK
UKHW040226290926
15471UKWH00001B/13
* 9 7 8 1 1 0 8 0 3 6 7 4 0 *